HIDDEN
But Now
REVEALED

A Biblical Theology of Mystery

G. K. BEALE AND
BENJAMIN L. GLADD

IVP Academic

An imprint of InterVarsity Press
Downers Grove, Illinois

InterVarsity Press
P.O. Box 1400, Downers Grove, IL 60515-1426
World Wide Web: www.ivpress.com
Email: email@ivpress.com

InterVarsity Press® is the book-publishing division of InterVarsity Christian Fellowship/USA®, a movement of students and faculty active on campus at hundreds of universities, colleges and schools of nursing in the United States of America, and a member movement of the International Fellowship of Evangelical Students. For information about local and regional activities, write Public Relations Dept., InterVarsity Christian Fellowship/USA, 6400 Schroeder Rd., P.O. Box 7895, Madison, WI 53707-7895, or visit the IVCF website at www.intervarsity.org.

All Scripture quotations, unless otherwise indicated, are taken from the New American Standard Bible®, *copyright 1960, 1962, 1963, 1968, 1971, 1972, 1973, 1975, 1977, 1995 by The Lockman Foundation. Used by permission.*

Cover design: Cindy Kiple
Interior design: Beth McGill
Images: angel: ©wynnter/iStockphoto
 old paper: ©Rouzes/iStockphoto
 The Last Judgment by Pieter Jansz Pourbus at Groeningemuseum, Bruges, Belgium/©Lukas—Art in Flanders VZW/The Bridgeman Art Library

ISBN 978-0-8308-2718-3 (print)
ISBN 978-0-8308-9683-7 (digital)

Printed in the United States of America ∞

Library of Congress Cataloging-in-Publication Data
Beale, G. K. (Gregory K.), 1949-
 Hidden but now revealed : a biblical theology of mystery / G. K.
Beale and Benjamin L. Gladd.
  pages cm
 Includes bibliographical references and index.
 ISBN 978-0-8308-2718-3 (pbk. : alk. paper)
 1. Mystery—Biblical teaching. 2. Bible. New Testament—Theology.
I. Gladd, Benjamin L. II. Title.
 BS2545.M87B43 2014
                                                    230'.041—dc23

| **P** | 24 | 23 | 22 | 21 | 20 | 19 | 18 | 17 | 16 | 15 | 14 | 13 | 12 | 11 | 10 | 9 | 8 | 7 | 6 | 5 | 4 | 3 | 2 | 1 |
| **Y** | 35 | 34 | 33 | 32 | 31 | 30 | 29 | 28 | 27 | 26 | 25 | 24 | 23 | 22 | 21 | 20 | 19 | 18 | 17 | 16 | 15 | 14 |

Contents

Preface

This book has been a long time coming. Both of us worked on this topic, to some degree, for our doctoral work. Greg Beale partly worked on how the book of Daniel's conception of "mystery" connects to areas of Judaism and the book of Revelation. His dissertation was published as *The Use of Daniel in Jewish Apocalyptic Literature and in the Revelation of St. John* (Lanham, MD: University Press of America, 1984), and he then further explicated his view of mystery in the New Testament in a later book, *John's Use of the Old Testament in Revelation,* JSNTSup 166 (Sheffield: Sheffield Academic Press, 1998). Ben Gladd, as a doctoral student of Greg Beale at Wheaton College, wrote a dissertation on how mystery in the book of Daniel influences early Judaism and 1 Corinthians, which was later published as *Revealing the* Mysterion: *The Use of Mystery in Daniel and Second Temple Judaism with Its Bearing on First Corinthians,* BZNW 160 (Berlin: Walter de Gruyter, 2008).

By combining our research on this subject, we believed that the project would be a natural fit. We asked InterVarsity Press whether they would be interested in publishing a biblical theology of mystery. They graciously obliged. At the beginning of the project, we were somewhat surprised that no one had attempted to write a complete study of mystery in the New Testament or to reflect on the biblical-theological implications of such a study. The topic seemed ripe for the picking. We soon realized why that may have been the case: the more we investigated the notion of mystery, the more difficult the project became. A quick search of the key word *mystery* (Greek *mystērion*) in the New Testament yields some interesting results. The term is nestled in discussions of key doctrines: the nature of the end-time kingdom (Mt 13 and par.), the crucifixion (1 Cor 2), the restoration of Israel (Rom 11), the relationship between Jews and Gentiles (Eph 3; Col 1), and so on. These texts are notoriously complicated in their own right and are the object of tireless debate among scholars. Meticulously working through these difficult texts required a considerable amount of time and energy.

Not only are the texts in question difficult to interpret, they also take center stage in how the two Testaments relate to one another. This is one of the reasons why mystery piques our interest: the New Testament writers employ the term *mystery* to signal a unique relationship between the Testaments. Our desire to launch this project lies in our conviction, though a minority view, that the New Testament authors, without exception, use the Old Testament contextually. That is, the New Testament authors respect to one degree or another the Old Testament authors' meaning in the original Old Testament context. The concept of mystery is a relatively untapped avenue into this debate. Because this area of biblical hermeneutics is so heavily debated, even among evangelicals, we wrote this book with an eye on this debate.

To obtain a good overview of this book, we recommend that readers first read chapter one on the use of mystery in Daniel, as this chapter forms the backbone of the entire project and is indispensable. In each subsequent chapter, we make reference to this first chapter. After reading chapter one, we recommend that the reader read through the body of each chapter to get the overall flow of the argument before extensive examination of the footnotes. For those wishing for further hermeneutical reflection on how mystery functions in the New Testament use of the Old Testament, we have included as an appendix an adaptation of Greg Beale's forthcoming essay on the cognitive peripheral vision of the biblical authors.

Our goal for this project is that the church would gain a greater appreciation for the concept of mystery and the intersection of the Old and New Testaments. The gospel itself contains both "old" and "new" elements that stand in continuity and discontinuity with the Old Testament.

Both authors are grateful for our wives, who continually illustrate God's goodness to us. Indeed, they play an integral role in the "marital mystery" of Ephesians 5:31-32.

We would also like to thank the students who diligently labored on this manuscript: Josh Darsaut and David Barry.

Above all, we are grateful to God who gave us the desire to write this project and the energy to complete it. Our prayer is that this book would give glory to him alone.

English translations of Scripture follow the New American Standard Bible (NASB) unless otherwise indicated.

The edition of the Greek Old Testament that is used is Alfred Rahlfs, ed., *Septuaginta*, revised and corrected by Robert Hanhart (Stuttgart: Deutche Bibelgesellschaft, 2006). In Daniel there are two distinct Old Testament Greek translations known as "Old Greek" and "Theodotion." Outside of Daniel, the Greek Old Testament will be referred to variously as the "Greek Old Testament" or "Septuagint" (sometimes abbreviated a the "LXX"). The English version of the Greek Old Testament cited is *A New English Translation of the Septuagint* (New York: Oxford University Press, 2007), unless otherwise noted. We emphasized key words or phrases in the NASB by underlining them, and we preserved the NASB's own italics that signal inserted English words with no formal Hebrew/Aramaic/Greek equivalent.

References to the Greek New Testament are from the Nestle-Aland *Novum Testamentum Graece* (Stuttgart: Deutsche Bibelgesellschaft, 1993). Our references to the Dead Sea Scrolls come primarily from the edition of F. G. Martinez, *The Dead Sea Scrolls Translated* (Boston: Brill, 1994); sometimes reference is made to *The Dead Sea Scrolls Study Edition*, ed. F. Garcia Martinez and Eibert J. C. Tigchelaar, 2 vols (Boston: Brill, 2000).

The primary sources of various Jewish works were ordinarily consulted, referred to, and sometimes quoted, in the following English editions: *Mekilta de-Rabbi Ishmael*, vols. 1-3, trans. and ed. J. Z. Lauterbach (Philadelphia: Jewish Publication Society of America, 1976); *The Fathers According to Rabbi Nathan*, trans. Judah Goldin (New York: Schocken Books, 1974); *The Midrash on Psalms*, trans. and ed. W. G. Braude, Yale Judaica Series 13:1-2 (New Haven, CT: Yale University Press, 1976); *Midrash Rabbah*, vols. 1-10, ed. H. Freedman and M. Simon (London: Soncino, 1961); *The Old Testament Pseudepigrapha*, vols. 1-2, ed. J. H. Charlesworth (Garden City, NY: Doubleday, 1983), though sometimes reference is made to the *Apocrypha and Pseudepigrapha of the Old Testament*, vol. 2, ed. R. H. Charles (Oxford: Clarendon, 1977); *The Aramaic Bible: The Targums*, ed. M. McNamara (Collegeville, MN: Liturgical, 1987).

References to ancient Greek works, especially those of Philo and Josephus (including English translations), are from the Loeb Classical Library unless otherwise noted. References and some English translations of the apostolic fathers come from *The Apostolic Fathers*, trans. J. B. Lightfoot and J. R. Harmer, ed. M. W. Holmes (Grand Rapids: Baker, 1992).

G. K. Beale and Benjamin Gladd

Abbreviations

1–3 En.	*1–3 Enoch*
1–4 Macc	1–4 Maccabees
1QH	*Hodayot* or *Thanksgiving Hymns*
1QM	*Milḥamah* or *War Scroll*
1QpHab	*Pesher Habbakuk*
1QS	*Serek Hayaḥad* or *Rule of the Community*
2 Bar.	*2 Baruch*
2 Clem.	*2 Clement*
ABRL	Anchor Bible Reference Library
AGJU	Arbeiten zur Geschichte des antiken Judentums und des Urchristentums
AHD	*The American Heritage Dictionary of the English Language*, 4th ed. Edited by Joseph P. Picket. Boston: Houghton Mifflin Harcourt, 2006.
Ant.	Josephus, *Jewish Antiquities*
Apoc. Ab.	*Apocalypse of Abraham*
Apoc. Pet.	*Apocalypse of Peter*
Apoc. Zeph.	*Apocalypse of Zephaniah*
Ascen. Isa.	*Ascension of Isaiah*
BA	*Biblical Archeologist*
Barn.	*Barnabas*
BDAG	Bauer, W., F. W. Danker, W. F. Arndt, and F. W. Gingrich. *Greek-English Lexicon of the New Testament and Other Early Christian Literature.* 3rd ed. Chicago: University of Chicago Press, 2000.
BDF	Blass, F., A. Debrunner, and R. W. Funk. *A Greek Grammar of the New Testament and Other Early Christian Literature.* Chicago: University of Chicago Press, 1961.
BECNT	Baker Exegetical Commentary on the New Testament
Bib	*Biblica*
BRS	Bible Resource Series
BS	Biblical Series

BZNW	Beihefte zur Zeitschrift für die neutestamentliche Wissenschaft
CBQ	*Catholic Biblical Quarterly*
CD	*Damascus Document*
Cher.	Philo, *De Cherubim*
CNT	Commentaire du Nouveau Testament
ConBNT	Coniectanea biblica: New Testament Series
COQG	Christian Origins and the Question of God
Diogn.	*Epistle to Diognetus*
DPL	*Dictionary of Paul and His Letters.* Edited by G. F. Hawthorne, R. P. Martin and D. G. Reid. Downers Grove: InterVarsity Press, 1993.
EBC	Expositor's Bible Commentary
ECC	Eerdmans Critical Commentary
EDNT	*Exegetical Dictionary of the New Testament.* 3 vols. Edited by Horst Balz and Gerhard Scheider. Grand Rapids: Eerdmans, 1993.
EGGNT	Exegetical Guide to the New Testament
Eph.	Ignatius, *To the Ephesians*
ExpTim	*Expository Times*
GTJ	*Grace Theological Journal*
HSCP	*Harvard Studies in Classical Philology*
HTR	*Harvard Theological Review*
IBC	Interpretation Bible Commentary
ICC	International Critical Commentary
Ios.	Philo, *De Iosepho*
ISBE	*International Standard Bible Encyclopedia*
IVPNTC	InterVarsity Press New Testament Commentaries
JBL	*Journal of Biblical Literature*
JETS	*Journal of the Evangelical Theological Society*
JNES	*Journal of Near Eastern Studies*
Jos. Asen.	*Joseph and Aseneth*
JSJSup	Journal for the Study of Judaism Supplement Series
JSNTSup	Journal for the Study of the New Testament Supplement Series
JSOTSup	Journal for the Study of the Old Testament Supplement Series
JSP	*Journal for the Study of the Pseudepigrapha*
JSPSup	Journal for the Study of the Pseudepigrapha Supplement Series
JTS	*Journal of Theological Studies*

LAE	*Life of Adam and Eve*
LCL	Loeb Classical Library
Leg.	Philo, *Legum allegoriae*
Legat.	Philo, *Legatio ad Gaium*
LNTS	Library of New Testament Studies
Magn.	Ignatius, *To the Magnesians*
Mart. Ascen. Isa.	*Martyrdom and Ascension of Isaiah*
Midr.	*Midrash*
MNTC	Moffat New Testament Commentary
Mos.	Philo, *De vita Mosis*
NCBC	New Century Bible Commentary
NETS	New English Translation of the Septuagint
NIBC	New International Bible Commentary
NICNT	New International Commentary on the New Testament
NICOT	New International Commentary on the Old Testament
NIDNTT	*New International Dictionary of New Testament Theology.* 4 vols. Edited by Colin Brown. Grand Rapids: Zondervan, 1979.
NIGTC	New International Greek Testament Commentary
NIV	New International Version
NIVAC	New International Version Application Commentary
NovTSup	Novum Testamentum Supplement Series
NSBT	New Studies in Biblical Theology
NTM	New Testament Monographs
OED	*Oxford English Dictionary.* 2nd edition.
OG	Old Greek translation
OTL	Old Testament Library
par.	parallel(s)
PNTC	Pillar New Testament Commentaries
Praem.	Philo, *De praemiis et poenis*
Pss. Sol.	*Psalms of Solomon*
PTMS	Pittsburgh Theological Monograph Series
RestQ	*Restoration Quarterly*
RevQ	*Revue de Qumran*
SBJT	*Southern Baptist Journal of Theology*

SBLECL	Society of Biblical Literature Early Christianity and Its Literature
SBLEJL	Society of Biblical Literature Early Judaism and Its Literature
SBLMS	Society of Biblical Literature Monograph Series
SBLSBS	Society of Biblical Literature Sources for Biblical Study
SBT	Studies in Biblical Theology
Sim.	*Similitudes* (*1 Enoch 37-71*)
SJT	*Scottish Journal of Theology*
SNTSMS	Society for New Testament Studies Monograph Series
Somn.	Philo, *De somniis*
Spec.	Philo, *De specialibus legibus*
SRB	Supplementi alla Rivista Biblica
STDJ	Studies on the Texts of the Desert of Judah
T. Benj.	*Testament of Benjamin*
T. Gad	*Testament of Gad*
T. Iss.	*Testament of Issachar*
T. Jac.	*Testament of Jacob*
T. Job	*Testament of Job*
T. Jos.	*Testament of Joseph*
T. Jud.	*Testament of Judah*
T. Levi	*Testament of Levi*
T. Mos.	*Testament of Moses*
T. Naph.	*Testament of Naphtali*
T. Zeb.	*Testament of Zebulun*
TDNT	*Theological Dictionary of the New Testament.* 10 vols. Edited by Gerhard Kittel and Gerhard Friedrich. Grand Rapids: Eerdmans, 1977.
Tg. Onq.	*Targum Onqelos*
Tg. Ps.-J.	*Targum Pseudo-Jonathan*
Theod	Theodotion
TJ	*Trinity Journal*
TNIV	Today's New International Version
TNTC	Tyndale New Testament Commentaries
TOTC	Tyndale Old Testament Commentaries
TynBul	*Tyndale Bulletin*
VT	*Vetus Testamentum*

VTSup	Vetus Testamentum Supplement Series
WBC	Word Biblical Commentary
Wis	Wisdom of Solomon
WTJ	*Westminster Theological Journal*
WUNT	Wissenschaftliche Untersuchungen zum Neuen Testament
ZBK	Zürcher Bibelkommentare

Introduction

WHEN READING THROUGH THE FOUR GOSPELS, one is immediately confronted with a difficult problem: Why are Israel and its leaders unable to grasp fully Jesus' identity and mission? Jesus himself claims that he is the climax of Israel's history and that the entire Old Testament anticipates his arrival, yet why is he not welcomed with open arms? Are not the Jewish leaders, the Old Testament scholars of their day, steeled in their resolve to quell Jesus' mission to restore Israel? One of Jesus' core teachings concerns the establishment of God's eternal kingdom on the earth, which will take place through his ministry, but Israel by and large rejects Jesus' kingdom message.

When Jesus hangs on the cross, the disciples flee for their lives. When the women report to the disciples that Jesus has been raised from the dead, the disciples are reticent to believe. Yet how can the apostle Paul state in 1 Corinthians 15:3-4 that "Christ died for our sins <u>according to the Scriptures</u>, and that he was buried, and that he was raised on the third day <u>according to the Scriptures</u>"? If the crucifixion and the resurrection were predicted in the Old Testament, then why were the disciples slow to believe? Jesus himself predicted his death and resurrection on several occasions! It appears, then, that even though the Old Testament anticipates Jesus and his ministry, there is some aspect of unexpectedness or *newness* to Jesus' identity and mission, which some would say cannot be found at all in the Old Testament.

Another poignant example is Jesus' interaction with the two men on the way to Emmaus. Jesus castigates them for being "slow of heart to believe in all that the prophets have spoken" (Lk 24:25). Surprisingly, Jesus then goes on to demonstrate to them that the whole Old Testament ultimately points to him. A similar event occurs in John's Gospel in the midst of Jesus' interactions with the Jewish leaders: "You search the Scriptures because you think that in them you have eternal life; it is these that testify about Me; and you are unwilling to come to Me so that you may have life" (Jn 5:39-40). Jesus' words cut deeply as they expose his method of interpreting the Old Testament—the person of Jesus unlocks the ultimate meaning of the entire Old Testament. Simply put, the Jewish leaders failed to interpret the Old Testament correctly, but we must ask why. Were they not the biblical scholars of their day?

The same can be said for how the Old Testament is used in the New Testament. On a number of occasions, New Testament authors cite the Old Testament in creative ways, ways that seemingly have little to do with the original intent of the Old Testament authors. An often-cited example of this is found in Ephesians 5:31-32, where the writer cites Genesis 2:24 and applies it to Christ and the church: "'For this reason a man will leave his father and mother and be united to his wife, and the two will become one flesh.' This is a profound mystery—but I am talking about Christ and the church" (NIV). By all appearances, the union between Adam and Eve is viewed as ultimately pointing to Christ and the church. Christ, the author believes, is really "there" in the original context in Genesis 2:24. Is there not a "new" layer of meaning in the Genesis text that was not in the mind of the Old Testament author but was in the mind of the New Testament author? Do New Testament writers "read in" new ideas to the Old Testament texts that they cite? And if so, how can we consider there to be a consistent unity to the whole Bible?

Israel's unbelief in Jesus, Jesus' hermeneutical method and Paul's use of Genesis 2:24 share a common thread: some believe that the New Testament, while resuming Israel's story, does not stand in continuity with the Old Testament. Accordingly, an element of discontinuity or "newness" runs through the entire New Testament. Depending on the topic, some elements tend to stand more in continuity with the Old Testament and others seem to be in discontinuity. The New Testament writers, on occasion, tip their hat to this notion of continuity/discontinuity by employing the term *mystery*. They tether this term to important topics such as the nature of the latter-day kingdom (Mt 13 and par.), Jesus' messiahship (1 Cor 2:7), the resurrection (1 Cor 15), the relationship between Jews and Gentiles (Eph 3) and the timing of Israel's restoration (Rom 11). By using the term *mystery*, a term from the book of Daniel that embodies both continuity and discontinuity, the New Testament writers expect their audiences to understand that the topic under discussion contains both of these elements. In other words, the term *mystery* alerts the reader that the topic at hand stands both in continuity and discontinuity to the Old Testament.

The purpose of this book is to unpack the relationship between the Old and New Testaments. We will explore all the occurrences of the term *mystery* in the New Testament and listen carefully to how the New Testament writers understand the issue of continuity and discontinuity. Throughout the book we will unpack how continuity and discontinuity relate. Studying the notion of mystery ought to sharpen our understanding of how the Old Testament relates to the New.

When modern-day readers of the New Testament happen upon the word *mystery,* images such as Sherlock Holmes pop into their heads. The first entry for *mystery* in *The American Heritage Dictionary of the English Language* defines it as something "that is not fully understood or that baffles or eludes the understanding; an enigma."[1] This modern definition of mystery is unfortunately imported into the New Testament's use of the word without any thought of what the word meant to the original, target audience. Therein lies the problem faced by Westerners in the twenty-first century when we read our Bible—unless we properly and patiently study biblical words and concepts, we will inevitably import our own preconceptions into Scripture. A brief example of this is the ubiquity of crosses in the Western culture. Crosses are affixed to cars, dangle from celebrities' necks and are tattooed on professional athletes. In the first century, no one would have dared do such a thing; it would have been the equivalent of adorning a gold-plated electric chair or a noose around the neck. In the first century, Romans and Jews viewed crucifixion not as a sign of religious devotion but as a symbol of treachery and moral bankruptcy.

When we approach the New Testament, we must resist the temptation to read Scripture anachronistically. By performing word studies in their context, evaluating the Jewish background, and studying the Old and New Testaments in their contexts, we are on more solid hermeneutical ground. So, when we attempt to study the biblical conception of mystery in the New Testament, we must pay attention to how mystery functions in the Old Testament and in Jewish writings. To ignore the Old Testament and Jewish background of the term is to cut off much of its meaning from the New Testament, leaving us with a greatly impoverished portrait of it.

---

[1]*AHD*, p. 1163.

We will define *mystery* generally as *the revelation of God's partially hidden wisdom, particularly as it concerns events occurring in the "latter days."* As we will see, scholars are on the right track when they define *mystery* as *divine wisdom that was previously "hidden" but has now been "revealed."* We will attempt to sharpen this definition, but generally speaking this widely held understanding of the biblical mystery is correct. Augmenting this definition, *mystery* often means something close to our modern-day denotation—knowledge that is somewhat baffling. In general accordance with the contemporary understanding, several Old Testament and New Testament texts describe individuals not understanding or grasping the mystery. What makes the term *mystery* so dynamic, even complex, is that the biblical writers sometimes use two definitions *simultaneously*: (1) God's wisdom has finally been disclosed, but nevertheless (2) his wisdom remains generally incomprehensible to nonbelievers. The biblical conception of mystery envelops both of these notions.

The problem with word-focused projects such as the one we undertake here is that an interpreter can easily import too much meaning into a word. That is, the term can become overloaded with meaning; too much theology gets packed into a single word. James Barr launches this critique at the multivolume *Theological Dictionary of the New Testament*. Barr criticized *TDNT* by asserting that it failed to take into account that a single word is unable to grasp the totality of a theological concept.[2] Indeed, different words can express the same theological concept.

Since scholars have long noted that *mystery* is a technical term in the New Testament,[3] Barr's protestations generally do not apply to the study of this word. With technical terms, the same theological concepts, even complex ones, can be attached wherever they occur, though of course the immediate context gives more specific meaning to how the terms are used. Moisés Silva notes, "Technical or semitechnical terms *refer to* or *stand for* defined concepts or ideas; . . . these concepts are true referents. . . . Insofar as a word can be brought into a

---

[2]James Barr, *The Semantics of Biblical Language* (New York: Oxford University Press, 1961), pp. 206-62.

[3]E.g., Douglas J. Moo, *Epistle to the Romans*, NICNT (Grand Rapids: Eerdmans, 1996), p. 714; David Aune, *Prophecy in Early Christianity and the Ancient Mediterranean World* (Grand Rapids: Eerdmans, 1983), p. 250; Gerd Luedemann, *Paul, Apostle to the Gentiles: Studies in Chronology*, trans. F. Stanley Jones (Philadelphia: Fortress, 1980), p. 240; Frederick David Mazzaferri, *The Genre of the Book of Revelation from a Source-Critical Perspective* (Berlin: Walter de Gruyter, 1989), p. 213; George Eldon Ladd, *A Theology of the New Testament*, rev. ed. (Grand Rapids: Eerdmans, 1993), p. 421.

one-to-one correspondence with an extralinguistic object or entity, to that extent the word may be subjected to the concordance-based, word-and-thing, historico-conceptual method typified by *TDNT*" (italics original).[4] Nevertheless, even with a technical term, it is possible to have a particular concept in mind without using the specific word. For example, at a number of places in the New Testament the concept of mystery exists, whereas the explicit term is lacking.

Although *mystery* is a technical term and carries the same general concept wherever it is used, we must be cautious about committing the fallacy of "illegitimate totality transfer," where a word is assumed to retain all of its possible semantic meanings in a given context.[5] In other words, we must be careful not to overload a word with too much meaning. To avoid such pitfalls, we must cautiously and carefully investigate the immediate context of each use of the term *mystery* and examine its connection with other words and phrases.

One might question the legitimacy of this project. Why write an entire book about one word that occurs just twenty-eight times in the New Testament and only a few times in the Old Testament? The answer lies not so much with the word itself, though that is important, but with those concepts that are tethered to it. The Synoptic Gospels, for example, tie the notion of God's end-time kingdom with mystery (Mt 13:11 and par.). Paul even weds the term with the crucifixion in 1 Corinthians 2:1, 7. Once we have grasped the meaning and significance of mystery, we can then turn to topics such as the establishment of God's latter-day kingdom and the crucifixion and explore how this word affects our understanding of such topics. In sum, we have two primary goals:

1. Define the Old and New Testament conception of mystery and grasp its significance.

2. Articulate as precisely as possible those topics that are found in conjunction with the term *mystery* in its various uses throughout the New Testament.

The net result of our investigation ought to sharpen our understanding of various topics, such as kingdom, crucifixion, the relationship between Jews and Gentiles, and so on. It may not be a coincidence that most of the occurrences of *mystery* are linked to Old Testament quotations and allusions. The New Testament authors at times have been given a new "revelation" about pre-

---

[4]Moisés Silva, *Biblical Words and Their Meaning: An Introduction to Lexical Semantics* (Grand Rapids: Zondervan, 1983), p. 107.

[5]Barr, *Semantics*, p. 218; cf. D. A. Carson, *Exegetical Fallacies*, 2nd ed. (Grand Rapids: Baker, 1996), p. 45, who warns that even technical words can become "overloaded" with meaning.

viously revealed Scripture. A revelation about revelation! An additional benefit of this study is a more accurate view of the relationship between the two Testaments. As we will attempt to show, our study of the use of *mystery* will shed significant light on how other Old Testament texts are used to indicate fulfillment in the New where the word *mystery* is not found.

Before venturing into this project, it is important to discuss the presuppositions and hermeneutical approach that underlie the way we will interpret Scripture in this book.[6] The first important presupposition underlying this study is the divine inspiration of the entire Bible, both Old and New Testaments. This foundational perspective means that there is unity to the Bible because it is all God's Word. While there is certainly significant theological diversity, it is not ultimately irreconcilable diversity. Therefore, tracing common themes between the Testaments becomes a legitimate and healthy pursuit. Though interpreters differ about what are the most significant unifying themes, those who affirm the ultimate divine authorship of Scripture have a common database with which to discuss and debate.

Another important presupposition is that the divine authorial intentions communicated through human authors are accessible to contemporary readers. Though no one can exhaustively comprehend these intentions, they can be sufficiently understood, especially for the purposes of salvation, sanctification and the glorification of God.

Intertextuality will receive much attention in this work, though it is better to refer to inner-biblical allusion than to the faddish word *intertextuality*. A number of concerns must be kept in mind when working in this area. First, the interpreter must demonstrate that a later text is literarily connected to an earlier text (whether, e.g., by unique wording or a unique concept or both). We will draw some connections where other interpreters might not. This field contains minimalists and maximalists. Minimalists are leery of seeing allusive literary connections, so even if they do acknowledge them, they remain apprehensive about teasing out the interpretative implications. Indeed, many New Testament scholars would not even see that the original meanings of some Old Testament texts have anything to do with the New Testament use of them, even when formal quotations of such texts exist. On the opposite end of the spectrum, we are willing to explore the possibility of more legitimate allusions than others

---

[6]This section on intertextuality is adapted from G. K. Beale, *We Become What We Worship: A Biblical Theology of Idolatry* (Downers Grove, IL: IVP Academic, 2008), pp. 21-25.

might. We certainly try to avoid reading into the text meaning that does not exist; instead, we will attempt to give what we think is a reasonable explanation for each literary connection and its significance in the immediate context. All such proposed connections have degrees of possibility and probability. We will only propose "probable" connections, though not all will agree with the probability of our connections or our interpretations of them.

Some commentators speak of "echoes" in distinction to "allusions." This distinction ultimately may not be that helpful for a number of reasons. First, some scholars use the two terms almost synonymously.[7] Second, those who clearly make a qualitative distinction between the terms view an echo as containing less volume or verbal coherence from the Old Testament than an allusion. Thus the echo is merely a reference to the Old Testament that is not as clear a reference as is an allusion. Another way to say this is that an echo is an allusion that is *possibly* dependent on an Old Testament text, in distinction to a reference that is clearly or *probably* dependent. Therefore, we will not pose criteria for discerning allusions in distinction to criteria for recognizing echoes.[8] It is fine to propose specific criteria for allusions and echoes, so readers can know how an interpreter is making judgments. However, the fact that scholars differ over specifically what criteria are best has led us to posit more general and basic criteria for allusions and echoes. At the end of the day, it is difficult to come up with hard and fast criteria that can be applicable to every Old Testament allusion or echo in the New Testament. A case-by-case study must be made.

Probably the most referred-to criteria for validating allusions is that offered by Richard Hays.[9] He discusses several criteria, which has the cumulative effect of pointing to the presence of an allusion.

---

[7]E.g., see Richard B. Hays, *Echoes of Scripture in the Letters of Paul* (New Haven, CT: Yale University Press, 1989), pp. 18-21, 30-31, 119; yet on the other hand Hays at other times clearly distinguishes between quotation, allusion and echo, representing Old Testament references on a descending scale (respectively) of *certain, probable* and *possible* (pp. 20, 23-24, 29).

[8]Echoes may also include an author's unconscious reference to the Old Testament, though such references are more subtle and more difficult to validate. See, e.g., G. K. Beale, "Revelation," in G. K. Beale and D. A. Carson, *Commentary on the New Testament Use of the Old Testament* (Grand Rapids: Baker Academic, 2007), pp. 319-21; and Christopher A. Beetham, *Echoes of Scripture in the Letter of Paul to the Colossians* (Boston: Brill, 2009), pp. 20-24, 34-35, for discussion of the possibility of distinguishing conscious from unconscious allusions and echoes, though Beetham sees a clear distinction between "allusion" and "echo." His argument for such a distinction is the best that we have seen.

[9]Hays, *Echoes of Scripture,* pp. 29-32, further elaborated in his *The Conversion of the Imagination* (Grand Rapids: Eerdmans, 2005), pp. 34-44. We have added a few of our own explanatory comments to Hays's criteria and have revised some. See also Beetham, *Echoes of Scripture in Colossians,* pp. 28-34, who also follows and expands somewhat on Hays's criteria.

1. The source text (the Greek or Hebrew Old Testament) must be available to the writer. The writer would have expected his audience on a first or subsequent readings to recognize the intended allusion.

2. There is a significant degree of verbatim repetition of words or syntactical patterns.

3. There are references in the immediate context (or elsewhere by the same author) to the same Old Testament context from which the purported allusion derives.

4. The alleged Old Testament allusion is suitable and satisfying in that its meaning in the Old Testament not only thematically fits into the New Testament writer's argument but also illuminates it and enhances the rhetorical punch.

5. There is plausibility that the New Testament writer could have intended such an allusion and that the audience could have understood it to varying degrees, especially on subsequent readings of his letters. Nevertheless, it is always possible that readers may not pick up an allusion intended by an author (this part of the criterion has some overlap with the first). Also, if it can be demonstrated that the New Testament writer's use of the Old Testament has parallels and analogies to other contemporary Jewish uses of the same Old Testament passages, then this enhances the validity of the allusion.

6. It is important to survey the history of the interpretation of the New Testament passage in order to see whether others have observed the allusion. This is, however, one of the least reliable criteria in recognizing allusions. Though a study of past interpretation may reveal the possible allusions proposed by others, it can also lead to a narrowing of the possibilities, since commentators can tend to follow earlier commentators and since commentary tradition always has the possibility of distorting or misinterpreting and losing the fresh and creative approach of the New Testament writers' inner-biblical collocations.

Hays's approach is one of the best ways of discerning and discussing the nature and validity of allusions (though he likes the term "echoes"), despite the fact, as we have seen, that some scholars have been critical of his methodology.[10]

---

[10]For a sampling of scholars favorable to Hays's approach, see Benjamin L. Gladd, *Revealing the Mysterion: The Use of Mystery in Daniel and Second Temple Judaism with Its Bearing on First Corinthians*, BZNW 160 (Berlin: Walter de Gruyter, 2008), pp. 3-4nn5, 9. See likewise G. K. Beale, *A Handbook on the New Testament Use of the Old Testament: Exegesis and Interpretation* (Grand Rap-

Ultimately, what matters most is the uniqueness of a word, word combination, word order or even a theme (if the latter is especially unique).

Nevertheless, it needs to be remembered that weighing the evidence for recognizing allusions is not an exact science but a literary art. Readers will make different judgments on the basis of the same evidence, some categorizing a reference as probable, and others viewing the same reference as only possible, or even so faint as to not merit analysis. Some may still wonder, however, whether an author has intended to make a particular allusion. They may wonder, if the author really intended to convey all the meaning from an Old Testament text, should the author not have made the connection with that text more explicit? In some of these cases, it is possible that later authors (like Paul) may have merely presupposed the Old Testament connection in their mind, since they were deeply entrenched in the Old Testament Scriptures. This would not mean that there is no semantic link with the Old Testament text under discussion, but rather that the author was either not conscious of making the reference or was not necessarily intending his audience to pick up on the allusion or echo. In either case, identification of the reference and enhancement of meaning that comes from the context of the source text may well disclose the author's underlying or implicit presuppositions, which form the basis for his explicit statements in the text.

With this intertextual discussion in mind, we can now proceed to our approach in evaluating mystery in the Old Testament, early Judaism and the New Testament. Occurring only nine times in the canonical Old Testament, the technical term *mystery* (Aramaic *rāz*) is found in the book of Daniel, whereas *mystērion* (Greek) occurs twenty-eight times in the New Testament. For the most part, early Judaism is deeply indebted to Daniel's conception of mystery, employing both the Aramaic and Greek terms for "mystery" a few hundred times. Our project will begin with an analysis of *mystery* in Daniel, followed by a brief survey of the term in early Judaism. Once we have established the ap-

---

ids: Baker Academic, 2012), pp. 32-35, on which this section on echoes, allusions and Hays's methodology has been based (and which also discusses scholars unfavorable to Hays's approach). Helpful works that discuss similar criteria as Hays for identifying allusions made by latter Old Testament writers of earlier Old Testament passages are, among others, Richard L. Schultz, *The Search for Quotation: Verbal Parallels in the Prophets,* JSOTSup 180 (Sheffield: Sheffield Academic Press, 1999), pp. 222-39; B. D. Sommer, "Exegesis, Allusion and Intertextuality in the Hebrew Bible: A Response to Lyle Eslinger," *VT* 46 (1996): 479-89, who also cite sources in this respect for further consultation. For a case-by-case analysis of significant inner-biblical allusions, see, e.g., Michael Fishbane, *Biblical Interpretation in Ancient Israel* (Oxford: Clarendon, 1985).

propriate background of *mystery,* we will then proceed to investigate each occurrence in the New Testament.

One may ask why we have decided to write on the topic of mystery, since there exist other surveys on this topic. Our desire to write this project stems from the lack of an exegetical and biblical-theological analysis of *mystery,* and especially of how the word informs the relationship between the Old Testament and the New Testament. Some of the older surveys of mystery do evaluate each occurrence of *mystery* in the Bible but are notoriously brief and largely void of detailed interaction with the immediate contexts. On the other hand, several monographs have been written on mystery as it pertains to a certain book or theme, and these works tend to be much more exegetically driven. Our project attempts to fill this gap by analyzing each occurrence of the word and paying special attention to the immediate context. We intend to unpack each occurrence of *mystery* by focusing on the surrounding Old Testament allusions and quotations, that occur in association with most of the uses of *mystery.* In other words, examining Old Testament quotations and allusions helps unlock the content of the revealed mystery. Part of the upshot of our work will be to confirm that, indeed, the older approach of understanding the New Testament's view of mystery against the background of pagan religions is not the best approach,[11] but rather, in line with more relatively recent studies, that the New Testament concept should be mainly understood in light of the Old Testament (and to a lesser degree Jewish developments of the Old Testament).

This project is intended for students, scholars, pastors and laypeople who seriously engage the Scriptures. This project is particularly complex, as it engages several extraordinarily difficult texts. Much ink has been spilled debating these texts, and scholars continue to dispute many of these passages. We have attempted to make this project more accessible by limiting our interaction with secondary sources (commentaries, journals, etc.) and focusing on the primary sources (the Old Testament and Jewish sources). We have also placed many discussions of relevant Old Testament and Jewish texts at the end of each chapter in excursuses, allowing the reader to grasp more easily the flow of the argument in the main body of the chapter. We intend the excursuses to provide further substantiation of the arguments in the main body.

Our hope is that scholars and students will benefit from the broad nature

---

[11]See chap. 11 below for a discussion of this "history of religions" approach.

of the investigation, especially the ways in which the term *mystery* is linked to Old Testament references (and the relevant bibliography). We hope that pastors and students will benefit from this project because of its emphasis on how the two Testaments relate. The New Testament often incorporates Old Testament quotations and themes but expresses them in new ways, though still retaining some continuity with the Old Testament. It may be helpful for lay readers to ignore some of the detailed discussions contained in the footnotes and focus on the body. We have attempted to keep the work at a level for both seriously interested laypeople, as well as students and scholars. For those looking for more detailed exploration of Old Testament and Jewish themes or texts, as noted, we have placed many of these discussions in excursuses at the ends of the chapters.

Each use of *mystery* that we will study in the New Testament will be conducted in the same general methodological manner: we will first examine the immediate New Testament context of each occurrence. We will then explore the Old Testament and Jewish background in each case. Some usages simply will not require as much Old Testament or Jewish background investigation. At the end of each study of *mystery* in the New Testament, we will attempt to show how it stands in both continuity and discontinuity with the Old Testament and Judaism. The New Testament employs the term *mystery* in a variety of ways and applies it to a number of doctrines and ideas. Since the scope of this project is fairly broad, we are forced to keep our surveys relatively brief and to the point. Chapter one, though, serves as the backbone to the project, so we often refer back to that chapter and the concepts contained therein.

1

The Use of *Mystery* in Daniel

As we will see when we come to the use of *mystery* in the New Testament,[1] the use of the term sometimes, if not often, has its background in its use in Daniel 2 and Daniel 4. Therefore, we begin the first substantive chapter of our book with a study of *mystery* in Daniel.

The word *mystery* plays a pivotal role in the book of Daniel. The term encapsulates both the symbolic form of revelation and the interpretation. In addition, *mystery* is associated with an end-time element that accompanies the content of the revelation. In order for us to grasp the nature and significance of *mystery*, we must pay close attention to the book of Daniel's narrative.

Understanding the Old Testament and the early Jewish background of the New Testament is crucial to grasping its meaning and application.[2] Ignoring this background material is a little like watching a sequel to a movie but never the original; the audience would be unfamiliar with the characters and plotline. Similarly, studying only the New Testament's use of *mystery* (*mystērion*) without any knowledge of its use in Daniel or Jewish literature will inevitably lead to a skewed understanding.

As scholars have argued in recent years, the New Testament's use of *mystery* remains tethered to the book of Daniel. But the list of those who have developed significantly the concept of mystery in the book of Daniel is surprisingly brief. The discussions are generally restricted to side comments and brief remarks from other studies. Even seminal works on the Jewish nature of the

---

[1]E.g., see the following chapters on Mt 13; 1 Cor 2; Eph 3; 2 Thess 2; and Revelation.
[2]Used with permission, this chapter is adapted from Benjamin L. Gladd, *Revealing the* Mysterion: *The Use of Mystery in Daniel and Second Temple Judaism with Its Bearing on First Corinthians*, BZNW 160 (Berlin: Walter de Gruyter, 2008), pp. 17-50.

term dedicate only a paragraph or so to this topic.[3] We, though, will work through both Daniel's and the Jewish conception of mystery in some detail, since this chapter will lay a proper foundation for the remainder of this project.[4]

The book of Daniel and early Judaism present mystery as a revelation concerning end-time events that were previously hidden but have been subsequently revealed. Critical to understanding the biblical mystery is the nature of hiddenness. *We will argue that the revelation of mystery is not a totally new revelation but the full disclosure of something that was to a significant extent hidden.* It is this tension between mystery being a revelation of something not completely hidden yet hidden to a significant extent that we hope to tease out in this chapter and, indeed, in the book. We will unpack the book of Daniel's conception of mystery by relating it to the hymn in Daniel 2:20-23, observing the twofold form of mystery and noting its relationship to latter-day events. After we examine Daniel's understanding of mystery, we will then briefly sift through a few prominent occurrences in early Judaism.

MYSTERY IN DANIEL

It is no wonder that a book in which a king constructs a huge statue, a person is tossed into a pit of lions, four ghastly beasts arise out of the water only to be judged by a figure riding on the clouds, and hostile opponents wage war against Israel and blaspheme God continues to pique the interest of many. The book of Daniel also displays a somewhat unique view of the disclosure of God's wisdom as the revelation of a mystery. Further developing the Old Testament understanding of wisdom, Daniel presents God's wisdom as manifesting itself in the form of symbolic communication that is indeed mysterious, communication that must be interpreted by an angel or a divinely gifted individual. While previous expressions of wisdom in the Old Testament contain such features (e.g., Joseph interprets Pharaoh's symbolic dreams in Gen 41), the book of Daniel further develops these expressions: the primary manner in which God communicates within the book of Daniel is through symbolism (dreams,

---

[3]Raymond Brown, *The Semitic Background of the Term "Mystery" in the New Testament*, BS 21 (Philadelphia: Fortress, 1968), pp. 7-8; Günther Bornkamm, "μυστήριον, μυέω," in *TDNT* 4:814-15; Markus Bockmuehl, *Revelation and Mystery in Ancient Judaism and Pauline Christianity*, WUNT 36 (Tübingen: Mohr Siebeck, 1990; repr., Grand Rapids: Eerdmans, 1997), pp. 15-16, 48, 101-2.

[4]G. K. Beale, *The Use of Daniel in Jewish Apocalyptic Literature and in the Revelation of St. John* (Lanham, MD: University Press of America, 1984), pp. 12-22; G. K. Beale, *John's Use of the Old Testament in Revelation*, JSNTSup 166 (Sheffield: Sheffield Academic Press, 1998), pp. 215-16; Gladd, *Revealing the Mysterion*, pp. 17-50.

writing on the wall, etc.). But not only is the mode of the communication developed, the content is as well. Nestled within the symbolic communication are highly charged end-time events. The book of Daniel has much to say about what will transpire in the "latter days." A great persecution and rampant false teaching will befall the Israelites in the end time, but eventually the enemy will be put down. God will raise the righteous Israelites from the dead, judge the ungodly and establish his eternal kingdom.

The English word *mystery* in Daniel is a translation of an Aramaic noun (*rāz*) that appears a total of nine times in the book (Dan 2:18, 19, 27-30, 47; 4:9 [4:6 MT]). Each time the word is used, the Greek translations of Daniel consistently render it *mystērion* ("mystery"). Understanding the term *mystery* requires us to connect it with Daniel's conception of wisdom. We will now proceed to analyze *mystery* and its companion word and concept, *wisdom,* throughout the book of Daniel.

The first two uses of *mystery* prominently occur in Daniel 2, which narrate that Nebuchadnezzar "dreamed dreams," but with great consternation, for his "spirit was troubled" (Dan 2:1). Nebuchadnezzar envisions a magnificent colossus that possessed a head of gold, chest and arms of silver, belly and thighs of bronze, legs of iron, and feet mixed with clay and iron (Dan 2:32-33). Despite its seemingly impregnable stature, a rock that was "cut out without hands" (Dan 2:34) smashes the statue's feet, resulting in a total decimation of the colossus. The "rock" then grows into a mountain filling the entire earth (Dan 2:35). Daniel then interprets the enigmatic dream and relates to Nebuchadnezzar that the four parts of the statue symbolize four kingdoms (which are often interpreted as Babylon, Medo-Persia, Greece and Rome). The fourth and final kingdom, the iron and clay feet, is eclipsed by God's eternal kingdom that "put an end to all these kingdoms" (Dan 2:44). The rock plays a central role in the establishment of this latter-day kingdom, as it could symbolize a divinely appointed individual (Judaism interpreted the rock as messianic) or simply the eternal kingdom itself (Dan 2:45).

Before Daniel interprets the dream, the king summons the Babylonian diviners and commands them to relate the dream because his "spirit is anxious to understand the dream" (Dan 2:3). But because the Babylonian wise men are unable to relate to the king either the dream or the interpretation (Dan 2:4, 7, 10-11), Nebuchadnezzar decrees that all the wise men in Babylon are to be destroyed (Dan 2:12-13). After catching wind of this drastic measure from Arioch

(Dan 2:14-15), Daniel approaches the king and begs for time, so that he may "declare the interpretation" to Nebuchadnezzar (Dan 2:16).

Following his plea, Daniel and his friends "request compassion from the God of heaven" concerning "this mystery" (Dan 2:17-18), and God subsequently answers their request in Daniel's night vision (Dan 2:19). Immediately following the reception of the mystery, Daniel blesses God through a hymn. At this juncture in the narrative, the reader is presented with a key text for understanding the entire book of Daniel. In this respect, Daniel 2:17-19, which has two uses of *mystery*, says,

> Then Daniel went to his house and informed his friends, Hananiah, Mishael and Azariah, about the matter, so that they might request compassion from the God of heaven concerning this <u>mystery</u>, so that Daniel and his friends would not be destroyed with the rest of the wise men of Babylon. Then the <u>mystery</u> was revealed to Daniel in a night vision.

In Daniel 2:18, *mystery* appears with the demonstrative pronoun *this*, referring to the preceding discussion: Nebuchadnezzar demands to know the dream he had and its interpretation (Dan 2:4-6, 9, 16). Daniel labels the king's dream and its meaning a "mystery." Since Nebuchadnezzar's request included both the dream and its interpretation, *mystery* encompasses both of these components. However, it is likely that Nebuchadnezzar himself knew the content of the dream but did not know the interpretation.[5]

The analogy with Nebuchadnezzar's dream in Daniel 4 points further to the king having knowledge of the content of the dream. The reason the king asks his diviners in Daniel 2 for not only the dream's interpretation but also its content is to validate that whoever gave the interpretation had also received supernaturally the content of the dream, thus also validating the interpretation. Nebuchadnezzar had two symbolic dreams, and he knew both dreams were symbolic (Dan 2:1-3; 4:5-6). Since both dreams were symbolic, Nebuchadnezzar summoned the Babylonian wise men, and after they failed to interpret the dreams he summoned

---

[5]According to Dan 2:16, Daniel requests additional time, so that he may disclose "the interpretation to the king." It is possible that *mystery* here only includes the dream's interpretation and not the dream itself. This, however, does not do justice to the surrounding context. The dream and its interpretation are mentioned together in Dan 2:4, 5, 6, 7, 9, 26. Nebuchadnezzar desires to know the content of the dream, but it must be interpreted. When Daniel requested time to declare the interpretation to the king, he *assumed* that the dream would be part of this disclosure. Therefore, both the dream and its interpretation are a mystery (see Brown, *Semitic Background*, p. 7; Beale, *Use of Daniel*, p. 13).

Daniel. The point is that King Nebuchadnezzar was aware that his dreams required an additional revelation of the symbolism, the interpretation of which remained a mystery to him. We will address below whether or not he was *completely* unaware of the interpretation of the symbolic dreams.

Thus far, the term *mystery* includes the dream and its interpretation (from Daniel's viewpoint), but the psalm in Daniel 2:20-23 lends further insight into the relationship between mystery and wisdom. The impetus for this psalm is the disclosure of the mystery to Daniel: "Then the mystery was revealed to Daniel in a night vision. Then Daniel blessed the God of heaven." Therefore, the contents of Daniel 2:20-23 should directly relate to the nature of mystery. Since these verses significantly affect Daniel 2 and the nature of mystery, we will analyze the passage and then relate it to the immediate and broader context.

The Hymn of Daniel 2:20-23

Daniel 2:20-22 uniquely describe the character of God and his relationship to the mystery:

> 20a Let the name of God be blessed forever and ever,
> 20b For wisdom and power belong to Him.
> 21a It is He who changes the times and the epochs;
> 21b He removes kings and establishes kings;
> 21c He gives wisdom to wise men
> 21d And knowledge to men of understanding.
> 22a It is He who reveals the profound and hidden things;
> 22b He knows what is in the darkness, and the light dwells with Him.

Line 20b states the reason for the blessing in 20a: "Let the name of God be blessed . . . for wisdom and power belong to him." Moreover, 20b is defined in the following lines (21a-22b) and appears to be central: wisdom and power originate from God alone. Lines 21a-21b describe God's power—he "changes the times" by "removing kings"—whereas lines 21c-22a concern God disclosing his wisdom—"he gives wisdom . . . and knowledge. It is he who reveals the profound and hidden things." Line 22b grounds 21c-22a, stating the basis for that disclosure: "He who reveals the <u>profound and hidden things</u> . . . [because] he knows what is in the darkness, and the light dwells with him." In sum, Daniel exalts and blesses God because he is truly powerful and wise. He exercises his power by removing and establishing kings and discloses his wisdom because he is all knowing.

The second section, Daniel 2:23, shifts from the third person to second, high-lighting God's actions but with reference to Daniel.[6]

> 23a To You, O God of my fathers, I give thanks and praise,
>
> 23b For You have given me wisdom and power;
>
> 23c Even now You have made known to me what we requested of You,
>
> 23d For You have made known to us the king's matter.

Daniel's praise to God is clearly exhibited in line 23a ("To You . . . I give thanks and praise") and grounded by lines 23b-d. We again detect notions of wisdom, power and revelation in 23b. God's deliverance of Daniel from distress can be seen in line 23b: "You have given me wisdom." Lines 23c-d further unpack God giving Daniel wisdom: "You have made known to me what we requested of you, for you have made known to us the king's matter." The first section, lines 20b-22b, is therefore rehearsed in the second section, yet narrowly referring to Daniel.

Keeping this psalm in mind, we are able to draw a few important conclusions. The first section (Dan 2:20-22) articulates God "removing" and "establishing" kings and giving wisdom to "wise men." In the second section (Dan 2:23), God gives Daniel wisdom concerning the rise and fall of kings (i.e., Nebuchadnezzar). To take this one step further, Daniel has already labeled this disclosure a "mystery" in Daniel 2:18-19. Therefore, according to Daniel 2:23 (which assumes Dan 2:20-22), *mystery may be initially and generally defined as the complete unveiling of hidden end-time events.*

At its most basic level, the term *mystery* concerns God *revealing* his wisdom. This accounts for the high appropriation of revealing or disclosing vocabulary throughout the book of Daniel. The verb "to reveal" (Aramaic *gālâ*) appears eight times, referring to God "disclosing" either "mysteries" (Dan 2:19, 28-30), "profound and hidden things" (Dan 2:22) or a visionary "message" (Dan 10:1). The disclosure of God's wisdom is the common denominator of each of these passages.

Therefore, although revelatory language is lacking in Daniel 4, it is still valid to call Nebuchadnezzar's dream in this chapter a "revelation." The same characterization can also be applied to Daniel's visions in Daniel 7–12. Furthermore, in Daniel 7:1, Daniel "saw a dream and visions" that are likely analogous to Nebuchadnezzar's dreams in Daniel 2 and Daniel 4. Just as God delivers his

---

[6]G. T. M. Prinsloo, "Two Poems in a Sea of Prose: The Content and Context of Daniel 2.20-23 and 6.27-28," *JSOT* 59 (1993): 97.

wisdom to Daniel to know and interpret the dreams of Nebuchadnezzar in Daniel 2–4, God directly discloses his wisdom to Daniel in Daniel 7–12 and furnishes Daniel with wisdom to understand them.

Form of the Mystery

A distinctive characteristic of Daniel is the nature of twofold revelation in contrast to other places in the Old Testament where the prophets directly receive God's revelation. Our aim in this section is to outline the basic structure of wisdom in the book of Daniel. This analysis will encompass its two major features: initial and partial revelation followed by a subsequent and fuller interpretation.

In Daniel 2, Nebuchadnezzar dreams and desires to know the interpretation (Dan 2:1-13). God reveals both the dream and the interpretation—the mystery—to Daniel in a "night vision" (Dan 2:19), outlined in Daniel 2:31-45. This disclosure of God's wisdom is marked by the term *interpretation* (Aramaic *pešer*), which is used thirty-four times in Daniel. The term *pešer* has been extensively discussed, especially in Near Eastern[7] and Qumran studies,[8] but for our present purposes, we will only discuss how it relates to *mystery* in Daniel.

The term *interpretation* may harken back to Genesis 40–41, where the cupbearer and baker had dreams and Joseph delivered their "interpretations" (Gen 40:5-19). Likewise, Pharaoh's dream cannot be interpreted by anyone except Joseph (Gen 41:14-32). Just as Joseph delivers the interpretation to the baker, the cupbearer and Pharaoh, so Daniel interprets for Nebuchadnezzar.

We will now evaluate Nebuchadnezzar's dream in Daniel 4 and direct our attention to a subtle yet important feature of the mystery, since the word appears there also (Dan 4:9: "no mystery baffles you [Daniel]"). It appears that Nebuchadnezzar has some insight into the symbolic meaning of his dream *before* Daniel discloses the dream's interpretation. This observation affects our general understanding of mystery at a fundamental level. On this basis, we will argue that *mystery* is not a radically new revelation but a disclosure of something that was largely (but not entirely) hidden.

Following the model set in Daniel 2, king Nebuchadnezzar has another revelatory dream in Daniel 4, motivating him once again to summon the Baby-

---

[7]Michael Fishbane, *Biblical Interpretation in Ancient Israel* (Oxford: Clarendon, 1985), pp. 454-56.
[8]E.g., W. H. Brownlee, "Biblical Interpretation Among the Sectaries of the Dead Sea Scrolls," *BA* 14 (1951): 54-76.

lonian diviners. In contrast to Daniel 2 where the king does not reveal the dream, this time Nebuchadnezzar reveals to them the content of his dream: "I related the dream to them, but they could not make its interpretation known to me" (Dan 4:7). Nebuchadnezzar not only demonstrates knowledge of his dream to Daniel, but also a *partial* understanding of its interpretation. The dream describes the story of a huge cosmic tree that provided food for all the animals (Dan 4:10-12). But in Daniel 4:13, the dream progresses (note the introductory formula in Dan 4:13a introducing an angelic interpreter), and an angelic messenger supplements the dream and gives a partial interpretation. When the angel communicates the destruction of the tree, he interprets the tree as a *person*:

> He shouted out and spoke as follows:
> "Chop down the tree and cut off its branches,
> Strip off its foliage and scatter its fruit;
> Let the beasts flee from under it
> And the birds from its branches.
> Yet leave the stump with its roots in the ground,
> But with a band of iron and bronze *around it*
> In the new grass of the field;
> And let him be drenched with the dew of heaven,
> And let him share with the beasts in the grass of the earth.
> Let his mind be changed from *that of* a man
> And let a beast's mind be given to him,
> And let seven periods of time pass over him." (Dan 4:14-16)

Though the Aramaic third person pronoun remains the same throughout this passage (masculine singular), referring to the tree and then to a person represented by the tree, the angel clearly interprets the tree as a prominent figure in Daniel 4:15-16. Within the dream report that Nebuchadnezzar receives, an angel interprets the tree as a royal figure.[9] One Greek translation (Old Greek) of Daniel 4 is particularly relevant in that the translation explicitly attributes partial understanding of the dream to Nebuchadnezzar (see excursus 1.1 below).

In Daniel 4:10-15, Nebuchadnezzar envisions a cosmic tree. Not coincidentally, cosmic trees elsewhere in the Old Testament symbolize prominent nations or individual kings. Ezekiel 17:23 (Israel), Ezekiel 31:1-2, 18 (the king of

---

[9]The mention of an angel in the Greek translation of Dan 2:11 (OG) who gives an interpretation points further to the similar nature of the Daniel 2 and Daniel 4 vision narratives.

Egypt) and Ezekiel 31:3-17 (Assyria) all contain language very similar to Daniel 4:12. In Daniel 4:5, Nebuchadnezzar states, "I saw a dream and <u>it made me fearful</u>; and these fantasies as I lay on my bed and <u>the visions in my mind kept alarming me</u>." It is possible to understand the king's fearful reaction to the dream strictly as an effect of the bizarre dream. On the other hand, it is also very possible that the king's behavior stems from *his suspicion that the dream may apply to him*. Nebuchadnezzar's dream in Daniel 4 follows his dream in Daniel 2, whereby the eventual destruction of the Babylonian Empire is symbolically portrayed in the annihilation of the golden head (Dan 2:32-35), which further suggests that the king senses that this second dream was also about his demise. Moreover, that the king had some sense of the dream's interpretation of the interpretative portion of the mystery (Dan 2:36-45) may be suggested from observing that Daniel describes king Nebuchadnezzar's rule much in the same way that the angel describes the cosmic tree in Daniel 4:11-12.

> You, O king, are the king of kings, to whom the God of heaven has given the kingdom, the power, the strength and the glory; and wherever the sons of men dwell, *or* the <u>beasts of the field</u>, or the <u>birds of the sky</u>, He has given *them* into your hand and has caused you to rule over them all. You are the head of gold. (Dan 2:37-38)

> The tree grew large and became strong
> And its height reached to the sky,
> And it *was* visible to the end of the whole earth.
> Its foliage *was* beautiful and its fruit abundant,
> And in it *was* food for all.
> The <u>beasts of the field</u> found shade under it,
> And the <u>birds of the sky</u> dwelt in its branches,
> And all living creatures fed themselves from it. (Dan 4:11-12)

The tight connection between Daniel 2 and Daniel 4 is well documented, and if the connection between the two chapters is valid, then the king most likely believed that his vision of the cosmic tree somehow involved himself, even before Daniel interpreted it for him. Whether or not this is the case, Daniel's interpretation of Nebuchadnezzar's dream in Daniel 4:19-27 is a further unpacking or full interpretation of a partially existing interpretation, which was already known by the king himself. The king already knew that the symbolic tree that was felled represented some leader or king somewhere, and, if he had a sense that the dream was about his own demise, then he knew even more about the interpretation of the symbolic dream. In other words, Daniel more fully interprets the king's dream *and* a partial (perhaps very partial) interpretation of it that the king already possessed!

It may be the case that Nebuchadnezzar's dream in Daniel 2 follows suit. According to Daniel 2:30b, Daniel claims to interpret "for the purpose of making the interpretation known to the king, and <u>that you may understand the thoughts of your mind</u>" ("thoughts" already in his mind, which may have been more than the mere recollection of the symbolic dream; cf. Dan 7:1). This verse may very well reveal that Nebuchadnezzar had *some* insight into the interpretation of his dream in Daniel 2.

Similar to Daniel 4, the king was "was troubled and his sleep left him," and he was "anxious to understand the dream" (Dan 2:1-3). Though Nebuchadnezzar withholds the symbolic dream from the Babylonian wise men, he may very well have told Daniel a portion of his dream and, perhaps, even told Daniel part of what he thought the dream meant. It is difficult to say either way, as the text is silent. Nevertheless, if Daniel 2 and Daniel 4 involve similar content, identical characters (the king, Nebuchadnezzar, the Babylonian diviners and Daniel) and the same revelatory framework (both are labeled a "mystery": Dan 2:18-19; 4:9), then what is true of the dream report in Daniel 4 may well also be true of dream report of Daniel 2. Thus, because of the close connections between Daniel 2 and Daniel 4, Nebuchadnezzar may also have already had some degree of insight into the symbolic meaning of his dream in Daniel 2 before it was fully interpreted by Daniel.

The remainder of Daniel generally follows the established pattern of initial, partial revelation and a subsequent interpretation. In Daniel 5 a twofold pattern of cryptic revelation and interpretation surfaces (Dan 5:7-8, 15-17, 24-28). The cryptic revelation (like the dreams) is the inscription on the wall (Dan 5:5-9). Only Daniel has the ability to give an accurate interpretation. As in Daniel 1–6, the disclosing of wisdom in Daniel 7–12 is couched in the typical two-part structure. Daniel 7 has long been considered to be linked with Daniel 2, since the four beasts are likened to four kingdoms. In addition to this thematic tie, cryptic revelation and its interpretation closely resembles Daniel 2; 4; 5. Like Nebuchadnezzar and Belshazzar, Daniel seeks an interpretation in Daniel 7:16 ("So he told me and made known to me the <u>interpretation</u> of these things") and Daniel 7:19 ("Then I desired to know the exact meaning of the fourth beast").

As in Daniel 7, Daniel desires to receive an interpretation in Daniel 8:15-17:

"When I, Daniel, had seen the vision, I sought to understand it; . . . I heard the voice of a man between *the banks of* Ulai, and he called out and said, 'Gabriel, give this *man* an understanding of the vision'" (cf. Dan 8:18-19). Like the preceding episodes, this cryptic revelation is interpreted through an angelic messenger (Dan 8:19-26).

Daniel 9 differs from Daniel 7–8, since Daniel does not receive an initial vision (Dan 9:22-23); instead, Daniel reads from Jeremiah's prophecy concerning the "seventy years" (Jer 25:11-12; 29:10). But it is worth noting that Jeremiah received the seventy-years prophecy "as the word of the Lord" (Dan 9:2). Thus, Daniel is reading what God *revealed* to Jeremiah. Daniel "observes" what God revealed to Jeremiah and understands that the interpretation of Jeremiah's prediction included seventy literal years of captivity for Israel (Dan 9:2). In addition, God delivers a further interpretation to Daniel in a vision (Dan 9:22-23) concerning "Jeremiah's revelation" and, again, through an angel (Dan 9:22-23, 24-27). It is likely that the angel's interpretation was a figurative (or perhaps typological) understanding of Jeremiah's prophecy.[10] The point is that Daniel understood the initial meaning of God's revelation to Jeremiah but then the angel gives a further interpretation, which is based on an understanding of the initial revelation. Again, an idea of "partial hiddenness—fuller revelation" is expressed here. Likely Daniel had little understanding of the angel's further interpretation of Jeremiah, except that this interpretation was based on and arose from his literal understanding of the original prophecy.

Daniel 10–12 constitutes the final vision of the book. This visionary experience further develops the themes found in Daniel 7–8,[11] as well as Daniel 2. Unlike the previous visions, this one does not explicitly use the two-tiered approach (cryptic then revealed revelation). It may, however, imply this distinction, for in Daniel 10:21 the angel is not delivering direct revelation: "I will tell you what is inscribed in the writing of truth." The notion of "inscribing" and

---

[10]On which see, e.g., Meredith G. Kline, "The Covenant of the Seventieth Week," in *The Law and the Prophets: Old Testament Studies Prepared in Honor of Oswald Thompson Allis*, ed. John H. Skilton (Phillipsburg, NJ: P & R, 1974), pp. 452-69. Though Kline denies that Dan 9:24-27 is an "interpretation" or "reinterpretation" of Jeremiah's prophecy, we believe it is allowable within Kline's framework to see Dan 9:24-27 as drawing out typological implications of the historical fulfillment of Jeremiah's prophecy of Israel's seventy years of captivity (see pp. 454, 460-64, which may point to a typological interpretation). In this respect, see the close verbal parallel in the LXX between 2 Chron 36:21-22, Lev 26:34 and Jer 25:12, all of which prophesy Israel's seventy-year captivity and show an intertextual connection. On the verbal parallels linking these three texts, see further G. K. Beale, *The Erosion of Inerrancy in Evangelicalism* (Wheaton: Crossway, 2008), pp. 139-42.

[11]Tremper Longman, *Daniel*, NIVAC (Grand Rapids: Zondervan, 1999), p. 245.

"writing" strongly allude to Daniel 5 with the writing on the wall (Dan 5:24-25) and may suggest that the angel is functioning in an interpretative role.[12]

Significantly, Daniel understands the interpretation of the dream revealed to him in Daniel 2, as well as the later elaboration of end-time visions and declarations of it in Daniel 10–12 (see Dan 10:1, 11-14), where Daniel is said to have understood the "word" and vision of Daniel 10–12. Nevertheless, he still does not understand the vast majority of this later revelatory elaboration, as Daniel 12:4, 8-9 makes clear (e.g., note Dan 12:8: "I heard but could not understand"). That the elaborated prophecy is to be "concealed and sealed" (Dan 12:4, 9) refers both to the time during which it remains unfulfilled and the time during which it is not understood. Fulfillment thus brings with it greater understanding. In this respect, we have Daniel initially having no understanding of the revelatory dream in Daniel 2, then having a significantly greater understanding of the dream later in Daniel 2, and then the subsequent elaboration of the Daniel 2 and Daniel 7 eschatological vision in Daniel 10–12 reaffirms Daniel's basic understanding of the end-time events. Finally, however, in Daniel 12:4, 8-9 it is evident that even Daniel still only has a partial understanding of these events, since a much greater apprehension of what he has seen and heard in Daniel 11:1–12:3 can only come with the fulfillment of the visionary prophecy.

Therefore, in our analysis we can determine that wisdom in Daniel is characterized by a twofold structure: symbolic and interpretative revelation. Revelation has taken the form of dreams, writing, previous prophecy and visions. It would therefore be a mistake to bifurcate any of these forms of revelation, since each of these modes is an expression of God's revealed wisdom. Revelation, albeit in several mediums, such as dreams, writing and Old Testament Scripture, remains largely hidden until the fuller interpretation has been provided. Note, however, that a partial interpretation of a dream report can be embedded within the initial revelation of the dream. The *full* interpretation remains unknown to individuals, even to the seer (i.e., Nebuchadnezzar, Daniel). It is not until the fuller interpretation has been given that the initial, hidden revelation as a mystery is understood. And even then it is only when the end-time events prophesied in the vision are fulfilled that even fuller understanding comes (e.g., note the emphasis on the "wise ones" who enjoy significant insight during the unfolding of the end-time events: Dan 11:33-35; 12:3, 10).

---

[12]Cf. David W. Gooding, "The Literary Structure of the Book of Daniel and Its Implications," *TynBul* 32 (1981): 68.

Though our study affirms the general maxim that mystery constitutes a revelation that was previously hidden but now has been revealed, we refine this definition by adding that the initial, symbolic revelation was not entirely hidden, though most of it was unknown. The idea of "partial hiddenness—fuller revelation" is apparent in Daniel 2 and Daniel 4, the only places in Daniel where the word *mystery* actually occurs. Thus subsequent revelation discloses the fuller meaning of end-time events. We have endeavored to show that this idea of "partial hiddenness—fuller revelation" is apparent not only in Daniel 2 and Daniel 4 but also in Daniel 9. There is not sufficient space within the scope of this book to analyze in any depth Daniel 5, Daniel 7–8 and Daniel 10–12 to see if the same notion is expressed there. It is possible that such an idea is not apparent in these other passages, though one might expect that the subsequent revelations in Daniel would follow the pattern of the earlier ones, especially since they recapitulate one another (especially Dan 2 is recapitulated to a great extent in Dan 7, and to varying degrees in Dan 8, Dan 9 and Dan 10–12). In this respect, we briefly discussed Daniel 10–12 and saw there that the fulfillment of the end-time visions and prophecies indeed do bring with them even fuller understanding of these prophecies hitherto partially understood by Daniel. Thus, there is in Daniel actually a threefold pattern: (1) little understanding of a prophetic vision (possibly by Nebuchadnezzar in Dan 2, and by Nebuchadnezzar and Daniel in Dan 4), (2) followed by an interpretation that reveals greater understanding of the prophecy, which (3) is then followed by fulfillment of the prophecy, bringing with it an even greater understanding than before.

THE END-TIME COMPONENT OF THE MYSTERY

Wisdom, according to the book of Daniel, is related to knowledge about eschatological events. By *eschatological,* we mean those events that are to take place in the "latter days." The phrase "latter days" and synonymous expressions refer to the end time and are used throughout the Old Testament. In the Old Testament, these expressions pertain among other things to a time of distress (Deut 4:30; 8:16; Ezek 38:8, 16), the restoration of Israel (Is 2:2; Jer 23:20; 30:24; Hos 3:5; Mic 4:1), and a ruler who ushers in peace and prosperity to Israel (Gen 49:1; Num 24:14). In Daniel 2:28, Daniel expresses one of the most insightful characteristics of the mystery: "There is a God in heaven who reveals mysteries, and He has made known to King Nebuchadnezzar what will take place in the latter days." Daniel closely conveys to Nebuchadnezzar two concepts: his God is a "revealer of mysteries," and this mystery in Daniel 2 specifically pertains to the "latter days." In Daniel 2:29, Daniel further develops this notion: "O king, *while* on your bed your thoughts turned to what would take place in the future [OG: "in the latter days"] and He who reveals mysteries has made known to you what will take place."

The end-time terminology in Daniel 2:28-29 is very appropriate given the content of the dream. The colossus represents four kingdoms that are eventually crushed by a "stone" (Dan 2:35, 44-45) and eclipsed by a "kingdom which will never be destroyed . . . but it will itself endure forever" (Dan 2:44). In Daniel 2:45, Daniel summarizes the climax of the dream, using latter-day terminology: "Inasmuch as you saw that a stone was cut out of the mountain without hands and that it crushed the iron, the bronze . . . the great God has made known to the king what will take place in the future [OG: "in the latter days"]." The remainder of Daniel touches on this main theme—God's kingdom ultimately will overthrow all others, including Nebuchadnezzar's.

Some commentators in their analysis of the term *mystery* tend to view Daniel 4 as noneschatological and disparate from Daniel 2, but this position does not take into account Daniel 4's relationship with Daniel 2. According to Daniel 2:21, God

> changes the times and the epochs;
> He removes kings and establishes kings.

In an almost striking fashion, Daniel 4:28-33 is an example/fulfillment of God "removing" a king (Dan 2:21; 4:31) and an immediate fulfillment of the mystery in Daniel 4:10-26.[13] In fact, part of the vision of Daniel 2 concerns Babylon as the first kingdom (the head of gold), and Daniel 4 focuses on a beginning judgment of this kingdom's king, which is partly prophesied in Daniel 2 (though the judgment in Dan 4 is not consummate as in Dan 2, but within the context of the book of Daniel it could be seen as leading up to such a decisive judgment).

Daniel 7–12 describes in more detail the end-time events that are outlined in Daniel 2. As in Daniel 2, four kingdoms are eclipsed by God's eternal kingdom (Dan 7:11-14). The idea of mystery in Daniel 7 represents four beasts being identified as four kingdoms that are eclipsed by God's reign. The concept of mystery in Daniel 8 is markedly eschatological (Dan 8:17-26).

Daniel's final vision in Daniel 10–12 likewise contains end-time language. In

---

[13]Beale, *Use of Daniel*, p. 15.

Daniel 10:14, an angelic messenger prefaces the upcoming visionary content: "Now I have come to give you an understanding of what will happen to your people in the latter days, for the vision pertains to the days yet *future*."[14] The eschatological events in Daniel 11–12 comprise the rise and fall of kings and the antagonism of Antiochus IV and an end-time opponent(s). A remnant will remain despite this affliction and will eventually be vindicated at the resurrection.

In sum, the content of the unveiled mystery pertains to events that take place in the latter days. These eschatological events primarily include a final tribulation, the rise and fall of Israel's antagonists, the establishment of God's end-time kingdom and finally the vindication of Israel's righteous.

Conclusion

Revelation of a mystery can be defined roughly as God fully disclosing wisdom about end-time events that were mostly hitherto unknown (Dan 2:20-23). He primarily communicates his wisdom through dreams and visions mediated by either an individual or angel. In the first half of the book, God gives his wisdom to both Nebuchadnezzar and Daniel, while in Daniel 7–12 only Daniel receives God's wisdom (via the interpreting angel).

The structure of the mystery in Daniel 2 and Daniel 4 entails a twofold characteristic—an individual receives a symbolic dream followed by a full interpretation. Elsewhere in the book this structure is also found in visions (Dan 7, 8, 10–12), writing (Dan 5) and previous prophecy (Dan 9). The two-tiered component of the mystery signals the hidden nature of the revelation and its subsequent interpretation—largely hidden but now more fully revealed. The initial revelation was not entirely hidden but only partially, and the subsequent revelation discloses the fuller meaning of end-time events.

Excursus 1.1: The Greek Old Testament's Interpretation of Daniel 4

The Old Greek translation of Daniel 4, one of the earliest commentaries on the book of Daniel, attests to the angel's initial interpretation of the dream (see table 1.1; the underlined wording represents the Greek expansion of the Aramaic text). The Theodotion Greek rendering is much more in line with the Masoretic Text (MT), whereas the Old Greek greatly expands the angel's initial

---

[14]Synonymous eschatological language is also found in Dan 11:20, 27, 35; 12:4, 7, 9, 13 (cf. 11:13). Though these verses do not use the phrase "latter days," they use terms such as *end* and *appointed time*.

interpretation. The most notable difference occurs in the last verse, where the Old Greek reads, "I [Nebuchadnezzar] described the dream for him, and he [Daniel] showed me its interpretation [*pasan tēn synkrisin*]" (Dan 4:15 [Dan 4:18 Eng.]). Both the MT and Theodotion read simply "interpretation" (Aramaic *pišrā;* Greek *to synkrima*). The Old Greek at this point may suggest that the king did indeed have a partial understanding or interpretation of his dream before the fuller interpretation was granted. The addition of the Old Greek in Daniel 4:14a, which is part of the dream revealed to the king, is interesting in this respect: "and he was delivered into prison and was bound by them with shackles and bronze manacles. I marveled exceedingly at all these things, and my sleep escaped from my eyes." It is clear here that a very significant person and not a tree is in mind, which was part of the cause of the king's "marveling" and his loss of sleep. This points further to the king realizing part of the interpretation of the symbolism of the tree in the dream itself, before its subsequent interpretation by Daniel; the king realized that the tree symbolized a significant person who was being depicted as being judged, and he may well have suspected that this person was himself. Daniel's subsequent interpretation clarified and more fully revealed this picture to the king.

Table 1.1

Masoretic Text (NASB)	Old Greek	Theodotion
Dan 4:10 Now *these were* the visions in my mind *as I lay* on my bed: I was looking, and behold, *there was* a tree in the midst of the earth and its height *was* great.	**Dan 4:7 (10)** I was sleeping, and lo, a tall tree was growing on the earth. Its appearance was huge, and there was no other like it.	**Dan 4:7 (10)** Upon my bed I was looking, and lo, a tree was at the center of the earth, and its height was great.
Dan 4:11 The tree grew large and became strong And its height reached to the sky, And it *was* visible to the end of the whole earth.	**Dan 4:8 (11)** And its appearance was great. Its crown came close to heaven, and its span to the clouds, filling the area under heaven. The sun and the moon dwelled in it and illuminated the whole earth.	**Dan 4:8 (11)** The tree grew great and strong, and its top reached as far as heaven, and its span to the ends of the whole earth.
Dan 4:12 Its foliage *was* beautiful and its fruit abundant, And in it *was* food for all. The beasts of the field found shade under it, And the birds of the sky dwelt in its branches, And all living creatures fed themselves from it.	**Dan 4:9 (12)** Its branches were about thirty stadia long, and all the animals of the earth found shade under it, and the birds of the air hatched their brood in it. Its fruit was abundant and good, and it sustained all living creatures.	**Dan 4:9 (12)** Its foliage was beautiful, and its fruit abundant, and food for all was on it. And the wild animals dwelled under it, and the birds of the air lived in its branches, and from it all flesh was fed.

Masoretic Text (NASB)	Old Greek	Theodotion
Dan 4:13 I was looking in the visions in my mind *as I lay* on my bed, and behold, an *angelic* watcher, a holy one, descended from heaven.	**Dan 4:10 (13)** I continued looking in my sleep; lo, an angel was sent in power out of heaven.	**Dan 4:10 (13)** I continued looking in the vision of the night while on my bed, and lo, <u>there was an Ir</u>, and a holy one descended from heaven.
Dan 4:14 He shouted out and spoke as follows: "Chop down the tree and cut off its branches, Strip off its foliage and scatter its fruit; Let the beasts flee from under it And the birds from its branches.	**Dan 4:11 (14)** And he called and said: "Cut it down, and destroy it, <u>for it has been decreed by the Most High to uproot and render it useless.</u>"	**Dan 4:11 (14)** And he called mightily, and thus he said: "Cut down the tree, and pluck out its branches, and strip off its foliage, and scatter its fruit. Let the animals be shaken beneath it, and the birds from its branches.
Dan 4:15 "Yet leave the stump with its roots in the ground, But with a band of iron and bronze *around it* In the new grass of the field; And let him be drenched with the dew of heaven, And let him share with the beasts in the grass of the earth.	**Dan 4:12 (15)** And thus he said: "Spare one of its roots in the ground <u>so that he may feed on grass like an ox with the animals of the earth in the mountains,</u>	**Dan 4:12 (15)** "Nevertheless, leave the growth of its roots in the ground and with a band of iron and bronze, and he will lie in the tender grass of the outdoors and in the dew of heaven. And his lot will be with the animals in the grass of the earth.
Dan 4:16 "Let his mind be changed from *that of* a man And let a beast's mind be given to him, And let seven periods of time pass over him.	**Dan 4:13 (16)** "and his body may be changed from the dew of heaven, and he may graze with them for seven years	**Dan 4:13 (16)** "His heart will be changed from that of humans, and the heart of an animal will be given to him, and seven seasons will be altered over him.
Dan 4:17 "This sentence is by the decree of the *angelic* watchers And the decision is a command of the holy ones, In order that the living may know That the Most High is ruler over the realm of mankind, And Bestows it on whom He wishes And sets over it the lowliest of men."	**Dan 4:14 (17)** "<u>until he acknowledges</u> that the Lord of heaven has authority over everything which is in heaven and which is on the earth and does with them whatever he wishes." [14a] <u>It was cut down before me in one day, and its destruction was in one hour of the day. And its branches were given to every wind, and it was dragged and thrown away. He ate grass with the animals of the earth. And he was delivered into prison and was bound by them with shackles and bronze manacles. I marveled exceedingly at all these things, and my sleep escaped from my eyes.</u>	**Dan 4:14 (17)** "The sentence is <u>by meaning of Ir,</u> and the demand is the word of holy ones in order that those alive may know that the Most High is Lord of the kingdom of humans, and he will give it to whom he will, and he will set over it what is contemned of humans."

Masoretic Text (NASB)	Old Greek	Theodotion
Dan 4:18 "This is the dream *which* I, King Nebuchadnezzar, have seen. Now you, Belteshazzar, tell *me* its interpretation, inasmuch as none of the wise men of my kingdom is able to make known to me the <u>interpretation</u> [*pišrāʾ*]; but you are able, for a spirit of the holy gods is in you.	**Dan 4:15 (18)** And when I arose in the morning from my bed, I called Daniel, the ruler of the savants and the leader of those who decide dreams, and I described the dream for him, and he showed me its <u>entire interpretation</u> [*pasan tēn synkrisin*].	**Dan 4:15 (18)** This is the dream that I, King Nabouchodonosor, saw. And you, Baltasar, tell the meaning, since all the sages of my kingdom are unable to explain to me <u>the meaning</u> [*to synkrima*]. But you, Daniel, are able, because a holy, divine spirit is in you.

If this is a correct understanding of the Old Greek, it shows what the Greek translator thought was the meaning of the Aramaic text of Daniel 4, and it is in line with our earlier definition of *mystery* in this chapter—an initial, *partially* hidden revelation that is subsequently more fully revealed.

2

THE USE OF *MYSTERY* IN EARLY JUDAISM

MYSTERY NOT ONLY FEATURES PROMINENTLY in the book of Daniel but also in early Judaism. Indeed, the term is a favorite in the Dead Sea Scrolls (DSS), a literary corpus that includes a number of diverse texts (apocryphal and pseudepigraphical works, sectarian documents, Old Testament texts, etc.). The Dead Sea Scrolls appear to have been composed between the third century B.C. and the first century A.D. by the Qumran community, a Jewish sect living just north of the Dead Sea in the desert, whose writings included commentaries on the Old Testament, rules for entrance into and conduct in their community, and a text that details their preparation for an eschatological war.

The Qumran community had quite a penchant for the term *mystery*. The Dead Sea Scrolls employ the term well over a hundred times, using it not unlike the book of Daniel. What makes this term remarkably difficult to survey is the various ways in which the Qumran community picked it up and used it. We will attempt to trace some of the more prominent and creative usages, establishing a foundation together with our earlier study in Daniel that will be of use to us throughout the remainder of the project.

The sectarian group at Qumran was not the only Jewish group that deemed the term important. Mystery crops up in Jewish apocalyptic texts such as *1 Enoch, 2 Baruch, Sibylline Oracles* and elsewhere. These Jewish texts give us insight into how Jews living in different contexts understood the term. In recent years, a few scholars have examined mystery in these Jewish texts, and there is no need to retrace their steps.[1] Our intention is to survey, albeit briefly, a few

---

[1]For a thorough survey of the term in early Judaism, see Benjamin L. Gladd, *Revealing the* Mysterion:

of the more prominent texts where mystery is referred to and developed. The hope is to give a representative sampling, though we acknowledge that the brevity results in a lack of nuance that a more thorough analysis could give. To make the information more manageable, we will proceed topically in accordance with our analysis of Daniel and synthesize the material in the Dead Sea Scrolls and other Jewish texts. As we will see below, *mystery* retains its eschatological and twofold characteristics of a revelation that is partially hidden and, subsequently, more fully revealed.

MYSTERY IN THE DEAD SEA SCROLLS

Mystery and eschatology. There is a body of literature in Qumran that is commonly called *Sapiential Work A* or *4QInstruction*, a text that was probably not written at Qumran.[2] Within this body of wisdom literature, the term *mystery* and the phrase "mystery of existence" is profound and in accord with the previous uses in the *Book of Mysteries*. Some of the most pertinent texts in *4QInstruction* are the following:

> [Consider the mystery of] existence and grasp the birth-times of salvation, and know who will inherit glory and t[oi]l. (4Q417 1 I, 10-11 = 4Q416 2 I, 5-6; see 4Q417 2 I, 2)

> Concerning the entry of years and the exit of periods [. . .] everything which happened in it, why it was, and what will be in it [. . .] its period which God uncovered to the ear of those who understand the mystery of existence. (4Q418 123 II, 2-4)

In light of these texts[3] and others,[4] we are able to observe a few peculiarities of the "mystery of existence." First, the phrase "mystery of existence" entails knowledge of God's redemptive plans, specifically, plans about past, present

---

The Use of Mystery in Daniel and Second Temple Judaism with Its Bearing on First Corinthians, BZNW 160 (Berlin: Walter de Gruyter, 2008), pp. 51-107; Markus Bockmuehl, *Revelation and Mystery in Ancient Judaism and Pauline Christianity*, WUNT 36 (Tübingen: Mohr Siebeck, 1990; repr., Grand Rapids: Eerdmans, 1997); and more recently, Samuel I. Thomas, *The "Mysteries" of Qumran: Mystery, Secrecy, and Esotericism in the Dead Sea Scrolls*, SBLEJL 25 (Atlanta: Society of Biblical Literature, 2009).

[2]Matthew J. Goff, *The Worldly and Heavenly Wisdom of 4QInstruction*, STDJ 50 (Boston: Brill, 2003), p. 227.

[3]While there is a lacuna in 4Q417 1 I, 10-11, it is likely that "mystery" is to be partly supplied in it because of the parallelism with 4Q418 123 II, 2-4, where "the mystery of existence" occurs without any lacuna.

[4]See also 4Q417 2 I, 6-13 = 4Q418 43-35 I, 4-10.

and future events. 4Q418 123 II, 2-4 summarizes this well: "concerning the entry of years and the exit of periods [. . .] everything which happened in it, why it was, and what will be in it." The mystery, therefore, concerns all cosmic activities—from beginning to end. In particular, the "mystery of existence" is often related to end-time judgment elsewhere in the Qumran literature.[5] Even though the phrase encompasses and highlights events related to the latter days, eschatology is but a natural extension of the larger category of the mystery of existence. In other words, the mystery of existence is the entire determined plan of God over the created realm.[6] Second, *mystery* appears to include pragmatic issues and not just redemptive-historical matters, including various pragmatics such as marriage, poverty and filial relationships.[7] Since reference to mystery primarily involves God's activity within the created order (e.g., creation, judgment), then social and moral issues ought also to fall in step with the created order. To put it another way, one must discern[8] and live in accordance with God's design of the cosmos and of history.

Mystery and hermeneutics. In recent years, scholars have looked to the Dead Sea Scrolls in search for a clearer understanding of Jewish hermeneutics. Of particular interest among these commentators is a group of texts that provide commentary on the Old Testament (known as the *pešarîm*). The term *mystery* appears only three times in these texts, yet all three occurrences generate significant insight. The first two are found in the famed commentary on Habakkuk:

> And God told Habakkuk to write what was going to happen to the last generation, but he did not let him know the consummation of the era. And as for what he says: "So that may run the one who reads it." Its interpretation concerns the Teacher of Righteousness, to whom God has made known all the mysteries of the words of his servants, the prophets. For the vision has an appointed time, it will have an end and not fail. Its interpretation: the final age will be extended and go beyond all that the prophets say, because the mysteries of God are wonderful. (1QpHab VII, 1-8)

---

[5]E.g., 4Q416 2 I, 5-6 = 4Q417 1 I, 10-11; 4Q418 77 2-4 = 4Q416 7 1-3.

[6]Torleif Elgvin, "Wisdom and Apocalypticism in the Early Second Century BCE: The Evidence of 4QInstruction," in *The Dead Sea Scrolls Fifty Years after Their Discovery*, ed. Lawrence H. Schiffman, Emanuel Tov and James C. VanderKam (Jerusalem: Israel Exploration Society, 2000), p. 235.

[7]E.g., 4Q416 2 III, 8-10 = 4Q416 9-10; 4Q416 2 III, 13-15.

[8]The Qumran community placed great emphasis on the ability or inability to discern divinely revealed mysteries (1QHa IX, 21; XV, 2-3; 1QS XI, 3; CD-A II, 14; 4Q418 123 II, 4). An individual of the "flesh" lacks the ability to understand and comprehend, whereas the "spiritual" person ascertains deep knowledge.

Even though God spoke to the prophet Habakkuk concerning "what was going to happen," according to the commentary, he did not primarily divulge *when* this would take place: "He [God] did not let him know the consummation of the era."[9] In other words, the Teacher of Righteousness, the primary authoritative figure at Qumran, has received complete revelation previously given to the prophet Habakkuk—an uncanny resemblance to the prophet Daniel.[10] Not only has God revealed the timing and content of Habakkuk's prophecy to the Teacher but also the *complete* meaning of the prophecy (!): "to whom God has made known all the mysteries of the words of his servants, the prophets." This conveys the idea that despite revelation given to the Old Testament prophets, there remained a time when God would issue a second and much more complete disclosure. The Teacher did not receive a revelation in absolute discontinuity to Old Testament prophecy, but a revelation that nuances the precise timing of end-time events. This final revelation is called appropriately "mysteries"—revelation that was previously veiled to the Old Testament prophets but has now been revealed to the Teacher (cf. 1QpHab II, 7-10). According to 1QHᵃ X, 13, the Teacher is also called a "knowledgeable mediator" or, more aptly, a "mediator of knowledge," which refers to one of his primary roles within the community. John J. Collins, representing the vast majority of scholarship, labels the Teacher as "the official mediator of revelation for the community."[11]

Second, the commentary follows a rather predictable structure that appears to be rooted in the book of Daniel: an Old Testament passage is cited followed by the word *interpretation,* while the verse subsequently is applied to the local situation at Qumran. According to Daniel, the initial vision is relatively meaningless without proper decipherment or "interpretation." Thus, in the same manner, Qumran viewed Old Testament prophetic texts as a "vision" or something that required decoding,[12] for the Qumran writers did not emphasize re-

---

[9]F. F. Bruce, *Biblical Exegesis in the Qumran Texts* (Grand Rapids: Eerdmans, 1959), p. 9; G. K. Beale, *The Use of Daniel in Jewish Apocalyptic Literature and in the Revelation of St. John* (Lanham, MD: University Press of America, 1984), pp. 37-38.

[10]Some commentators suggest that the Teacher analogously functions like the prophet Daniel. See William H. Brownlee, *The Midrash Pesher of Habakkuk,* SBLMS 24 (Missoula, MT: Scholars Press, 1979), pp. 30, 112; Bruce, *Biblical Exegesis,* pp. 16-17; Beale, *Use of Daniel,* p. 36.

[11]John J. Collins, *The Apocalyptic Imagination: An Introduction to Jewish Apocalyptic Literature,* 2nd ed., BRS (Grand Rapids: Eerdmans, 1998), p. 151.

[12]Daniel Patte, *Early Jewish Hermeneutic in Palestine,* SBLDS 22 (Missoula, MT: Scholars Press, 1975), pp. 300-308; I. Rabinowitz, "Pesher/Pittaron: Its Biblical Meaning and Its Significance in the Qumran Literature," *RevQ* 8 (1973): 229-30.

velatory visions or apparently did not experience such visions.[13] *Therefore, in Qumran Old Testament texts, particularly prophecies are hidden mysteries, lacking a full or complete interpretation.*

MYSTERY IN THE TARGUMS

Like in the Dead Sea Scrolls, the term *mystery* appears once more to be an eschatologically charged term in some of the Aramaic Targums (first century B.C. to fifth century A.D.). The Targums are Aramaic translations of the Old Testament, which often give us some insight into how Jews interpreted the Old Testament.

The Targum of Genesis 49 has undergone much expansion, yet in the midst of this elaboration the notion of mystery plays a pivotal role.[14] We will quote at length Neofiti's Aramaic translation of Genesis 49:1:

> And Jacob called his sons and said to them: "Gather together and I will tell you *the concealed* <u>secrets,</u> *the hidden ends, giving of the rewards of the just, and the punishment of the wicked, and what the happiness of Eden is." The twelve tribes gathered together and surrounded the bed of gold on which our father Jacob was lying after* <u>the end</u> *was revealed to him and that the determined end of blessing and the consolation might be communicated to them. As soon as* <u>the end</u> *was revealed to him, the mystery was hidden from him. They hoped that he would relate to them the determined end of the redemption and the consolation. As soon as* <u>the mystery</u> *was revealed to him, it was hidden from him and as soon as the door was opened to him, it was closed from him.*[15]

This targumic expansion explicitly connects mystery with several apocalyptic features that we have already discussed at length. First, "mysteries" in Genesis 49 entail knowledge of the "end," the "rewards of the just," the "punishment of the wicked" and the "happiness of Eden." Each of these is a common end-time notion, appearing throughout Judaism, especially in apocalyptic literature (e.g., *1 En.*; *2 Bar.*). Furthermore, the revelation of "mysteries" concerning the "end"

---

[13]Qumran apparently believed, however, that they participated in the heavenly realm by partaking in and issuing forth divine revelation. The community, according to the *Songs of Sabbath Sacrifice*, join with the angels in the expressions of heavenly revelations and mysteries (4Q400 2, 1-3; 4Q401 14 II, 2-8; 4Q403 1 II, 18-27).

[14]See Bockmuehl, *Revelation and Mystery,* pp. 94-96, for additional discussion and elaboration on mystery and other revelatory concepts in the Targums.

[15]Italics represent targumic expansion, and underlined text reflects our emphasis.

or "latter days"[16] is probably a direct allusion to Daniel 2:28-29 (see table 2.1). Apparently, the Targums perceived a tension in Jacob's revelation concerning the end and his prophetic blessing on his children in Genesis 49:2-27, for Jacob received revelation concerning the very end of history but failed to relate the specifics to his offspring. The Targums ease the tension by commenting that the disclosed mystery—the latter-day specificities—was revealed for a short period of time then subsequently hidden.

Table 2.1

Genesis 49:1 (Neofiti)	Daniel 2:28
"As soon as the end was revealed to him, the mystery was hidden from him. . . . As soon as the mystery was revealed to him."	"There is a God in heaven who reveals mysteries, and he has made known to King Nebuchadnezzar what will take place in the latter days."

Nevertheless, the thrust of the passage is that Jacob received a revelation or mystery concerning end-time events. According to the book of Daniel, the term *end* expresses an eschatological conception, since it is repeatedly located in eschatological contexts throughout and appears to be interchangeable with the phrase "latter days."[17] Thus there does appear to be an awareness of the Danielic mystery in Genesis 49:1 (Neofiti).[18]

In sum, the word *mystery*, though often used noneschatologically in the Targums,[19] still retains its apocalyptic flavor on some occasions. The coupling of the term with the "end" or "latter days" shows that *mystery* can be eschatological in the Targums.

Conclusion

The following is a summary of the relevant facets of mystery in Judaism, which

---

[16]The MT of Gen 49:1 explicitly uses the phrase "latter days," thus linking it with other eschatological texts (e.g., Is 2:2; Dan 2:28). Note also strong end-time overtones in the use of *mystery* in the Num 24:14-17 Targum, where also "the end of the last days" occurs.

[17]Dan 8:19; 9:27; 11:13, 27; 12:13; cf. Dan 11:35; 12:4, 7.

[18]Roger Syrén, *The Blessings in the Targums: A Study on the Targumic Interpretations of Genesis 49 and Deuteronomy 33*, Acta Academiae Aboensis 64/1 (Abo: Abo Akademi, 1986), p. 121. Martin Mc-Namara also suggests that the same language "shows dependence on apocalyptic texts, e.g., Dan 2:18, 28, 30, 47f." *Targum Neofiti 1: Genesis: Translated, with Apparatus and Notes* (Collegeville, MN: Liturgical, 1992), p. 215.

[19]In some instances, the term *mystery* in the targumic literature means a heavenly "secret/council" (Mic 4:12; Ps 25:14; 89:8; 91:1; 111:1; Job 15:8; 29:4) or simply a mundane "secret" or "counsel" (Gen 49:6 [*Tg. Onq.*]; Josh 2:1; Judg 4:21; 9:31; 1 Sam 18:22; 24:5; 2 Kings 6:11; Ezek 13:9; Ps 55:15; 64:3; 83:4; Job 19:19; Prov 3:32; 11:13; 15:22; 20:19; 25:9; Ruth 3:7).

is in line with its meaning in the book of Daniel that we discussed in the preceding chapter. (1) Mystery is eschatological—that is, it concerns those events that take place in the "latter days." On the one hand, the end-time content of *mystery* can be very general, but more often than not, the term refers to a specific aspect of the latter days, such as rewards for the righteous and judgment or a particular feature within the process of redemptive history. (2) Central to the revelatory nature of mystery is its twofold aspect—an initial, generally hidden, revelation is often disclosed, followed by a subsequent fuller (even surprising) interpretation of its meaning.[20]

EXCURSUS 2.1: *MYSTERY* IN *FIRST ENOCH* AND OTHER JEWISH TEXTS

First Enoch: The Book of Watchers. First Enoch (second century B.C.) is comprised of five works: *The Book of Watchers, The Book of Similitudes, The Book of Astronomical Writings, The Book of Dream Visions* and *The Book of the Epistle of Enoch. The Book of Watchers* (*1 En.* 1–36) is probably the earliest of the Enochic works. It describes the heavenly journey of Enoch and the egregious sin of the fallen angels. The first use of the technical term *mystery* occurs in 8:3B: "All these [Watchers] began to reveal mysteries [*anakalyptein ta mystēria*] to their wives and children" (our translation).[21] In addition, another similar occurrence is located in 9:6: "And they [Azaz'el and the other fallen angels] revealed eternal secrets [*edēlōsen ta mystēria tou aiōnos*] which are performed in heaven." These passages are in the context of the Watchers' *illicit* revelations to humans. For example, in 1 Enoch 7:1, they showed humankind "magical medicine" and "incantations" (cf. 8:1-3; 10:7; 65:6; 69:1-16). The Aramaic renders this as "[sor]cery, incanta[tions]" ([*lḥr*]*št wlks*[*pt'*]; 4Q202 II, 19). The root of the second word, *ḥrš*, is found in the Old Testament to refer to an "enchanter" or "magician" (e.g., Is 3:3). Moreover, in his recent commentary, Nickelsburg contends that the second word should read *'*[*špt'*] ("conjurations") and not *kš*[*pt'*] ("incantations").[22] If he is correct, then this word recalls the book of

---

[20]There could be a debate about new developed meanings in Judaism, especially Qumran, concerning whether or not these new meanings are a consistent development of the meaning of the Old Testament texts or whether these developed meanings are completely unrelated to the meaning of the Old Testament texts. For the most part, we lean toward the former view, though there is not space to argue that here.

[21]The Aramaic is very similar to the Greek: "[And all began] [to reveal] secrets [*(lgly)h rzyn*] to their wives" (4Q202 IV, 5 = 4Q202 III, 5).

[22]George W. E. Nickelsburg, *1 Enoch*, Hermeneia (Minneapolis: Fortress, 2001), 1:197-99.

Daniel, for the root *ʾšp* ("conjure") is exclusively used in Daniel 1–5.[23] The subtle
allusion to the book of Daniel reinforces the programmatic nature of Daniel's
conception of mystery.

Juxtaposed with the Watchers' revelation, Enoch stands as the divinely sanc-
tioned recipient of revelation (1:2). His heavenly journey begins in 14:8, with
his first stop at the divine throne room, where he participates in the heavenly
temple and receives a commission (14:9–16:3). He will be the official "scribe of
righteousness" (12:4; cf. 13:4-6; 14:1-16:4; 82:1) that records and disseminates
revelation. This ascent to heaven—soon to become a Jewish tradition—is close
to the Qumran participation in heavenly worship that we encounter in the
Songs of Sabbath Sacrifice.[24] Enoch traverses the ends of the cosmos throughout
the majority of the book (18:10–36:4).

In the book of Daniel, revelation is transmitted through "dreams" and "visions" (e.g., Dan 2:3, 19; 4:5). Compared to Enoch, Daniel's revelations are far
less cosmological; there are no journeys or visitations. But there are several
similarities, namely, a focus on eschatology (including end-time judgment)—
an emphasis on the afterlife, throne room and angels. Yet for this study, we need
to note the medium of revelation that undergirds these two apocalyptic works:
revelation or mystery in Daniel primarily manifests itself within the dream
reports, and Enoch receives penetrating "mysteries" as he ascends to the
heavenly throne and tours the cosmos.

Other prominent Jewish texts. Two distinct categories of mystery emerge
from the Jewish work the *Testaments of the Twelve Patriarchs*. On the one hand
mystery can mean a secret between individuals or parties (*T. Zeb.* 1:6; *T. Gad*
6:5), while other occurrences of the term function similarly to the book of
Daniel. The *Testament of Levi* is couched in a highly apocalyptic setting, and
the *Testament of Judah* 12:6-7 and 16:3-4 resonate well with other Jewish documents that speak of hidden teaching (e.g., 4Q416 2 III, 8-10; 4Q416 2 III, 13-15).
Therefore, the *Testaments of the Twelve Patriarchs* incorporate both a secular
and an apocalyptic perspective of mystery.

Philo employs the concept of mystery in application to the mystery religions,
while retaining a commitment to Judaism (e.g., *Leg.* 3.71, 100; *Cher.* 48-49).
Philo seeks to combine a Hellenistic worldview and Hebrew "orthodoxy." We
thus get pagan mystery rituals garbed in a cloak of Judaism. Josephus, though

---

[23]Dan 1:20; 2:2, 10, 27; 4:7; 5:7, 11, 15.
[24]Collins, *Apocalyptic Imagination*, p. 54.

using the term *mystery* several times, does not reflect the usual Semitic connotation. Instead, he limits the word to the common Hellenistic usage (e.g., *Ant.* 19.30, 71, 104).

The Apocrypha, except for Wisdom of Solomon 2:21-22, do not significantly develop the end-time notion of mystery (e.g., Sir 27:16-17; Tob 12:7, 11; 2 Macc 13:21). The apocryphal writers rarely depend on or even acknowledge the apocalyptic side of the term.

3

THE USE OF *MYSTERY*
IN MATTHEW

WE EXPLORED IN THE LAST TWO CHAPTERS how mystery originates and is used in the book of Daniel and how it continues to be used in a similar manner in parts of early Judaism. Somewhat unique to Daniel is the nature of twofold revelation, in contrast to other places in the Old Testament where the prophets directly receive God's revelation. We determined that mystery encompasses two major features: initial and partial revelation, then subsequent and significantly fuller interpretation. Revelation has taken the form of dreams, writing, previous prophecy and visions, which is clearest in Daniel 2; 4; 9. A very partial interpretation of a dream report is embedded within the initial revelation. The fuller interpretation remains unknown to individuals, even to the seer (i.e., Nebuchadnezzar, Daniel). It is not until the full, even surprising, interpretation has been given that the initial, largely hidden revelation is fully understood. According to Daniel, the mystery also pertains to events that take place in the "latter days," events that largely include a final tribulation, the rise and fall of Israel's antagonists, the establishment of God's end-time kingdom and finally the vindication of Israel's righteous.

Turning to the four Gospels, we quickly notice that one of Jesus' core teachings concerns the establishment of God's eternal kingdom on the earth, which will take place through his ministry. Israel, however, rejects Jesus' kingdom message. On the one hand, the Gospels present Jesus' kingdom proclamation to be the fulfillment of Old Testament promises. Yet, on the other, Jesus' teaching about the kingdom differs from Old Testament and Jewish expectations. The Gospel writers attempt to resolve this tension in a number of ways. Central to their resolution is the notion of mystery. The Synoptic Gospels employ the term *mystery* to capture the nature of Jesus' end-time kingdom, a kingdom that stands in both continuity and discontinuity with the Old Testament.

With Adolf von Harnack's work *What is Christianity?* came the zenith of German liberalism. For him and others like him (e.g., Reimarus, Strauss, Wrede), the brilliance of Jesus' ministry rested not on his actions (the cross or resurrection) but his teachings. At the heart of Jesus' career, according to these scholars, lies moralism. Like the collapse of a house of cards, this moralistic reductionism of Jesus and the Gospels quickly came to an end with the pioneering work of Albert Schweitzer (and his predecessor, Johannes Weiss). Schweitzer argued for a much more contextual approach for the historical Jesus, an approach that examined Jesus' career in light of early Judaism.[1] Current debates over the historical Jesus are in a very real sense still indebted to Schweitzer's seminal work.

In this Schweitzerian era, scholars are continually refining their portrait of the historical Jesus in light of the Old Testament and early Judaism. At the center of Jesus' ministry are his teachings and actions concerning the kingdom of God. Jesus speaks to the nature of the kingdom more than any other topic in the Gospels, and at the center of his kingdom message is its *paradoxical* nature. Though the term *mystery* occurs only a handful of times in the Synoptics, it plays a pivotal role in Jesus' teaching on the end-time kingdom.

The importance of the term *mystery* has not gone unnoticed in synoptic studies. George Eldon Ladd claims, "'The mystery of the kingdom' is the key to the understanding the unique element in Jesus' teaching about the Kingdom."[2] We believe Ladd is correct. As we will see, much of Jesus' ministry and mission concerns the nature of the kingdom, but Jesus' conception of the kingdom generally departs from Old Testament and Jewish expectations. How does Jesus' conception of the kingdom differ from that of the Old Testament and Judaism? It is the purpose of this chapter to try to answer this question. We will examine the use of *mystery* in Matthew's Gospel and determine how it functions in its

---

[1]Albert Schweitzer, *The Quest of the Historical Jesus: A Critical Study of Its Progress from Reimarus to Wrede,* 3rd ed., trans. W. Montgomery (London: Black, 1956).
[2]George Eldon Ladd, *The Presence of the Future: The Eschatology of Biblical Realism* (Grand Rapids: Eerdmans, 1974), p. 227.

immediate and wider context. As we will see, mystery remains tied to the book of Daniel both in its content (the advent of the end-time kingdom) and in its form (the partially hidden and more fully disclosed revelation).

IMMEDIATE CONTEXT

The word *mystery* (*mystērion*) occurs three times in the Synoptics (Mt 13:11; Mk 4:11; Lk 8:10). The term is found at pivotal points within each Gospel and consistently used in relation to Jesus' teaching concerning the nature of the kingdom. Each Gospel writer employs the term immediately following the parable of the sower and before Jesus' interpretation of it. For our purposes, we need only determine the significance of the term in the narrative of the Synoptics. Since Matthew's Gospel delivers the fullest elaboration, we will primarily interact with his narrative, while keeping an eye on the other two Synoptic accounts.

Though Matthean scholars debate the overall structure of the book, many are convinced that the teaching sections constitute much of the overall structure.[3] Matthew 13 constitutes the third discourse section in Matthew's Gospel and may indeed be the primary one.[4] Like the other two Synoptic Gospels, this discourse specifically addresses the nature of the kingdom. It seeks to answer the ongoing problem that keeps occurring up to this point in Jesus' ministry and will continue to do so—why do some understand the kingdom and embrace Jesus' message, while others do not?[5]

The key passage for our study is Matthew 13:10-17:

> And the disciples came and said to Him, "Why do You speak to them in parables?" Jesus answered them, "To you it has been granted to know the mysteries of the kingdom of heaven, but to them it has not been granted. For whoever has, to him *more* shall be given, and he will have an abundance; but whoever does not have, even what he has shall be taken away from him. Therefore I speak to them in parables; because while seeing they do not see, and while hearing they do not hear, nor do they understand. In their case the prophecy of Isaiah is being fulfilled, which says,

---

[3]E.g., David L. Turner, *Matthew,* BECNT (Grand Rapids: Baker Academic, 2008), pp. 8-10; D. A. Carson, *Matthew,* EBC (Grand Rapids: Zondervan, 1984), pp. 50-51.

[4]See, for example, Craig Keener, *The Gospel of Matthew: A Socio-Rhetorical Commentary* (Grand Rapids: Eerdmans, 1999), p. 371.

[5]R. T. France, *Gospel of Matthew,* NICNT (Grand Rapids: Eerdmans, 2007), p. 499.

'YOU WILL KEEP ON HEARING, BUT WILL NOT UNDERSTAND;
YOU WILL KEEP ON SEEING, BUT WILL NOT PERCEIVE;
FOR THE HEART OF THIS PEOPLE HAS BECOME DULL,
WITH THEIR EARS THEY SCARCELY HEAR,
AND THEY HAVE CLOSED THEIR EYES,
OTHERWISE THEY WOULD SEE WITH THEIR EYES,
HEAR WITH THEIR EARS,
AND UNDERSTAND WITH THEIR HEART AND RETURN,
AND I WOULD HEAL THEM.'

"But blessed are your eyes, because they see; and your ears, because they hear. For truly I say to you that many prophets and righteous men desired to see what you see, and did not see *it*, and to hear what you hear, and did not hear *it*."

The chapter begins with the parable of the sower (Mt 13:3-8). After hearing the parable, the disciples, probably reflecting the sentiment of the crowd (Mt 13:2), remain baffled: "Why do you speak to the people in parables?" (TNIV). Jesus responds to their question by claiming, "to you it has been granted to know the mysteries of the kingdom of heaven, but to them it has not been granted."[6] The "outsiders" or the "crowd" (Mt 13:2), Jesus says, do not have access to the revealed mysteries and therefore are unable to grasp the nature of his kingdom proclamation. He explains why he speaks in parables to the crowd (Mt 13:12-13) by recalling the quotation from Isaiah 6:9-10 in Matthew 13:14-15. After stating the purpose of the parables, Jesus affirms that the disciples, unlike the crowds, are able to understand: "But blessed are your eyes, because they see; and your ears, because they hear" (Mt 13:16). In addition to their unique understanding, the disciples have insight that even Old Testament prophets did not have:

---

[6]Mark and Luke differ slightly from Matthew's statement that "to them [*ekeinois*] it [knowledge of the mysteries of the kingdom] has not been granted" (Mt 13:11). Mark's account reads, "those who are outside [*exō*] get everything in parables" (Mk 4:11), and Luke's is quite similar: "to the rest [*loipois*] it is in parables" (Lk 8:10). Matthew's peculiar wording may reflect a more apocalyptic appropriation of the nature of mystery. By claiming that the knowledge of mysteries is simply not divulged to "them" or "outsiders," Matthew taps into the well-established theme of God sovereignly choosing those to whom he divulges apocalyptic wisdom. For example, God's dealings with Daniel are paradigmatic. In Dan 2:17-18, Daniel prays that God would reveal to him (and not the "wise" Babylonians) Nebuchadnezzar's dream and its interpretation. After God answers Daniel's prayer (Dan 2:19), Daniel extols God in Dan 2:20-23. In the hymn of Dan 2:20-23, God is viewed as the one who divulges wisdom to the "wise": "He gives wisdom [or mysteries] to wise men and knowledge to men of understanding" (Dan 2:21b). This identical theme is again rehearsed in Dan 2:30: "This mystery has not been revealed to me for any wisdom residing in me more than in any other living man, but for the purpose of making the interpretation known." Thus Jesus' disclosure of wisdom to a select group, which is enhanced in Matthew's account, follows the pattern of Daniel.

"For truly I say to you that many prophets and righteous men desired to see what you see, and did not see *it*, and to hear what you hear, and did not hear *it*" (Mt 13:17). Matthew's Gospel is the only Synoptic Gospel to include this verse in conjunction with mystery. This verse taps into a common theme essential to the notion of mystery—its hiddenness. Since mystery naturally entails some form of hiddenness, we will now sketch, albeit briefly, Daniel's conception of hiddenness and relate it to what we find here in Matthew's Gospel.

HIDDENNESS IN DANIEL AND MATTHEW

The term *mystery* appears to possess two levels of hiddenness: "temporary hiddenness" and "permanent hiddenness."[7] By "temporary hiddenness" we mean the partially hidden nature of revelation that is undisclosed over a period of time that eventually gives way to a final, more complete form of revelation. "Permanent hiddenness," on the other hand, is more concerned with the ongoing hidden nature of mystery. Even when the revelation has reached its completed state of disclosure, the fuller meaning of the revelation remains elusive to some individuals.

The book of Daniel speaks to both characteristics. The concept of mystery can refer to the hidden nature of God's redemptive-historical plan. Daniel 2:28 addresses this specific theme: "there is a God in heaven who reveals mysteries, and he has made known to King Nebuchadnezzar what will take place in the latter days." Here the interpretation of the revelation of the statue seen in a dream is initially veiled for the most part from Nebuchadnezzar. In the immediate context, the revelation is interpreted clearly to refer to the end-time establishment of God's eternal kingdom and the overthrow of the pagan empires (Dan 2:36-45; cf. Dan 4:19-27; 5:25-28; 7:15-27; 8:15-26). This example falls under the category of "temporary hiddenness."[8]

The second aspect of hiddenness (permanent hiddenness) also occurs in Daniel. Daniel 12:8-9 describes Daniel not being able to understand the preceding prophetic verbal and visionary revelation (Dan 10:1–12:3): "I heard but I could not understand." An angel responds and says these "words are concealed and sealed up until the end time," when they will be fulfilled. Then

---

[7]For further reflection on this theme, see Benjamin L. Gladd, *Revealing the* Mysterion: *The Use of Mystery in Daniel and Early Judaism with Its Bearing on First Corinthians*, BZNW 160 (Berlin: Walter de Gruyter, 2008), pp. 133-36.

[8]The theme of "temporary hiddenness" also has precedent in Judaism—e.g., see 1QpHab VII, 1-8.

Daniel 12:10 says that at the time of fulfillment, "none of the wicked will understand, but those who have insight will understand" and consequently be "blessed" (Dan 12:12). Thus, while both believers (e.g., Daniel) and unbelievers did not understand prophecies about the end time,[9] when the fulfillment comes, unbelievers will continue to lack understanding, though true saints will understand: "The king spoke to Daniel and said, 'Truly your God is the God of Gods and the Lord of kings, the only one who reveals <u>hidden mysteries</u>, because you are able to disclose this mystery" (Dan 2:47, our translation).

Throughout Daniel's narrative, mystery is largely veiled from Nebuchadnezzar (Dan 2, 4), as he is unable to understand most of the dream.[10] Even the Babylonian wise men are puzzled by Nebuchadnezzar's dreams. Similarly, Belshazzar feebly attempts to interpret the writing on the wall by summoning his wisest advisors in Daniel 5. The same can be said for Daniel, who, despite his inspired ability in Daniel 2 and Daniel 4, fails to understand for the most part his own revelations in Daniel 7–12. These examples of "permanent hiddenness" illustrate the principle that mystery is veiled to some and revealed to others, setting a pattern for later usage of the term.[11]

Sketching this established pattern of hiddenness in Daniel is important as we understand the nature of mystery in Matthew, where we detect both forms of hiddenness. In Matthew 13:10, the disciples ask Jesus why he speaks "in parables." Jesus responds by saying that he reveals "mysteries" to them—namely, the disciples—but to the crowds he does not reveal such mysteries. Jesus grounds this statement in Matthew 13:14-15 by quoting Isaiah 6:9-10:

> In their case the prophecy of Isaiah is being fulfilled, which says,

---

[9]Recall our earlier qualification of this in chap. 2: even unbelievers like Nebuchadnezzar, and presumably the Babylonian wise men, possessed *some* knowledge of the end-time prophecy of Dan 2, as a result of Daniel's revelatory interpretation of the king's dream. However, they did not have the moral ability to apply it wisely to their lives. And, furthermore, while Daniel understands the interpretation of the dream revealed to him, as well as the later elaboration of end-time visions and declarations (see Dan 10:1, 11-14!), nevertheless he does not understand the vast majority of this later revelatory elaboration (Dan 12:4, 8-9). The elaborated prophecy is to be "concealed and sealed" (Dan 12:4, 9) and refers both to the time during which it remains unfulfilled and to the time during which it is not understood. Its fulfillment brings with it greater understanding.

[10]See Raymond Brown, *The Semitic Background of the Term "Mystery" in the New Testament*, BS 21 (Philadelphia: Fortress, 1968), p. 43; and D. Deden, "Le 'Mystère' paulinien," *Ephemerides theologicae lovanienses* 13 (1936): 429-30, who connect the theme of "hiddenness" in Dan 2 with 1 Cor 2.

[11]For examples of "permanent hiddenness" in early Judaism, see 1QHa IX, 21; XXI, 4-5; CD-A II, 14; 4Q268/4QDamascus Document 1 7-8.

'You will keep on hearing, but will not understand;

You will keep on seeing, but will not perceive;

For the heart of this people has become dull,

With their ears they scarcely hear,

And they have closed their eyes,

Otherwise they would see with their eyes,

Hear with their ears,

And understand with their heart and return,

And I would heal them.'

This quotation is riddled with difficulties and has received much scholarly attention. For our purposes we only need to make a few observations.

The link between "seeing"/"hearing" and mysteries is that divine enablement is required to understand unveiled wisdom—that is, *mysteries.* In the Synoptics Jesus often commands the crowds and the disciples to "hear" or "understand" his teaching. Often this is expressed as "he who has ears, let him hear."[12] Jesus claims that "mysteries" have been given to the disciples (Mt 13:11) and that "blessed are your eyes, because they see; and your ears, because they hear" (Mt 13:16). In addition, Jesus interprets the parables to the disciples in Matthew 13:37-43, further indicating that he is illuminating cryptic revelation. Matthew 11:25-27 unpacks this identical theme and relates it to the nature of the kingdom and Jesus' messiahship (see Mt 11:1-24): "At that time Jesus said . . . 'You have hidden these things from *the* wise and intelligent and have revealed them to infants'" (Mt 11:25). Thus, there is in Matthew both temporary hiddenness for believers and permanent hiddenness for those in intractable unbelief.

Temporary hiddenness, especially in Matthew's account, refers to the nature of the kingdom that differs from Old Testament and Jewish expectations (see excursus 3.1). In Matthew 13:17, this characteristic is explicit: "For truly I say to you that many prophets and righteous men desired to see what you see, and did not see *it,* and to hear what you hear, and did not hear *it.*" Old Testament prophets and righteous men were not privy to the "mysteries of the kingdom," since they were largely hidden from them. Jesus is now unveiling previously and mostly hidden end-time revelation.[13] Here two distinctions among believers experiencing temporary hiddenness should be made. First, there is the be-

---

[12]Mt 11:15; 13:9; Mk 4:9, 23; 8:18; Lk 8:8; 14:35. Cf. Acts 7:51; 28:27; Rom 11:8; 1 Cor 2:9; Rev 2:7, 11, 17, 29; 3:6, 13, 22; 13:9. For further discussion, see G. K. Beale, *John's Use of the Old Testament in Revelation,* JSNTSup 166 (Sheffield: Sheffield Academic Press, 1998), pp. 236-39.

[13]See especially Joel Marcus, "Mark 4:10-12 and Marcan Epistemology," *JBL* 103 (1984): 557-74.

lieving covenant community that stretches from the Old Testament epoch on into the New Testament age. Old Testament saints only understood much of Old Testament prophecy very partially, but saints of the new covenant age understood it more fully. Second, there are believers living during the time of Jesus' ministry who initially had a limited understanding like those of the Old Testament age, but then they experienced enlightenment from Jesus' teaching and came to a significantly fuller understanding of Old Testament prophecy.

Permanent hiddenness or veiling is pervasive in this passage, not only occurring in Matthew 13 and parallels but also in much of Jesus' revelatory acts and teachings.[14] For example, in Matthew 13 Jesus tells the parable of the sower: "When anyone hears the word of the kingdom and does not understand it, the evil one comes and snatches away what has been sown in his heart" (Mt 13:19). Here Jesus explicitly refers to permanent hiddenness—the inability to comprehend latter-day revelation. For a time, even the disciples are unable to grasp the revelation, which is why they asked for the parable to be explained in Matthew 13:36.[15] Joel Marcus is right to argue that "part of the content of 'the mystery of the kingdom' is precisely the division of humanity into the blind and the *illuminati*."[16] Virtually all of Jesus' parables and deeds are veiled or characterized by some form of permanent hiddenness. This is not to say that everything Jesus does is a "mystery"; rather it simply demonstrates the ubiquity and importance of this theme in Jesus' ministry. Those who have "eyes to see" comprehend Jesus' message, but those who are "blind" are unable to penetrate the full meaning of the revelation.[17] In the Gospels, the disciples oscillate be-

---

[14]See, for example, Mt 11:25: "You have hidden these things from the wise and intelligent and have revealed them to infants."

[15]The passive verb "to you it has been granted [*dedotai*] to know the mysteries of the kingdom" should be understood as a divine passive, since it is God who reveals mysteries (Dan 2:20-23; see France, *Gospel of Matthew*, p. 511).

[16]Marcus, "Mark 4:10-12," p. 564.

[17]Several scholars argue that Matthew intends the reader to identify the disciples with the "wise ones" of Dan 11:33-35; 12:3; 12:10, e.g., David E. Orton, *The Understanding Scribe: Matthew and the Apocalyptic Ideal*, JSNTSup 25 (Sheffield: Sheffield Academic Press, 1989), p. 147. This connection seems justified in that the Hebrew text of Dan 11:33 highlights the role of the "wise" as one communicating their wisdom to "the many," whereas one of the Greek translations of Daniel (Theodotion) emphasizes the understanding of the "wise ones": "And the intelligent [*hoi synetoi*] of the people will have understanding [*synēsousin*] in many things" (11:33a; Theodotion; NETS). Though the word group for "understanding" (*syniēmi*) is relatively common in the New Testament, in Matthew this word takes on special meaning in several key verses, especially Mt 13:13-15, 19, 23, 51; 15:10. The wise ones were prophesied to gain understanding in the "latter days" (Dan 10:14; 11:35). One of the points of Jesus' discourse on the kingdom is that the latter-day kingdom has begun through Jesus. It makes much sense then that the advent of the wise ones also begins to be inaugu-

tween comprehension and inability to perceive. At times they understand, though not fully, Jesus' identity and mission (e.g., Mk 8:29), and at other times they lack insight (e.g., Mk 8:17). Similar to the disciples, the crowds are often-times viewed as unable to comprehend Jesus' mission, though occasionally they have insight. The Jewish leadership, however, appears hardened and unable to perceive. Consequently, for some the revelation is only temporarily hidden, while for others it is permanently hidden.[18]

PSALM 78:2 IN MATTHEW 13:35

One of Jesus' unique traits as presented by the Synoptics is his desire to speak publically in parables. In Matthew 13:34, Matthew claims that Jesus only spoke to the outsiders or the crowds in parables: "All these things Jesus spoke to the crowds in parables, and He did not speak to them without a parable." But if Jesus desires that his audience gain understanding, then why not speak openly? The notion of parables is tethered to this theme of hiddenness, particularly "permanent hid-denness." Critical to our understanding of hiddenness and the notion of mystery is the use of Psalm 78:2 in Matthew 13:35: "*This* was to fulfill what was spoken through the prophet: 'I will open my mouth in parables; I will utter things hidden since the foundation of the world'" (Mt 13:35). It is worthwhile to note the dif-ference between Matthew's text and the Greek Old Testament (LXX) (see table 3.1).

Table 3.1

Psalm 77:2 LXX (Eng. Ps 78:2)	Matthew 13:35
"I will open my mouth in a parable; I will utter problems from of old."	"I will open my mouth in parables; I will utter things hidden since the foundation of the world."
anoixō en parabolais to stoma mou, phthegxomai problēmata ap' archēs.	*anoixō en parabolais to stoma mou, ereuxomai kekrymmena apo katabolēs [kosmou].*
"I will open my mouth in a parable; I will utter dark sayings of old" (MT)	

The first clause is identical in both texts, but the second differs significantly.

---

rated in and through the disciples. They are "blessed" (Mt 13:16) in fulfillment of Dan 12:12 ("blessed is he who keeps waiting and attains to the" fulfillment).

[18]It should be noted that there is a kind of "middle" group: unbelievers who are temporarily hardened and lack understanding, but then their ears are opened and they understand and join the group of enlightened believers. However, it is clear that some remain permanently hardened and without understanding.

For our purposes we need only to take note of Matthew's use of "things hidden" in contrast to the Greek Old Testament's rendering of *problēmata* (lit. "hindrances" or "problems").[19] In the immediate context of Psalm 78:2, the psalmist commands the audience to heed or "listen" to his instruction (Ps 78:1). The psalmist claims that he has "heard" and "known" the message, which the "fathers have told" (Ps 78:3) and promises to "not conceal them from their [the fathers'] children." In other words, the psalmist is simply passing on "riddles" or enigmas from one Israelite generation to another (see Ps 78:9-72). Intriguingly, Matthew substitutes the substantive *kekrymmena* ("things hidden") for the LXX's *problēmata*.[20] Matthew's conspicuous use of *kekrymmena* ("things hidden") in contrast to the Greek Old Testament's *problēmata* ("hindrances" or "problems") may reflect his attempt to connect the notion of mystery to the kingdom parables in Matthew 13.

Since the concept of mystery includes the notion of revealing hidden wisdom (see above), mystery is naturally associated with the various forms of the word *hidden* (expressed by the Greek stem *kryp–* in the Old Testament and early Judaism; cf. Dan 2:47; 1 Cor 2:7; Eph 3:9; Col 1:26).

This connection between mystery and "hiddenness" helps explain the function of the notable quotation in Matthew 13:35. According to Matthew, the quotation partly explains why Jesus speaks in parables—he is announcing "hidden things" or end-time mysteries pertaining to the latter-day kingdom. Jesus' teaching concerning the "mysteries of the kingdom" typologically corresponds to the psalmist declaring the "works of God" to another Israelite generation (Ps 78:7).

By "typological" we mean that Jesus sees that what the psalmist was describing about Israel in the Old Testament foreshadowed the generation of those living at the time of Jesus. Both figures are declaring "hidden things" or "parables" from one generation to another.[21] Moreover, the psalmist's making

---

[19]The MT uses the word *ḥîdâ* ("riddle"), which denotes an enigma or "riddle" (Num 12:8; Ezek 17:2; Hab 2:6; Ps 49:4; Prov 1:6; see esp. Judg 14:12, 14-19) or "difficult question" (1 Kings 10:1; 2 Chron 9:1). In Ps 78:2, the word falls in line with the denotation of a riddle, since it parallels the word "parable" (*māšāl*).

[20]Of the seventeen occurrences of *ḥîdâ* ("riddle"), eleven of them are translated by the LXX as *problēma* ("hindrance" or "problem"). The remaining six are rendered as *ainigma* ("riddle": Num 12:8; 1 Kings 10:1; 2 Chron 9:1; Prov 1:6; Dan 8:23) and *diēgēma* ("narrative" or "account of events": Ezek 17:2). This reinforces the idea that Matthew's rendering of *kekrymmena* ("hidden things") instead of *problēmata* ("problems") is unique.

[21]See Craig L. Blomberg, "Matthew," in *Commentary on the New Testament Use of the Old Testament*, ed. G. K. Beale and D. A. Carson (Grand Rapids: Baker Academic, 2008), p. 49.

known the revelation about Israel's repeated disobedience to and rejection of God's revelation in the Old Testament pointed forward to the same thing on the part of Israel to whom Jesus came. Just as Israel of old repeatedly did not respond positively to God's parabolic revelation, so it was in Jesus' ministry. Nevertheless, a remnant is preserved in both cases. A remnant of old Israel understood and obeyed God's word, so only a remnant will understand Jesus' parables. Psalm 78:4 includes a forward-pointing reference to a time when understanding of the psalmist's "parables" concerning Israel's repeated unbelief would be grasped by God's true end-time people.

Matthew's rendering of Psalm 78:2 reinforces the hidden nature of mystery to the outsiders or to those who lack "eyes to see" and "ears to hear." They are simply unable to grasp unveiled revelation. The quotation also corresponds to the temporary hiddenness of the mystery. God has, in eternity past ("since the foundation of the world"), planned that the kingdom ought to be introduced in an inaugurated stage and not only consummated form, though he did not divulge it clearly until the coming of Jesus.

Parables in general, though hotly debated,[22] lend themselves to be associated with the notion of mystery. Parables must be decoded or interpreted. In a similar way, mystery, according to Daniel, is characterized by a similar twofold structure: symbolic and interpretative revelation. The initial revelation remains largely incoherent to individuals, even to the seer (e.g., Nebuchadnezzar, Daniel). It is not until the interpretation has been given that the initial, hidden revelation becomes sensible. Perhaps this is one of the reasons why the term *mystery* is found in a cluster of paradigmatic parables within the Synoptics. R. T. France seems to be in agreement with this assessment when he states, "Parables are 'hidden things.' In this way the medium (parables) is itself integral to the message it conveys (the secrets of the kingdom of heaven)."[23]

Mysteries of the Kingdom

Now that we have a better grasp of the hidden nature of mystery, let us turn to its content. Jesus' statement that "to you it has been granted to know the mysteries of the kingdom of heaven" (Mt 13:11) is perhaps not as direct as we would like. What is the precise meaning of the phrase "mysteries of the kingdom"?

---

[22]For a thumbnail sketch of the past and current issues, see Klyne R. Snodgrass, *Stories with Intent: A Comprehensive Guide to the Parables of Jesus* (Grand Rapids: Eerdmans, 2008), pp. 1-59.

[23]France, *Gospel of Matthew*, p. 500.

The phrase "mysteries of the kingdom of heaven" (*ta mystēria tēs basileias tōn ouranōn*) should probably be rendered as "mysteries belonging to the kingdom of heaven" (the genitive *tēs basileias* ["of the kingdom"] should be understood as a genitive of possession). Linguistically, we should note that out of twenty-eight occurrences of *mystery* (*mystērion*)[24] in the New Testament only four occur in the plural, two of which are in the Synoptics (Lk 8:10; 1 Cor 13:2; 14:2). The plural, however, is also found in the book of Daniel (Dan 2:28-29, 47, OG/Theodotion). Perhaps the plural reflects an effort to connect Jesus' teaching with Daniel 2 (see below).[25]

Mark and Luke render this idea as "mystery/mysteries of the kingdom of God" (Mk 4:11; Lk 8:10), whereas Matthew renders it "mysteries of the kingdom of <u>heaven</u>" (cf., e.g., Mt 3:2; 4:17; 5:3, 10, 19-20; 7:21; 8:11; 10:7). In his work on the notion of heaven and earth in Matthew, Jonathan T. Pennington cogently argues that Matthew's preference for "heavenly" language stems not from a desire to avoid the title "God" but to draw a distinction between heaven and earth.[26] In addition, Matthew's heaven terminology refers to the *arrival of the heavenly kingdom on earth.* The heavenly dimension irrupts into the earthly ministry of Jesus. "Matthew's choice to regularly depict the kingdom as τῶν οὐρανῶν [*tōn ouranōn* {lit. "of heavens"}] is designed to emphasize that God's kingdom is not like earthly kingdoms, stands over against them, and will eschatologically replace them (on earth)."[27] We would only add that this end-time kingdom "of heaven" has begun its descent and has initially broken into the earthly sphere. Indeed, the key words *mystery* (*mystērion*), *kingdom* (*basileia*) and *heaven* (*ouranos*) only occur in two passages—Matthew 13:11 and Daniel 2:28. Matthew most likely uses these terms to signal the initial fulfillment of Daniel's long-awaited kingdom.

To get to the heart of the matter, what does Jesus mean by "mysteries of the kingdom of heaven"? Commentators have understood this phrase in a number of different ways. Schweitzer argued that it refers to the great harvest in contrast to the kingdom's insignificant beginnings,[28] and Otto Piper surmises that it

---

[24]Note, however, that *mystery* is missing in 1 Cor 2:1 in some manuscripts.

[25]Otto A. Piper, "The Mystery of the Kingdom of God," *Interpretation* 1 (1947): 196, suggests that the plural noun refers to "various implications of that secret."

[26]Jonathan T. Pennington, *Heaven and Earth in the Gospel of Matthew,* NovTSup 126 (Boston: Brill, 2007; repr., Grand Rapids: Baker, 2009).

[27]Ibid, p. 321.

[28]Albert Schweitzer, *The Mystery of the Kingdom of God: The Secret of Jesus' Messiahship and Passion,* trans. Walter Lowrie (New York: Macmillan, 1950), p. 108.

refers to Jesus' incarnation.[29] In the immediate context, the revealed mystery is directly related to the parable of the sower and the following parables concerning the kingdom. The Old Testament prophecies appear to view the establishment of the end-time kingdom to be a decisive overthrow of God's enemies at one consummate point at the very end of world history (e.g., Gen 49:9-10; Num 24:14-19; Dan 2:35, 44-45; see excursus 3.1 for a survey of this theme in the Old Testament and Judaism).

Strictly speaking, the discourse on the "mysteries of the kingdom" in Matthew 13 is the longest passage on the topic and comprises some forty-nine verses, compared to Mark's thirty-one and Luke's fourteen verses. Matthew's Gospel is the fullest and contains far more parables concerning the mystery of the kingdom.[30] We will thus primarily focus our attention on Matthew's portrait and interact with Mark and Luke where appropriate.

In each Synoptic Gospel, the phrase "mysteries of the kingdom" is tied to Jesus' response to the disciples' question, "Why do you speak to them in parables?" (Mt 13:10).[31] Jesus explains that a complete disclosure of the nature of the kingdom is restricted to his disciples. Matthew 13:13-15 explains the hiddenness of the revelation and the inability of the "crowds" or the "outsiders" to perceive the revelation. Then in Matthew 13:16-17 the disciples are able to comprehend the revelation because they have the ability to understand latter-day revelation (see above). The parable of the sower primarily addresses not the content of the kingdom but the reception of it (Mt 13:18-23). Only those who both embrace the message of the kingdom and persevere or "bear fruit" (Mt 13:23) will gain entrance into the kingdom.

After explaining the nature of parables (Mt 13:12-23), Jesus expounds on the *nature* of the kingdom (Mt 13:24-52). The key term *kingdom* (*basileia*) is found twelve times in Matthew 13. Typically, the parables are introduced with the general formula "the kingdom of heaven may be compared to" (Mt 13:24) or "the kingdom of heaven is like" (Mt 13:31; see Mt 13:33, 44, 45, 47, 52). This is

---

[29]Piper, "Mystery of the Kingdom," p. 190; cf. G. W. Barker, "Mystery," in *ISBE* 3:452.

[30]Matthew and Luke have two notable differences from Mark. They both read, "To you it has been granted *to know the mysteries of the kingdom* [*gnōnai ta mystēria*]" (Mt 13:11; Lk 8:10), whereas Mark includes "To you has been given *the mystery* [*to mystērion*] of the kingdom" (Mk 4:11). Matthew and Luke add "to know" and include the plural "mysteries." The significance of these differences is opaque, but we can at least suggest that Matthew and Luke may be textually independent of Mark here.

[31]Mark's Gospel records that in addition to the Twelve, "others around him" (TNIV) questioned Jesus concerning parables (Mk 4:10; cf. Mk 3:34).

contrasted with Jesus' interpretation of the parable of the sower that begins with "When anyone hears the word of the kingdom" (Mt 13:19).

The second parable, regarding the tares (Mt 13:24-30), describes a field owner who sowed good seed, but while he was sleeping his enemy came and sowed tares (Mt 13:24-25). As a result, the tares and the wheat grew *together*, making it difficult to separate them (Mt 13:26-28). The owner thought it wise to allow the wheat and the tares to flourish concurrently (Mt 13:29). Only at the harvest will the wheat and the tares be ultimately separated. Fortunately, the parable is interpreted a few verses later (Mt 13:36-43), because of the apparent lack of understanding (Mt 13:36). In the interpretation, the field constitutes the world, the good seed are the sons of the kingdom, and the tares are the sons of the evil one (Mt 13:38). The point of the parable could not be clearer: *the kingdom citizens and the unrighteous individuals dwell together.*[32]

What makes Jesus' teaching about the kingdom a "mystery" is the contrast with the Old Testament and Jewish expectation of the kingdom. One of the main tenants of the prophesied latter-day kingdom is the *consummate* establishment of God's kingdom directly preceded by the ultimate destruction of unrighteousness and foreign oppression. The advent of the Messiah would signal the death knell of evil empires. Pagan kings and their kingdoms were to be destroyed or "crushed" (Dan 2:44), and the Messiah would "shatter all their substance with an iron rod" (*Pss. Sol.* 17:24). Such a defeat and judgment would be decisive and happen all at once at the end point of history. But here Jesus claims that the advent of the Messiah and the latter-day kingdom does not happen all at once, since a complete defeat and judgment of the wicked does not occur. Paradoxically, two realms coexist—those who belong to the kingdom and those who belong to the "evil one."

Joel Marcus, in commenting on the mystery in Mark 4, is right to include

---

[32]The parable of the tares in Matthew's account is similar to Mark's parable of the seed (Mk 4:26-29). Mark claims that the "kingdom of God is like a man who casts seed upon the soil" (Mk 4:26). The farmer is not aware of *how* the seeds transform into "mature grain." Seeds simply grow by themselves, independent of human action: "The soil produces crops by itself; first the blade, then the head, then the mature grain in the head" (Mk 4:28). In the same manner, the kingdom is inaugurated and grows and expands independent of human achievement. (Note the contrasting view of the kingdom portrayed in the *War Scroll* [1QM]—the Qumran community physically overtakes their enemies in one decisive victory—and Jesus' teaching on the same subject, which affirms that the victorious kingdom begins spiritually and is consummated after a considerable interval of time.) At the end of the age, the kingdom will arrive consummately: "When the crop permits, he [the owner] immediately puts in the sickle, because the harvest has come" (Mk 4:29).

Mark 3:23-27 in his definition of the "mystery of the kingdom." He then goes on to make several accurate conclusions:

> When 3:23-27 is taken together with the parable of the sower, the following emerge as components of "the mystery of the kingdom": (a) the fact that God causes there to be *two* kingdoms, that of God and that of Satan, which are in deadly opposition to each other (3:23-26); (b) the fact that in Jesus' ministry the kingdom of Satan is routed (3:27); (c) the fact that, in spite of (b), the kingdom of Satan can still in certain ways impede the kingdom of God (4:3-8). All three points may be subsumed under the rubric "the collision of the kingdoms." The "mystery of the kingdom of God" thus has to do with God's strange design of bringing his kingdom in Jesus Christ, yet unleashing the forces of darkness to blind human beings so that they oppose that kingdom.[33]

Commentators generally affirm this position and agree that the revealed mystery of the kingdom comprises the unique and unexpected inauguration of the latter-day kingdom in and through Jesus' ministry.[34] The eschatological kingdom, in a very real sense, has begun through Jesus. Jesus' defeat of the devil during his wilderness temptation is nothing short of the fulfillment of Old Testament promises that portray God annihilating Israel's enemy through the Messiah. But the true enemy of Israel is not ultimately Rome—but Satan.[35] Jesus as the "stone" that had been "cut out without hands" (Dan 2:34) has "crushed" the devil and his demonic forces. (Mt 21:44 likely includes allusion to this Daniel passage: "and he who falls on this stone will be broken to pieces; but on whomever it falls, it will scatter him like dust.") Moreover, Jesus' exorcism of demons is a result of his victory over the devil and further advancement of the kingdom. Matthew 12:28 says, for example, "But if I cast out demons by the Spirit of God, then the kingdom of God has come upon you." At the very end of the age, the physical enemies of God (behind whom stand Satan and the forces of evil) will be completely and finally defeated. We thus have an already-and-not-yet end-time defeat of evil: first the unseen powers of evil in the first century and then the physical opponents of God and his people at the eschaton.

Returning to Matthew 13, the inclusion of two more parables—the hidden

---

[33]Marcus, "Mark 4:10-12," p. 567.

[34]E.g., Barker, "Mystery," p. 452; Günther Bornkamm, "μυστήριον, μυέω," *TDNT* 4:818-19; Brown, *Semitic Background*, pp. 32-36; H. Krämer, "μυστήριον," *EDNT* 2:449; Werner Kelber, *The Kingdom in Mark: A New Place and a New Time* (Philadelphia: Fortress, 1974), pp. 25-43; G. R. Beasley-Murray, *Jesus and the Kingdom of God* (Grand Rapids: Eerdmans, 1986), pp. 103-7.

[35]N. T. Wright, *Jesus and the Victory of God*, COQG 2 (Minneapolis: Fortress, 1996), pp. 451-61.

treasure and the costly pearl (Mt 13:44-46)—demonstrate the immense worth or inauguration of the latter-day kingdom. This is again illustrated in the enigmatic saying found in Matthew 13:52: "Therefore every scribe who has become a disciple of the kingdom of heaven is like a head of a household, who brings out of his treasure <u>things new and old</u>." Here the kingdom is likened to a scribe or writer who furnishes "things new and old." Whatever the precise identification of all the details may be, the main thrust is that Jesus' teaching concerning the kingdom involves both "new" and "old" insights. In other words, his teaching stands in both continuity and discontinuity with the Old Testament (see also Lk 10:21-24).[36] The continuity of Jesus' teaching is that the already-and-not-yet kingdom truly fulfills Old Testament latter-day prophecies concerning the kingdom (e.g., Gen 49; Num 24; Dan 2). The kingdom has come! On the other hand, the discontinuity refers to the inaugurated nature of the kingdom and its nonconsummative presence. Mysteriously, the arrival of the kingdom does not signal the *complete* destruction of Israel's enemies and the devil, as the Old Testament and Judaism appear to depict. Sin, wickedness and rebellion persist, whereas the expectations of God's kingdom affirmed that all sin and wickedness would be extinguished forever.

The kingdom has been *inaugurated but remains to be consummately fulfilled.* Scholars label this framework the "already-and-not-yet," and it is commonly referred to as "inaugurated eschatology." Jesus teases out this paradigm through the parable of the tares' emphasis on the consummate judgment of the wicked:

> The enemy who sowed them is the devil, and the harvest is the end of the age; and the reapers are angels. So just as the tares are gathered up and burned with fire, so shall it be at the end of the age. The Son of Man will send forth His angels, and they will gather out of His kingdom all stumbling blocks, and those who commit lawlessness, and will throw them into the furnace of fire; in that place there will be weeping and gnashing of teeth. Then the RIGHTEOUS WILL SHINE FORTH AS THE SUN in the kingdom of their Father. He who has ears, let him hear. (Mt 13:39-43)

Jesus also speaks of the consummate restoration of the righteous through resurrection (Mt 13:43), where he partially quotes from Daniel 12:3. In its immediate context, the passage refers to the general resurrection. The righteous are consummately restored and the wicked are punished: "Many of those who

---

[36]France, *Gospel of Matthew*, pp. 546-47.

sleep in the dust of the ground will awake, these to everlasting life, but the others to disgrace *and* everlasting contempt. 'Those who have insight will shine brightly like the brightness of the expanse of heaven, and those who lead the many to righteousness, like the stars forever and ever'" (Dan 12:2-3). The quotation of Daniel 12:3 in Matthew 13:43 signals the yet-future fulfillment of this passage. In other words, when God consummately restores the kingdom at the end of the age, then the Danielic prophecy will be ultimately fulfilled.

Jesus' already-and-not-yet conception of the kingdom is found throughout each remaining parable in Matthew 13. The parable of the dragnet in Matthew 13:47-50 rehearses the point of the parable of the tares:

> Again, the kingdom of heaven is like a dragnet cast into the sea, and gathering *fish* of every kind; and when it was filled, they drew it up on the beach; and they sat down and gathered the good *fish* into containers, but the bad they threw away. So it will be at the end of the age; the angels will come forth and take out the wicked from among the righteous, and will throw them into the furnace of fire; in that place there will be weeping and gnashing of teeth.

Fish are gathered in a net and then separated on the beach. The good fish are preserved in containers, whereas the bad fish are thrown away (Mt 13:48). Like the tares and the wheat dwelling together in the same field, the good and the bad fish exist in the same sea. The upshot is that despite the commencement of the latter-day kingdom, those who participate in the kingdom coexist with those who do not. The judgment at the "end of the age" will determine the good fish from the bad (Mt 13:49-50).

The parable of the mustard seed (Mt 13:31-32) and the parable of leaven (Mt 13:33) illustrate this precise point:

> He presented another parable to them, saying, "The kingdom of heaven is like a mustard seed, which a man took and sowed in his field; and this is smaller than all *other* seeds, but when it is full grown, it is larger than the garden plants and becomes a tree, so that THE BIRDS OF THE AIR come and NEST IN ITS BRANCHES." He spoke another parable to them, "The kingdom of heaven is like leaven, which a woman took and hid in three pecks of flour until it was all leavened."

The kingdom is likened to a mustard seed that is sown and "is smaller than all other seeds, but when it is full-grown, it is larger than the garden plants and becomes a tree" (Mt 13:31-32; see also Mk 4:30-32; Lk 13:18-19). Similarly, the kingdom is inaugurated and begins small but eventually grows into a full-blown tree and arrives in its consummate form. Accordingly, in contrast to Old Testament expectations of the kingdom that viewed the fullness of the kingdom coming all at once at the end, Jesus says that the mystery of his kingdom is that it is beginning in a small way and will grow over an extended period of time. In the parable of leaven, a woman takes some leaven and hides it in "three pecks of flour" (Mt 13:33). The leaven eventually seeps throughout the flour until "it was all leavened" (Mt 13:33). The point here is that, whereas the Old Testament expectation was that when the kingdom came, it would come suddenly and be seen visibly in its completeness by all eyes, now the disclosed mystery of the kingdom is that the kingdom has come but it appears at first to be invisible but nevertheless growing, until it reaches maturity, when all eyes will finally see it.

The emphasis in these two parables is slightly different from the parable of the tares. Though the "mustard seed" exists in the midst of other "seeds" and "garden plants," the general thrust of the parable together with the leaven parable is the *slow but sure growth of the kingdom and its eventual dominion.*[37]

The upshot of the disclosed mystery of the kingdom is that it is somewhat different from Old Testament and Jewish expectations of the kingdom, which foresaw that it would come (1) very visibly for eyes to see, (2) all at once, (3) in its complete fullness, (4) when all of God's enemies would be decisively defeated and (5) the saints would be separated from the ungodly, the former receiving reward and the latter punishment. The kingdom's mystery that is revealed is that it commences (1) for the most part invisibly, so that one must have spiritual eyes to perceive it, (2) in two stages (already-and-not-yet), (3) growing over an extended time from one stage to the last stage. (4) God's opponents are not defeated immediately all together, but the invisible satanic powers are first subjugated and then at the end of time, all foes will be vanquished and judged, and (5) saints are not being separated from the ungodly in the beginning stage of the kingdom, but such a separation will occur on the last day, when Jesus' followers receive their reward and the latter punishment.

---

[37]The parable of the mustard seed ends with a partial Old Testament quotation or strong allusion: "THE BIRDS OF THE AIR come and NEST IN ITS BRANCHES" (Mt 13:32). The quotation seems to be dependent on Dan 4:12. In Dan 4, the tree celebrates the greatness of Nebuchadnezzar's kingdom, whereas the quotation in Mt 13:32 extols the greatness of the long-awaited Danielic kingdom of Dan 2. God's kingdom has ironically cut down (cf. Dan 4:14-15, 23), as it were, the "trees" of the nations, and replaced them with an eternal one.

THE PRESENCE OF *MYSTERY* IN THE SYNOPTICS

One question that scholars rarely ask in determining the presence and significance of the term *mystery* in the Synoptics is why it is found only in this particular discourse. The term is found throughout Paul's writings and a few times
in Revelation but only three times here in the Synoptics (all occurrences are in
the same discourse). Why is this the case? Perhaps we can offer one suggestion:
the Synoptics employ the term at a crucial juncture—Jesus' teaching concerning the end-time kingdom. Not only does the term evoke several salient
features such as temporary and permanent hiddenness, it also recalls the narrative of the book of Daniel, particularly Daniel 2, where "mystery" and
"kingdom" are intertwined. The point could not be any clearer: the end-time
kingdom of Daniel has begun to be fulfilled in and through Jesus. This explains
why the term *mystery* is not connected to any other theme in the Synoptics (or
John's Gospel, for that matter) but restricted to Jesus' teaching on the latter-day
kingdom.[38] Pennington, in reference to Matthew's kingdom of heaven language,
claims, "*Matthew, drinking deeply at the waters of Daniel, has developed his
kingdom of heaven language and theme from the same motif and similar language in Daniel 2–7*" (italics original).[39] For example, part of the Daniel 2
prophecy refers not only to mystery but also "the God of heaven [who] will set
up a kingdom" (Dan 2:44). The reason for this, we think, is that Matthew (and
the other Synoptic authors) is signaling that the long-awaited Danielic kingdom
has begun to be fulfilled in and through Jesus.

CONCLUSION

Jesus labels his teaching here in Matthew 13 (and par.) as the "mysteries of the
kingdom." It is labeled a "mystery" because it was partially hidden in the Old
Testament that the latter-day kingdom would be fulfilled in two stages or in an
already-and-not-yet manner. The Old Testament predicted that the kingdom
would be established all at once at the very end of time, but the revealed mystery

---

[38]So e.g., see George Eldon Ladd, *The Presence of the Future: The Eschatology of Biblical Realism*
(Grand Rapids: Eerdmans, 1974), pp. 223-25. Wright similarly argues that the eschatological kingdom of Dan 2 is bound up with Jesus' teaching in the parable of the sower (*Jesus and the Victory of
God*, pp. 231-32). See also David Wenham, "The Kingdom of God and Daniel," *ExpTim* 98 (1987):
132-34; Craig A. Evans, "Daniel in the New Testament: Visions of God's Kingdom," in *The Book of
Daniel: Composition and Reception*, ed. John J. Collins and Peter W. Flint (Boston: Brill, 2001),
2:510-14.

[39]Pennington, *Heaven and Earth*, p. 289.

of the kingdom is that its timing has occurred in an unexpected manner: it has come "already" but it is "not yet" completed. Its consummation will come at some distant future point. This is the main feature of the revealed mystery of the kingdom. This means that the kingdom would begin in a very small form and grow over an extended time from one stage to the last stage, until it reaches its full maturity at the last day. Thus Old Testament saints understood the basic meaning of the kingdom prophecies in their consummate form but did not perceive at all clearly that they would begin fulfillment in an inaugurated manner for a period of time. This was not in contradiction to the meaning of the prophecies from the Old Testament vantage point but a fuller understanding about the timing of their fulfillment. Indeed, even the Old Testament perspective contained an inkling of an inaugurated period of fulfillment of kingdom prophecies (e.g., see Ps 110:1-2).

To sum up, the Old Testament prophesied that the end-time kingdom would be established by the defeat of every one of Israel's enemies all together and all at once, yet Jesus proclaims that his kingdom exists in simultaneity with his opponents' kingdom. The kingdom of God has indeed been installed and the deathblow to Satan and his forces has been dealt, but without consummation. At the very end of all things, every single enemy will be defeated. Second, the kingdom commences for the most part invisibly, not visibly as in Old Testament expectations, so one must have special insight to perceive it. Third, saints are not being separated from the ungodly in the beginning stage of the kingdom, but such a separation will occur on the last day, when Jesus' followers receive their reward and the latter punishment.

Israel and its leaders by and large were unable to grasp the mystery of the kingdom. They failed to understand that God's end-time kingdom would occur first spiritually—an initial fulfillment that resulted in the overlap of the righteous and unrighteous. God would then consummately establish his latter-day kingdom at the end of the age in both a spiritual and physical form.

EXCURSUS 3.1: EXPECTATION OF THE LATTER-DAY KINGDOM IN THE OLD TESTAMENT AND EARLY JUDAISM

Old Testament expectation. The Old Testament expectation of the coming kingdom is obviously significant. However, the theme conceptually spans large tracts of texts and is thematically related to other latter-day concepts such as the coming messianic ruler, new creation, judgment upon Israel's enemies and its restoration, the pouring out of the Spirit, the new covenant, and so forth (see Is 43:1-8; 65:17; 66:22; Jer 31:33). Thus we are unable to survey all the material in detail. We will therefore provide only a cursory overview of this theme by touching on a few significant texts as examples and narrowly focusing on the expectation of the latter-day kingdom.

Perhaps one of the easiest ways to broach this topic is to review Old Testament texts that explicitly link the notion of "latter days" (or a synonymous eschatological expression) with the advent of God's kingdom.[40] The phrase "latter days," found throughout the Old Testament, should be viewed as an eschatological time period.[41] At times, it can refer to a time of distress (Deut 4:30; 8:16; Ezek 38:8, 16) and the restoration of Israel (Is 2:2; Jer 23:20; 30:24; Hos 3:5; Mic 4:1). But this expression is often coupled with the kingdom.

The first occurrence of the phrase is in Genesis 49:1: "Assemble yourselves that I may tell you what will befall you <u>in the days to come</u> [bĕʾaḥărît hayyāmîm, lit. 'in the latter days']."[42] Though some reject the eschatological connotations of the expression in this passage, represented by many translations (NASB, TNIV, NRSV),[43] we ought to conceive it as pertaining to the end times. A few verses later, Jacob describes the future of Judah:

> Judah is a lion's whelp. . . .
> The scepter shall not depart from Judah,
> Nor the ruler's staff from between his feet,
> Until Shiloh comes,
> And to him *shall* be the obedience of the peoples. (Gen 49:9-10)

Judah is to rule over his enemies (Gen 49:8, 11-12; cf. Is 63:1-3) and be mighty as a lion (Gen 49:9). He will rule until all the nations pay obeisance to him (Gen 49:10). Judah's victory is not seen as merely a local phenomenon but a decisive

---

[40]See also G. K. Beale, "Eschatological Conception of New Testament Theology," in *Eschatology in Bible & Theology*, ed. Kent E. Brower and Mark W. Elliott (Downers Grove, IL: InterVarsity Press, 1997), p. 14. Synonymous eschatological language is also found in Dan 11:20, 27, 35; 12:4, 7, 9, 13 (cf. Dan 11:13, 35). Though these verses do not use the phrase "latter days," they use terms such as *end* and *appointed time*.

[41]See John T. Willis, "The Expression *beʾacharith hayyamim* in the Old Testament," *RestQ* 22 (1979): 54-71.

[42]The brief discussion of "latter days" in the Pentateuch is adapted from G. K. Beale, *A New Testament Biblical Theology: The Unfolding of the Old Testament in the New* (Grand Rapids: Baker Academic, 2011), pp. 88-102.

[43]G. W. Buchanan, "Eschatology and the 'End of Days,'" *JNES* 20 (1961): 188-93, esp. p. 189; J. P. M. Van Der Ploeg, "Eschatology in the Old Testament," in *Oudtestamentische Studiën*, ed. A. S. Van Der Woude (Boston: Brill, 1972), pp. 89-99.

and ultimate victory over all possible enemies of Israel. Genesis 49:8-10 is a climactic point in Israel's history and thus represents an eschatological zenith point of Jacob's prophecy. This prophesied king from Judah will defeat the end-time enemy, like Adam should have done (Gen 49:9-10) and will be rewarded with living in a climactic new creation environment (Gen 49:11-12).

The second appearance of the expression "in the latter days" occurs in Numbers 24:14: "And now, behold, I [Balaam] am going to my people; come, and I will advise you what this people will do to your people in the days to come." As in Genesis 49:1, this phrase also is not a mere vague reference to the future but a specific, eschatological one.[44] That Numbers 24:14 alludes to Genesis 49:1-10 is evident from the following: (1) virtually the same wording in Genesis 49:9 occurs in Numbers 24:9, "He couches, he lies down as a lion, and as a lion who dares rouse him?"; (2) the repetition of "scepter" in Genesis 49:10 and Numbers 24:17; (3) Numbers 24:8, like Genesis 49, explicitly refers to the "nations" as Israel's enemies who are to be defeated; (4) new creation imagery is found in both Genesis (Gen 49:11-12, 22, 25-26) and Numbers (cf. Num 24:7b-9 with Num 24:5-7).

> How fair are your tents, O Jacob,
> Your dwellings, O Israel!
> Like valleys that stretch out,
> Like gardens beside the river,
> Like aloes planted by the Lord,
> Like cedars beside the waters.
> Water will flow from his buckets,
> And his seed *will be* by many waters,
> And his king shall be higher than Agag,
> And his kingdom shall be exalted. (Num 24:5-7)

The depiction of Numbers 24:5-8 is also associated with the Abrahamic promise (cf. an increase of "seed" in Num 24:7, and the "blessing and cursing" in Num 24:9 repeats Gen 12:3b). There may also be an echo of the original Adamic commission (note "king" and "kingdom" in Num 24:7 and "dominion" in Num 24:19) and of the manner in which the promised seed in Gen 3:15 ("he shall bruise you on the head") is to defeat the divine enemy (cf. "a scepter . . . shall crush through the forehead of Moab" in Num 24:17).

---

[44]This is confirmed by its allusion to Gen 49, the context of the phrase in Num 24, and its use in later biblical and extrabiblical literature.

Balaam's discourse to Balak climaxes in Numbers 24:17-19 as he describes a
messianic-like king arriving and defeating Israel's enemies:

> I see him, but not now;
> I behold him, but not near;
> A star shall come forth from Jacob,
> A scepter shall rise from Israel,
> And shall crush through the forehead of Moab,
> And tear down all the sons of Sheth.
> Edom shall be a possession,
> Seir, its enemies, also will be a possession,
> While Israel performs valiantly.
> One from Jacob shall have dominion,
> And will destroy the remnant from the city.

Part of this prophecy ("Edom shall be a possession") is alluded to in Amos 9:12a
("that they [Israel] may possess the remnant of Edom"), a prophecy of Israel's
end-time defeat of the nations at the time of her restoration (Amos 9:11) to her
land, described in paradisiacal language, much like that in Genesis 49:11-12 and
Numbers 24:6-7 (cf. Amos 9:13-15: "the mountains will drip sweet wine"; "they
will also plant vineyards and drink their wine, and make gardens and eat their
fruit"; "they will not again be rooted out from their land").

Consummate ruling over the nations and establishing God's kingdom climaxes in the book of Daniel. As we saw in chapter one above, Daniel con-
tributes to this theme by outlining the successive pagan kingdoms and their
ultimate defeat through a "stone made without hands," preparing the arrival of
God's eternal kingdom. The statue in Daniel 2 symbolizes four world kingdoms
that are eventually smashed by a "stone" (Dan 2:35, 44-45)—an image that is
interpreted messianically in the New Testament.[45] The pagan kingdoms were
eclipsed by a "kingdom which will never be destroyed" (Dan 2:44). Daniel
claims that the fulfillment of his prediction will take place in the future: "There
is a God in heaven who reveals mysteries, and he has made known to King
Nebuchadnezzar what will take place in the latter days [OG: *ep' eschatōn tōn
hēmerōn*]" (Dan 2:28). Similarly, Daniel 2:45 says, "Inasmuch as you saw that a
stone was cut out of the mountain without hands and that it crushed the iron,
the bronze . . . God has made known what will occur in the latter days [Our

---

[45]See G. K. Beale, *The Temple and the Church's Mission*, NSBT 17 (Downers Grove, IL: InterVarsity
Press, 2004), pp. 185-88.

translation. OG: *ta esomena ep' eschatōn tōn hēmerōn*]." In other words, a "stone" representing an end-time agent of God will destroy the pagan kingdoms in the "latter days" and install God's consummate kingdom (Dan 2:35, 44-45).

Daniel 7:11-12 graphically portrays the destruction of the four beasts, namely, the four kings/kingdoms (cf. Dan 7:17): "I kept looking until the beast was slain, and its body was destroyed and given to the burning fire. As for the rest of the beasts, their dominion was taken away." As a replacement, the Son of Man receives the authority to rule over God's eternal kingdom:

> One like a Son of Man was coming . . .
> And to Him was given dominion,
> Glory and a kingdom,
> That all the peoples, nations and *men of every* language
> Might serve Him.
> His dominion is an everlasting dominion
> Which will not pass away;
> And . . . will not be destroyed. (Dan 7:13-14)

Most of the book of Daniel touches on this main theme; God's kingdom will consummately overthrow Israel's enemies (including Nebuchadnezzar's; Dan 4:4-33; 5:5-30; 7:1-27; 8:1-26; 10:1-12:13).[46] Gooding contends rightly, "The total message of the book [of Daniel], then, is nothing less than a survey, part historical and part prophetic, of the whole period of Gentile imperial rule from Nebuchadnezzar's first assault on Jerusalem and the removal of its Davidic king until the abolition of all Gentile imperial power and the setting up of the Messianic kingdom."[47]

All of these Old Testament prophecies appear to view the establishment of the end-time kingdom to be a decisive overthrow of God's enemies at one consummate point at the very end of world history.

---

[46]Other relevant Old Testament texts prophesying the future establishment of God's kingdom at the end of time are the following: "I will raise up your descendant after you, who will come forth from you, and I will establish his kingdom. He shall build a house for My name, and I will establish the throne of his kingdom forever. . . . Your house and your kingdom shall endure before Me forever; your throne shall be established forever" (2 Sam 7:12-13, 16; cf. 1 Chron 17:11-14; 22:10); "There will be no end to the increase of *His* government or of peace, / On the throne of David and over his kingdom, / To establish it and to uphold it with justice and righteousness / From then on and forevermore. / The zeal of the LORD of hosts will accomplish this" (Is 9:7; cf. Is 2:1-22; 11:1-16; Jer 23:5-8; Ezek 40–48); see also Psalm 2.

[47]David W. Gooding, "The Literary Structure of the Book of Daniel and Its Implications," *TynBul* 32 (1981): 68.

Early Judaism's expectation. The advent of God's end-time kingdom permeates early Judaism, since it is often associated with general restoration and judgment texts. Examining all relevant texts in detail is a massive undertaking and beyond the scope of this project. A number of studies exist that have already canvassed the appropriate literature, so there is no need to survey the material once more.[48] Like the Old Testament and in allusion to the Old Testament, the early Jewish literature generally highlights decisive and consummative judgment upon the wicked, vindication of the righteous, the Messiah's rule over Israel and its enemies, and the return from exile. We need only to sample a few representative texts.

> Undergird him with the strength to destroy the unrighteous rulers . . . in wisdom and in righteousness to drive out the sinners from the inheritance; to smash the arrogance of sinners like a potter's jar; to shatter all their substance with an iron rod; to destroy the unlawful nations with the word of his mouth; at his warning the nations will flee from his presence; and he will condemn sinners by the thoughts of their hearts. He will gather a holy people whom he will lead in righteousness; and he will judge the tribes of the people that have been made holy by the Lord their God. He will not tolerate unrighteousness (even) to pause among them, and any person who knows wickedness shall not live with them. For he shall know them that they are all children of their God. He will distribute them upon the land according to their tribes; the alien and the foreigner will no longer live near them. He will judge peoples and nations in the wisdom of his righteousness. And he will have gentile nations serving him under his yoke, and he will glorify the Lord in (a place) prominent (above) the whole earth. And he will purge Jerusalem (and make it) holy as it was even from the beginning, (for) nations to come from the ends of the earth to see his glory, to bring as gifts her children who had been driven out, and to see the glory of the Lord with which God has glorified her. And he will be a righteous king over them, taught by God. There will be no unrighteousness among them in his days, for all shall be holy, and their king shall be the Lord Messiah. (*Pss. Sol.* 17.22-32, first century B.C.)

> And when these things come to pass and the signs occur . . . then my son will be revealed, whom you saw as a man coming up from the sea. And when all the nations hear his voice . . . and an innumerable multitude shall be gathered together, as you saw, desiring to come and conquer him. But he will stand on the top of Mount Zion. And Zion will come and be made manifest to all people,

---

[48]E.g., G. R. Beasley-Murray, *Jesus and the Kingdom of God* (Grand Rapids: Eerdmans, 1986).

prepared and built, as you saw the mountain carved out without hands. And he, my Son, will reprove the assembled nations for their ungodliness . . . and will reproach them to their face with their evil thoughts and with the torments with which they are to be tortured . . . and he will destroy them. . . . Those who are left of your people, who are found within my holy borders, shall be saved. Therefore when he destroys the multitude of the nations that are gathered together, he will defend the people who remain. (*4 Ezra* 13.32-49, first century A.D.)

This Son of Man whom you have seen is the One who would remove the kings and the mighty ones from their comfortable seats and the strong ones from their thrones. He shall loosen the reins of the strong and crush the teeth of the sinners. He shall depose the kings from their thrones and kingdoms (*1 En.* 46.4-5, first century B.C.)

Like sparks that you saw, so will their kingdom be; they will rule several year[s] over the earth and crush everything; a people will crush another people, and a province another provi[n]ce. Until the people of God arises and makes everyone rest from the sword. His kingdom will be an eternal kingdom, and his paths in truth. (4Q248 II, 1-5; cf. 1Q28b V, 1-29, third century B.C. to first century A.D.)

Language of "destroying the unlawful nations" (*Pss. Sol.* 17.23), "reproving the assembled nations for their ungodliness" (*4 Ezra* 13.37) and "deposing the kings from their thrones and kingdoms" (*1 En.* 46:5) is a common theme in texts that describe the final defeat of evil kingdoms and the complete form of the coming end-time kingdom. Texts such as these portray the consummate destruction of pagan nations and their inhabitants for their unceasing rebellion against God and particularly the Messiah.[49] For example, in the above quotation, *Psalms of Solomon* 17:24 says, "To shatter all their substance with an iron rod." By the first century A.D., early Judaism waited expectantly for the overthrow of the Roman Empire. The Maccabbean conflict left an indelible mark on Judaism— Israel's enemies must be overthrown all at once. This can be aptly illustrated by Josephus's interpretation of the fourth kingdom in Daniel 2, a kingdom he identified with the Roman Empire:[50] "These misfortunes our nation did in fact

---

[49]See esp. *T. Mos.* 10:1-7: "Then his kingdom will appear throughout his whole creation. Then the devil will have an end. . . . For the Heavenly One will arise from his kingly throne. Yea, he will go forth from his holy habitation with indignation and wrath on behalf of his sons. And the earth will tremble, even to its ends shall it be shaken. . . . For God Most High will surge forth, the Eternal One alone. In full view will he come to work vengeance on the nations. Yeah, all their idols will he destroy." Cf. Wis 3:8; *3 En.* 44.8; *4 Ezra* 2.10-14; *1 En.* 62.2-9; *2 En.* 31.3-6 [J]; 58.3 [J]; 4Q174 1 I, 1-19; 4Q213 1 II +2, 1-19; 4Q387a 3 III, 1-12; 4Q554 2 III, 14-22.

[50]F. F. Bruce, *A Mind for What Matters: Collected Essays* (Grand Rapids: Eerdmans, 1990), pp. 19-31;

come to experience under Antiochus Epiphanes, just as Daniel many years before saw and wrote that they would happen . . . Daniel also wrote about the empire of the Romans" (*Ant.* 10.275-76; cf. 11.336-39). In this light, the Jews expected the last shoe of Daniel's prophecy to drop: the destruction of this last fourth kingdom of evil by the Messiah and God.

In the *War Scroll* (1QM), the Qumran community scrupulously planned for the eschatological attack against their enemies, including those who were apostate within Israel. In 1QM I, 1-2, this notion is explicit: "The first attack by the sons of light will be launched against the lot of the sons of darkness, against the army of Belial, against the band of Edom and of Moab . . . who are beings helped by the violators of the covenant." The book goes on to describe in great detail the specificities of the attack by the Qumran warrior-saints (e.g., their banners, shields, cavalry formations, trumpets; see columns I-XIX). In column XI, the Qumran community is identified with the "star" of Jacob (Num 24:17-19): "Thus you [the Lord] taught us from ancient times saying, 'A star will depart from Jacob, a sceptre will be raised in Israel.' . . . By the hand of your anointed ones, seers of decrees, you taught us the ti[mes of] the wars of your hands . . . to fell the hordes of Belial" (5-8). Throughout the DSS, the latter-day kingdom receives much discussion and is greatly anticipated, since the community held that it was currently living in the "latter days" (e.g., 4Q174 1 I, 19).

Positively, the Messiah will rule over Israel ushering in God's consummate kingdom (*Pss. Sol.* 18.5: "May God cleanse Israel . . . for the appointed day when his Messiah will reign") and the new creation.[51] At this time, Gentiles will flee to Jerusalem in submission (*Pss. Sol.* 17.31: "nations to come from the ends of the earth to see his glory, to bring as gifts her children"). As a result of the Messiah's victory over pagan nations, peace and joy will be ubiquitous: "And [after he] has sat down in eternal peace on the throne of the kingdom, then joy will be revealed and rest will appear. And then health will descend in a dew, and illness will vanish, and fear and tribulation and lamentation will pass away" (2 *Bar.* 73.1-2). All of Jerusalem will be deemed "holy" (*Pss. Sol.* 17.30: "he will purge Jerusalem, [and make it] holy"). God will thoroughly restore Israel, and

---

Louis H. Feldman, *Josephus's Interpretation of the Bible* (Los Angeles: University of California Press, 1998), pp. 629-69; Paul Spilsbury, "Flavius Josephus on the Rise and Fall of the Roman Empire," *JTS* 54 (2003): 1-24.

[51]On the general theme of the restoration of the latter-day kingdom, see *T. Jud.* 17.5-6; *T. Iss.* 5.7; *T. Jos.* 19.12; *T. Jac.* 7.27; *T. Mos.* 10.1-10; *1 En.* 25.7; 91.12-17; *3 En.* 48A.10; *Syb. Or.* 3.46-60; 3.635-730; 3.767-95; 14.352-60; *2 Bar.* 39.7; 73.1.

righteousness will reign (*Pss. Sol.* 17.26: "he will gather together a holy people, whom he will lead in righteousness").

Thus, as in the Old Testament, so in early Jewish writings, the defeat of God's enemies and the establishment of God's kingdom were to occur decisively and completely all at once at the very end of world history.

4

THE USE OF *MYSTERY*
IN ROMANS

IN THE PREVIOUS CHAPTER, WE EXAMINED THE USE OF *mystery* in the book of Matthew. Jesus disclosed to his disciples that the kingdom arrived for the most part invisibly, in two stages (already-and-not-yet), and would grow over an extended time from one stage to the last stage. God's enemies are not defeated immediately and all together, as the Old Testament predicted (the only exception perhaps being Ps 110:1), but the invisible satanic powers are first subjugated and then consummately defeated at the end of time. Lastly, the saints are not being separated from the ungodly in this initial stage of the kingdom but dwell in the midst of wicked individuals.

Paul's discussion of mystery in the book of Romans is not far removed from Matthew's (and the Synoptics') conception of mystery, since both of them generally concern the nature of God's eternal kingdom. Whereas Matthew's treatment of mystery is more concerned with the establishment of the kingdom, Paul in Romans details the *order* in which people groups participate in the end-time kingdom.

The Gospels present Jesus as first pursuing the restoration of ethnic Israelites, followed by the salvation of the Gentiles. According to Matthew 10:1-6, Jesus commissions the Twelve to avoid first proclaiming the kingdom message to Gentiles but to pursue the conversion of ethnic Jews: "These twelve Jesus sent out after instructing them: 'Do not go in *the* way of *the* Gentiles, and do not enter *any* city of the Samaritans; but rather go to the lost sheep of the house of Israel" (Mt 10:5-6). Certainly, Jesus made overtures to the conversion of Gentiles, but only after he brought about Israelite restoration (e.g., Mt 8:5-11). The same pattern of salvation is readily apparent in the book of Acts. Acts is programmatically structured around this principle: "You shall be My witnesses both in Jerusalem, and in all Judea and Samaria, and even to the remotest part of the earth" (Acts 1:8). Luke's description of Paul's journeys also testifies to this phenomenon. After first delivering the gospel to the Jews in the synagogues, Paul turns to the Gentiles because of Jewish unbelief: "Paul and Barnabas spoke out boldly and said, 'It was necessary that the word of God be spoken to you first; since you repudiate it and judge yourselves unworthy of eternal life, behold, we are turning to the Gentiles'" (Acts 13:46).

This established pattern in the Gospels and Acts is somewhat difficult to reconcile with the book of Romans. Paul begins and concludes Romans with a clear statement about "Jew first, then Gentile" (Rom 1:16; 2:9-10; 15:8-9). On the other hand, he reverses the order in Rom 11:11-12: "But by their [Israel's] transgression salvation *has come* to the Gentiles, to make them [Israel] jealous. Now if their transgression is riches for the world and their failure is riches for the Gentiles, how much more will their [Israel's] fulfillment be!" How do we resolve these two statements? Within Romans itself, tension exists between these two truths, and it has been difficult for commentators to resolve this tension.

MYSTERY IN ROMANS 11

The resolution, we believe, is bound up with the unveiled mystery in Romans 11:25 and its relationship to a key portion of Deuteronomy. The plot line from Deuteronomy 27–32 appears to be the only place in the Old Testament where salvation is first given to Gentiles, which then leads to Israel's jealous emulation and their eventual restoration. Deuteronomy 27–32 is somewhat peculiar, since everywhere else in the Old Testament, it is prophesied that Israel's salvation leads to Gentile salvation (e.g., Is 49:5-6).

The second occurrence of the revealed mystery (Rom 16:25-26) may be related to the earlier use of *mystery* in Romans 11:25-26. Genesis 49 and Psalm 2 state that when the end-time king of Israel arrives, he will bring about a forced submission of the Gentile enemies. The apostle, however, claims that these Old Testament prophecies have already begun fulfillment at Christ's first coming but in an unanticipated manner. The task of the remainder of this chapter is to elaborate on our approach to Paul's understanding of mystery in Romans 11 and 16, especially with respect to the relationship of Jews and Gentiles and particularly the order of their salvation.

Mystery and the salvation of ethnic Israel. We will now turn to Romans
11:11-27:

> I say then, they did not stumble so as to fall, did they? May it never be! But by
> their transgression salvation *has come* to the Gentiles, to make them jealous.
> Now if their transgression is riches for the world and their failure is riches for the
> Gentiles, how much more will their fulfillment be! But I am speaking to you who
> are Gentiles. Inasmuch then as I am an apostle of Gentiles, I magnify my ministry,
> if somehow I might move to jealousy my fellow countrymen and save some of
> them. For if their rejection is the reconciliation of the world, what will *their* ac-
> ceptance be but life from the dead? If the first piece *of dough* is holy, the lump is
> also; and if the root is holy, the branches are too.
>
> But if some of the branches were broken off, and you, being a wild olive, were
> grafted in among them and became partaker with them of the rich root of the
> olive tree, do not be arrogant toward the branches; but if you are arrogant, *re-
> member that* it is not you who supports the root, but the root *supports* you. You
> will say then, "Branches were broken off so that I might be grafted in." Quite right,
> they were broken off for their unbelief, but you stand by your faith. Do not be
> conceited, but fear; for if God did not spare the natural branches, He will not
> spare you, either. Behold then the kindness and severity of God; to those who
> fell, severity, but to you, God's kindness, if you continue in His kindness; oth-
> erwise you also will be cut off. And they also, if they do not continue in their
> unbelief, will be grafted in, for God is able to graft them in again. For if you were
> cut off from what is by nature a wild olive tree, and were grafted contrary to
> nature into a cultivated olive tree, how much more will these who are the natural
> *branches* be grafted into their own olive tree?
>
> For I do not want you, brethren, to be uninformed of this mystery—so that
> you will not be wise in your own estimation—that a partial hardening has hap-
> pened to Israel until the fullness of the Gentiles has come in; and so all Israel will
> be saved; just as it is written,

"THE DELIVERER WILL COME FROM ZION,
HE WILL REMOVE UNGODLINESS FROM JACOB."
"THIS IS MY COVENANT WITH THEM,
WHEN I TAKE AWAY THEIR SINS."

Paul resumes the issue of the restoration of Israel in Romans 11, by claiming
that God has not rejected ethnic Jews but has preserved a remnant, even in
midst of dire circumstances (Rom 11:1-10). Paul uses himself (Rom 11:1) and the
Old Testament story of the "seven thousand men who have not bowed the knee

to Baal" (Rom 11:2-4; 1 Kings 19:10-18) to prove that God has never failed to keep his promise to preserve Israel. Romans 11:5 states, "In the same way then, there has also come to be at the present time a remnant according to God's gracious choice." Just as God preserved a remnant in the Old Testament, he is presently doing the same. Paul's incisive point in Romans 9:6 that not all Israelites are part of true Israel sharpens and clarifies Romans 11.

The next section details the role of Gentiles in God's plan. Strangely, through Israel's disbelief (Rom 11:7-10), Gentiles have become part of God's true end-time people: "By their [Israel's] transgression salvation has come to the Gentiles" (Rom 11:11). With the Gentiles participating in the new covenant community, Jews become jealous and this jealousy causes them to return to the Lord (Rom 11:11b, 14). In Romans 11:17-24, Paul employs a tree metaphor to illustrate the relationship between three parties: Jesus, the Gentiles and the Jewish people. Some view the root to be the faithful patriarchs and the promises to them.[1] We think this needs some qualification: the root represents the patriarchal promises that have begun fulfillment in Christ (which we believe Rom 1:2-4 and Rom 9:4-5 bear out, and Rom 15:13 confirms [where Christ is the fulfillment of "the root of Jesse" in Is 11:10]). Thus the focus of the root is on Jesus (Rom 11:18; 15:12),[2] the wild olive branches constitute the Gentiles (Rom 11:17) and the natural branches are ethnic Jews (Rom 11:18). The natural branches have been broken off and replaced by the wild olive branches, but the natural branches are being grafted back into their own tree. In other words, a remnant of ethnic Jews is in the process of being restored to true Israel (Rom 11:18). Though the ethnic Jews were "broken off" (Rom 11:19-20a), the Gentiles are in no position to boast about their position before God (Rom 11:20b). Gentiles, like Jews, will be punished for their disobedience but rewarded for belief and obedience (Rom 11:21-22). Romans 11:23-24 reaffirm the salvation (present and future) of Jews: "They [ethnic Jews] also . . . will be grafted in, for God is able to graft them in again" (Rom 11:23). Romans 11:24, in contrasting the Gentiles' unique "grafting" into the olive tree, highlights the restoration of ethnic Jews. Paul grounds this assertion in Romans 11:25-26: "For I do not want you, brethren, to be uninformed of this mystery—so that you will not be wise in your own estimation—a partial hardening has happened to Israel until the

---

[1]Douglas J. Moo, *The Epistle to the Romans,* NICNT (Grand Rapids: Eerdmans, 1996), p. 704.
[2]Cf., e.g., Svetlana Khobnya, "'The Root' in Paul's Olive Tree Metaphor (Romans 11:16-24)," *TynBul* 64 (2013): 257-73.

fullness of the Gentiles has come in and in this manner all Israel will be saved" (our translation).[3] In other words, the apostle informs his audience how ethnic Jews are and will be saved—Gentile inclusion acts as a catalyst for Jewish salvation. When Gentiles come to faith in Jesus the Messiah, some ethnic Jews will become jealous and likewise embrace Christ.

Gentile salvation and the restoration of Israel. In Romans 11, why do we have the order of "Gentile first, then Jew," instead of "Jew first, then Greek"? This reversal from the Old Testament expectations of "Jew first, then Greek" (which Paul himself states in Rom 1:16 and Rom 15:8-9) is what Romans 11:25 labels as a mystery. It is likely that those Jews first hearing and accepting the gospel at Pentecost and shortly thereafter in Jerusalem (Acts 2–7) represent the beginning fulfillment of the order of "Jew first, then Greek." This is clear from the progression of the book of Acts, which depicts the beginning of Gentile salvation in Acts 8; 10–11 (the Ethiopian eunuch and Cornelius) after first focusing on Jewish salvation in Acts 1–7. Then Acts 13 to the end of the book focuses primarily on Gentile salvation. It is evident from Acts 13:46-51 and onward that only a remnant of Jews will saved from there on, and that the majority of those to be saved will be Gentiles. This latter part of Acts then represents the pattern of the church composed predominately of Gentiles with a minority of Jews, which would appear to be the circumstance motivating Paul's strategy in Romans 11 to provoke Jews to jealousy by the influx of Gentiles being saved.

Romans fully endorses the "Jew first, then Gentile" pattern of the Old Testament (Rom 1:16; 15:8-9), while Romans 11 reflects on the notion that during the majority of the church age most believers will be Gentiles, along with a remnant of Jews being saved at the same time (as evident in Acts 13–28). Paul interprets this reality to mean that God has planned that the greater influx of Gentile believers will spark a remnant of Jewish believers also to come to faith until the end of the age. In this way, Paul argues for "Gentile first, then Jew." Paul does not try to defend this twofold pattern from the early history of the church where the pattern developed, as testified to in Acts. Instead, he roots it in the Old Testament.

This twofold pattern was a "mystery" from the Old Testament perspective.

---

[3]We understand "all Israel" in Rom 11:26 as a reference to all elect ethnic Jews who are converted beginning from the first century to Christ's second coming (we realize this is much debated, but we do not have space to discuss the debate nor to present the evidence supporting our conclusion; nevertheless, this conclusion does not significantly affect the present discussion).

That there would be two stages of the fulfillment of Jewish and Gentile redemption was not clearly foreseen by the Old Testament: (1) an initial salvation of Jews consisting of the majority of the redeemed, then Gentiles, and then (2) a second longer stage of Gentiles composing the majority of the saved, which would spark off a remnant of Jews being saved. This is a mystery because such an *explicit* chronological two-stage salvation cannot be found in the Old Testament. Is this two-stage salvation a revealed mystery in that it is a *completely* foreign idea to the Old Testament? We think not, but how can one explain that the Old Testament contained the seeds of such a two-stage salvation?

We think that at least part of the answer to this question lies in understanding Paul's quotation of Deuteronomy 32:21 in Romans 10:19 and its further development in Rom 11:13-14:

> But I say, surely Israel did not know, did they? First Moses says,
>
> "I WILL MAKE YOU JEALOUS BY THAT WHICH IS NOT A NATION,
> BY A NATION WITHOUT UNDERSTANDING WILL I ANGER YOU." (Rom 10:19)
>
> I say then, they did not stumble so as to fall, did they? May it never be! But by their transgression salvation *has come* to the Gentiles, to make them jealous. . . . But I am speaking to you who are Gentiles. Inasmuch then as I am an apostle of Gentiles, I magnify my ministry, if somehow I might move to jealousy my fellow countrymen and save some of them. (Rom 11:11-14)

In Deuteronomy 31–32 God is metaphorically portrayed as Israel's husband, who is angry to find his spouse in love with someone else, and as Israel's father, who is pained to see his daughters and sons profligate and ungrateful. On the one hand, Deuteronomy 32:21 appears not to refer to Israel's salvation but to speak of Israel's judgment by other nations before restoration. Israel's jealousy and anger over the Gentiles refers to their displeasure in being judged by the Gentiles instead of themselves being in a position to conquer the Gentiles. On the other hand, Deuteronomy 32:21 appears to suggest that God "making Israel jealous" alludes to her envying the role of the nations. Israel should have been judging the pagan nations, but because of Israel's unfaithfulness, God was using the wicked nations to judge Israel. Thus, Israel was envious in that she desired to be in the redemptive-historical position of the nations dispensing punishment. In this respect, Israel would be "provoked to envy" of the nations (see excursus 4.1 for more interaction with the immediate context of Deut 32).

John Murray affirmed about Romans 10:19 that "Israel would be provoked to jealousy and anger because another nation which had not enjoyed God's covenant favour as Israel had would become the recipient of the favour which Israel had despised."[4] Douglas J. Moo concludes that in Romans 11:11, which develops Romans 10:19, Paul "thinks that the Jews, as they see the Gentiles enjoying the messianic blessings promised first of all to them, will want those blessings for themselves."[5] These two assessments are compatible with the meaning that we have just formulated for the idea of jealousy (*parazēlaō*) in Deuteronomy 32:21 (see excursus 4.1), though Paul understands this verse in two major ways that are not clear from the Hebrew text—that is, he sees it (1) in the light of the Septuagint's rendering to refer to the eschatological period[6] when God would provoke Israel to jealousy by transferring his covenant favor from them to the nations, and (2) in a messianic context.[7]

Thus it is understandable that Paul in Romans 10:19 could perceive Deuteronomy 32:21 in its context to refer to Israel's judgment and restorative salvation in the latter days and affirm that Israel knew about the plot their national story would follow in relation to the Gentiles, especially since Deuteronomy 27–32 repeatedly says that it is to be a "witness" against Israel in the end times.[8] Paul's clear understanding of Israel's jealousy in a positive sense is rooted not only in Deuteronomy 32:21, but in the entire context of Deuteronomy 27–32, which makes his positive development more comprehensible.

Paul identifies present Israel's judgment of hardening and the Gentiles' salvation followed by Israel's redemption with the same prophesied storyline in

---

[4]John Murray, *The Epistle to the Romans 9–16*, NICNT (Grand Rapids: Eerdmans, 1959), p. 62.

[5]*Moo, Romans*, p. 688.

[6]Deut 32:20 (LXX) translates "I will see what their end will be" (MT) by "and I will show what will happen to them at the end [*ep' eschaton*]" (so NETS). A number of manuscripts read the fuller phrase "in the latter days" (*ep' eschatōn tōn hēmerōn*) (e.g., B [Vatinacus] 707 W1-54´), in addition to Latin manuscripts and the Armenian and Syro-Hexaplaric versions, which shows that a significant strain of the LXX exegetical tradition understood Deut 32:20-21 in an eschatological sense. It is widely agreed that Paul has depended on the LXX of Deut 32:21, but has adapted it because of his context, so that the directly preceding verse setting Rom 11:21 in an eschatological context would likely be within Paul's purview.

[7]The focus of excursus 4.1 is on the background of the order of Jew and Gentile salvation, since that is the focus of the mystery in Rom 11:24-26. However, why Paul can place Deut 32:21 within a messianic context is beyond the purview here because of space considerations. However, we think the solution lies in reflecting on the citations from Is 65:1-2 in Rom 10:20-21 in comparison with the prophecy about the coming "redeemer" in Is 59:20-21 that is cited Rom 11:26.

[8]So David Lincicum, *Paul and the Early Jewish Encounter with Deuteronomy*, WUNT 2.284 (Tübingen: Mohr Siebeck, 2010), p. 162.

Deuteronomy. That Paul is very familiar with this Deuteronomic plot line is evident from his quotations of Deuteronomy 29:4 in Romans 11:8 (concerning Israel's hardening) and Deuteronomy 32:42 (LXX) in Romans 15:10, where the nations are to rejoice with God's people Israel. Thus Paul read Deuteronomy 27–32 as broadly prophesying (1) Israel's disobedience, hardening and judgment, (2) the covenantal favor being given to the Gentiles, (3) Israel subsequently being provoked to jealousy by such Gentile favor, and (4) all of this finally leading to Israel's redemption.[9]

Does Paul derive this order of salvation merely from his own observation that the majority of those being saved were Gentiles, and was it his hope that this would provoke Israel to jealousy to want this salvation too? *The plot line from Deuteronomy appears to be the only place in the Old Testament where covenant favor (i.e., restoration) is first shown to Gentiles, which then is to spark off Israel's jealous emulation, leading to their restoration.* This seems to be the best explanation of where Paul derived his understanding of the unveiled mystery in Romans 11:25-27: Gentile salvation first, then Israel's salvation.[10] Why was it a mystery? Because everywhere else in the Old Testament, Israel's salvation is prophesied to spark off Gentile salvation (e.g., Is 49:5-6). Even within Deuteronomy the same pattern is prophesied, as we will see below. Yet Deuteronomy 32:21 would appear to prophesy the reverse pattern of "Gentile first and then Jew," though this interpretation only becomes clearer in the broader context of Deuteronomy 27–32. How can Deuteronomy prophesy both to occur in the eschaton? It is a mystery. However, the way redemption is actually accomplished fulfills both patterns: the majority of the first Christians were converts from Judaism, followed by Gentiles composing the majority of the church, as the pattern in Acts reveals. Yet as Acts unfolds, the Gentiles predominantly compose the church with only a minority of Jews, which Paul interprets in Romans 11 as the pattern of "Gentile first, then Jew provoked to jealousy and salvation."[11] It is only the

---

[9]Following Lincicum (ibid., pp. 164-65) again in the remainder of this paragraph. Lincicum's view is supported by and compatible with that of J. Ross Wagner, *Heralds of the Good News,* NovTSup 101 (Boston: Brill, 2002), pp. 190-201.

[10]See Lincicum, *Paul and the Jewish Encounter,* p. 165, who asks if the prophesied narrative in the Song of Moses might "account for how Paul arrives at the 'mystery' of the final salvation of Israel in Rom. 11:25-27." However, he does not answer this question in any substantial manner.

[11]This does not necessitate the view that the majority of Israel will be saved at the very end of the eschatological period, which Lincicum and others seem to assume. The mere preponderance of Gentiles in the church who witness to Jews is sufficient for this second stage pattern of "Gentile

actual fulfillment that shows how this mystery of the order of salvation is unraveled.

The use of Deuteronomy 29:22–30:19 in Romans 11. Deuteronomy 32:21, however, might be seen by some as too unclear to establish any pattern of restoration of "Gentile then Jew," since, as we have seen, some think it refers only to another nation coming to judge Israel.[12] We think the argument so far from Deuteronomy 32:21 supports this pattern, but is there any other passage in the Old Testament where such an order may be reflected, which may have enhanced Paul's own understanding of the redemptive-historical order? There are not many references to the nations in Deuteronomy 27–32. We have seen that one reference pertains to the restoration of the nations in Deuteronomy 32:43, where the nations are exhorted to rejoice together with God's people Israel. Yet no redemptive-historical order of salvation is given there.

However, a second significant passage about the nations is Deuteronomy 29:22–30:10, which may reflect a "Gentile first, then Israel" order of restoration (see excursus 4.2). How would Paul have looked at Deuteronomy 29:22–30:19? Though Deuteronomy 29:22-28 is not explicit about the nations' salvific restoration, it carries overtones pointing in that direction. This suggests that Paul could well have understood it in the way we have argued. If so, the tension between "Gentile salvation first, then Israel" and "Israel salvation first, then the nations" would have been even more pronounced, since nowhere in Deuteronomy, except Deuteronomy 32:21, or in the rest of the Old Testament, is there a reference to Gentiles being saved first. Rather, whenever

---

first, then Jew" to hold. For the direction of our own approach to the passage, see some examples in the following articles: O. Palmer Robertson, "Is There a Distinctive Future for Ethnic Israel in Romans 11?" in *Perspectives on Evangelical Theology*, ed. Stanley N. Gundry and Kenneth S. Kantzer (Grand Rapids: Baker, 1979), pp. 209-27; Benjamin L. Merkle, "Romans 11 and the Future of Ethnic Israel," *JETS* 43 (2000): 709-21; and Anthony A. Hoekema, *The Bible and the Future* (Grand Rapids: Eerdmans, 1979), pp. 139-47. All of these sources argue that "all Israel" in Rom 11:26 refers not to a mass conversion of ethnic Israel at the very end of the church age but to the entire remnant of ethnic Israel who are redeemed throughout the interadvent age until the very end of time. Other commentators argue similarly but contend that "all Israel" consists of both Gentiles and Jews—e.g., John Calvin, *Acts 14-18; Romans 1-16*, Calvin's Commentaries (Grand Rapids: Baker, 1984), 16:437. There are many commentators who argue that Rom 11:26 does prophesy that the majority of Israel will be saved at the very end of the interadvent era—e.g., see Murray, *Romans 9-16*, pp. 96-100; and R. L. Saucy, *The Case for Progressive Dispensationalism* (Grand Rapids: Zondervan, 1993), pp. 250-63.

[12]E.g., see C. E. B. Cranfield, *A Critical and Exegetical Commentary on the Epistle to the Romans*, ICC (Edinburgh: T & T Clark, 1979), 2:539; see also R. H. Bell, *Provoked to Jealousy: The Origin of the Jealousy Motif in Romans 9-11*, WUNT 2.63 (Tübingen: Mohr, 1994), pp. 209-14.

a sequence is stated in the Old Testament, it is always Israel that is prophesied to be saved first in the latter days, and then the Gentiles (e.g., Is 42:6; 49:1-6; 60:1-2; 66:19; Zech 8:23). Deuteronomy 29:22–30:10; 32:21 are the only possible places in all of the Old Testament where the sequence of restoration is reversed. Paul may have perceived that part of the decretive divine "secret" in Deuteronomy 29:29 had in mind the conundrum of how the Gentiles could be saved first, and then the Jews, while at the same time other biblical prophecies have Israel being saved first, and then the Gentiles. This Deuteronomic secret would appear to be partly behind what Paul calls a revealed "mystery" in Romans 11:25. Perhaps not unrelated to Paul's perspective, later Judaism viewed Deuteronomy 29:29 as referring to the relationship of Jews and Gentiles or to the "age to come."[13] That Deuteronomy 29:22-29; 32:21 are susceptible of a "Gentile first, then Jew" order of restoration but are not explicit about this would seem to fit with the notion of mystery in the Synoptics and Paul elsewhere, where revealed mysteries refer to realities that were not fully revealed in the Old Testament but have now been fully revealed.[14] In other words, it was largely hidden in the Old Testament that the Gentiles would serve as a catalyst to Israel's salvation (though Deut 27–32 appears to suggest this order), but it was fully revealed to Paul that God had decreed the Gentile-Jewish order of salvation. This order of salvation was, to some small degree, anticipated in the Old Testament, but it was not explained in detail and later Old Testament prophecies do not develop it.

The language of "secret" and "revealed" from Deuteronomy 29:29 is vocab-

---

[13] According to *Midr. Psalms* 87.6, "The secret things belong to the Lord our God" in Deut 29:29 [29:28 MT] refers to the time when God "out of the heathen will bring Israel to the King Messiah," and at that time "God will take priests and Levites not only out of the children of Israel that are brought, but also out of the nations that bring the children of Israel," as Is 66:21 says. Then the Midrash asks, "Where [in the books of Moses] did God say this?" And the answer is given that Deut 29:28 [29] affirmed this. *Mekilta De-Rabbi Ishmael* 12.60-64 says the same thing about the relation of Is 66:21 and Deut 29:28, but does not specify that Gentiles are included among the "priests and Levites." These midrashic comments do not refer to the problem of an order of salvation, but they do refer to the close relationship of Jew and Gentile salvation being part of God's "secret." *The Fathers According to Rabbi Nathan* 34 affirms that Deut 29:28 [Deut 29:29 Eng.] asserts that things "not revealed to us . . . will be revealed to us in the age to come."

[14] Recall that in Mt 13 the "revelation of mysteries" referred not to a completely new revelation of the fulfillment of Old Testament kingdom prophecies but to the surprising manner in which those prophecies were being fulfilled. We will also see subsequently in Paul that the revelation of mysteries is not the manifestation of a completely new reality but the unexpected manner of fulfillment of an Old Testament prophecy, which was already understandable to some degree in the Old Testament itself.

ulary typically used in apocalyptic contexts, and sometimes "secret" is virtually synonymous with the unveiled mystery in the Greek Old Testament (LXX) and in Paul's epistles.[15] Strikingly, Paul refers in Romans 16:25-26 to "the revelation of the mystery which has been kept secret [not *kryptos* but a synonymous verbal form of *sigaō*] . . . but now has been manifested [*phaneroō*, a verbal form of *phaneros*] and . . . made known to the nations."

In the Romans 16 passage the apostle sees the focus of the mystery as the same as in Romans 11:25-27. Paul has experienced the resolution to the Deuteronomic secret or "mystery"; indeed, the first to be saved in the eschaton were Jews in Jerusalem and Judea, and then the Jewish Christian witness went out to the Gentiles resulting in their salvation. However, there came a point early in the Jewish Christian witness that the majority of Jews rejected the gospel message and the majority of those who accepted were Gentiles. Paul then in Romans 11:11-14 says that the decretive order of salvation for the remainder of the interadvent age is Gentile first and then Jew, hoping that the success of the gospel among the Gentiles would "provoke to jealous zeal" the Jews, leading to their salvation.[16]

---

[15]The LXX of Deut 29:29 has *krypta* for "secret things" and *phanera* for "manifest things." These words are found in apocalyptic contexts elsewhere in the LXX: Wis 7:21 (*krypta kai emphanē*, "secret and manifest"); Sir 1:30 ("the Lord reveal your secret things"); Sir 3:21-22 (an allusion to Deut 29:29); Sir 4:18 (wisdom "will reveal to him her secret things"). Dan 2:47 is especially relevant because of its explicit eschatological context: God "brings to light hidden mysteries [*mystēria krypta*] because you have been able to disclose this mystery [*mystērion*]"; cf. Sir. 11:4. Likewise, *phaneros* is used in the following apocalyptic contexts in the Greek Old Testament (Prov 15:11; 16:2; Is 64:1-2; 2 Macc 12:41; 3 Macc 6:18). In the New Testament *kryptos* is used in an apocalyptic manner in Mt 10:26; Lk 12:2; Rom 2:16. 1 Cor 3:13 uses *phaneros* in the same way. Significantly, forms of *both kryptos* and *phaneros* are used in an apocalyptic manner in Mk 4:22 (linked to "mystery" in Mk 4:11); Lk 8:17 (linked to "mystery" in Lk 8:10); Jn 7:4; 1 Cor 4:5 (linked to "mystery" in 1 Cor 4:1); 1 Cor 14:25; 2 Cor 4:2; Eph 5:12-13; Col 1:26 (where "mystery" is equated with "hidden"!); 1 Tim 3:16 (where the "mystery" is "made manifest").

[16]The presupposition that *Jesus Christ is the true Israel, summing up in himself the Israelite nation* might also help us to understand the mystery. Accordingly, Christ as true Israel sparks off the initial salvation of Jews (as recorded in Acts 1–12). If ethnic Jews wanted to be part of true Israel, they needed to trust in and identify with Christ, the one who sums up true Israel in himself. Then the first Jewish Christians in Israel carry the good news to the Gentiles, who are saved. Thus, the first stage of salvation ("to the Jew first, then Greek") is achieved through Christ, the true Israel, sparking off Jewish salvation and afterward Gentiles are saved through Jewish evangelism. It is important to note that in this first stage of salvation in which Gentiles are subsequently saved, they, like Jewish believers, identify with Christ, the true Israel, and so Gentiles also become part of true Israel. For arguments in favor of the church being true Israel, see further G. K. Beale, *A New Testament Biblical Theology: The Unfolding of the Old Testament in the New* (Grand Rapids: Baker Academic, 2011), pp. 651-749.

Mystery in Romans 16

Christ and the mystery. The term *mystery* is found once again in Romans 16:25-26:

> Now to Him who is able to establish you according to my gospel and the preaching of Jesus Christ, according to the revelation of the mystery which has been kept secret for long ages past, but now is manifested, and by the Scriptures of the prophets, according to the commandment of the eternal God, has been made known to all the nations, *leading* to obedience of faith.

The mystery of Romans 16 is stated only very generally and most likely entails some idea of the reversal of salvific patterns discussed in Romans 11. Most acknowledge that the concluding phrase "made known to all the nations, *leading* to obedience of faith" is a repetition of Romans 1:5, "to bring about the obedience of faith among all the Gentiles." Some have observed that Psalm 2:8 ("I will surely give the nations as your inheritance") stands behind this expression in Romans 1:5.[17] Psalm 2:8 may be alluded to in Roman 1:5 *and* Romans 16:16. In addition to Psalm 2:8 playing a role in Romans 1:4-5, Genesis 49:10 appears to lie behind the notable phrase "<u>obedience of</u> faith among all <u>the nations</u>" in Romans 1.[18]

Table 4.1

Genesis 49:10b	Romans 1:4-5 (cf. almost identically Rom 16:25)
"<u>To him</u> [the coming Israelite conqueror] . . . *shall be* <u>the obedience of the peoples</u>."	"<u>Jesus Christ</u> . . . through whom we have received grace and apostleship <u>to bring about *the* obedience</u> of faith among all <u>the Gentiles</u> [lit. *nations*]."

We will briefly explore the validity of the Genesis allusion for both Romans 1 and Romans 16, and then discuss its interpretative significance in relation to the Psalm 2 allusion and, finally, to the meaning of *mystery* in Roman 16. The close resemblance of the two expressions in Romans 1 and Romans 16 points to an allusion to Genesis 49:10 (see table 4.1), especially since Judaism and Revelation 5:5 identify the ruler of the Genesis passage respectively with the

---

[17]See D. B. Garlington, "Obedience of Faith in the Letter to the Romans," *WTJ* 52 (1990): 203. Rom 1:3-4 may well be an echo of Ps 2:7: "I will surely tell of the decree of the Lord: he said to me, 'You are my Son, today I have begotten you.'"

[18]See Garlington, "Obedience of Faith," p. 203, who appears to see some degree of reference both to Gen 49:10 and Ps 2:8-9, but he only cites the references and does not develop his view; see also Chip Anderson, "Romans 1:1-5 and the Occasion of the Letter: The Solution to the Two-Congregation Problem in Rome," *TJ* 14 (1993): 38, who elaborates more on a definite connection to Gen 49.

Messiah and Jesus. Such an allusion also fits nicely with Psalm 2:8, since both prophetically picture the forced submission of Gentiles by the Messiah. The Genesis background is also appropriate for the Romans 16 context for two reasons: (1) virtually the identical phrase is found there, and (2) Genesis 49:1 introduces the entire chapter as a prophecy which is to occur "in the latter days" ("I will tell you what will befall you in the latter days"—our translation). Romans 16:25-26 speaks of "the Scriptures of the prophets" which have been fulfilled "now" at the turn of the ages, a conceptual reference to the inauguration of the latter days.[19]

Once again we see the term *mystery* attached closely to an Old Testament reference, perhaps even two references (if Psalm 2 is also in mind). Genesis 49 and Psalm 2 (as well as, perhaps, Num 24) agree that when the end-time king of Israel comes, he will bring about a forced submission of the Gentile enemies. Paul no doubt still holds this to be true: it will happen at the very end of history, when Jesus returns to consummate the eternal kingdom already inaugurated.

On the other hand, he sees that the two prophecies (or at least Gen 49) have already begun fulfillment at Christ's first coming but in an unanticipated manner: *antagonistic Gentiles have begun to yield themselves voluntarily to the Messiah's reign by the "obedience of faith"*—that is, "by the obedience which consists in faith and the obedience which is the product of faith."[20] It was a mystery from the Old Testament perspective that Genesis 49 (Ps 2 and Num 24) could be speaking about *voluntary* obedience of Gentile *enemies,* but now Paul sees that this mysterious prophecy has begun fulfillment unexpectedly by Gentiles being taken into "captive obedience" through trusting in the gospel. We again find continuity and discontinuity upheld in the New Testament use of *mystery.*

Mystery and Scripture. Romans 16:25-26 is one of the clearest texts that pairs the Old Testament with mystery: "revelation <u>of the mystery</u> [*mystēriou*] which has been kept secret for long ages past, but is now manifested, and by <u>the Scriptures of the prophets</u> [*graphōn prophētikōn*] . . . made know to all the nations." Paul states two characteristics of mystery here: (1) the unveiled mystery has been hidden or "kept secret" for "long ages past." As we have seen, this aspect of mystery is often either implied or explicitly mentioned in the Old

---

[19]Anderson, "Romans 1.1-5," p. 38, has made this observation previously with respect to Rom 1 but not Rom 16.

[20]For this understanding of the genitival phrase, see Garlington, "Obedience of Faith," pp. 223-24.

Testament, Judaism and the New Testament. It refers to the previously hidden nature of God's wisdom with reference to a particular prophetic theme or passage. We have labeled this phenomenon "temporary hiddenness" and discussed it at some length.[21] (2) The revelation of the mystery has occurred in the "prophetic writings." The phrase "Scriptures of the prophets" most likely refers to the Old Testament corpus as a whole or at least vast portions of it.[22] The much fuller meaning of certain passages in the Old Testament, Paul claims, is a "mystery" that has only now been revealed. In other words, the meaning of the Old Testament (or portions of it) was only *partially* understood to the original audience, but now that Christ has come, a much fuller meaning of these texts is available.[23] In the context, Genesis 49 and Psalm 2 are immediately in mind, but Paul's statement appears to be applied elsewhere. As we have seen and will continue to see, mystery in Romans 11 and Romans 16 is again wedded to Old Testament texts or concepts.

CONCLUSION

On the one hand, Romans fully endorses the "Jew first, then Gentile" pattern that is clearly found in the Old Testament (Rom 1:16; 15:8-9), whereas Romans 11 suggests that during the majority of the church age most believers will be Gentiles (along with a Jews being saved at the same time or, as some hold, at a future time). God has decreed that the influx of Gentile believers will function as a catalyst for Jewish believers who also come to faith until the end of the age. In this way, Paul argues for "Gentile first, then Jew."

This twofold pattern was a "mystery" from the Old Testament perspective. The Old Testament did not clearly predict the following two-stage fulfillment of Jewish and Gentile redemption: (1) an initial salvation of Jews as the majority of the redeemed, then Gentiles, and then (2) a second longer stage of Gentiles composing the majority of the saved during the course of the inaugurated end-time age, which would then spark off a remnant of Jews being saved. Though

---

[21]See pp. 60-66 above.

[22]E.g., Bockmuehl, *Revelation and Mystery*, p. 207; Romano Penna, *Il «Mysterion» Paolino*, SRB 10 (Brescia: Paideia, 1978), p. 43.

[23]Regarding Paul's understanding of mystery here in Rom 16 and elsewhere, some make a distinction between Christ himself being the end-time revelation of mystery and Paul's interpretation of Old Testament writings as they pertain to Christ as the mystery. While there is indeed a distinction here, both of these concepts are so organically tied together that we will treat them as a whole. See, though, our brief discussion of the role of Christ in the New Testament conception of mystery in our conclusion on pp. 321-26.

the Old Testament does not fully develop this doctrine, it does contain a few passages that in seed form appear to anticipate this phenomenon.

Paul read Deuteronomy 27–32 as broadly prophesying (1) Israel's disobedience, hardening and judgment, (2) the covenantal favor being given to the Gentiles, (3) Israel subsequently being provoked to jealousy by such Gentile favor, and (4) finally all of this leading to Israel's redemption. The plot line from Deuteronomy appears to be the only place in the Old Testament where salvation is first given to Gentiles, which then leads to Israel's jealous emulation and their eventual restoration. This seems to be the best explanation of where Paul derived his understanding of the unveiled mystery in Romans 11:25-27: Gentile salvation first, then Israel's salvation. Why was it a mystery? Because elsewhere in the Old Testament it is clear only that Israel's salvation leads to Gentile salvation (e.g., Is 49:5-6).

According to the New Testament, the way redemption is actually accomplished fulfills both patterns: the majority of the first Christians were converts from Judaism, which sparked off initial Gentile salvation, as the pattern in Acts reveals. Yet as Acts unfolds, the Gentiles predominately compose the church with only a minority of Jews, which Paul interprets in Romans 11 as the pattern of "Gentile first, then Jew provoked to jealousy and salvation." It is only the actual fulfillment that shows how this mystery of the order of salvation is unraveled.

The second occurrence of *mystery* in Romans (Rom 16:25-26) may be related to the earlier use of the term in Romans 11:25-26, primarily with respect to the topic of the Gentiles. Genesis 49 and Psalm 2 claim that when the end-time king of Israel arrives, he will bring about a forced submission of the Gentile enemies. Paul certainly still holds this to be true, as it will happen at the very end of history when Jesus returns to establish consummately the eternal kingdom. On the other hand, the apostle states that two Old Testament prophecies have already begun fulfillment at Christ's first coming but in an unanticipated manner. Paul states that the mystery was "kept secret" but has now been revealed "by the Scriptures of the prophets." The full meaning of portions of the Old Testament was inaccessible to the original audience, but now that Christ has come, a much fuller meaning of these texts is unveiled.

EXCURSUS 4.1: THE OLD TESTAMENT CONTEXT OF DEUTERONOMY 32:21

Deuteronomy 32:21 occurs in the larger segment of Deuteronomy 27–32. This segment sets before Israel future blessings for faithful obedience (e.g., Deut

28:1-14) and curses of exile for unbelief and disobedience (e.g., Deut 28:15-68). Yet woven throughout the section are actual predictions that indeed Israel will not trust in God and will violate his commandments, so that they will be punished by going into exile and suffering there. Israel will first disobey God and experience the curse of the suffering of exile (e.g., Deut 29:19-28; 31:16-21), but afterward Israel will believe God and experience the blessings of restoration from exile back to the promised land (e.g., Deut 30:1-10). At the time of their deliverance and restoration, some of the Gentiles will also participate in being restored to God, along with Israel (Deut 32:43). This mention of Gentile restoration (implied by the expression, "Rejoice, O nations, with his people") occurs explicitly only once in Deuteronomy 27–32. It appears that this Gentile restoration will occur at the same general time of Israel's future restoration, though no particular order of "Jew first, then Gentile" or vice versa is given, as it is later found in Isaiah's prophecies (e.g., Is 49:1-6), where the order of "Jewish salvation then Gentile salvation" is explicit.

Paul quotes from Deuteronomy 32:21 to indicate that Old Testament Israel knew about the gospel that saves Jew and Gentile (cf. Rom 10:12-13, as it forms part of the argument leading up to the Deut 32 quotation in Rom 10:19). The apparent problem, according to some commentators, however, is that Deuteronomy 32:21 appears not to refer to Israel's salvation but to speak of Israel's judgment by other nations before their restoration[24] (seemingly developing Deut 28:25, 33, 36, 49-52).[25] Accordingly, Israel's "jealousy" and "anger" over the Gentiles refers to their displeasure in being judged by the Gentiles instead of themselves being in a position to defeat Gentiles.

A second view of Deuteronomy 32:21, however, is that God "making Israel jealous" alludes to Israel "envying" the role of the nations. It was Israel that should have been judging the enemy nations, but because of Israel's unfaithfulness, God was using the nations to judge Israel. Thus Israel was "envious" in that it wanted to be in the redemptive-historical position of the nations meting out punishment. In this respect, Israel would be "provoked to envy" of the nations. Accordingly, Israel's "anger" would refer to a displeasure at not being in the position the nations were now to be in, which implied a

---

[24]See again, for example, Cranfield, *Romans*, 2:539; cf. also Bell, *Provoked to Jealousy*, pp. 209-14.

[25]On the other hand, the judgment of the nations is also referred to (e.g., Deut 32:41). Presumably, Israel's judgment precedes the judgment of the nations, since it is the latter that is the divine instrument of the former's judgment.

desire to be in that position. This view of the "jealousy" and "anger" is pointed to by the same likely meaning of the two words in the first part of Deuteronomy 32:21: Israel made God "jealous" and "angry" with her worship of idols (so also in Deut 32:16-18). This response is not mere anger but a displeased jealousy because God desired for himself the worship Israel gave instead to the idols. This positive element in the notion of jealous anger arises from a "response to the violation of a close and exclusive relationship."[26] The language of "provoking to anger" and "provoking to jealousy" in Deuteronomy 31–32 expresses the emotions of God as a husband to Israel, who is angry to find his spouse in love with someone else, and to God as the father of Israel, who is pained to see his daughters and sons profligate and ungrateful.[27] Just as a husband who finds his wife with another man is angry yet still wants her love, so it is with God and Israel. Correspondingly, for God to show covenant favor to another nation in Deuteronomy 32:21 is for the purpose of causing Israel not only anger but a jealousy that includes a desire to be in the position of the favored Gentiles. Thus, Deuteronomy 32:21 is placed in a context where God's ultimate goal is the reconciliation of Israel's covenant loyalty.[28]

Thus Israel's being "provoked to jealousy" because of God's covenantal favor to the nations was designed so that Israel would be envious and want to possess the restored covenantal relationship to God that the nations were experiencing. Being "provoked to anger" would have a similar meaning. This restorative notion is also likely included in Deuteronomy 32:21, since for Israel to be in the position of the nations would mean for them first to be restored to God and then to follow his will in dominating and inheriting the nations, which was their original calling. Certainly the segment of Deuteronomy 27–32 repeatedly refers to both Israel's salvific restoration (Deut 30:2-10; 32:36, 43) and that of the nations (Deut 32:43; cf. also Deut 29:22-28).

The two above views are not that far apart but would appear to be entailed in one another. Could one not be passionately displeased and angry about not possessing something that someone else had (view 1) and at the same time be passionately jealous about what was not possessed and want to possess it (view 2)? Could not Deuteronomy 32:21 be packed with both notions, especially since both meanings are connoted by both the Hebrew (*qānâ*) and Greek (*parazēlaō*)

---

[26]Wagner, *Heralds*, p. 195.
[27]See the many Old Testament references adduced in support of this in ibid., p. 195.
[28]Cf. ibid., p. 198.

words? And could not these notions entail to some degree the idea of Israel's desire to be restored back into a position of fulfilling her original mandate to dominate and inherit the nations of the earth?[29]

There are at least three factors that may contribute to having a positive perspective of the nations in Deuteronomy 32:21. First, "the language of vengeance is applied to 'adversaries,' 'those who hate me,' and 'the enemy,' but never to Gentiles *per se*."[30] Thus this kind of adversarial language is not something applicable to all Gentiles.[31] Second, there are several passages that speak very positively about Gentiles, two of which occur in the literary segment of Deuteronomy 27–32 (Deut 4:6; 26:18-19; 32:43; 33:19).[32] Third, the Song of Moses itself (Deut 32) is explicitly about what must occur "in the latter days" (*eschaton tōn hēmerōn;* Deut 31:29), which is reiterated in the LXX of Deuteronomy 32:20 ("in the end" [*ep' eschatōn*] or "in the latter days" [*ep' eschatōn tōn hēmerōn*]). In fact, the end-time focus may best explain several of the Song's atypical features (e.g., no significant mention of past notable events: the covenants, the exodus, the patriarchal references).[33] This focus is enhanced further by the

---

[29]See Robert Jewett, *Romans: A Commentary,* Hermeneia (Minneapolis: Fortress, 2007), pp. 645-46, who sees that "since the preposition παρά makes the attached verb transitive, rendered here with 'make x' or 'provoke to x,' the translation issue centers on the verb ζηλόω," which he then understands to have four main ranges of meaning: "(1) holy zeal in the sense of Israel's holy war [citing in support, Phil 3:6; Heb 10:27 and LXX Zeph 1:18; Ezek 36:6]; (2) hostility that derives from zeal or jealousy [citing in support Acts 15:17-18, and in LXX 1 Macc 1:24-26]; (3) jealousy itself [citing in support Acts 7:9; 1 Cor 13:4, and in LXX Gen 30:1 and Sir. 37:10]; and (4) emulation or the desire to attain a goal [citing in support 1 Cor 12:31; 2 Cor 9:2; Titus 2:14, and in LXX Sir. 51:18; see also Philo, *Praem.* 89]." *Parazēlaō* refers in the LXX to: (1) provoking God to jealous anger, i.e., God jealously desired Israel's worship that Israel gave to her idols, which raised his ire (Deut 32:21a; 1 Kings 14:22; Ps 78:58); (2) a righteous person being jealous (and perhaps consequently angry) of the unrighteous who prosper, so that the righteous desire to be in the position of the ungodly prosperous (Ps 36:1, 7; likely also Ps 36:8, and perhaps Sir 30:3). In light of the other uses of *parazēlaō*, especially in Deut 32:21a, it would appear that Israel being "provoked to jealousy" in Deut 32:21b refers to jealously desiring to be in the victorious position of the nations and being angry about not being in such a position, as the end of v. 21 explicitly says, "I will anger them with a nation void of understanding." Paul uses *parazēlaō* four times, once in quoting Deut 32:21 in Rom 10:19 and twice in Rom 11:11, 14. The use in Rom 10:19 appears to have the same "jealous anger" notion as in Deuteronomy, while the latter two uses draw out the positive nuance of the jealousy from Rom 10:19 in terms of Israel's desire to be in the favorable position of the nations, an idea likely included in Deut 32:21 itself. The remaining New Testament use is in 1 Cor 10:22, where Paul says the Corinthians should not "provoke God to jealousy" with their idol worship, which entails God's jealous desire to have them worship him instead and his consequent anger that some are worshipping idols.

[30]Lincicum, *Paul and the Jewish Encounter,* p. 161.

[31]E.g., Deut 32:43 distinguished redeemed nations from the Gentile "adversaries."

[32]On the textual problem of Deut 32:43, see below.

[33]See again Lincicum, *Paul and the Jewish Encounter,* p. 161, for the last two points, though he men-

Septuagint's translation of the Hebrew in Deuteronomy 32:29 that Israel would discern "their end [future]" by their "time to come." In fact, the full Hebrew of this verse has, "Would that they were wise, that they understood this [the reason for their judgment in Deut 32:22-27], that they would discern their future!" But the LXX has "They had no sense to understand these things [the reason for their judgment in Deut 32:22-27]. Let them accept them for the time to come." Accordingly, the past generation of Israel was lacking in understanding of God's ways, but the future generation living in the latter days is exhorted finally to understand these things.

EXCURSUS 4.2: THE POSSIBLE OLD TESTAMENT CONTEXT OF DEUTERONOMY 29:22–30:10

Deuteronomy 29:22–30:10 may suggest a "Gentile first, then Israel" order of restoration. While speculative, we believe it is worth including this excursus for consideration as background material, especially since no one else has ever suggested it. The passage deserves to be quoted at length:

> Now the generation to come, your sons who rise up after you and the foreigner who comes from a distant land, when they see the plagues of the land and the diseases with which the LORD has afflicted it, will say, "All its land is brimstone and salt, a burning waste, unsown and unproductive, and no grass grows in it, like the overthrow of Sodom and Gomorrah, Admah and Zeboiim, which the LORD overthrew in His anger and in His wrath." All the nations will say, "Why has the LORD done thus to this land? Why this great outburst of anger?" Then *men* will say, "Because they forsook the covenant of the LORD, the God of their fathers, which He made with them when He brought them out of the land of Egypt. They went and served other gods and worshiped them, gods whom they have not known and whom He had not allotted to them. Therefore, the anger of the LORD burned against that land, to bring upon it every curse which is written in this book; and the LORD uprooted them from their land in anger and in fury and in great wrath, and cast them into another land, as *it is* this day."
>
> The secret things belong to the LORD our God, but the things revealed belong to us and to our sons forever, that we may observe all the words of this law.
>
> So it shall be when all of these things have come upon you, the blessing and the curse which I have set before you, and you call *them* to mind in all nations where the LORD your God has banished you, and you return to the LORD your

---

tions only Deut 32:43 with respect to a positive view of the Gentiles.

God and obey Him with all your heart and soul according to all that I command you today, you and your sons, then the LORD your God will restore you from captivity, and have compassion on you, and will gather you again from all the peoples where the LORD your God has scattered you. If your outcasts are at the ends of the earth, from there the LORD your God will gather you, and from there He will bring you back. The LORD your God will bring you into the land which your fathers possessed, and you shall possess it; and He will prosper you and multiply you more than your fathers.

Moreover the LORD your God will circumcise your heart and the heart of your descendants, to love the LORD your God with all your heart and with all your soul, so that you may live. The LORD your God will inflict all these curses on your enemies and on those who hate you, who persecuted you. And you shall again obey the LORD, and observe all His commandments which I command you today. Then the LORD your God will prosper you abundantly in all the work of your hand, in the offspring of your body and in the offspring of your cattle and in the produce of your ground, for the LORD will again rejoice over you for good, just as He rejoiced over your fathers; if you obey the LORD your God to keep His commandments and His statutes which are written in this book of the law, if you turn to the LORD your God with all your heart and soul. (Deut 29:22–30:10)

This segment from Deuteronomy 29–30 is striking, since it *could* be read as giving a future order of the nations' restoration (in Deut 29:22-29) followed by Israel's restoration (Deut 30:1-10). What would be striking about this is that directly after the prophecy of the nations' restoration and right before the narrative of Israel's subsequent restoration is a reference to the "secret things" that "belong to the LORD our God" (Deut 29:29), which were not revealed to others at the time. The "secret things" refer to what precedes (including Deut 29:22-28 concerning Gentile restoration) and would appear to refer also to Deuteronomy 30:1-10, so that Deuteronomy 29:29 is a transition between the two sections. If this analysis is going in the right direction, then the pattern of "Gentile restoration first, then Jewish restoration later" would be viewed as a divine "secret."

Most commentators affirm that Deuteronomy 29:22-29 is merely a rhetorical declaration that expresses the nations' recognition and astonishment about the dire condition of Israel in exile, such as in 1 Kings 9:8-9; 2 Kings 21:12; Jeremiah 19:8; 22:8-9; 49:17 [about Edom]; Jeremiah 50:13 [about Babylon]; Lamentations 2:15; Ezekiel 27:35-36; and Ezekiel 16:14.[34] For example,

---

[34]See J. A. T. Thompson, *Deuteronomy,* TOTC (Downers Grove, IL: InterVarsity Press, 1974), p. 283, for an ancient Near Eastern parallel to such expressions.

1 Kings 9:8-9, which is fairly representative of the other parallels, says,

> And this house will become a heap of ruins; everyone who passes by will be as-
> tonished and hiss and say, "Why has the LORD done thus to this land and to this
> house?" And they will say, "Because they forsook the LORD their God, who
> brought their fathers out of the land of Egypt, and adopted other gods and wor-
> shiped them and served them, therefore the LORD has brought all this adversity
> on them.

These passages outside of Deuteronomy, however, are brief in expressing the
nations' astonishment about Israel's judgment, and also express the nations'
disdain over Israel's suffering, whereas Deuteronomy 29:22-29 goes into more
detail about how the nations reflected on Israel's predicament and does not
contain the note of disdain. In particular, the Deuteronomy 29 passage contains
the following differences from the expressions of proverbial-like disdain found
elsewhere in the Old Testament: (1) it is much longer in its description; (2) it
says that God's anger brought upon Israel "every curse which is written in this
book" (Deut 29:27). Some commentators see this as being an added editorial
comment at a later time, or they see it as an anonymous rhetorical reply to the
question about "why the Lord has done thus to the land?" However, it could
also easily be the nations answering their own question, in which case the nations are speaking positively of that "which is written in this book" [of Deuter-
onomy] (note in this respect, that the question of Deut 29:24 starts with "And
all the nations shall say . . ." and the reply begins in the next verse with "Then
they shall say . . ."). Accordingly, the nations would be affirming the fulfillment
of the true predictions in Deuteronomy.[35] This, at least, would appear to be a
plausible way later readers like Paul would have understood the passage.
(3) Deuteronomy 29:22 starts the section off by saying that it is not only people
from the nations (the foreigner) who will observe Israel's future devastation but
also "the last generation,[36] your [Israel's] sons, who rise up after you." This "last
generation" of Israel would appear to refer to those Israelites in the latter days
who give a positive perceptive evaluation of Israel's past devastation by God, so
that the "foreigner's" evaluation should be put on the same positive par with
that of this later Israelite generation's positive perception, as the wording makes
clear: "now the generation to come, your sons who rise up after you, and the

---

[35]Or, if this is not the reply of the nations but is anonymous, the nations may be seen as positive
witnesses to this reply.

[36]Most translations render *haddôr hāʾaḥărôn* as "the generation to come."

foreigner who comes from a distant land . . ."[37] But this leaves us with an enigma: the Israelite "generation to come" in Deuteronomy 29:22-23 is positively testifying about the fulfillment of past Israel's curse, which then precedes future Israel's restoration (Deut 30:1-10), and that future restored Israelite nation is distinguished from the Israelite "generation to come" in Deuteronomy 22:22 repeatedly by "you," "your" and so on in Deuteronomy 30:1-10. How does this Israelite "generation to come" relate to the restoration of Israel in Deuteronomy 30:1-10? The Deuteronomy 29 text itself does not clarify this. At the least, the two—the Gentile and the later Israelite generation—give their testimony at the same time. Could it be, however, in the light of Paul's view of fulfillment, that the subsequent Israelite generation is the initial Israelite remnant saved at the very beginning of the eschatological period that testifies together with the saved Gentiles to the rest of unsaved Israel throughout the remainder of the end-time period? Despite this problem, the focus of the witness in Deuteronomy 22:22-28 is on the Gentile testimony.

These three unique ideas were not included in the above proverbial or rhetorical passages of 1 Kings 9 and other like expressions. Taken together, these three distinctives, along with the lack of expressions of disdain, suggest that the nations are truly reflecting on Israel's predicament, and that they are learning from it or are God's witnesses to it, or both. The only commentator who takes this general line of argument is P. D. Miller, who, while not making the above three observations, nevertheless says,

> At least they [the nations] serve in this book as indirect witnesses and interpreters of what the Lord is doing. This is first seen in 4:6 . . . It may be too much to suggest the nations [in Deut. 29:28] are Israel's teachers, but the work of God in Israel is once again set within the context of world history. Not only does that larger history serve as the plane on which God's story with Israel is worked out, but in these indirect ways the other nations are seen as witnessing, reflecting upon, and

---

[37]If Deut 29:22a is to be punctuated with a comma after the phrase "your sons who rise up after you," then "the foreigner" is to be identified as living during the Israelite "generation to come" or if the comma is removed then the "foreigner" is part of that "generation to come." Either way, the meaning is close. That Israel's restoration occurs in the end times is apparent from the context of Deuteronomy: "in the latter days, you will return to the Lord" (Deut 4:30); Israel's return is directly preceded by their sin and judgment, which leads directly up also into the "latter days," directly before their restoration (so also Deut 31:29; 32:20 [LXX]; 31). For the eschatological context for Israel's restoration, see also *Tg. Ps.-J.* on Deut 30:4, which says "*the Memra* of the Lord [will] gather *you* [Israel] *through the mediation of Elijah, the great high priest,* and from there *he will bring you near through the mediation of the King Messiah.*"

comprehending that story even though it is not their own. The divine work through the prophets draws those nations even more directly into the story, confirming the word at the beginning (Gen. 12:1-3) that Israel's way was never for its own sake alone but a part of God's purposes for all the families for the earth.[38]

This comes very close to saying that the nations' reflection on Israel's predicament and their witness to it is part of their positive response to God's revelation in Deuteronomy and thus inextricably linked to their own restoration to God. This positive view of the nations in this passage fits with several comments elsewhere in Deuteronomy about the nations that are also positive with respect to their response to God's revelation. Though most of the references to the "nations" or "peoples" in Deuteronomy are negative (referring, e.g., to their defeat by Israel or to their idolatry), there are at least four significant passages that express a more optimistic view of the nations:

> So keep and do *them,* for that is your [Israel's] wisdom and your understanding in the sight of the peoples who will hear all these statutes and say, "Surely this great nation is a wise and understanding people." (Deut 4:6)

> The LORD has today declared you to be His people, a treasured possession, as He promised you, and that you should keep all His commandments; and that He will set you high above all nations which He has made, for praise, fame, and honor; and that you shall be a consecrated people to the LORD your God, as He has spoken. (Deut 26:18-19).

> Rejoice, O nations,[39] *with* His people;
> For He will avenge the blood of His servants,
> And will render vengeance on His adversaries,
> And will atone for His land *and* His people. (Deut 32:43)

> They will call peoples *to* the mountain;
> There they will offer righteous sacrifices;
> For they will draw out the abundance of the seas,
> And the hidden treasures of the sand. (Deut 33:19)

---

[38]P. D. Miller, *Deuteronomy,* Interpretation (Louisville, KY: Westminster John Knox, 1990), pp. 211-12.

[39]The MT, LXX and Targum all have the "nations rejoicing" either for or with "his people," Israel, and the vast majority of English translations render Deut 32:43 in the same way. Paul himself quotes the LXX to this effect in Rom 15:10. However, Qumran's translation (4QDeut⁹) of this verse omits "rejoice, O nations, with his people" and reads instead "rejoice, O heavens, together with him" (followed for the most part by the NRSV). It would appear that the Qumran reading has omitted part of the original Hebrew (which the MT maintains) and that the MT likewise has omitted part of the proto-MT (which Qumran maintains). Both likely reflect the composite earliest original Hebrew text.

In Deuteronomy 4:6 the nations would be able to perceive that Israel was "a wise and understanding people," and to witness to that fact. Deuteronomy 26:18-19 affirms that God setting Israel "high above all nations" should bring about "his [i.e., God's] praise, [his] fame, and [his] honor" arising from the nations and their witness to God's mighty work on behalf of Israel.[40] On the other hand, the nations' witness to God's sovereign destruction of Israel in Deuteronomy 29:22-28 would appear to imply that the result of their witness would be the nations' "praising" and "honoring" God for these mighty acts, as in their witness to God's work in Deuteronomy 26:19. The above-mentioned Deuteronomy 32 and Deuteronomy 33 passages are important because they appear in the literary segment of Deuteronomy 28–32, and they come in the close context of our focus texts of Deuteronomy 29:22-29 and Deuteronomy 32:21. In the Deuteronomy 32 passage, the nations will "rejoice" at the eschatological time when Israel's enemies will be vanquished. The second passage affirms that Israel "will call peoples to the mountain," presumably referring to the latter days, when Israel's "law will go forth from Zion," "the mountain of the house of the Lord," when "all nations will stream, to it, and many peoples will say, 'Come, let us go up the mountain of the Lord'" (Is 2:1-3).

Consequently, if it is correct to see Deuteronomy 29:22-29 as referring to a positive response of the nations to God's revelation in his dealings with Israel, then the prophecy directly following, that Israel would respond to God in repentance and be restored (Deut 30:1-10), would, together with Deuteronomy 29:22-29, represent a redemptive-historical order of a positive Gentile response (i.e., Gentile restoration to God) followed by a positive response to God by Israel. Deuteronomy 29:29 ("the secret things belong to the Lord our God") becomes a transition between Deuteronomy 29:22-28 and Deuteronomy 30:1-10.[41] The "secret" aspect of Deuteronomy 29:29a would appear to include a reference to the preceding, including the notion about why God would redeem Israel out of Egypt and then proceed to harden their hearts (Deut 29:2-4), sparking their further sin (Deut 29:19-21, 24-27) and consequent judgment (Deut 29:22-28). But could its transitional function include a notion of why the

---

[40]It is possible that Deut 26:19 refers to "praise, fame, and honor" directed toward Israel by the nations, but it is God who has brought about Israel's blessing in fulfillment of his promise (Deut 26:18).

[41]Some commentators believe that Deut 29:29 belongs only to Deut 30:1-10, forming an inclusio with the Torah conclusion of Deut 30:10. Certainly, the notion of "revealing" in Deut 29:29b has its corollary in Deut 30:10, but there appears to be some link between Deut 29:29 and Deut 30:1-10, though commentators debate exactly what it refers to in the preceding verses.

nations first perceive a correct interpretation of God's dealings with Israel, and afterward Israel comes to this restorative perception? Part of the divine decretive secret of Deuteronomy 29:29 is that Gentiles appear to be restored first in the latter days, and then Israel. This would appear to be fairly anomalous, since even in Deuteronomy 4:6 it is Israel that first shows wisdom through their law, which is subsequently recognized by the nations. Likewise Deuteronomy 33:19 portrays Israel first at God's mountain and then "calling peoples to the mountain of God," apparently in the latter days.[42] How can these two apparently different notions be reconciled? Deuteronomy 29:29 claims that it is a decretive "secret." Compounding the secret is the observation that a later Israelite generation will positively testify together with the nations (Deut 29:22), which will then be followed by Israel's salvation in Deuteronomy 30:1-10. Who precisely is this later Israelite generation?

Of course, these enigmas would all dissolve if Deuteronomy 29:22-28 were understood to be purely rhetorical.

---

[42]Though the prophecy is ambiguous—but for that very reason part of its packed meaning would appear to include the eschaton.

5

THE USE OF *MYSTERY*
IN 1 CORINTHIANS

◆ ▨ ◆

WE DETERMINED THAT ALTHOUGH THE BOOK of Romans supports the "Jew first, then Gentile" pattern that is found throughout the Old Testament (Rom 1:16; 15:8-9), Romans 11 states that during the majority of the church age most believers will be Gentiles (along with a remnant of Jews who will be saved at the same time). Gentile believers, however, will spark off the salvation of Jewish believers.

Paul appears to have read Deuteronomy 27–32 as prophesying Israel's disobedience, hardening and judgment, and their covenantal favor being given to the Gentiles. Israel is then provoked to jealousy by such Gentile favor, leading to Israel's final redemption. Why was this a "mystery"? Because everywhere else in the Old Testament, Israel's salvation leads to Gentile salvation.

The revealed mystery in Romans 16:25-26 may be related to the earlier use of mystery in Romans 11:25-26. Genesis 49 and Psalm 2 claim that when the end-time king of Israel arrives, he will bring about a forced submission of the Gentile enemies. Paul claims that these two Old Testament prophecies have already begun fulfillment at Christ's first coming but in an unanticipated manner.

Having examined Paul's disclosure of the mystery in Romans 11 and Romans 16, we now turn to 1 Corinthians, an epistle that employs the term *mystery* at critical junctures. The first discussion of mystery occurs at the beginning of the letter, where Paul confronts a theological problem head on: Why did Jews crucify their Messiah? Were not the Jews for the most part eagerly anticipating the arrival of their king? Ratcheting up this dilemma is the Old Testament's prophetic role. The cross, according to Paul in 1 Corinthians 15:3, was anticipated in the Old Testament. Yet why did the majority of the Jews not recognize this crucial event as the culmination of God's prophetic design? Paul answers these knotty questions with one of the most elaborate discussions of mystery in all of his letters. The other uses of mystery in 1 Corinthians are not far removed from this discussion of the crucifixion.

Such was the climate when Paul arrived at Corinth—political and ecclesiastical factions, moral compromises, rampant idolatry, and the pursuit of fame and wealth. Some of what can be determined about Paul's ministry at Corinth comes from Luke's account in Acts 18. According to Luke, Paul arrived at Corinth during his second missionary journey immediately after his ministry at Athens (Acts 17:16-34). Luke records Paul's stint at Corinth as lasting a lengthy eighteen months (Acts 18:11). When Paul left Corinth and ministered at Ephesus, he wrote to the Corinthians concerning their immoral behavior (1 Cor 5:9). He then received reports from "Chloe's people" and possibly from "Stephanas, Fortunatus, and Achaicus," along with a letter from the Corinthians themselves, concerning a wide variety of problems within the Corinthian community, particularly divisiveness (1 Cor 1:11; 7:1; 16:17). Paul thus writes to the Corinthians once more, addressing these particulars in what we call "1 Corinthians."

With the exception of Ephesians, no other book in the New Testament employs the term *mystery* more than 1 Corinthians. Occurring six times in the epistle, *mystery* is found in key passages and plays a significant role in the overall purpose of the book. Commentators have connected the term with Daniel in the epistle but have not significantly developed that relationship, especially its relationship to Old Testament Scripture.[1]

In 1 Corinthians 2:1, 7, the revealed "mystery" is the paradoxical event of the crucifixion: Christ, at the moment of his death, became the sovereign king. Not only is God's wisdom the event of the crucifixion, but as in other early instances, it also triumphs over all forms of human wisdom. Paul in 1 Corinthians 4:1 uses himself and Apollos as examples of what leaders ought to be: "stewards of mysteries" and "servants of Christ." As a Daniel figure, the apostle's goal is to remain faithful in his role as mediating God's revelation (1 Cor 4:2). Even though Paul does not give any clues with respect to the content of "mysteries" in 1 Corinthians 13:2; 14:2, both of these occurrences ought to be read against

---

[1]Used with permission, the material in this chapter is adapted from Benjamin L. Gladd, *Revealing the Mysterion: The Use of Mystery in Daniel and Second Temple Judaism with Its Bearing on First Corinthians*, BZNW 160 (Berlin: Walter de Gruyter, 2008), pp. 108-262.

the Old Testament and Jewish background. Last, the revealed mystery concerns the transformation of believers into the image of Christ, the Last Adam (1 Cor 15:51).

THE MYSTERY OF THE CROSS IN 1 CORINTHIANS 2:1, 7

Immediate context. Before studying 1 Corinthians 2, it is helpful to see how the last part of 1 Corinthians 1:17-31 leads into it:

> For Christ did not send me to baptize, but to preach the gospel, not in cleverness of speech, so that the cross of Christ would not be made void.
>
> For the word of the cross is foolishness to those who are perishing, but to us who are being saved it is the power of God. For it is written,
>
> "I WILL DESTROY THE WISDOM OF THE WISE,
> AND THE CLEVERNESS OF THE CLEVER I WILL SET ASIDE."
>
> Where is the wise man? Where is the scribe? Where is the debater of this age? Has not God made foolish the wisdom of the world? For since in the wisdom of God the world through its wisdom did not *come to* know God, God was well-pleased through the foolishness of the message preached to save those who believe. For indeed Jews ask for signs and Greeks search for wisdom; but we preach Christ crucified, to Jews a stumbling block and to Gentiles foolishness, but to those who are the called, both Jews and Greeks, Christ the power of God and the wisdom of God. Because the foolishness of God is wiser than men, and the weakness of God is stronger than men.
>
> For consider your calling, brethren, that there were not many wise according to the flesh, not many mighty, not many noble; but God has chosen the foolish things of the world to shame the wise, and God has chosen the weak things of the world to shame the things which are strong, and the base things of the world and the despised God has chosen, the things that are not, so that He may nullify the things that are, so that no man may boast before God. But by His doing you are in Christ Jesus, who became to us wisdom from God, and righteousness and sanctification, and redemption, so that, just as it is written, "LET HIM WHO BOASTS, BOAST IN THE LORD."

First Corinthians 1:17-18 constitutes Paul's thesis statement: the message of the cross permanently transforms believers' behavior and worldview. The only way for the Corinthians to alter their factional conduct is to embrace the message of the cross. Most now to some degree admit that the phrase "in cleverness of speech" in 1 Corinthians 1:17 denotes worldly Greco-Roman rhetorical practices. The content, not the delivery, of the message delivers people from plight. In particular, the goal of the rhetoric prized in Corinth was aimed at persuading the audience in any way possible toward the speaker's desires. If Paul succumbed to such worldly rhetoric in his ministry, the cross would be emptied of its power (1 Cor 1:17). In contrast to the "cleverness of speech," Paul preaches the "word of the cross" (1 Cor 1:18).[2] To the outsiders, the message of the cross is weak and foolish, but to those who believe, the cross is salvation and power. First Corinthians 1:19-25 is the basis for the proposition in 1 Corinthians 1:18a: "The word of the cross is foolishness to those who are perishing." The world's wisdom, alluring to the Corinthians, is unable to grasp Christ's work on the cross. Moreover, not only is God's wisdom beyond humanity's reach, but also his wisdom *trumps* all human wisdom (Is 29:14; 1 Cor 1:19), even the wisdom of the culturally sophisticated (1 Cor 1:20-21). Both Jews and Greeks alike examine the message of the cross and regard it as absurd (1 Cor 1:22-25).

Paul further interprets 1 Corinthians 1:19-25 in 1 Corinthians 1:26-28 by explaining that God works contrary to human reason: "God has chosen the foolish things of the world to shame the wise, and God has chosen the weak things of the world to shame the things which are strong" (1 Cor 1:27). God's purpose is that "no man may boast" (1 Cor 1:29). True wisdom, Paul claims, is found in Christ: "Let him who boasts, boast in the Lord" (1 Cor 1:31; Jer 9:23).

Now in 1 Corinthians 2:1-9 Paul builds on what he has said in the previous chapter:

> And when I came to you, brethren, I did not come with superiority of speech or of wisdom, proclaiming to you the mystery of God. For I determined to know nothing among you except Jesus Christ, and Him crucified. I was with you in weakness and in fear and in much trembling, and my message and my preaching

---

[2]The sophistic movement at Corinth during Paul's ministry there has stimulated much scholarly interest in the past several years. Several seminal works have appeared, refining the social context of 1 Corinthians and Paul's response to it: e.g., Bruce Winter, *Philo and Paul Among the Sophists,* SNTSMS 96 (New York: Cambridge University Press, 1997); Duane Litfin, *St. Paul's Theology of Proclamation: 1 Corinthians 1–4 and Greco-Roman Rhetoric,* SNTSMS 79 (New York: Cambridge University Press, 1994). Wisdom, so treasured at Corinth, was a type of sophistic wisdom. The exact contents of this wisdom are quite difficult to ascertain, but it is probably safe to assume that sophistic wisdom was alluring, philosophical, and human-centered. Rhetorically gifted individuals paraded this wisdom, hoping to gain a following by their persuasive rhetoric. The Corinthians were jockeying with each other by aligning themselves with one sophist over another, thus, pitting the leaders (and themselves) against each other.

were not in persuasive words of wisdom, but in demonstration of the Spirit and of power, so that your faith would not rest on the wisdom of men, but on the power of God. Yet we do speak wisdom among those who are mature; a wisdom, however, not of this age nor of the rulers of this age, who are passing away; but we declare God's wisdom, a mystery that has been hidden and that God destined for our glory before time began; *the wisdom* which none of the rulers of this age has understood; for if they had understood it they would not have crucified the Lord of glory; but just as it is written,

"THINGS WHICH EYE HAS NOT SEEN AND EAR HAS NOT HEARD,
AND *which* HAVE NOT ENTERED THE HEART OF MAN,
ALL THAT GOD HAS PREPARED FOR THOSE WHO LOVE HIM."

In 1 Corinthians 2:1-5, Paul is an example of preaching in conformity to the content of the gospel (1 Cor 1:18-25). He arrives at the Corinthian church not using ungodly rhetorical methods (1 Cor 2:1), because he desires "only to know Christ and him crucified." Paul's method conforms to his message: "I was with you in weakness and in fear and in much trembling, and my message and my preaching were . . . in demonstration of the Spirit and of power" (1 Cor 2:3-4; cf. 1 Cor 1:17). The purpose of coming "in weakness and in fear" is that the Corinthians' faith may not "rest on the wisdom of men, but on the power of God" (1 Cor 2:5). For Paul, faith must be wholly placed in the message of the cross, nothing more or less.

In these first five verses of 1 Corinthians 2, Paul rehearses the manner in which he proclaimed the "mystery" (1 Cor 2:1) or message of the cross, whereas in 1 Corinthians 2:6-16 he describes the nature of that wisdom. First Corinthians 2:6-9 relates the *accessibility* of that wisdom. The first part of 1 Corinthians 2:6 outlines how this wisdom is accessible to believers or the "mature." On the other hand, to those of "this age" and the "rulers of this age," such wisdom remains inaccessible (1 Cor 2:6b). First Corinthians 1:7 then contrasts the negative statement in 1 Corinthians 2:6b and further unpacks how this wisdom is indeed a revealed mystery and for the believers' benefit: "But we speak wisdom hidden in a mystery, which God predestined before the ages for our glory." Then 1 Corinthians 2:8 proceeds to explain the "hidden wisdom" of the previous verse—how the "rulers of this age" did not understand the wisdom of the cross, because if they had, they would not have crucified Christ. This conclusion is supported by an Old Testament quotation in 1 Corinthians 2:9, the hardening of the rulers and the ability of the believers to understand the cross. Before we unpack the content of *mystery* in 1 Corinthians 2:7, we must first take notice of a cluster of allusions to the book of Daniel and the nature of hiddenness. Both of these discussions aid us in recovering the meaning of the mystery in 1 Corinthians 2.

The use of Daniel in 1 Corinthians 1–2. Scholars have long noted the presence of several allusions to the book of Daniel in 1 Corinthians 1–2. The following proposed allusions to Daniel are subtle, but their cumulative effect within the same context points to the plausibility that they are present to some degree. The difficulty, though, lies in *why* Paul echoes Daniel in the midst of writing the first few chapters of this epistle. We will first cover some of the more prominent allusions to Daniel and then attempt to offer a solution to this perplexing problem.

Several scholars argue that the salient hymn of Daniel 2:20-23 lies behind 1 Corinthians 2:6-16, and they have good reason to think so.[3] As we previously argued, Daniel 2:20-23 is central for understanding Daniel's conception of mystery. We believe that the hymn encapsulates the nature of mystery, spanning almost the entire book of Daniel. Though the precise term *mystery* (*mystērion*) does not occur in this hymn, it is almost assuredly implied, for it represents the process of God disclosing his wisdom to the "wise" and to Daniel. Furthermore, God's revelation in Daniel 2:20-23 is referred to repeatedly as a "mystery" in Daniel 2:27-30, 47.

This use of *mystery* in Daniel 2 is likely behind Paul's repeated use of the very same word in 1 Corinthians 2:1, 7,[4] as evident from the following commonalities between the two:

1. Daniel 2 refers to a "mystery" revealed to an evil ruler who does not fully understand the revealed interpretation (cf. 1 Cor 2:8).

2. The interpretation of the mystery is understood by the godly prophet who receives the revelation and passes it on to others (1 Cor 2:10-16).[5]

---

[3]H. H. Drake Williams, *The Wisdom of the Wise*, AGJU 49 (Boston: Brill, 2001), p. 167; Hans Hübner, *Biblische Theologie des Neuen Testaments* (Göttingen: Vandenhoeck & Ruprecht, 1993), 2:121.

[4]On the textual problem of *mystery* (*mystērion*) or *testimony* (*martyrian*), see Gladd, *Revealing the Mysterion*, pp. 123-26. The textual support for both of these variants is strong, though *mystērion* receives slightly better attestation (P[46] ℵ A). The determining factor is, however, the immediate context of the passage. 1 Cor 1–2 is saturated with apocalyptic language, which reinforces the probability that Paul would again use the apocalyptic word, *mystērion*. 1 Cor 4:1 must also play a key role in the debate: "Let a man regard us . . . as stewards of the mysteries of God." The variant *mystērion* simply makes the most sense in light of external and internal considerations.

[5]The highly charged and debated "mature" in 1 Cor 2:6 may even reflect a similar theme that is sig-

3. The prophet understands the revealed mystery because God revealed it to him by his Spirit (cf. Dan 4:9 [parallel with Dan 2:20-21] and 1 Cor 2:10-16).[6]

4. To know this mystery is to have "wisdom."

5. The mystery concerns the establishment of the kingdom in the end times (for Paul's relevant end-time language, cf. 1 Cor 2:7-8 with 1 Cor 7:31; 10:11).

6. The emphasis on *wisdom* together with *power*,[7] along with the comment that Daniel has received insight from God, seems to suggest that Daniel 2:20-23 is part of the Old Testament background to 1 Corinthians 2:6-16.

Why Daniel? If indeed 1 Corinthians 1–2 contains Danielic allusions, why does Paul draw on Daniel? Is it merely for rhetorical flavor, or is there a deeper and more penetrating reason? It seems that Paul uses these allusions as a vehicle for communicating the mystery of the cross. These allusions to Daniel are vital for Paul's argument. The references to Daniel provide the basis as to why the meaning of the cross, so grand and pivotal in the process of redemptive history, remains elusive to the foolish but wisdom to the wise. The allusions may pull double duty by signaling the fulfillment of God's eschatological triumph over wisdom (Dan 2:1-16, 25-30) and the beginning of his eternal reign over all earthly kingdoms (Dan 2:44-45). The book of Daniel, therefore, is significant for Paul's overall thought in 1 Corinthians 1–2. Once again, Daniel's narrative plays an important role in the New Testament understanding of mystery.

Hiddenness of the mystery. What makes mystery so difficult for readers to

---

nificantly developed in Daniel and later Jewish literature. "Those who have insight among the people will give understanding to the many" (Dan 11:33; see Dan 12:3). Accordingly, those who have "insight" are the only ones privy to special revelation and subsequently impart such revelation to others.

[6]The role of the Spirit in the process of revelation may further suggest an intertextual or at least a thematic link between 1 Cor 2:10-13 ("For to us *God revealed them through the Spirit;* for the Spirit searches all things, *even the depths of God*") and Dan 4:9, where Nebuchadnezzar describes Daniel as one who has "a spirit of the holy gods" and "no mystery baffles" him (cf. Dan 2:11; 4:18; 5:11, 14). Even the language of "revealing" and "depths of God" in 1 Cor 2:10 may likewise allude to Dan 2:22: "It is he who reveals the profound and hidden things."

[7]Some suggest that the combination of *power* and *wisdom* in 1 Cor 2:4-6 is a reference to Dan 2:20 (MT); Dan 2:23 (MT, Theodotion). See G. K. Beale, *John's Use of the Old Testament in Revelation*, JSNTSup 166 (Sheffield: Sheffield, 1998), p. 252; H. Hübner, *Vetus Testamentum in Novo* (Göttingen: Vandenhoeck & Ruprecht, 1997), 2:230. *Power* (*dynamis*) occurs four times in 1 Cor 1:18, 24; 2:4, 5; *wisdom/wise* (*sophia/sophos*) appears 20 times in 1 Cor 1:19–2:16.

grasp is that the term is multifaceted, and its presence is expressed in a number of related themes in 1 Corinthians 1–2. One notable theme is "hiddenness": "We declare God's wisdom, hidden in a mystery" (1 Cor 2:7a, our translation).[8] Notice how Paul links *mystery* with the adjectival participle *hidden* (*apokekrymmenēn*). As we have seen in our chapters on Daniel and Matthew, hiddenness is a cardinal feature of the term. We distinguished between "temporary hiddenness" and "permanent hiddenness." Temporary hiddenness concerns the hidden nature of the revelation and its eventual revelation. For a period of time, the revelation was hidden from humanity. On the other hand, permanent hiddenness refers to an enduring or constant veiling of the revelation even after its manifestation, as the revelation is only able to be perceived by a few (e.g., the character Daniel).

If we apply this twofold characteristic of mystery to 1 Corinthians 1–2, we are able to unlock a few difficult texts. Since the term refers to the message of the cross (1 Cor 1:18-31), the event of the crucifixion was hidden from mankind but has now been revealed. We can now better understand 1 Corinthians 2:7: "We declare God's wisdom, hidden in a mystery, which God destined for our glory before the ages" (our translation).

In addition to God previously hiding the ironic nature of Christ's death from all of humanity, the message of the cross *continues* to be hidden from unbelievers: "wisdom which none of the rulers of this age has understood; for if they had understood it they would not have crucified the Lord of glory" (1 Cor 2:8). Not only was God's plan hidden in the past, but it also was hidden from the "rulers of this age" and unbelievers. On the other hand, says Paul, believers at the same time have insight into the mystery of the cross. We see this explicated in 1 Corinthians 2:10-16: "For to us God revealed them [that is, the mystery] through the Spirit" (1 Cor 2:10a).

In keeping with the theme of hiddenness, 1 Corinthians 2:9 provides the basis for the proposition that the "rulers of this age" did not understand the event of the crucifixion (1 Cor 2:7-8). The use of Isaiah 64:4 in 1 Corinthians 2:9

---

[8]Scholars disagree on what *en mystēriō* ("in a mystery") modifies. Some think *en mystēriō* modifies the verb *laloumen* ("we speak"), thus rendering it "we speak mysteriously" or "we speak God's wisdom in a mystery" (NASB, ASV). Such a translation connotes Paul speaking in secret, which would seem to contradict Paul's theology as a whole and makes little sense in the immediate context. Another option, the far more popular one, is to take *en mystēriō* with the noun *sophian* ("wisdom") (ESV, NRSV, NIV). The latter translation fits the context much better, for the emphasis is on the nature of apocalyptic wisdom: "we declare God's wisdom, hidden in a mystery."

is important but beyond the scope of this project.[9] Though many have been puzzled over the origin of the quotation and its use in 1 Corinthians 2:9, a thorough analysis of the original context fits well within Paul's thought. Sensory organ language (focusing on eyes, ears and heart) is frequently used for the perceiving redemptive events and revelation. Paul contrasts the rulers' lack of perception of God's redemptive plan with the insight of the Spirit-filled believer. As a result of their hardened condition and their dulled spiritual senses, they crucified Jesus. But since Paul and the Corinthians have Spirit-enabled senses, they can understand the redemptive event of the cross. The "mature" (1 Cor 2:6) and the "spiritual" (1 Cor 2:15) are those who have eyes to see and a heart that can comprehend the end-time revelation of the cross.

Wisdom and mystery in 1 Corinthians 1–2. Paul's use of *mystery* in 1 Corinthians 2:1, 7 appears on the surface as God's salvation in Christ. This particular use of the term *mystery* is perhaps more difficult to define and articulate than its use in 1 Corinthians 15:51, Romans 11:25 and Ephesians 3:4-6, where the term is still difficult to define. Yet in 1 Corinthians 1–2, the unveiled mystery is likened to a scattered mosaic; one has to assemble all the different pieces, taking into account the contours and coloring, the different shapes and sizes. Once all the pieces are joined together, it is necessary to stand back and examine the picture that emerges.

The first factor in helping us understand the notion of mystery here is the relationship between the word *mystery* and the "wisdom" of 1 Corinthians 1–2. Starting from 1 Corinthians 2:7 and working backward, we perceive that the revealed mystery constitutes the "wisdom" of God. Here Paul states, "We speak God's *wisdom,* which is hidden in a mystery." In other words, *the divine wisdom that Paul has been discussing throughout 1 Corinthians 1–2 can be labeled as a "mystery"* (1 Cor 1:21, 24, 30; 2:6). In referring to Christ in 1 Corinthians 2:2, 8, it is highly probable that Paul primarily has in mind the concept of the Old Testament and Jewish expectation of the Messiah (see excursus 5.1 for a brief survey).

According to the Old Testament, the Messiah refers above all to the "king of Israel." The Lord promises to restore and reign over his people through his Messiah. In 2 Samuel 7, God promised David that his descendants would rule over Israel. The Old Testament traces this promise and its fulfillment in the former and latter prophets. *The Messiah, a descendant of David, would be*

---

[9]For an extended discussion on the use of Is 64:4 in 1 Cor 2:9, see Gladd, *Revealing the* Mysterion, pp. 136-50.

instrumental in bringing about the establishment of God's eternal kingdom and destruction of Israel's enemies. That much is clear. Bound up with this phenomenon is the arrival of the new exodus, making possible forgiveness of sins, pouring out of the Spirit, the dawn of the new creation, and so on. Regarding the suffering aspect of the Messiah, a few passages seem to hint that the Messiah would suffer to some extent, but this suffering is not a cardinal aspect of his ministry. Messianic suffering is the means by which God will restore his people.[10]

The mystery of the cross. With a basic grasp of the messianic expectations in the first century, we can appreciate the mystery of the crucifixion in 1 Corinthians 2. In the first few chapters of this book, we attempted to demonstrate that the revealed mystery is the full revelation of God's partially hidden wisdom in the Old Testament. In the pre-Christian epoch, this wisdom was largely hidden, but it has now been more fully made known or revealed. But how is the cross a revealed mystery in 1 Corinthians 2? Scholars answer this problem differently. Some commentators argue that the term *mystery* refers to God's general salvation in Christ with the cross as its focal point. Paul, though, points us in a different direction by giving us a few clues in the immediate context. The following points are several clues that, when synthesized, hopefully offer a clearer picture about what is the revealed mystery concerning Christ.

Lord of glory. An immediate clue is found in 1 Corinthians 2:8b: "For if they [the rulers] had understood it [the mystery] they would not have crucified the Lord of glory." The combination of "Lord" (*kyrios*) and the crucifixion is unique in Paul. Nearly every time that Paul mentions the cross, he uses the titles "Christ" or "Jesus Christ."[11] (The only exception is found in Galatians

---

[10]The Old Testament appears to conceive of a suffering Messiah figure in such Old Testament texts as Is 53 and Dan 9:26 (cf. also Gen 3:15, Dan 9: and Zech 12:10; 13:7). The New Testament also perceives a suffering Messiah in the Old Testament: e.g., Lk 24:25-27: "And he [Jesus] said to them, 'O foolish men and slow of heart to believe in all that the prophets have spoken! Was it not necessary for the Christ to suffer these things and to enter into his glory?' Then beginning with Moses and with all the prophets, he explained to them the things concerning himself in all the Scriptures" (cf. Jn 5:39-47). 1 Cor 15:3-4 affirms that the Old Testament anticipated a suffering Messiah: "For I delivered to you as of first importance what I also received, that Christ died for our sins according to the Scriptures, and that he was buried, and that he was raised on the third day according to the Scriptures." Likewise, 1 Pet 1:10-11 says, "As to this salvation, the prophets who prophesied of the grace that *would come* to you made careful searches and inquiries, seeking to know what person or time the Spirit of Christ within them was indicating as he predicted the sufferings of Christ and the glories to follow."

[11]E.g., 1 Cor 1:17, 23; 2:2; 2 Cor 13:4; Gal 3:1; 6:12; Phil 2:8; 3:18; Col 1:20; 2:14.

6:14: "in the cross of our Lord Jesus Christ.") Not only is the title "Lord" peculiar, but so is its modifier "of glory" (*tēs doxēs*). This precise title, the "Lord
of glory," is used nowhere else in the New Testament or in the Greek translation of the Old Testament.[12]

This title is, however, found throughout the prominent Jewish document of
1 Enoch. In 1 Enoch 22.14, Enoch venerates God after receiving a vision: "At that
moment I blessed the Lord of Glory [*ton kyrion tēs doxēs*] and I said, 'Blessed
be my Lord, the Lord of righteousness who rules forever.'" A few chapters later,
the angel Uriel relates to Enoch the particularities of the judgment of the
wicked and the righteous: "There will be upon them the spectacle of the
righteous judgment. . . . The merciful will bless the Lord of Glory [*ton kyrion
tēs doxēs*], the Eternal King" (*1 En*. 27.3). Enoch responds to this insight and
praises God: "At that moment, I blessed the Lord of Glory [*ton kyrion tēs doxēs*]
and gave him the praise that befits his glory" (*1 En*. 27.5).

The title "Lord of glory" in 1 Enoch is representative of the throne room
tradition in Jewish apocalypticism. There has been much discussion in recent
years of the idea of God's heavenly throne room in Jewish apocalyptic literature.
For our purposes, we simply need to note that in 1 Corinthians 2:8 Paul likely
taps into a Jewish tradition with his use of the title "Lord of glory." He takes
what was a Jewish title that describes the transcendent Lord and applies it to
Christ. By labeling Christ as the "Lord of glory," the apostle is, in effect, desig-
nating Christ as the exalted, preeminent and supreme divine ruler.

Messiah. We mentioned above that the word for "Messiah" is rendered *christos*
("Christ") in Greek. This refers to the messianic king of Israel. This is significant
when reading the New Testament, particularly those sections that deal with Jesus'
suffering and death. The first-century Jewish reader (or Gentile who was familiar
with the Old Testament) would immediately pick up on the Old Testament/
Jewish background. When reading 1 Corinthians 1–2, we too must keep the significance of this title in mind. Paul is referring to the death of the king of Israel.

In 1 Corinthians 1:17 and following, we perceive a slight shift in titles, for the
title "Lord" is not used until 1 Corinthians 2:8. The apostle transitions from
"Lord Jesus Christ" (1 Cor 1:2-9) to "Christ crucified" (1 Cor 1:23). The titles
"Christ" and "Jesus" are exclusively attached to the crucifixion in 1 Corinthians
1:17, 23, 30; 2:2. It is possible that Paul uses these titles for stylistic reasons, but

---

[12]Jas 2:1 does, however, come close to the title "Lord of glory": "Do not hold your faith in our glorious
Lord Jesus Christ with an attitude of personal favoritism."

that is unlikely. Since the revealed mystery is tied to the crucifixion of the *Messiah,* Paul is careful how he nuances this relationship. Paul states in 1 Corinthians 1:17, "Christ did not send me to baptize, but to preach the gospel, not in cleverness of speech, that the cross of Christ would not be made void." And again in 1 Corinthians 1:23, "we preach Christ crucified." Finally, this is reaffirmed in 1 Corinthians 2:2, "I determined to know nothing among you except Jesus Christ, and him crucified." In sum, Paul highlights the kingly messianic nature of Jesus as it relates to his horrific death on the cross.

Power. Along with the exalted nature of the long-awaited Messiah, the notion of power is repeated in 1 Corinthians 1–2 and tethered to the cross in 1 Corinthians 1:18: "For the word of the cross is foolishness to those who are perishing, but to us who are being saved it is the power of God." A few verses later this theme is repeated in 1 Corinthians 1:23- 24: "Christ crucified, to Jews a stumbling block and to Gentiles foolishness, but to those who are the called . . . Christ the power of God" (cf. 1 Cor 2:4). Above we noted that power in this context is a reference to Daniel 2:20, 23. Power, according to Daniel 2:20, 23, 37, is the establishment and removal of earthly kings from their thrones and the establishment of God's eternal kingdom (Dan 2:21, 36-45). This is further illustrated in Daniel 2:44-45, where a kingdom "which will never be destroyed" eclipses the fourth and final kingdom. By combining Daniel's notion of power with the crucifixion, *Paul invokes overtones of God installing his latter-day kingdom through the Messiah's death.*

Cross of suffering. That Christ is the exalted Lord of glory is only half the unveiled mystery. The other side of the coin is the crucifixion. We already have noted the prominence of the cross in 1 Corinthians 1–2 (1 Cor 1:17-18, 22-25; 2:1-2, 8). For the Jews, the cross is a "stumbling block" and to the Gentiles it is "foolishness" (1 Cor 1:23). Fortunately, we do not need to spend much time developing this thought, because the Jewish and Greco-Roman perspectives on the cross are apparent.[13] In the first century, the cross was the symbol of rejection and cursing. Deuteronomy 21:23 is a passage associated with the cross in the first century[14] and quoted by Paul in Galatians 3:11 in reference to Christ. Deuteronomy 21:22-23 states, "If a man has committed a sin worthy of death

---

[13]See M. Hengel, *Crucifixion: In the Ancient World and the Folly of the Message of the Cross* (Philadelphia: Fortress, 1977); David W. Chapman, *Ancient Jewish and Christian Perceptions of Crucifixion,* WUNT 244 (Tübingen: Mohr Siebeck, 2008).

[14]See 4QpNah (4Q169) 3 + 4 4-9; 11QTemple (11Q19) LXIV, 6-13.

and he is put to death, and you hang him on a tree . . . (for he who is hanged is accursed of God)." The cross symbolizes utter rejection and being accursed by God, the epitome of shame.

Conclusion: A crucified king. The cumulative effect of the aforementioned points is striking. We noted the prominence of Jesus' titles, their association with the crucifixion (Lord Jesus Christ, the Messiah or Christ crucified, the Lord of glory) and the peculiar language of "power." By investigating both the regal notions associated with the coming Messiah and the scandal of the cross, we arrive at the uncovering of the mystery in 1 Corinthians 2. *The disclosed mystery is the exalted, kingly, divine Messiah affixed to the cross.*[15] While Jesus is suffering a shameful death on the cross, he is simultaneously the supreme divine ruler—"the Lord of glory,"[16] which as we saw in Judaism is a phrase used only of God in his heavenly throne room. Therefore, the making known of the mystery in 1 Corinthians 2:1, 7 is *the Messiah, divine Lord of glory reigning at the same time he is defeated and accursed.* Fee comments, "One may have a Messiah, or one may have a crucifixion; but one may not have both—at least not from the perspective of a merely human understanding. *Messiah* meant power, splendor, triumph; *crucifixion* meant weakness, humiliation, defeat."[17] We may go further: as the Lord of glory,[18]

---

[15]For those who generally agree that the mystery entails Jesus suffering as the Messiah, see, e.g., Gordon D. Fee, *First Epistle to the Corinthians*, NICNT (Grand Rapids: Eerdmans, 1987), p. 105; Garland, *1 Corinthians*, 95; Richard Hays, *First Corinthians*, IBC (Louisville, KY: Westminster John Knox, 1997), pp. 43-44; Seyoon Kim, *The Origin of Paul's Gospel*, WUNT 4 (Tübingen: Mohr Siebeck, 1981; repr., Grand Rapids: Eerdmans, 1981), pp. 80-81; Günther Bornkamm, "μυστήριον, μυέω," *TDNT* 4:819; Raymond Brown, *The Semitic Background of the Term "Mystery" in the New Testament*, BS 21 (Philadelphia: Fortress, 1968), p. 41; D. A. Carson, "Mystery and Fulfillment," in *Justification and Variegated Nomism: Volume 2—The Paradoxes of Paul*, ed. D. A. Carson, Peter T. O'Brien and Mark A. Seifrid (Grand Rapids: Baker, 2004), pp. 416-17; F. F. Bruce, *1 and 2 Corinthians*, NCBC (London: Marshall, Morgan & Scott, 1971; repr., Grand Rapids: Eerdmans, 1986), p. 39.

[16]The phrase is either an adjectival genitive ("glorious Lord") or a possessive genitive ("the Lord who possesses glory"), though Anthony C. Thistleton, *The First Epistle to the Corinthians*, NIGTC (Grand Rapids: Eerdmans, 2000), p. 247, refers to this as a qualitative genitive.

[17]Fee, *1 Corinthians*, p. 75.

[18]One could contend that Paul's reference to "the Lord of glory" refers only to Jesus in his post-resurrection exalted state in heaven, but it appears that this phrase expresses part of what was hidden, the "hidden wisdom," which was part of the essence of the mystery (1 Cor 2:8). Jesus being "the Lord of glory" is part of what "the rulers of this age" did not understand (1 Cor 2:8) or did not have eyes to see (1 Cor 2:9a). See Thistleton, *1 Corinthians*, p. 247, who says that "Lord of glory belongs to a broader contrast in Paul in which glory relates to the cross (Gal 6:14)," so that Paul can say in this Galatians text that he "boasts . . . in the cross of our Lord Jesus Christ." Jesus as "Lord of glory" is "now defined in terms of the wonder of his self-giving in the cross," so that Paul views Jesus in 1 Cor 2:8 as having been glorified through the event of the crucifixion itself. On the other hand, see Kim, *Origin of Paul's Gospel*, pp. 78-80, who contends that Christ as "the Lord of

Jesus is being identified with the ruling God in his suffering and crucifixion!

Though a suffering messiah was to some degree anticipated, messianic suffering does not play a central role in the Old Testament and especially in Jewish thought. Worldly wisdom could not conceive that the Messiah could be crucified, much less be seen as a *glorious divine ruler actually exercising ruling power while being defeated.* This understanding of the Messiah develops Old Testament and Jewish expectations. Thus Paul portrays Jesus as executing his divine *messianic* office at the moment of the crucifixion. The revelation of this mystery was not clearly seen formerly by God's Old Testament prophets; it was largely hidden.

But were there subtle intimations in the Old Testament of such an ironic rule in the midst of suffering? There is not space to elaborate on this in substantial degree, but a few suggestions may indicate fruitful avenues for further exploration. For example, the Servant of Isaiah 53 suffers vicariously for the remnant of Israel, so that in the midst of his suffering actual "healing" (Is 53:5), redemption from death (Is 53:8) and justification (Is 53:11) was taking place for his people. May we not say that these positive spiritual realities in the midst of suffering were part and parcel of the Messiah's spiritual exercise of rule in delivering his people from death and the powers of death, after which he was to receive a more overt reward (Is 53:12)? Another example of a king ruling in the midst of suffering would be David, who in so many ways was typological of the ultimate Davidic king, Jesus. In David's exile and suffering while Absalom was attempting to hunt him down and kill him, David was still a king exercising rule over the remnant of Israel who followed him and conducting battles and winning victory over the enemy (albeit the inner-covenantal enemy led by his own son).

If these and other intimations in the Old Testament itself of ironic ruling in the midst of suffering have any merit, then they may serve as seedbeds from which the Old Testament intimations were clarified by the later revelation of the

---

glory" was revealed from heaven to Paul at the Damascus experience, after Christ had ascended to the heavenly realm (appealing to "glory of Christ" in 2 Cor 4:4 and "glory of the Lord" in 2 Cor 3:18, both of which, Kim asserts, have to do with allusions to Paul's Damascus christophany; cf. also Phil 3:21). While this is likely included, it would seem that Christ's glory was already present at the cross in hidden form, since the revelation is said to be not only for Paul but also for "those who love him" (1 Cor 2:9) and for Christians in general ("us," 1 Cor 2:10; "we," 1 Cor 2:12; the "spiritual" person, 1 Cor 2:15; "we," 1 Cor 2:16). If Christ was truly "Lord of glory" (which we have seen to be a divine title) at his heavenly exaltation, he certainly was divine at his crucifixion and possessed such glory, though it was hidden.

"mystery" of Christ. So the declaration of the mystery of a crucified Lord of glory in 1 Corinthians 2 is "new" but, on the other hand, it may clarify what was already implied or hinted at in the Old Testament. Thus there remains some continuity between the Old Testament and 1 Corinthians 2, yet the latter also contains new revelation that in surprising ways clarifies the older anticipations.

PAUL AS A "STEWARD OF MYSTERIES" IN 1 CORINTHIANS 4:1

The members of the church in Corinth are deemed fleshly, because they pit one leader over another (1 Cor 3:1-4; see 1 Cor 1:10-13). Paul therefore attempts to remedy this situation by furnishing a series of examples for the Corinthians to imitate. After agricultural and architectural temple metaphors in 1 Corinthians 3, Paul moves on to the third metaphor of serving the church as "servants of Christ" and "stewards of the mysteries of God" (1 Cor 4:1). Paul's stewardship of mysteries, like his planting and building activities (1 Cor 3:8, 14-15), incurs a strict judgment (1 Cor 4:3-5). Paul defends his stewardship by emphasizing his sole accountability to the Lord. The full passage in 1 Corinthians 4 needs to be set forth here in order that the reader may recall it readily to mind:

> Let a man regard us in this manner, as servants of Christ and stewards of the mysteries of God. In this case, moreover, it is required of stewards that one be found trustworthy. But to me it is a very small thing that I may be examined by you, or by *any* human court; in fact, I do not even examine myself. For I am conscious of nothing against myself, yet I am not by this acquitted; but the one who examines me is the Lord. Therefore do not go on passing judgment before the time, *but wait* until the Lord comes who will both bring to light the things hidden in the darkness and disclose the motives of *men's* hearts; and then each man's praise will come to him from God. (1 Cor 4:1-5)

In the past, commentators have not attempted much exploration of the background behind the phrase "stewards of the mysteries of God" in 1 Corinthians 4:1, but most now admit that the term *mysteries* in this context stands squarely in the stream of Judaism (scholars typically see Paul's use of *mystery* in 1 Cor 2:7 behind 1 Cor 4:1).

Paul's office as a "steward" is similar to his other roles in 1 Corinthians 3:6-15. The first metaphor in 1 Corinthians 3—Paul as a planter—recalls several Old Testament texts that speak of a "cultivated field" or "vineyard," and probably suggests that Paul views himself as a latter-day servant in God's field. The imagery of planting and building most likely refers to several other Old Testament and Jewish texts about the temple.[19] If these Old Testament texts are in mind in these two metaphors (which appears plausible), then it may not be a matter of coincidence that additional Old Testament texts may lie behind Paul's final metaphor concerning stewardship.

If the Danielic background of mystery in 1 Corinthians 2:1, 7 is still in mind in 1 Corinthians 4:1, the clause "one be found faithful" (1 Cor 4:2) could echo the person of Daniel in Daniel 6:4 (see table 5.1). Daniel 6:4 does not explicitly say that Daniel was "found faithful" but it comes very close to saying that.

Table 5.1

Daniel 6:4 Theod. (Dan 6:4 MT)	1 Corinthians 4:2
"They could not find any pretext or corruption against him, because he was faithful."	"In this case, moreover, it is required of stewards that one be found trustworthy."
MT: "they could find no ground of accusation or *evidence of* corruption, inasmuch as he was faithful, and no negligence or corruption was *to be* found in him."	
Theodotian: *pasan prophasin kai paraptōma kai amblakēma ouch heuron kat autou hoti pistos ēn*	*hōde loipon zēteitai en tois oikonomois, hina pistos tis heurethē*

Furthermore, in Daniel 2:45, the interpretation of the dream by Daniel is called "faithful": "the dream is true and its interpretation is *trustworthy [pistē]*" (OG). The verb "to be faithful" or "certain" (*'mn*) is used only three times in the book of Daniel (Dan 2:45; 6:5, 24) and is always translated with the Greek cognate *pist-* (the verb *pisteuō* occurs in Dan 6:24). In Daniel 2:45, the revelation of the mystery by Daniel is deemed "faithful" (cf. Rev 22:6), for the message entails end-time events that have already come to pass during the ministry of Daniel (e.g., Dan 4:28-37; 5:30), and those events which are certain to occur but await final fulfillment. Therefore, in light of the book of Daniel, *both* the message from Daniel *and* the messenger are deemed faithful.

Though Paul's "faithfulness" may be analogous to both the figure of Daniel and the declaration of the Danielic mystery, these connections do not exhaust the significance of a faithful steward in 1 Corinthians 4:1-5. Paul considers himself to be in a mediatory position between God and the Corinthians, which

---

[19]Ex 31:4; 35:31-32, 35; 1 Kings 5–6; 2 Chron 3–4; Ps 92:12-15; Ezek 17:5, 7; 1QS VIII, 5; 1QH VIII, 4-11; CD I, 7; cf. G. K. Beale, *The Temple and the Church's Mission*, NSBT 17 (Downers Grove, IL: InterVarsity Press, 2004), pp. 246-52.

may suggest that he regarded himself as a "wise one" (Dan 12:3) or at least functioning in a similar capacity as did Daniel, the faithful conveyer of God's revelation to others.[20]

MYSTERIES OF PROPHECY AND TONGUES IN 1 CORINTHIANS 13:2; 14:2

In 1 Corinthians 12–14, spiritual gifts become the central theme. These Spirit-enabled gifts are for the community as a whole (1 Cor 12:12-31) and not to be utilized for self-adulation. Without love, these gifts become useless (1 Cor 13:1-13). Tongues, though very attractive to the Corinthians, ought to be restricted to one's prayer closet (1 Cor 14:3, 14-17), unless they are interpreted, resulting in the edification of the body (1 Cor 14:5). Prophecy, on the other hand, is much more public and beneficial for the community (1 Cor 14:1, 3, 5-12, 20-33), since the church understands the message and is edified.

Content of "all mysteries." In 1 Corinthians 13:2 Paul says: "If I have *the gift of* prophecy, and know all mysteries and all knowledge; and if I have all faith, so as to remove mountains, but do not have love, I am nothing." Determining the exact content of *mysteries* in 1 Corinthians 13:2, difficult though it may be, is still attainable to some degree, since Paul provides a few clues in the immediate context. If we connect Paul's use of *mystery* here in 1 Corinthians 13:2 with his other uses in 1 Corinthians 2:1, 7; 4:1; 15:51 and elsewhere in the New Testament, its content may become clearer. In 1 Corinthians 2, the unveiled mystery is Christ's paradoxical work on the cross, while in 1 Corinthians 4:1 Paul commands the Corinthians to regard him as a steward of apocalyptic wisdom. In 1 Corinthians 15:51, the mystery involves the nature of the resurrection, as we will soon see. We noted that mystery in Daniel and early Judaism pertains to various end-time issues: the eternal reign of God, the oppression of the righteous Israelites, defeat of the saints' enemies, and so forth. Thus the content of the mystery in 1 Corinthians 13:2 by inference at least includes some association generally with latter-day realities. Paul declares that though he may possess eschatological wisdom and knowledge, without love such special insight is worthless.

Tongues and mysteries. The apostle says in 1 Corinthians 14:2, "For one who speaks in a tongue does not speak to men but to God; for no one understands,

---

[20]The Teacher of Righteousness, an eminent figure in the Qumran community, may also be considered a "steward of mysteries," much like the description of Paul that we find here in 1 Cor 4:1 (1QS IX, 18-19 = 4Q256 XVIII, 1-3; 4Q258 VIII, 3-4; cf. 1QS IX, 12-14, 20 = 4Q259 III, 2-17).

but by the Spirit he speaks <u>mysteries</u> [*mystēria*]." This verse provides the basis for (*gar*) the previous exhortation—"especially that you may prophesy" (1 Cor 14:1)—and breaks it into two parts: "The one who speaks in a tongue does not speak to men but to God" and "For no one understands him, but by the Spirit he speaks mysteries." The second part of 1 Corinthians 14:2 grounds the first— "one who speaks in a tongue speaks to God, <u>because no one understands</u>, but by the Spirit speaks mysteries" (our translation).

There are a few different ways to define "mysteries" in 1 Corinthians 14:2. Some take the term in a mundane sense (i.e., the one speaking in tongues simply communicates "secrets" to God),[21] while others take this clause adverbially—"speaking mysteriously"[22] or as a reference to pagan mystery cults.[23] Finally, "mysteries" could refer to speaking revelations back to God via the empowerment of the Spirit.[24] In light of these possibilities, the last option may be best in the immediate context. But whatever one concludes, one ought to remain very tentative, as interpretative clues are scant.

Since Paul's use of "mystery" in 1 Corinthians 14:2 is certainly ambiguous, the search for a closely related passage might yield a better grasp of this verse; we need not journey too far, for we quickly arrive at 1 Corinthians 13:2. We have already discussed Paul's use of mystery in 13:2—"all mysteries and knowledge"— and surmised that "mysteries" refers there to end-time revelations (see 1 Cor 14:25). The same is probably true of "mysteries" in 1 Corinthians 14:2.

Tongues of men and angels. Setting us on the right track in our search for the nature of "mysteries" of 1 Corinthians 14:2, Paul divulges an interesting hint in 1 Corinthians 13:1, "If I speak with the tongues of men and angels, but do not have love, I have become a noisy gong or a clanging cymbal." That tongues and angels are associated with each other in 1 Corinthians 13:1 is significant, since tongues are found in connection to angelic speech in early Judaism.

---

[21]E.g., Fee, *1 Corinthians*, p. 656; Thiselton, *1 Corinthians*, pp. 1085-86; Peter T. O'Brien, "Mystery," in *DPL*, pp. 621-23; Chrys Caragounis, *The Ephesian Mysterion: Meaning and Content*, ConBNT 8 (Lund: Gleerup, 1977), p. 27.

[22]Joseph Coppens, "'Mystery' in the Theology of Saint Paul and Its Parallels at Qumran," in *Paul and Qumran: Studies in New Testament Exegesis*, ed. Jerome Murphy-O'Connor (Chicago: Priority, 1968), pp. 137-38.

[23]H. W. House, "Tongues and the Mystery Religions at Corinth." *Bibliotheca sacra* 140 (1983): 134-50; A. E. Harvey, "The Use of Mystery Language in the Bible," *JTS* 31 (1980): 332.

[24]See Brown, *Semitic Background*, p. 47; James D. G. Dunn, *Jesus and the Spirit: A Study of the Religious and Charismatic Experience of Jesus and the First Christians as Reflected in the New Testament* (Philadelphia: Westminster Press, 1975; repr., Grand Rapids: Eerdmans, 1997), p. 244; Bornkamm, "μυστήριον," p. 822; Kim, *Origin of Paul's Gospel*, p. 78; by implication, Hays, *1 Corinthians*, p. 223.

Recently several scholars have conducted detailed studies of angelic prayer and worship in Judaism, making several pertinent conclusions.[25] In several Jewish texts, we find the visionary joining the angels in their veneration of God. The *Testament of Job* 48.3 (first century B.C. to first century A.D.) says, "But she [Hemera] spoke ecstatically in the angelic dialect, sending up a hymn to God in accord with the hymnic style of the angels. And as she spoke ecstatically, she allowed 'The Spirit' to be inscribed on her garment" (see also *T. Job* 49:1–50:3; *Mart. Ascen. Isa.* 9:33-36; 9:27-32; *Apoc. Zeph.* 8:1-5; *Sim.* 71:1-11).

Several texts found at Qumran likewise describe the speaker's identification with the angelic host,[26] but we will only cite a body of texts called the *Songs of Sabbath Sacrifice* (second century B.C.). Just as the angels possess and pronounce "mysteries" in these texts, so too the Qumran community possesses and proclaims divine wisdom. For the sake of space, only two pertinent texts from this body are cited here. The first refers to angels and the second to human saints:

> And the offering of their tongues [. . .] seven mysteries of knowledge in the wonderful mystery of the seven regions of the hol[y of holies. . . . The tongue of the first will be strengthened seven times with the *tongue* of the second to him. The tongue of the second to him will be strengthened] seven times with (that) of the third to [him. The tong]ue of the thi[rd will] be strengthened seven times. (4Q403 1 II, 26-28)

> Sing with joy, [those of you enjoying his knowledge,] [with rejoi]cing among the [wonderful] god[s. Proclaim his glory with the tongue of all who proclaim] [knowl]edge; [his wonderful] songs, [with the mouth of all who proclaim him. For he is] God of al[l who sing for ever, and Judge in his power over all the spirits of understanding.] Give thanks, all [majestic] divinities, [to the king of majesty; for to his glory all] [the divin]ities of knowledge give thanks, and al[l the spirits of justice give thanks to his truth. And they make their knowledge acceptable]. (4Q404 4, 2-7 = 4Q403 1 I; cf. also 4Q403 1 I, 36-42; 4Q405 4, 5, 6, 57, 58, 69)

In light of these passages from *Songs of Sabbath Sacrifice*, we are able to make a few observations: (1) angels/Qumranites praise God with their "tongues"; (2) this worship consists of celebrating God's holiness, knowledge and "mysteries";

---

[25]E.g., Bilhah Nitzan, *Qumran Prayer and Religious Poetry* (Boston: Brill, 1994), pp. 290-91; Esther G. Chazon, "Human and Angelic Prayer in Light of the Scrolls," in *Liturgical Perspectives: Prayer and Poetry in Light of the Dead Sea Scrolls*, ed. Esther G. Chazon, STDJ 48 (Boston: Brill, 2003), pp. 35-47.

[26]1QHa 26 top; 4Q471b 1-3; 1QHa XI, 20-23; see also 1QHa III, 21-22; 1QS XI, 5-9.

and (3) angelic/Qumran worship includes "enjoying" and "proclaiming" knowledge. Therefore, Paul's declaration that speaking in tongues (*glossolalia*) includes worship/prayer (1 Cor 14:14-19), "tongues of angels" (1 Cor 13:1) and "mysteries" (1 Cor 14:2) has some conceptual parallel with these documents. In fact, some of these parallels strike close to 1 Corinthians, showcasing the one who speaks in tongues as participating in angelic worship in the divine throne room. Perhaps this is part of the significance of 1 Corinthians 11:10: "The woman ought to have a symbol of authority on her head, <u>because of the angels</u>" when "praying or prophesying" (1 Cor 11:5; cf. 1 Cor 11:13), which likely refers to activities of Christian worship gatherings. When Christians came together to worship God, they considered themselves to be in the very presence of the angels and God, who was present in their midst, though in a different invisible and heavenly dimension (1 Cor 14:25; Acts 2:1-41; 10:44-47). At least textually it is difficult to link any of these texts to this situation at Corinth, but, at the very least, some sectors of Judaism promote the idea that humans were able to communicate in a heavenly dialect with the angels at the divine throne room. While there is likely no dependence of 1 Corinthians 14 on these Qumran texts, nevertheless, they may offer some general parallels to help explain conceptually part of what is going on.

Interpretation of tongues. If we are right about the revelatory nature of tongues and mysteries and their subsequent interpretation in 1 Corinthians 14, then we come admirably close to the pattern of wisdom in the book of Daniel. In Daniel, we saw how God revealed to Nebuchadnezzar the mystery concerning the statue (Dan 2:28-29) and then its interpretation to Daniel (Dan 2:19, 30, 47; 4:9). This same twofold pattern is likewise found in Qumran, particularly in its commentary on Habakkuk. Therefore, that Paul describes tongues as speaking mysteries makes much sense because of the well-established twofold pattern of apocalyptic wisdom.

Prophecy, as Paul adamantly contends, serves to edify the church. It is a revelation that has been given to the Christian prophet and subsequently related to the individual or community. In other words, prophecy is a revelation that has reached its intended goal—communal understanding and thus edification. Speaking in tongues, on the other hand, can be both without understanding or it can convey understanding. If tongues are left without an interpretation, then they are incomprehensible; even the individual does not understand their meaning (1 Cor 14:13-17). But, if the initial revelation receives a second or final revelation, then the entire revelation becomes apprehensible; the individual's mind or the community is edified (1 Cor 14:5, 14-15).

THE MYSTERY OF THE RESURRECTION IN 1 CORINTHIANS 15:51

First Corinthians 15:50-53 answers the question posed in 1 Corinthians 15:35 and serves as the culmination of Paul's argument. The entire relevant portion of the passage needs to be quoted before explanation of this difficult text.

> But someone will say, "How are the dead raised? And with what kind of body do they come?" You fool! That which you sow does not come to life unless it dies; and that which you sow, you do not sow the body which is to be, but a bare grain, perhaps of wheat or of something else. But God gives it a body just as He wished, and to each of the seeds a body of its own. All flesh is not the same flesh, but there is one *flesh* of men, and another flesh of beasts, and another flesh of birds, and another of fish. There are also heavenly bodies and earthly bodies, but the glory of the heavenly is one, and the *glory* of the earthly is another. There is one glory of the sun, and another glory of the moon, and another glory of the stars; for star differs from star in glory.
>
> So also is the resurrection of the dead. It is sown a perishable *body*, it is raised an imperishable *body;* it is sown in dishonor, it is raised in glory; it is sown in weakness, it is raised in power; it is sown a natural body, it is raised a spiritual body. If there is a natural body, there is also a spiritual *body.* So also it is written, "The first MAN, Adam, BECAME A LIVING SOUL." The last Adam *became* a life-giving spirit. However, the spiritual is not first, but the natural; then the spiritual. The first man is from the earth, earthy; the second man is from heaven. As is the earthy, so also are those who are earthy; and as is the heavenly, so also are those who are heavenly. Just as we have borne the image of the earthy, we will also bear the image of the heavenly.
>
> Now I say this, brethren, that flesh and blood cannot inherit the kingdom of God; nor does the perishable inherit the imperishable. Behold, I tell you a mystery; we will not all sleep, but we will all be changed, in a moment, in the twinkling of an eye, at the last trumpet; for the trumpet will sound, and the dead will be raised imperishable, and we will be changed. For this perishable must put on the imperishable, and this mortal must put on immortality. But when this perishable will have put on the imperishable, and this mortal will have put on immortality, then will come about the saying that is written, "DEATH IS SWALLOWED UP in victory. O DEATH, WHERE IS YOUR VICTORY? O DEATH, WHERE IS YOUR STING?" The sting of death is sin, and the power of sin is the law; but thanks be to God, who gives us the victory through our Lord Jesus Christ. (1 Cor 15:35-57)

In 1 Corinthians 15:50, Paul explicitly states what has been implicit thus far in 1 Corinthians 15:35-49: "flesh and blood cannot inherit the kingdom of God." Paul contends, probably in agreement with the Corinthians, that the "earthly" are unable to dwell in a "heavenly" environment. But unlike those in Corinth, Paul believes that God has the ability to refashion and transform those in their earthly bodies into heavenly ones, a point that he has previously made in 1 Corinthians 15:36-38. Paul emphatically declares that he is disclosing a mystery in explaining the transformation of all believers into the heavenly image of Adam (1 Cor 15:51-52). Therein lies the key that was "hidden" from the Corinthians in their misunderstanding that the earthly body could not dwell in a heavenly environment. First Corinthians 14:53 provides the basis for the unveiled mystery and further describes the nature of the transformation. Believers are transformed from their earthly existence to a heavenly one.

The mystery of transformation. There are those who contend that the revealed mystery in 1 Corinthians 15:51 does not refer to a specifically new doctrine, but is rather a general description of God's redemptive activity in Christ. On the other hand, many commentators affirm that the revealed mystery constitutes the transformation of only the living. Richard Hays argues accordingly: "The mystery is that *even the living will undergo transformation into a new form,* receiving their resurrection bodies without having to pass through death" (italics original).[27] This view places the emphasis on the living, whereas others advance a similar yet distinct view that the revealed mystery is the transformation of the living *and* the dead.[28] Perhaps we could frame the question in the following way: Does the revealed mystery refer to the new idea that living believers will be transformed into a resurrected existence without experiencing death, or is it that all will be transformed at the end?

In order for us to determine the precise content of the revealed mystery, we must remember the context. That transformation is stressed in the immediate context is apparent; however, Paul seems to nuance the revelation of the mystery in 1 Corinthians 15:51-52. After he declares, "I tell you a mystery," Paul

---

[27]Hays, *1 Corinthians*, p. 274; cf. Fee, *1 Corinthians*, p. 801; Carson, "Mystery and Fulfillment," p. 419; Kim, *Origin of Paul's Gospel,* 78; Bornkamm, "μυστήριον," p. 823; Markus Bockmuehl, *Revelation and Mystery in Ancient Judaism and Pauline Christianity,* WUNT 36 (Tübingen: Mohr Siebeck, 1990; repr., Grand Rapids: Eerdmans, 1997), p. 172.

[28]Joachim Jeremias, "Flesh and Blood Cannot Inherit the Kingdom of God (1 Cor 15:50)," *NT Studies* 2 (1955-56): 159; Brown, *Semitic Background,* 47; E.-B. Allo, *Première Épitre aux Corinthiens,* 2nd ed. (Paris: Gabalda, 1956), p. 432; Coppens, "'Mystery' in the Theology," p. 143.

immediately states a negative "we will not <u>all</u> sleep" along with the positive "but we shall <u>all</u> be changed."[29] The first use of "all" (*pantes*; v. 51a) refers to the "living" (obviously, only the living can die or "sleep"), whereas the "all" in the second clause (*pantes*; v. 51b) likely refers to both the living *and* the dead.[30] It is possible to understand the second "all" as referring to only the living; however, it seems preferable to include the living and the dead because of the wider and immediate context, where resurrection of the dead is clearly in mind (1 Cor 15:35-44, 55-56). Since 1 Corinthians 15:35, Paul has discussed at length the nature of earthly and heavenly bodies. So Paul advances the argument to the next level in 1 Corinthians 15:51, claiming that *everybody, both the living and the dead, will undergo a bodily transformation* (1 Cor 15:50: "flesh and blood cannot inherit the kingdom of God"). In addition, Paul's emphasis in 1 Corinthians 15:51-52 is not when but *how* the resurrection will take place. The somewhat chiastic form of this section is illuminating in this regard:

> Behold, I tell you a mystery
> > a We shall not all sleep,
> > > b but we shall all be <u>changed</u> (*allagēsometha*),
> > > > c in a moment, in the twinkling of an eye, at the last trumpet.
> > > c' for the trumpet will sound,
> > a' and the dead will be raised imperishable,
> > > b' and we shall be <u>changed</u> (*allagēsometha*).

The repetition of the verb "to be changed" highlights this theme. The first "change" refers to both the living and the dead (b), whereas the latter indicates the living (b').[31] We have come full circle to the problem posed in 1 Corinthians 15:50—"flesh and blood cannot inherit the kingdom of God"—so, the dead and the living will be transformed, in order to meet this demand. Therefore, *the revelation of the mystery solves the dilemma raised by Paul in 1 Corinthians 15:35, 50.* It does not narrowly refer to the transformation of the living, a situation that would only solve part of the problem, but the entire group of individuals, both the living and the dead.

First Corinthians 15:53 provides the basis for the revealed mystery in 1 Cor-

---

[29]See Gladd, *Revealing the Mysterion*, p. 251n90, for a discussion of the textual problems in 1 Cor 15:51-52.

[30]See Garland, *1 Corinthians*, p. 743.

[31]This line (b') probably only refers to the living, since only the dead are in view in the previous line (a').

inthians 15:51-52: the reason that believers must be transformed (1 Cor 15:51-52) is because "it is necessary that this perishable <u>must clothe itself</u> [*endyō*] with the imperishable and this mortal <u>must clothe itself</u> [*endyō*] with immortality" (our translation). This verse recalls the perishable and imperishable in the programmatic 1 Corinthians 15:50. Moreover, it explicitly describes further and explains the basis for the nature of the transformation of believers in 1 Corinthians 15:51-52: *the transformation—that is, the revealed mystery, is the appropriation of the last Adam's body by believers.* This is substantiated by 1 Corinthians 15:49: "Just as <u>we have borne</u> [or "worn," *ephoresamen*] the image of the earthly, we <u>will also bear</u> [or "wear," *phoresomen*] the image of the heavenly." These two verbs (*phoreō* and *endyō*) commonly refer to the wearing of clothes (as does 1 Cor 15:54, which also refers to "when the perishable <u>has been clothed</u> [*endyō*] with the imperishable, and the mortal *has been* <u>clothed</u> [*endyō*] with immortality"). Paul here views the transformation as putting on the garb of the "last Adam." First Corinthians 15:45-48 contrasts the two modes of existence— earthly and heavenly—and concludes that believers will be like the last Adam. The next verse then states more clearly what the previous verse has said: believers will bear the image of the heavenly Adam, just as Seth bore the image of his father, the first earthly Adam (1 Cor 15:49).[32] Though some commentators acknowledge the Old Testament background of Paul's language in 1 Corinthians 15:49-53, few draw out the implications.

Paul's view of clothing the body with Adamic garments. As we will see in excursus 5.2 at the end of this chapter, at least certain sectors of Judaism held two premises: (1) Adam was created in a glorious state and after the fall lost that glory, and (2) the righteous are to return to Adam's pre-fall state and therefore become like the original Adam. But does this picture fit Paul's view of Adam and the resurrection of believers? Is Paul advocating a return to the original, Adamic state? Those who have insisted that Paul is drawing on a Jewish, particularly apocalyptic, background stress that Paul is in agreement with contemporary and later Judaism. The problem with this commonly held view is that nowhere in Genesis is Adam clothed with *eschatological* garments. In addition, this interpretation does not take seriously enough the quotation of Genesis 2:7

---

[32]Note the allusion to Gen 5:3 in 1 Cor 15:49: Adam "became the father of a *son* [Seth] in his own likeness, according to his image"; see further Benjamin L. Gladd, "The Last Adam as the 'Life-Giving Spirit' Revisited: A Possible Old Testament Background of One of Paul's Most Perplexing Phrases," *WTJ* 71 (2009): 297-309.

in 1 Corinthians 15:45a: "So also it is written, 'The first MAN, Adam, BECAME A LIVING SOUL.'" First Corinthians 15:45b then says, "The last Adam *became* a life-giving spirit."

In 1 Corinthians 15:45, Paul regards the first Adam as "natural" (*psychikos*) and the last Adam as "spiritual" (*pneumatikos*). But what many fail to observe is that Paul's quote is from Genesis 2:7, a *pre-fall* text. The pre-fall Adam or the Adam ostensibly clothed with "garments of glory" is still reckoned as "natural," even though he had not yet sinned. Christ, on the other hand, has a *different* body of glory. This is precisely the point of 1 Corinthians 15:35-44 and, above all, of 1 Corinthians 15:45-49: Christ, the last Adam, differs from Adam; his new body is not a return to the pre-fall body but an entirely different body, recreated by the Spirit.[33]

Therefore, when Paul discusses the issue of transformation, he is not simply referring to the appropriation of the original Adamic garments but the transition into the body of the escalated last Adam (2 Cor 5:1-5; Phil 3:20-21; cf. 1 Jn 3:2). The implicit portrayal of having the old clothing of the former life stripped off and the more explicit reference to donning new clothing in 1 Corinthians 15:49-54 may well reflect a background of changing clothes in Genesis 3 itself. Genesis 3:7 says that directly after their sin Adam and Eve tried to cover their sinful nakedness by their own autonomous efforts: "they sewed fig leaves together and made themselves loin coverings." On the other hand, in an apparent expression of their beginning restoration to God after the fall (especially in light of Gen 3:20), Genesis 3:21 says, "and the LORD GOD made garments of skin for Adam and his wife, and clothed [*endyō*] them." The clear implication is that their first suit of clothes was taken off and replaced by divinely made clothing, indicating that the handmade clothing was associated with their alienated condition and sinful shame (Gen 3:7-11) and was an insufficient covering for those who have begun to be reconciled to God.[34] Paul may be using the Genesis 3 clothing language analogically, but perhaps he even uses it typologically, as we have seen he does with Genesis 2:7 above: at the consummation of the age, believers are seen to have discarded the clothes of the old fallen Adam and have

---

[33]See Andrew T. Lincoln, *Paradise Now and Not Yet: Studies in the Role of the Heavenly Dimension in Paul's Thought with Special Reference to His Eschatology* (Grand Rapids: Baker, 1991), pp. 51-52.

[34]That Adam's and Eve's "loin coverings" were not proper attire to wear in God's holy presence is clear from the fact that "they hid themselves from the presence of the Lord God" and still considered themselves "naked" (Gen 3:8-10); this view of the clothing in Gen 3:8 is also taken by *Sib. Or.* 1:47-49.

been clothed with the attire of the last Adam, with which Adam himself was proleptically clothed to indicate his restored relationship with God. Now the clothing represents the consummative restored relationship of the new humanity. As we have seen, this transformed consummative clothing is at the heart of the mystery in 1 Corinthians 15. Accordingly, part of the mystery may include Paul's typological understanding of the change of clothing narrated in Genesis 3.

Conclusion. We have discovered that Paul calls the transformation of believers both alive and dead a revealed mystery. We concluded that this transformation is the clothing of the believer's body (both the dead and those living at the very end of the age) with Christ's Adamic "clothes" or body. In 1 Corinthians 15:51-52, the revealed mystery is the transformation of believers from the natural body to the spiritual body and, according to 1 Corinthians 15:45, Christ is the one who transforms the body from one physical realm to another through the instrumentality of the Spirit.

But why would Paul call this a "mystery" that he is finally revealing? Is this revelation of the mystery a completely new revelation that cannot be found to any extent in the Old Testament? In the Old Testament, only a few passages explicitly speak of resurrection. Among these texts are Isaiah 26:19 and Daniel 12:2-3, which may subtly indicate transformation. After all, it can fairly easily be assumed that those who have died and whose bodies have decayed in the grave, will experience a transformation from the bodily decay to resurrection existence.

Nevertheless, the Old Testament does not *explicitly* teach a transformation of the body, so that this transformation may well be part of Paul's mystery in which he clarifies what was certainly implied. But what the Old Testament does not teach is that those *living and who have not died* at the very end of time, when the resurrection of the dead occurs, will also experience a bodily transformation into a new creational, resurrected being. Perhaps the rapture of Enoch and Elijah implied such a thing. And it would seem to make sense that those saints living at the time of the final resurrection of the dead would also need for their bodies to undergo an everlasting transformation fit for living in an eternal new creation. This Paul also brings out more clearly, so that it appears to be included in the revelation of the mystery. Neither does the Old Testament connect resurrection with the Adamic image of God, which we have seen is also part of Paul's mystery. But unlike the Old Testament, as we will see in excursus 5.2, many pockets of Judaism portray the resurrection as transformation—as a return to the pre-fall Adamic state. Paul differs even from his Jewish counterparts in that *he views the resurrection not as a return to Adam's pre-fall state but as a transformation into an escalated, eschatological Adamic condition*. The notion that the first Adam, in connection with other heightened blessings, would have experienced an escalated, latter-day blessing of such a transformation is hinted at in Genesis 1–3,[35] but now Paul makes this explicit. And Paul likely sees Adam's pre-fall condition in Genesis 2:7 (1 Cor 15:45a, "the first man, Adam, became a living soul") to be a typological foreshadowing of Jesus, the eschatological Adam, since this is how he unpacks 1 Corinthians 15:45a in 1 Corinthians 15:45b ("the last Adam *became* a life-giving spirit"). Likewise, part of the mystery may include Paul's typological understanding of the change of clothing narrated in Genesis 3. These typological uses are mysterious from the Old Testament perspective, since it was not clear that these Old Testament passages had a typological perspective.

To sum up, the following four aspects appear to be included in Paul's understanding of the mystery in 1 Corinthians 15:45-54, which were not clearly revealed in the Old Testament: (1) an end-time transformation of the body; (2) the consummative fulfillment of the Old Testament prophecies of the saints' resurrection identifies those resurrected saints as being transformed into the image of Adam, especially the escalated end-time image of the new Adam, the Messiah; (3) those *living* at the time of the resurrection of the dead will also experience a bodily transformation into a new creational resurrection life; (4) a typological understanding of Genesis 2:7 and of the narration of the clothing in Genesis 3. All four of these aspects of the mystery revolve around the conceptual notion of an unexpected transformation of the body.

Conclusion

In a community filled with factions, rivalry and competition, Paul delivers his remedy—the theology of the cross. If the Corinthians embrace the wisdom of the cross and adopt a cruciform lifestyle, then their divisions will cease. We concluded that the mystery in 1 Corinthians 2 is the paradoxical event of the crucifixion: at the moment of his death and defeat, Christ was, nevertheless, the sovereign "Lord of glory." That Israel's long-awaited glorious Messiah would

---

[35]On which see G. K. Beale, *A New Testament Biblical Theology: The Unfolding of the Old Testament in the New* (Grand Rapids: Baker Academic, 2011), pp. 39-46.

be crucified and put under a curse was generally hidden in the Old Testament.

The Corinthian believers were vying with one another by aligning with different leaders, which was an expression of worldly wisdom. First Corinthians 3:18-23 condemns those who conduct themselves according to the wisdom of "this age" (1 Cor 3:18) and instructs the community to not "boast in men" (1 Cor 3:21). On the other hand, 1 Corinthians 4:1-5 reveals how church leaders ought to live. Paul uses himself and Apollos as examples of what leaders ought to be: "stewards of mysteries" and "servants of Christ" (1 Cor 4:1). As a Danielic figure, the apostle's goal is to remain faithful to his role in mediating God's revelation of prophetic mysteries (1 Cor 4:2).

Even though Paul does not give any clues as to the content of the "mysteries" in 1 Corinthians 13:2; 14:2, we are still able to place both of these occurrences in the sphere of Old Testament and Jewish thought. The difficult expression "one who speaks in a tongue . . . speaks mysteries by the Spirit" (1 Cor 14:2) probably refers to an individual participating in angelic worship, similar to the situation at Qumran.

Apparently, some of the Corinthians could not grasp the mystery of the resurrection: God transforms individuals, both living and dead, through the resurrection from their old corruptible bodies to new-creational physical beings, bodies fashioned in the clothing of the image of the last Adam. Individuals will not return to the image of the first Adam, as Judaism had imagined, but will be transformed into the image of the "last Adam."

EXCURSUS 5.1: MESSIANIC EXPECTATIONS AND THE IDEA OF THE MESSIAH IN 1 CORINTHIANS 2:1-8

The Old Testament expectation of the latter-day Messiah. Scholars debate whether or not the Old Testament has much to say on this topic. Some opt for a minimal view that considers only a few texts to be explicitly messianic. Others, though, find a Messiah under every stone. The truth probably lies somewhere in between these two poles. A detailed survey of the Old Testament conception of the Messiah is beyond the scope of this project, so we will focus on primary sources and limit ourselves to the more explicit texts.[36] Moreover, we need to

---

[36]For more detailed discussions, consult Michael F. Bird, *Are You the One Who Is to Come? The Historical Jesus and the Messianic Question* (Grand Rapids: Baker Academic, 2009), pp. 31-62; John J. Collins, *The Scepter and the Star: The Messiahs of the Dead Sea Scrolls and Other Ancient Literature,* ABRL 10 (New York: Doubleday, 1995); N. T. Wright, *The New Testament and the People of God,* COQG 1 (Minneapolis: Fortress, 1992), pp. 307-20.

keep in mind that many of the following Old Testament texts are highly poetic and enigmatic, making it notoriously difficult to interpret them with great precision. Perhaps it may be best to speak of a messianic trajectory or "proto-messianism."[37] A chorus of Old Testament texts anticipates the coming Messiah; some texts sing louder than others, but all are unified by a common denominator—a figure will arrive in the "latter days," who will rule over Israel and bring about her restoration. To entertain only passages that explicitly mention "the Messiah" would be to commit the word-concept fallacy. It is entirely possible for an author to have a messianic or end-time kingly figure in mind but without using the term *Messiah*.

Genesis 3:15, though not explicitly "messianic," sets the stage for a development of messianic expectations, albeit in seed form (though some scholars dispute that this verse has anything to do with an eschatological figure who will defeat evil):

> And I will put enmity
> Between you and the woman,
> And between your seed and her seed;
> He shall bruise you on the head,
> And you shall bruise him on the heel.

One of the promises God makes to the primeval couple is that their descendants will form into two lines of progeny, a godly and an ungodly seed, and these two will continually wage war with one another. One of their descendants will eventually "bruise" or "crush" the head of the serpent (cf. Ps 91:13). In a highly poetic and stylized manner, the author promises that a mortal wound would be dealt to the serpent, the very embodiment of evil.

At the end of Genesis, Jacob blesses his twelve sons, and Judah receives a particular, special blessing:

> Judah, your brothers shall praise you;
> Your hand shall be on the neck of your enemies;
> Your father's sons shall bow down to you.
> Judah is a lion's whelp;
> From the prey, my son, you have gone up.
> He couches, he lies down as a lion,
> And as a lion, who dares rouse him up?
> The scepter shall not depart from Judah,

---

[37]Bird, *Are You the One?* p. 36.

Nor the ruler's staff from between his feet,
Until Shiloh comes,
And to him *shall be* the obedience of the peoples. (Gen 49:8-10; cf. 4Q252 V, 1-6)

According to this passage, in the "latter days" (Gen 49:1) a future ruler will descend from the tribe of Judah and conquer his (and Israel's) enemies. The result of this decisive victory is that the nations will pay obeisance to him (and Israel).

Numbers 24:17 is one of the more well-known texts. In it, a "star" is said to come from Jacob in the "latter days" (Num 24:14) that will "crush the foreheads of Moab"—a longtime enemy of Israel.

God covenants with David in 2 Samuel 7, wherein he promises to maintain a Davidic ruler in Jerusalem:

> When your days are complete and you lie down with your fathers, I will raise up
> your descendant after you, who will come forth from you, and I will establish his
> kingdom. He shall build a house for My name, and I will establish the throne of
> his kingdom forever. I will be a father to him and he will be a son to Me. (2 Sam
> 7:12-14; cf. 4Q174 1 I, 7-14)

God promises to "establish" the ruler's kingdom "forever," and this ruler will build God a temple or "house." The importance of 2 Samuel 7 cannot be overstated. Therein lies the genesis of an expectation of a Davidic figure who would one day rule over Israel and build God's glorious temple. The prophetic corpus is laced with references to the arrival of this Davidic ruler[38] and the restoration of Israel. Some of Israel's kings even serve as initial fulfillments of this Davidic promise.

Several psalms anticipate a Davidic ruler. Psalm 2:2, 6-7 (see also Ps 78; 132), for example, says,

> The rulers take counsel together
> Against the LORD and against His Anointed. . . .
>
> "But as for Me, I have installed My King
> Upon Zion, My holy mountain."
>
> "I will surely tell of the decree of the LORD:
> He said to Me, 'You are My Son,
> Today I have begotten You.'"

---

[38]E.g., Is 9:7; 16:5; Jer 22:4; Ezek 34:22-24; Hos 3:5; Mic 5:2; Amos 9:11; Hag 2:20-23; Zech 3:6-10;
4:1-14.

Of particular importance is Psalm 89. The psalmist recalls God's covenant to David throughout the psalm:

> I have made a covenant with My chosen;
> I have sworn to David My servant,
> "I will establish your seed forever
> And build up your throne to all generations." (Ps 89:3-4)

Later the psalmist goes on to say:

> But I [Yahweh] shall crush his adversaries before him,
> And strike those who hate him. . . .
>
> I also shall make him *My* firstborn,
> The highest of the kings of the earth. (Ps 89:23, 27)

Most likely these verses speak of the Davidic line, culminating in the establishment of *the* Davidic ruler, the Messiah. Psalm 110, though one of the most difficult psalms to interpret, anticipates not only a kingly Messiah but also a *priestly* one:

> The Lord [Yahweh] says to my Lord:
> "Sit at My right hand
> Until I make Your enemies a footstool for Your feet."
>
> The Lord has sworn and will not change His mind,
> "You are a priest forever
> According to the order of Melchizedek." (Ps 110:1, 4; cf. Heb 7:1-28)

The book of Isaiah, perhaps more than any other Old Testament book, prophesies of a latter-day ruler of Israel who will eliminate Israel's enemies and rule with righteousness and wisdom. Isaiah 11:1-5 describes this messianic figure, the "branch," in some detail:

> Then a shoot will spring from the stem of Jesse,
> And a branch from his roots will bear fruit. . . .
>
> But with righteousness He will judge the poor . . .
>
> And He will strike the earth with the rod of His mouth,
> And with the breath of His lips He will slay the wicked. (Is 11:1, 4-5; cf. Is 9:6-7)

Jeremiah 23:5 (cf. Jer 33:17-22) also refers to the same phenomenon using similar language:

I will raise up for David a righteous Branch;
And He will reign as king and act wisely
And do justice and righteousness in the land.

The messianic ruler in Isaiah 9:6-7; 11:1-5 probably should be identified with the Suffering Servant in the later portions of Isaiah. This Servant figure is the catalyst that brings about the release of Israel from Babylonian captivity and restores the righteous remnant (Is 42:1-9; 49:1-6; 50:4-9; 52:13–53:12). In the final song (Is 52:13–53:12), the Servant is prophesied to suffer for the sake of others:

He was despised and forsaken of men. . . .
Surely our griefs He Himself bore,
And our sorrows He carried. . . .
But He was pierced through for our transgressions,
He was crushed for our iniquities;
The chastening for our well-being *fell* upon Him,
And by His scourging we are healed.

His grave was assigned with wicked men,
Yet He was with a rich man in His death,
Because He had done no violence,
Nor was there any deceit in His mouth.

But the LORD was pleased
To crush Him, putting *Him* to grief;
If He would render Himself as a guilt offering,
He will see *His* offspring,
He will prolong *His* days,
And the good pleasure of the LORD will prosper in His hand. . . .
By His knowledge the Righteous One,
My Servant, will justify the many,
As He will bear their iniquities. (Is 53:3-5, 9-11)

This passage is fraught with difficulties—textual variants, the referent of the Servant (individual or corporate?) and the precise meaning of the highly stylized language. Nevertheless, at the very least, this passage was interpreted messianically in early Christianity (Mt 8:17; Lk 22:37; Acts 8:32; 1 Pet 2:22; *Sib. Or.* 8.257; *Ascen. Isa.* 4.21) and serves as part of the "messianic trajectory."

That the Messiah may suffer in some capacity is mentioned in one other passage. Daniel 9:25-26 seems to suggest that such a figure will be eventually put to death: "From the issuing of a decree to restore and rebuild Jerusalem until <u>Messiah</u> [*māšîaḥ*] the Prince *there will be* seven weeks and sixty-two weeks. . . . Then after the sixty-two weeks <u>the Messiah</u> [*māšîaḥ*] will be cut off and have nothing" (cf. also Zech 12:10). This passage is very difficult to interpret and leaves us more questions than answers. In any case, an "anointed one" will arrive on the scene after sixty-nine "sevens" or weeks and Jerusalem will be "rebuilt." Daniel 9:26 then states that after sixty-two "sevens" or weeks the anointed one "will be cut off and have nothing." Whether or not the passage concerns *the* latter-day messiah figure is difficult to determine. At the very least, a prominent Israelite leader (the "prince"?) will be put to death or "cut off." What tilts the scales in favor of a messianic interpretation is Daniel 9:24: "Seventy weeks have been decreed for your people and your holy city, to finish the transgression, to make an end of sin, to make atonement for iniquity, to bring in everlasting righteousness." The language of "bringing in everlasting righteousness" together with the "anointed one" in Daniel 9:25-26 recalls several messianic passages that have the identical theme in mind—the Messiah will usher in God's latter-day "righteousness" (Is 11:1-5; Jer 23:5; 33:15).

Many Old Testament passages speak clearly or at least hint at a coming messianic figure who will deliver Israel and redeem her from her plight. <u>The term *Messiah* (Heb *māšîaḥ;* Greek *christos*) means "anointed one." The verb "to anoint" (*māšaḥ*) connotes being set apart for a distinct purpose;</u> it occurs in various cultic contexts, such as the tabernacle and the altar (Ex 40:9-11). The term is also applied to individuals that are to be separated for a specific purpose—for example, Aaron (Lev 8:12), Saul (1 Sam 15:17) and David (2 Sam 12:7). The noun form is likewise applied to priests (Lev 4:3; 1 Sam 2:35) and kings (e.g., 1 Sam 24:6; 26:11), and to Cyrus, a pagan ruler (Is 45:1). The coming endtime king is actually called an "anointed one" or "Messiah" in <u>Psalm 2:2</u> (cf. Ps 2:7-9) and <u>Daniel 9:25-26</u> (cf. also 1 Sam 2:10).

In summary, according to the Old Testament, the Messiah refers above all to the coming "king of Israel." <u>The Lord promises to restore and reign over his people through his Messiah.</u> In 2 Samuel 7, God promised David that his descendants would rule over Israel. The Old Testament traces this promise and its fulfillment in the former and latter prophets. *The Messiah, a descendant of David, would be instrumental in bringing about the establishment of God's eternal kingdom and destruction of Israel's enemies.* That much is clear. Bound up with this phenomenon is the arrival of the new exodus, making possible forgiveness of sins, pouring out of the Spirit, the dawn of the new creation, and so on. Regarding the suffering aspect of the Messiah, a few passages seem to hint that the Messiah would suffer to some extent, but this suffering is not a cardinal aspect of his ministry. Messianic suffering is the means by which God will restore his people.[39]

It is against this Old Testament background that Paul's understanding of Jesus as a ruling, divine king in the midst of suffering in 1 Corinthians 2:1-8 expresses an unexpected fulfillment of the prophecies of the coming "Messiah."

Jewish expectation of the latter-day Messiah. Messianic expectations in early Judaism are notoriously difficult to synthesize, since the Jews at this time were greatly fragmented (e.g., Essenes, Pharisees, Sadducees, Zealots). Some groups were hotbeds of messianic fervor (e.g., Zealots), whereas others had minimal expectations in light of their political allegiance (e.g., Sadducees). Simply put, what is true for one group need not be true for the others. For our purposes, we need not discuss the full range of expectations or even attempt a full-blown synthesis; instead, we will survey several texts from a variety of pockets of Judaism and offer some initial conclusions.

Perhaps the lengthiest and most detailed account of the Messiah stems from *Psalms of Solomon* 17.21-46, a text that probably dates to the first century A.D.:

> See, Lord, and raise up for them their king, the son of David, to rule over your servant Israel. . . . Undergird him with the strength to destroy the unrighteous rulers, to purge Jerusalem from gentiles. . . . To shatter all their [the sinners] substance with an iron rod; to destroy the unlawful nations with the word of his mouth. (*Pss. Sol.* 17.21-22, 24)

Here the Messiah "purges" Israel from idolatrous contamination that was a result of Gentile occupation and practices (*Pss. Sol.* 17.11-15), and he will even-

---

[39]Recall that the New Testament writers express a clear understanding that the Old Testament conceives of a suffering messiah: e.g., see Lk 24:25-27: "And he [Jesus] said to them, 'O foolish men and slow of heart to believe in all that the prophets have spoken! Was it not necessary for the Christ to suffer these things and to enter into his glory?' Then beginning with Moses and with all the prophets, he explained to them the things concerning himself in all the Scriptures" (cf. Jn 5:39-47). 1 Cor 15:3-4 likewise affirms that the Old Testament anticipated a suffering messiah: "For I delivered to you as of first importance what I also received, that Christ died for our sins according to the Scriptures, and that he was buried, and that he was raised on the third day according to the Scriptures." Likewise, 1 Pet 1:10-11 says, "As to this salvation, the prophets who prophesied of the grace that would come to you made careful searches and inquiries, seeking to know what person or time the Spirit of Christ within them was indicating as he predicted the sufferings of Christ and the glories to follow."

tually annihilate the pagans or "sinners." Several verses later, the author(s) of the *Psalms of Solomon* predicts that the Messiah will be instrumental in the restoration of Israel by bringing the exiled Israelites back to Palestine: "He will gather a holy people . . . he will distribute them [the Israelites] upon the land according to their tribes" (*Pss. Sol.* 17.26-28). Once Israel is restored to her Promised Land, the Gentiles will subsequently convert to Judaism and be placed in a subservient role: "He [the Messiah] will have gentile nations serving him under his yoke. . . . Nations . . . [will] come from the ends of the earth to see his glory, to bring as gifts her children who had been driven out . . . their [the nations'] king shall be <u>the Lord Messiah</u>" (*Pss. Sol.* 17.30-32; cf. 18.7).

Second Baruch 30.1-5a (second century A.D.) associates the coming of the Messiah at the "end of times" with the resurrection of the righteous: "It will happen after these things when the time of the appearance of the Anointed One has been fulfilled and he returns with glory, that then all who sleep in hope of him will rise" (*2 Bar.* 30.1). Several chapters later the Messiah is prophesied to arrive when the "fourth kingdom" (Rome?) begins to decline: "It will happen when the time of its fulfillment is approaching in which it [the fourth kingdom] will fall, that at that time the dominion of my Anointed One . . . will be revealed" (*2 Bar.* 39.7). A few verses later, the Messiah will "convict him [the ruler of the fourth kingdom] of all his wicked deeds and will assemble and set before him all the works of his hosts. And after these things he will kill him" (*2 Bar.* 40.1-2).

Augmenting the Messiah's kingly rule, the *Testament of Levi* 18.2-9 (second century B.C.) paints the Messiah in prophetic and priestly colors.

> Then the Lord will raise up a new priest to whom all the words of the Lord will be revealed. . . . And his star shall rise in heaven like a king; kindling the light of knowledge as day is illumined by the sun. . . . In his priesthood the nations shall be multiplied in knowledge on the earth, and they shall be illumined by the grace of the Lord. (*T. Lev.* 18:2-3, 9)

The Messiah, according to the *Testament of Levi*, will function as a "priest," and part of the Messiah's priestly duties is to mediate knowledge to Israel and the nations.

Several documents at Qumran likewise highlight the Messiah's priestly role. For example, the Damascus Document (CD-A XII, 23) refers to "those who walk in them [Qumran's regulations], in the time of wickedness until there arises the ‹Messiah› of Aaron." Though scarcely any details are given concerning the Messiah, he is tied so closely to the priestly character Aaron that he is described as "the Messiah of Aaron." These passages and others like them (CD-B XIX, 10; XX, 1) suggest that Qumran expected two messiahs—a descendant of Aaron and a descendant of David. [40]

Of particular note is one of the Qumran commentaries, 4QIsaiah Pesher[a] (4Q161),[41] wherein Isaiah 11:1-5 is interpreted messianically:

> [The interpretation of the word concerns the shoot] of David which will sprout in the fi[nal days, since] [with the breath of his lips he will execute] his [ene]my and God will support him with [the spirit of c]ourage [. . .] [. . . thro]ne of glory, h[oly] crown and multi-colour[ed] vestments [. . .] in his hand. He will rule over all the pe[ople]s and Magog [. . .] his sword will judge [al]l the peoples. (4Q161 8-10 III, 18-22)

Though this passage is filled with textual gaps and some particulars elude us, it is evident that the Messiah will arrive on the scene in the "final days" and will overpower the wicked. God will support the Messiah in this mission. The Messiah will then be rewarded with a "throne of glory," a "crown" and special garments.

By no means have we given a detailed analysis of messianic expectations,[42] but the texts we have surveyed agree, more or less, with one another: not only the Old Testament but also early Judaism expected a coming Messiah to rule over Israel and judge the nations. That, generally speaking, is the common denominator. A few texts hint at a Messiah suffering (Is 52:13–53:12; Dan 9:25-26), but what must be kept in mind is that suffering is not what is emphasized in the Old Testament nor especially in Judaism. This Jewish background (which develops Old Testament expectations) underscores the Old Testament expectations of the Messiah, which further shows that Paul's understanding of Jesus in 1 Corinthians 2:1-8 expresses an unexpected fulfillment of the prophecies of the coming "Messiah."

EXCURSUS 5.2: ESCHATOLOGICAL TRANSFORMATION IN EARLY JUDAISM

Apocalyptic literature contains the most explicit references to the transfor-

---

[40]The Damascus Document (CD) dates approximately from the first century B.C. to the first century A.D.

[41]The Isaiah Pesher dates to the first century B.C.

[42]E.g., see also *4 Ezra* 12–13.

mation of the body. Like Paul in 1 Corinthians 15:50-54, these texts typically describe transformation as clothing the body with heavenly garments:

> The righteous and elect ones shall rise from the earth and shall cease being of downcast face. They shall wear the garments of glory. These garments of yours shall become the garments of life from the Lord of the Spirits. Neither shall your garments wear out. (*1 En.* 62.15-16)

> And the Lord said to Michael, "Go, and extract Enoch from [his] earthly clothing. And anoint him with my delightful oil, and put him into clothes of my glory." And so Michael did, just as the Lord had said to him . . . and I had become like one of his glorious ones, and there was no observable difference. (*2 En.* 22.8-10 [J]; cf. *2 Bar.* 51.3-10; *Apoc. Ab.* 13.14)

> And there I saw Enoch and all who (were) with him, stripped of (their) robes of the flesh; and I saw them in their robes of above, and they were like the angels who stand there in great glory. (*Ascen. Isa.* 9.9-10; cf. 4.16; 8.14-15; 9.17)

Even though some of these sources are later than the first century A.D. (e.g., *2 En.*, *Ascen. Isa.*), they nevertheless indicate the importance of this clothing theme. These apocalyptic texts clearly indicate that righteous individuals will be clothed with heavenly garments. The first text, *1 Enoch* 62.15 (second to first century B.C.), labels these clothes "garments of glory." In *2 Baruch* 51.3-10 and the *Ascension of Isaiah* 8.14-15; 9.9-10, the righteous are transformed "into the splendor of angels" (*2 Bar.* 51.5)[43] and become "equal to the angels" (*Ascen. Isa.* 8.15).

Genesis 3:21 may have stimulated the Jewish writers' emphasis on garments (as we saw earlier may likewise have influenced Paul in 1 Cor 15:49-54): "The LORD God made garments of skin for Adam and his wife, and clothed them". Early Judaism and even the rabbis speculated about Adam and Eve's garments. They claimed that Adam was first created in an exalted position, but, as a result of the fall, he was stripped of his glorious "robe." The *Life of Adam and Eve* (*Apocalypse*) is explicit: "And at that very moment my eyes were opened and I knew that I was naked of the righteousness with which I had been clothed. And I wept saying, 'Why have you done this to me, that I have been estranged from my glory with which I was clothed?'" (20.1-2).[44]

---

[43]*Second Baruch* dates approximately to the second century A.D., and the *Martyrdom and Ascension of Isaiah* from the second century B.C. to the fourth century A.D., the latter of which is a Christian document.

[44]Cf. *2 Bar.* 4:3; cf. 56:5–59:12; *Apoc. Adam* 1:2, 4-5; 13:14; *3 Bar.* 4:16 [Greek].

Here, Eve recounts the fall and the loss of "glory." A natural corollary to this concept is that the righteous will return to the pre-fall Adamic state, when God will clothe them with the original Adamic garb. Some Qumran texts appear to develop the Jewish notion that God will restore individuals to the original state of Adam:

> You [protect] the ones who serve you loyally, [so that] their posterity is before you all the days. You have raised an [eternal] name, [forgiving] offence, casting away all their iniquities, giving them as a legacy all the glory of Adam [and] abundance of days. (1QHᵃ IV, 14-15)

> He will sprinkle over him the spirit of truth . . . to make [them] understand the wisdom of the sons of heaven to those of perfect behavior. For those God has chosen for an everlasting covenant and to them shall belong all the glory of Adam. . . . For God has sorted them into equal parts until the appointed end and the new creation. (1QS IV, 21-25; cf. 4Q171 III 1 1-2; CD-A III, 19-20)

The Qumran community held that the righteous and faithful would obtain "all the glory of Adam." Apparently, they, like other sectors of Judaism, held a high view of Adam and the necessity of a return for saints to the pre-fall state.

6

THE USE OF *MYSTERY*
IN EPHESIANS

◆ ▣ ◆

OUR CHAPTER ON 1 CORINTHIANS LARGELY ENTAILED Paul's teaching
on the nature of the cross and Jesus' kingship (1 Cor 1–2). The Old Testament
and Jewish conception of the Messiah generally entails him ruling over Israel
and the nations as king. The Messiah, a descendant of David, would be instrumental in bringing about the establishment of God's eternal kingdom and the
destruction of Israel's enemies. A few passages appear to suggest that the
Messiah would suffer to some extent, and this suffering would be the means by
which God would restore his people. Paul, though, portrays Jesus as executing
his divine messianic prerogative at the moment of his suffering a painful death
on the cross. It was largely hidden in the Old Testament that the Messiah's reign
would be characterized by suffering and death. But the Old Testament does
bring together, in seed form, the twin themes of suffering and kingly rule (e.g.,
David's rule while in exile, Isaiah's Servant). We also noted Paul's discussion of
the believers' resurrection, and how the bodily transformation from the image
of the first Adam to the last Adam constituted an unveiled mystery, since the
Old Testament did not reveal clearly that the final resurrection would be a
transformation of not only dead but of living bodies into the image of an escalated eschatological Adam, the Messiah. Likewise, part of this mystery was that
Genesis 2:7 and Genesis 3 contained a typological perspective.

With an epistle that weaves mystery into the very fabric of its theology and
flow of thought, it is no wonder that Ephesians has garnered so much attention
from those seeking to discover the significance of mystery. The term *mystery*
occurs six times in the book, at crucial junctures (Eph 1:9; 3:3-4, 9; 5:32; 6:19).

The letter to the Ephesians answers one of the most perplexing questions in the establishment of the early, largely Gentile church: are the Gentiles, who have joined themselves to Jesus and thus to the end-time people of God, required to obey the Israelite commandments that demarcated the nation of Israel from the surrounding nations? For example, do the Gentiles in the latter days have to maintain the Israelite dietary regulations? What about circumcision?

COSMIC MYSTERY IN EPHESIANS 1[1]

Commentators have suggested rightly that mystery in Ephesians largely concerns the theme of unity, moving from the general to the specific.[2] Peter T. O'Brien is probably on the right track when he argues, "Christ is the starting point for a true understanding of the mystery in this letter, as elsewhere in Paul. There are not a number of 'mysteries' with limited applications, but one supreme 'mystery' with a number of applications."[3] Moving from broad to specific, Paul casts his net wide in Ephesians 1 and then tightens it as he progresses through the letter. The disclosed mystery in Ephesians 1 encapsulates the summation and unification of all things under the sovereign hand of Christ. Paul then gives a concrete example of such unification in Ephesians 3: the equality and unity between Jews and Gentiles in Christ. Ephesians 5 presents a further example of unity about which Paul received special insight—the union between Christ and the church mirrors the union between a husband and a wife (Eph 5:31-32). Finally, the last occurrence of *mystery* probably returns to the more general message of the gospel. In almost every case, *mystery* in Ephesians is directly linked to references to the Old Testament.

The Gospels clearly portray Jesus as the long-awaited Messiah who has come to restore Israel and conquer her inimical enemy Satan. It is not until Paul's letters that we learn about Christ functioning explicitly as a *cosmic* ruler. Scholars debate the idea of the "cosmic Christ," particularly how it relates to Gnostic myths. Gnostic sources, however, are later than the first century, so that it is not evident that Gnostic ideas would have been present in the first century,

---

[1]This project assumes Pauline authorship of the disputed letters (Ephesians, Colossians, 2 Thessalonians, and the Pastorals), since we do not find the arguments against Pauline authorship persuasive.
[2]Gregory W. Dawes, *The Body in Question: Metaphor and Meaning in the Interpretation of Ephesians 5:21-33*, Chrys Caragounis, *The Ephesian* Mysterion: *Meaning and Content*, ConBNT 8 (Lund: Gleerup, 1977), p. 118; Andrew T. Lincoln, *Ephesians*, WBC 42 (Waco, TX: Word, 1990), p. 35.
[3]Peter T. O'Brien, *Letter to the Ephesians*, PNTC (Grand Rapids: Eerdmans, 1999), p. 110.

at least in the form in which they appear later. Such studies are also misguided by failing to recognize that Paul's conception of the cosmic Christ is deeply rooted most of all in the Old Testament, and Paul even claims that Christ's role as cosmic ruler is a revealed "mystery." That is, it was not fully revealed in the Old Testament that the Messiah would become king over the cosmos, not only earth but also the heavens. Ephesians 1, as we will see, sets forth more clearly the scope, manner and result of Christ's cosmic rule.

Since we will be interacting with Ephesians 1:3-14, we will quote it at length:

> Blessed *be* the God and Father of our Lord Jesus Christ, who has blessed us with every spiritual blessing in the heavenly *places* in Christ, just as He chose us in Him before the foundation of the world, that we would be holy and blameless before Him. In love He predestined us to adoption as sons through Jesus Christ to Himself, according to the kind intention of His will, to the praise of the glory of His grace, which He freely bestowed on us in the Beloved. In Him we have redemption through His blood, the forgiveness of our trespasses, according to the riches of His grace which He lavished on us. In all wisdom and insight He made known to us the mystery of His will, according to His kind intention which He purposed in Him with a view to an administration suitable to the fullness of the times, *that is,* the summing up of all things in Christ, things in the heavens and things on the earth. In Him also we have obtained an inheritance, having been predestined according to His purpose who works all things after the counsel of His will, to the end that we who were the first to hope in Christ would be to the praise of His glory. In Him, you also, after listening to the message of truth, the gospel of your salvation—having also believed, you were sealed in Him with the Holy Spirit of promise, who is given as a pledge of our inheritance, with a view to the redemption of *God's own* possession, to the praise of His glory.

Content of the "mystery of His will." In order for us to determine the content of the mystery in Ephesians 1, we must first untangle Ephesians 1:8-10 and briefly discuss the logical flow of Paul's argument. The prepositional phrase "in all wisdom and insight" (Eph 1:8b) describes how God revealed the mystery. Similarly, the next two prepositional phrases "according to His kind intention which he purposed in Him" and "with a view to an administration suitable to the fullness of the times" also relate *how* God revealed the mystery. The former phrase probably indicates more specifically that the basis of God's revealing of the mystery lies in his own "kind intention," and the latter clause shows the purpose for which God set forth the mystery, giving us a fuller understanding of the mystery itself. The mystery has to do with Christ overseeing a "household management" (or "administration," *oikonomia*)[4] of the "fullness of the times" that refers to the latter days (Eph 1:10a).

Ephesians 1:10 further explains the previous phrase "for a household management" with the phrase, "that is, the summing up of all things in Christ, things in the heavens and things on the earth" (cf. the punctuation of the ESV, RSV, TNIV). The infinitive "summing up" (*anakephalaiōsasthai*) here should be understood as further explaining the previous noun, "household management" (or "administration"), which ultimately is a further explanation of the "mystery." In other words, Paul tells us what part of the revealed mystery is (!) "a household management—the summing up of all things in Christ, things in the heavens and things on the earth."

The expression "summing up" (*anakephalaiōsasthai*) here could also be defined as to "head up," to "restore" or to "unify."[5] "All things" are brought together or "summarized" in Christ. Perhaps a better way of translating this difficult expression is the rendering of the NIV: "to bring unity to all things in heaven and on earth under Christ." Lincoln observes, "1:10 then refers to the summing up and bringing together of the diverse elements of the cosmos in Christ as the focal point."[6] If the content of the mystery includes the unification of "all things" in Christ, then what does this mean precisely?

At this point we can say that Christ came to restore (or reconcile) a lost unity and harmony between heaven and earth, which had been plunged into disintegration because of sin. This is in line with the key parallel of Colossians 1:20-22, which affirms this very notion:

And through Him to reconcile all things to Himself, having made peace through

---

[4]The word *oikonomia* can be translated as "administration" or "household management." The word *oikonomos* was typically used in classical and Hellenistic Greek for a *steward* who manages the affairs of a household for the owner, so that *oikonomia* described the task of what the "household manager" did. Sometimes the "household manager" was a slave (the rabbis sometimes referred to a person who performed such a task conceptually as "a son of the house"), which was virtually equivalent to the *oikonomos*. The Gospels express this concept by referring to a servant over his master's house as a "slave" (see Mt 24:45, where *doulos* occurs; cf. also Joseph in *T. Jos.* 12). In the Greek Old Testament *oikonomos* refers to the manager of the affairs of "the household" of the king (e.g. Is 36:3, 22; 37:2).

[5]It seems that a consensus has emerged among commentators to define the verb *anakephalaiōsasthai* in this manner. See, for example, O'Brien, *Ephesians*, p. 111; Lincoln, *Ephesians*, pp. 32-33; Martin Kitchen, "The *anakephalaiōsis* of All Things in Christ" (PhD diss., University of Manchester, 1988).

[6]*Lincoln, Ephesians*, p. 33; cf. Markus Bockmuehl, *Revelation and Mystery in Ancient Judaism and Pauline Christianity*, WUNT 36 (Tübingen: Mohr Siebeck, 1990; repr., Grand Rapids: Eerdmans, 1997), p. 199.

the blood of His cross; through Him, *I say,* whether things on earth or things in heaven. And although you were formerly alienated and hostile in mind, *engaged* in evil deeds, yet He has now reconciled you in His fleshly body through death.

God's cosmic household had fallen into disorder and became wrecked and fragmented. Christ came as a household manager to put God's cosmic household back into order. *The main focus of the revelation of the mystery is that Christ is the point of reintegration and restoration of the original cosmic unity and harmony that had been lost at the fall of humanity, a fragmentation that had affected not only earthly but also the heavenly realm.* Hence, the notion of *anakephalaioō* is "to regather all things together under one head," so that Christ can rearrange them and put them back together again in their original order. All the affairs of the cosmic household are put under Christ's authorial head to reorder them.

As we will see, mystery here, in the context, consists of three organically related components essential to Christ's "regathering all things" under himself: (1) the scope of Christ's rule, (2) the instrumentation of Christ's rule and (3) the result of Christ's rule. Fortunately, Paul further unpacks Ephesians 1:8b-10 later on in the chapter, giving us more insight into Christ's work in "unifying all things in heaven and on earth":

> which [God's might] He brought about in Christ, when He raised Him from the dead and seated Him at His right hand in the heavenly *places,* far above all rule and authority and power and dominion, and every name that is named, not only in this age but also in the one to come. And He put all things in subjection under His feet, and gave Him as head over all things to the church, which is His body, the fullness of Him who fills all in all. (Eph 1:20-23)

The scope of Christ's rule. Ephesians 1:20-23 describes in greater detail the mystery in Ephesians 1:9-10 of the reunification of all things in heaven and earth under Christ. That Christ as "head" (*kephalē*) over all things on earth and "in the heavenlies" in Eph 1:20-23 probably expands on Christ as "heading up" (*anakephalaiōsasthai*) "all things . . . in the heavens and on the earth" in Eph 1:10. Therefore, we will spend some time explaining Paul's description of Christ in Ephesians 1:20-23, since it expands on the mystery in Ephesians 1:9-10. The first christological thread that we will develop is the extent of Christ's rule. As we have already seen in the previous chapter, one of the core elements of the coming Messiah is his role to rule over Israel and the surrounding nations. We have already concluded in the previous chapter that, according to the Old Testament and early Judaism, the Messiah was to come and defeat Israel's enemies in the "latter days," resulting in the new creation and the reconciliation of the pagan nations to the Lord (see excursus 5.1).

Here in Ephesians 1 the messianic rule also develops Old Testament and Jewish expectations: *Christ rules over the cosmos.* Paul states that Christ, literally, the "Messiah," unifies or sums up "all things . . . things in the heavens and things on the earth" (Eph 1:10). The phrase "all things" is explained as "things in the heavens and things on the earth."[7] This notion is further explained in Ephesians 1:20-22 but with the explicit language of Christ "ruling": "[God] seated Him [Christ] at His right hand in the heavenly *places,* far above all rule and authority and power and dominion . . . not only in this age but also in the one to come. And He put all things in subjection under His feet, and gave Him as head over all things" (note the underlined verbal parallels between 1:10 and 1:20-22). As most commentators agree, Christ is described here as reigning over not only earthly rulers but also cosmic heavenly authorities. These two texts and others like them make it exceptionally clear that *Christ executes his messianic prerogative as cosmic ruler—that is, ruler not only over the earth but also the heavens* (cf. Acts 2:32-35; 1 Cor 15:25-28, which focus on Christ's earthly rule; cf. Phil 2:9-11; Col 1:15-18; Rev 1:5-18, which include Christ's rule over both earth and the heavenly realms).

In sum, part of the divulged mystery in Ephesians 1:9 is the scope of the Messiah's rule. The Old Testament and early Judaism expected the coming Messiah to mediate God's reign *on the earth* and bring the pagan nations *on earth* under subjection. But Christ's coming, rule and exaltation to the right hand of the Father signaled Christ's reign not only over earthly rulers but also over inimical spiritual rulers in the heavenly regions. The scope of Christ's earthly and heavenly reign develops Old Testament and Jewish texts.[8] This is not to say that Christ's cosmic rule even over the heavenly realm is not without an Old Testament precursor. Clearly God rules over the cosmos, as many Old Testament texts demonstrate (e.g., Gen 2:4; 14:21; Deut 10:14). The New Testament squarely places Christ ruling alongside of the Lord. He rules just as his Father rules (Eph

---

[7]Caragounis, *Ephesian* Mysterion, pp. 143-46, posits that the book of Ephesians largely concerns the reconciliation or the "summing up" of two main groups—heavenly powers ("things in heaven") and the church ("things on the earth").

[8]Cf. Caragounis, *Ephesian* Mysterion, p. 117; Bockmuehl, *Revelation and Mystery*, p. 200; H. Krämer, "μυστήριον," *EDNT* 2:448; Raymond Brown, *The Semitic Background of the Term "Mystery" in the New Testament, BS* 21 (Philadelphia: Fortress, 1968), pp. 59-64.

1:20; Phil 2:9-11; Col 3:1). Christ's divine identity therefore must entail an earthly and heavenly sovereignty. Thus, in seed form, the Old Testament indeed anticipates the future cosmic reign of Christ precisely in its depiction of the Lord ruling over the same realm, and the New Testament clarifies this.[9]

That Ephesians is making explicit the Old Testament concept of the Messiah's reign even over heaven is further apparent from Ephesians 1:22, where Christ is viewed as ruler over heaven and earth, in elaboration of Ephesians 1:9-11. "[God] seated Him . . . far above all rule and authority and power and dominion . . . And He put all things in subjection under His feet, and gave Him as head over all things to the church" (Eph 1:21-22). In this vein, the first part of Ephesians 1:21 alludes to Daniel 7:14, 27 (see table 6.1).[10] These two texts agree both on a linguistic and conceptual level. First of all, while "rulers and authorities" might at first glance seem to be common wording found in many places elsewhere in Scripture, the word combination of *dominion* (*exousia*) and *rule* (*archē*) occurs in the Old Testament *only* in Daniel 7:14, 27.[11] To enhance this uniqueness "all rule" (*archēn pasōn*) and "all authorities" (*pasai hai exousiai*) are found in the Old Testament only in Daniel 7:27 (OG), as in Ephesians 1:21. In addition, note the common use of the notion of "heaven," though in Daniel 7:27 (Old Greek), the saints are given rule "under heaven" and in Ephesians 1:20-21 Christ rules "in the heavenlies." Christ's rule in the heavenlies may well have its closest precedent in Daniel 7:13, where the Son of Man is prophetically portrayed as "coming on the clouds of heaven [*ouranou*]" and receiving authority *in heaven* before "the Ancient of Days" to rule over the entire world, as elaborated in Daniel 7:13-14:

> With the clouds of heaven,
> One like a Son of Man was coming . . .
> And to Him was given dominion,
> Glory and a kingdom,
> That all the peoples, nations and *men of every* language
> Might serve Him. (MT)[12]

---

[9]In the Old Greek of Dan 7:13, the "Son of Man" is identified with God: "a son of man was coming on the clouds of heaven, and he came as the Ancient of Days." This is relevant, since we will see directly below that allusion to the scope of the Son of Man's rule from Dan 7:14 is made in Eph 1:21.

[10]Caragounis, *Ephesian* Mysterion, p. 126, also sees an allusion here to Dan 7:14 (cf. pp. 157-61).

[11]This combination does occur one other time in Prov 17:14, but "rule" there does not refer to "ruling powers" but to something that precedes something else: "sedition and strife *precede* want." Thus, the idea in Proverbs is completely different than in Dan 7.

[12]See R. T. France, *Jesus and the Old Testament* (Grand Rapids: Baker, 1982), p. 169, following T. W.

Table 6.1

Daniel 7:14, 27	Ephesians 1:20-21
7:14 (Theodotion): "And to him [the son of man] was given the rule [*hē archē*]. . . . His authority is an everlasting authority [*hē exousia autou exousia aiōnios*], which will not pass away, and his kingship will not be destroyed."	"[God] seated him [Christ] . . . in the heavenlies [*epouraniois*] far above all rule and authority [*pasēs archēs kai exousias*] and power and dominion, and every name that is named, not only in this age but also in the one to come."
7:27 (Old Greek): "And the kingdom and the authority [*exousian*] and the magnitude of all their kingdoms and of all rule [*archēn pasōn*] of the kingdoms, which are under heaven [*ouranon*], he [God] shall give to the holy people of the Most High, to reign over an everlasting kingdom, and all authorities [*pasai hai exousiai*] will be subjected to him and obey him until the conclusion of the world" (so likewise Dan 7:27 in Theodotion)	

While the focus in Daniel 7:13-14 is on a universal *earthly* rule, the use of *heaven* in Daniel 7:13, 27 (see above) and the mention of an evil heavenly "ruler" (*ho archōn*) of Persia (and of Greece, Dan 10:20)[13] and a good heavenly "ruler" (*archōn*) in Daniel 10:13 hint that this rule extends to the heavenly regions. In particular, that the rule of the "Son of Man" in Daniel 7:13-14 includes a future rule even over the heavenly regions is apparent from Daniel 10:13, 16-21, where a "Son of Man" (Dan 10:16 Theod.) gives revelation to Daniel that includes the "Son of Man" together with the angel Michael *presently* "fighting against the [heavenly] ruler of the Persians . . . and the [heavenly] ruler of the Greeks." In this respect, how could the "Son of Man" rule over the earthly realm of Persia and Greece in his future end-time universal earthly rule (so Dan 7:13-14), if this did not also mean that he would rule over the evil heavenly angelic counterparts and representatives of these earthly nations? That, in fact, the "Son of Man" in past history had already begun to rule victoriously over these evil heavenly forces points to his consummative eschatological rule over such forces. These are significant clues that point in the Old Testament itself to the coming Messiah's rule in both *earth and heaven,* which Christ is seen as fulfilling in Ephesians 1:9-10, 21-22.

One more consideration suggests that the Old Testament hinted at the

---

Manson, for the notion that the Son of Man is portrayed in Dan 7:13 as coming to the heavenly sphere to receive his authority from God.

[13]Though *archōn* is not used of "the prince of Greece" in Dan 10:20.

coming end-time king's rule over both earth and heaven. Since Adam should have ruled over the satanic serpent in Eden, but did not, the last Adam has come to do just that. This is consistent with Ephesians 1:22, where Psalm 8:5 is quoted ("he subjected all things under his feet"). This is one of the clearest ideal-Adam psalms in all of the Old Testament. It is also likely not coincidental that Psalm 8:2 speaks of strength coming from human weakness in order "to make the enemy and the revengeful cease." Psalm 8:2 likely is to be linked to part of the way the ideal, eschatological Adam rules in Psalm 8:5-8, which is a cosmic rule, alluding back to Genesis 1:26, 28.

If this connection between Psalm 8:2 and Psalm 8:5-8 and its Genesis 1 background is correct, then the serpent should likely be included among the enemies mentioned in Psalm 8:2, since he is the only enemy present in all of Genesis 1–3 whom Adam should have overcome.[14] Thus, Christ's cosmic rule over all evil powers, which dwell in heaven and are at work on earth, is partially found in the Old Testament but made clearer and more detailed in the New Testament.

Therefore, in light of the above, the disclosed mystery that Christ is regathering *all things in heaven and on earth* and setting them rightly in order under himself (Eph 1:10) is only hinted at in the Old Testament but clarified significantly in the New. This is part of the content of the mystery.

The instrumentation of Christ's rule. The means of Christ's Adamic rule and unification of all things under himself is through his death (Eph 1:7) and resurrection (Eph 1:20), and is likely included also as part of the revelation of the mystery. In Ephesians 1:9-10, Paul does not disclose how Christ achieved his victory, only that he is currently sovereign over "all things" in reordering them. But in Ephesians 1:19-20, the apostle indicates part of the way in which Christ

---

[14]The allusion to Dan 7 in Eph 1:21-22 noted in the directly preceding section is further confirmed by the quotation of Ps 8:7 (LXX) in Eph 1:22. The Adamic figure of Ps 8 (see Gen 1:27-28) conceptually stands behind the Son of Man figure in Dan 7, which develops the Gen 1:28 reiterations throughout the Old Testament, most prominently that of Ps 8:4-8. See G. K. Beale, *A Biblical Theology of the New Testament: The Unfolding of the Old Testament in the New* (Grand Rapids: Baker Academic, 2011), pp. 83-84. G. B. Caird concurs in his discussion of Dan 7: "In the judgment process whereby power passes to the Son of Man lies the fulfillment of the vision of human destiny in the eighth psalm, whereby the human race, humbled for a season, is to inherit glory and honour, with even the beasts subject to human authority. Thus Daniel 7 perserves the earliest known biblical midrash of Psalm 8." He then footnotes this statement with the following: "Here the backward progression would be Dan. 7 → Ps. 8:6 → Gen. 1:26." See G. B. Caird, *New Testament Theology*, ed. L. D. Hurst; Oxford: Clarendon: 1995), 378n57. Therefore, Paul may cite Ps 8 in Eph 1:22 to signal the fulfillment of the Adamic figure's (i.e., the "son of man" in Ps. 8:4) role of subjugating all of creation, which reinforces the Son of Man's role in ruling over all of creation.

fulfilled his messianic prerogative: "his [God's] mighty strength, which he ex-
erted in Christ <u>when he raised him from the dead</u> and seated him at his right
hand in the heavenly realms" (NIV). Note also the explicit mentioning of
Christ's death in Ephesians 1:7 that immediately precedes the "mystery": "In
Him we have <u>redemption through His blood</u>, the forgiveness of our trespasses."

We have already discussed this theme in some detail in the previous chapter, so
we will only briefly rehearse our conclusions. That the Messiah would suffer is
anticipated in the Old Testament and early Judaism, but suffering and death are
not *central* to his ministry. A few messianic texts speak of a messianic figure suffering in order to achieve Israel's restoration (cf. Is 53, in the context of Is 40–56;
Dan 9:26; Zech 13:7). Yet in the Gospels Jesus claims that suffering and death
occupy a cardinal role and are indicative of his messiahship and the end-time
kingdom (e.g., Mt 17:12; Mk 9:12). The "newness" of the revelation is not necessarily that the Messiah suffers but how prominent this notion is and especially the
extent to which it is so closely tied to his reign. *Christ's reign is bound up with his
death and defeat.* Surprisingly, at the very moment of his defeat, he executes his
messianic rule; he conquers in the very midst of defeat, a theme well-known in
the Gospel of John. In the Old Testament, neither the Messiah's death nor his
resurrection were clearly viewed as the instrumentations of the Messiah's coming
rule.[15] Indeed, the fact that the Messiah would rise from the dead is found only in
implicit form in the Old Testament and in Judaism.[16] These things about Christ's
ironic death then are also included to some degree in the unveiled "mystery" in
Ephesians 1 because of its connection to the mystery in Ephesians 1:9-10.

Likewise, Christ's resurrection is an unexpected event by which Christ
further exercised his rule and which was necessary to occur in order to restore
and unify all things under himself. It was not clear in the Old Testament that
the Messiah's resurrection would be a decisive event in achieving his end-time
kingship, but now this likely becomes part of the revealed mystery found in

---

[15]As suggested earlier, perhaps David's exile from Jerusalem while being pursued by his son, Absalom,
is an Old Testament hint that one could be a true king while, at the same time, being in exile or
suffering.

[16]The resurrection of God's people or of individual saints is found in the Old Testament (Deut 32:39,
cf. Ex 3:6; cf. Job 14:14 with 19:25-26; 1 Sam 2:6; Ps 16:9-10; 22:28-29; 49:14-16; 73:24; Is 25:7-9;
26:19; Ezek 37:1-14; Dan 12:1-2; Hos 6:1-3; 13:14). Perhaps only in Is 53:10-11 is there a reference
to the messianic Servant's resurrection but this is at best only implicit. The New Testament understands texts such as Ps 16:9-10 (see Acts 2:24-32) and Hos 6:1-3 (1 Cor 15:4) to refer to the Messiah's resurrection, likely according to the rationale that Jesus was the summation of true Israel or
the epitome of the righteous individual Israelite. Thus, since all faithful Israel was to be resurrected
at the very end of time, this must also include the faithful Israelite Messiah.

Ephesians 1:9-10. We have discussed already that the resurrection of Israel was clearly prophesied in the Old Testament and that this plausibly would have included the resurrection of the nation's coming Messiah. Genesis 3:15 prophesies the end-time leader's overcoming of suffering (the "bruising of his heel") by the end-time opponent, who is dealt a fatal blow. However, that this victory would occur by resurrection is certainly not apparent in Genesis 3:15. Nevertheless, that the prophecies of resurrection meant victory over death would have been understood as part of the meaning of the Old Testament prophecies of Israel's resurrection is likely. This probably implicitly included a victory over the evil forces causing death. To this degree, resurrection as a victory for the coming Messiah may be seen to have its roots implicitly in the Old Testament.

Indeed, 1 Corinthians 15:3-4 says that "Christ died for our sins according to the Scriptures and . . . was raised on the third day according to the Scriptures." Thus Paul sees the Messiah's resurrection to be predicted somewhere in the Old Testament. But where? Hosea 6:1-2 is one passage that many see prophesying the Messiah's resurrection (God "has wounded us. . . . He will revive us after two days; / He will raise us up on the third day / That we may live before him"). The primary reference of this prophecy is about the restoration of corporate believing Israel. Paul probably includes this passage as part of the "Scriptures" prophesying the Messiah's resurrection on the basis, as we noted just above, that the resurrection of Israel plausibly would have included the resurrection of the nation's coming Messiah, who summed up and represented end-time Israel in himself. Accordingly, then, Christ's resurrection as a victory over death and evil forces in Ephesians 1 would appear to be included in the revealed mystery, since it was not explicitly disclosed in the Old Testament. Yet this teaching has its roots there and was implicit there.

Again we perceive *continuity* and *discontinuity* with the Old Testament, particularly regarding how Christ achieved the reunification of all things (in Ephesians 1:10) (partly through his death and not only his resurrection). Throughout our study we have discovered that this is the case, and we will continue to argue that it is always the case in the New Testament uses of *mystery*.

The result of Christ's rule. Another element of the mystery in Ephesians 1 is the result of Christ's rule, though our comments here overlap somewhat with our discussion above about the "scope" of Christ's rule. This component receives the most attention in Ephesians 1:9-10: "the mystery of his will . . . the summing up [*anakephalaiōsasthai*] of all things in Christ." We argued above that the Greek verb *anakephalaiōsasthai* is best rendered as "summing up" or "unifying." The NIV is right to translate Ephesians 1:10 as: "to bring unity to all things in heaven and on earth under Christ." In a word, "all things" are brought together or "summarized" in Christ. For us to determine adequately the result of Christ's rule, we need to probe more deeply into the nature of the concept of cosmic unity, which is the focus of the mystery in Ephesians 1.

In the immediate context, "all things" are defined as "things in the heavens and things on the earth" (Eph 1:10). As noted above, the phrase "all things" is further specified as spiritual powers and entities ("all rule and authority and power and dominion, and every name that is named," Eph 1:21). The crucifixion and resurrection inaugurated the end-time restoration of the cosmos. The fallenness and fragmented nature of creation, in a very real sense, has been righted and brought under the cosmic control of Christ.

Colossians 1:16-20 closely resembles Paul's discussion of "all things" in Ephesians 1:10, 21. What makes this Colossians passage even more relevant to our text is the inclusion of the "reconciliation" of "all things."

> For by Him all things were created, *both* in the heavens and on earth, visible and invisible, whether thrones or dominions or rulers or authorities—all things have been created through Him and for Him. He is before all things, and in Him all things hold together . . . For it was the *Father's* good pleasure for all the fullness to dwell in Him, and through Him to reconcile all things [*apokatallaxai ta panta*] to Himself, having made peace through the blood of His cross; through Him, *I say*, whether things on earth or things in heaven.

Just as Christ is the one who brought about the first ordered and harmonious creation (Col 1:16-17), so is he the one to bring about order in the new creation.[17] Though hotly debated, this Colossians passage highlights the notion that the entire cosmos, because of Christ's death and resurrection, is in the process of being "renewed" and has come under Christ's rule (cf. Phil 2:10-11). Lohse rightly comments that the "universe has been reconciled in that heaven and earth have been brought back into their divinely created and determined order . . . the universe is again under its head and . . . cosmic peace has returned."[18] Even evil forces will be "reconciled" in the sense of undergoing a

---

[17]For a fuller explanation of the relation of the old creation to the new creation in Col 1:15-22, see G. K. Beale, "Colossians," in *Commentary on the New Testament Use of the Old Testament*, ed. G. K. Beale and D. A. Carson (Grand Rapids: Baker Academic, 2007), pp. 851-55.

[18]Eduard Lohse, *Colossians and Philemon*, Hermeneia (Minneapolis: Fortress, 1972), p. 59; cf. also

process of forced pacification under the hand of Christ. Of course, this is decisively and irreversibly inaugurated in Christ's first coming (especially spiritually) and consummated at his final coming (spiritually and physically). Some of the most significant aspects of this cosmic peace, pacification and unification will be unpacked in Ephesians 3 and Ephesians 5. We will have to wait until those later chapters to explain how the cosmic unity and restoration brought about through Christ was a mystery in the Old Testament and revealed in the New. This cosmic restoration and unity through Christ is likely the focus of the mystery in Ephesians 1:9.

THE ETHNIC MYSTERY IN EPHESIANS 3

After discussing Christ's cosmic rule and the subsequent unity of all things, Paul will continue the theme of unity in Ephesians 2–3. He specifies that one of the most significant ways in which Christ has begun to restore the fragmented cosmos is the unification of formerly alienated and hostile people groups. Just as "all things" are united in Christ, so Jews and Gentiles are joined together in him. We therefore ought to view the revealed mystery in Ephesians 3 as deeply rooted in, and an unpacking of, the cosmic mystery in Ephesians 1. In Ephesians 3, the apostle articulates how the mystery involves Gentiles participating in the new covenant community and become equal members along with believing Jews in that new community—by faith in Christ. But how or why is this a mystery? The remainder of this section will attempt to demonstrate what is the precise essence of the mystery in Ephesians 3. This passage is notoriously complex, so we will attempt to evaluate it from a number of angles and in some detail.

We will first examine the immediate context of the passage and then evaluate how Paul's discussion of the ethnic unity relates to the Old Testament and Judaism. We will also take note of Christ's role as true Israel and the implications for understanding the mystery here in Ephesians 3. At the end of our discussion, we will highlight an allusion to the book of Daniel that points further to our conclusions.

Immediate context. Ephesians 3 is one of the longest discussions of mystery in the New Testament and contains a wealth of insight into Paul's understanding of the unveiled mystery, so we will investigate this passage by making a number of observations.

Douglas J. Moo, *The Letters to the Colossians and Philemon*, PNTC (Grand Rapids: Eerdmans, 2008), pp. 136-37; Moo, "Nature in the New Creation: New Testament Eschatology and the Environment," *JETS* 49 (2006): 469-74.

For this reason I, Paul, the prisoner of Christ Jesus for the sake of you Gentiles—
if indeed you have heard of the stewardship of God's grace which was given to
me for you; that by revelation there was made known to me the mystery, as I
wrote before in brief. By referring to this, when you read you can understand my
insight into the mystery of Christ, which in other generations was not made
known to the sons of men, as it has now been revealed to His holy apostles and
prophets in the Spirit; *to be specific,* that the Gentiles are fellow heirs and fellow
members of the body, and fellow partakers of the promise in Christ Jesus through
the gospel, of which I was made a minister, according to the gift of God's grace
which was given to me according to the working of His power. To me, the very
least of all saints, this grace was given, to preach to the Gentiles the unfathomable
riches of Christ, and to bring to light what is the administration of the mystery
which for ages has been hidden in God who created all things; so that the man-
ifold wisdom of God might now be made known through the church to the rulers
and the authorities in the heavenly *places. This was* in accordance with the eternal
purpose which He carried out in Christ Jesus our Lord, in whom we have
boldness and confident access through faith in Him. Therefore I ask you not to
lose heart at my tribulations on your behalf, for they are your glory. (Eph 3:1-13)

Ephesians 3 begins with "For this reason," which refers to the preceding
context wherein Jews and Gentiles have been said to be "one." Paul claims that
Christ made both groups into one "by having loosed the dividing wall of the
barrier" (Eph 2:14). Though many have debated the precise identification of
Paul's metaphor, it is likely that he is referring to the Old Testament law. For in
Ephesians 2:15 he expands on the previous verse by explaining how Christ
made both groups into one body: "by abolishing in his flesh the enmity, which
is the Law of commandments contained in ordinances." This statement likely
focuses not as much on the redemptive significance of Christ's death (as the
parallel in Col 2:13-14, in fact, does) but on one of the crucial sociological *results*
of that death. Christ's death has affected a change in how people groups now
define themselves, especially with respect to the law's nationalistic tags that
formerly defined Israel as a peculiar ethnic nation.

The phrase "mystery of Christ" (Eph 3:4: *tō mystēriō tou Christou*) is only found
one other time in the New Testament: "so that we may speak forth the mystery of
Christ [*mystērion tou Christou*]" (Col 4:3). Christ is explicitly mentioned together
with mystery in a few other instances (Rom 16:25; Eph 5:32; Col 1:27; 2:2), but Colossians 4:3 remains the closest parallel. Determining the use of the genitive "of Christ"
(*Christou*) is difficult, but we suggest that it is an objective genitive: "the mystery

about Christ." This fits remarkably well in the immediate context. Ephesians 3:6 says, "the Gentiles are . . . fellow partakers of the promise in Christ Jesus." Again, in Ephesians 3:8: "this grace was given to preach to the Gentiles [about] the unfathomable riches of Christ." The significance of this objective genitive is that the revealed mystery in Ephesians 3:3-13, though it is applied to the way Gentiles relate to Jews, is so tethered to the Messiah that Paul can label it the "mystery about Christ."

We saw in our chapter on 1 Corinthians that permanent and temporal hiddenness play a key role in the Pauline literature. Ephesians 3:5 refers to what we designate as "temporary hiddenness." This characteristic of hiddenness concerns a particular revelation that was hidden from saints in the Old Testament or "other generations"[19] but has now been revealed to God's people with the latter-day coming of Christ (cf. Col 1:26).[20] Notice the almost formulaic expression: "in other generations was not made known to the sons of men, as it has now been revealed to His holy apostles and prophets."[21] The focus on the contrast between these two generations is probably not so much on the people groups themselves but *the age in which these people groups live.* The "other generations" and the "sons of men" lived in the old age, wherein God partially hid this mystery. On the other hand, the "apostles" and "prophets" are part of the new age—the age in which God has revealed the mystery. This is borne out by the salient term *now (nyn).* In the Pauline corpus, this term often signals the turning of the ages (e.g., Rom 8:22; 11:30; 16:26; 2 Cor 5:16; 6:2; 2 Tim 1:10).

Content of the mystery. Now that we have briefly discussed Ephesians 3:1-13, we will focus on the content of the revealed mystery. Ephesians 3:6 gets to the heart of the mystery in this chapter: "to be specific [*einai*], that the Gentiles are fellow heirs and fellow members of the body, and fellow partakers of the promise in Christ Jesus through the gospel." The verse begins with further explanation or clarification that unpacks the content of the revealed mystery in Ephesians 3:3-4: "by revelation there was made known to me the mystery . . . when you read you can understand my insight into the mystery of Christ."

---

[19]In the Old Testament, the expression "other generations" (*heterais geneais*) is a contrast between the present generation and the past/future generation (e.g., Deut 29:21; Judg 2:10; Ps 47:14 LXX). Here Paul uses it to draw a distinction between incomplete or partial knowledge of the mystery in the Old Testament and its fuller revelation in the New Testament.

[20]See also Col 1:26: "*that is*, the mystery which has been hidden from the past ages and generations, but has now been manifested to his saints" (cf. 1 Pet 1:10-12).

[21]Nils Alstrup Dahl, *Jesus in the Memory of the Early Church* (Minneapolis: Augsburg, 1976), pp. 32-33, is right to note the formulaic expression of the mystery being at one time "hidden" but "now revealed."

There are generally three views on the content of the revealed mystery. Dispensationalists and progressive dispensationalists claim that the content of the mystery here is the general, spiritual equality between Jews and Gentiles, which was not revealed at all in the Old Testament. That is, both groups have full access to God in Christ, are equal members in the body (the church) and enjoy complete salvation in Christ.[22]

On the other hand, a number of commentators argue that the content of the revealed mystery is the complete equality between Jews and Gentiles, who both equally comprise the church as *true* Israel.[23] That the Gentiles are part of Israel according to "the promise" would appear to be clear from this verse and the previous passage (Eph 2:11-22). The question is, however, whether or not that notion constitutes the unveiled mystery in Ephesians 3:6. Caragounis, for example, claims, "This . . . is the content of the *mysterion* in ch. 3. The weight of emphasis is on the Gentiles rather than on the Jews, since what is new in this connection is not the salvation of the Jews, but the participation of the Gentiles in redemption and in the Body of Christ."[24]

If the mystery concerns the Gentiles sharing in Israel's inheritance, then Ephesians 3:6 is merely a restatement of what has already been established in Ephesians 2, though it is an important restatement. The Gentiles, according to these scholars, are now on equal footing as true Israelites with the ethnic believing Jews. Ephesians 2:12 states that in Old Testament times Gentiles were "alienated from the commonwealth of Israel," but now in Ephesians 3:6 they are said to be "fellow members of the body," that is "of the body" of Israel from which they were formerly separated according to Ephesians 2:12. Also, Ephesians 2:12 has said that Gentiles formerly were "strangers to the covenants of promise" for Israel, but now Ephesians 3:6 says they are "fellow partakers of the promise," which, in the light of Ephesians 2:12, is the promise made to

---

[22]See, for example, Harold W. Hoehner, *Ephesians: An Exegetical Commentary* (Grand Rapids: Baker, 2002), pp. 445-48; Robert L. Saucy, "The Church as the Mystery of God," in *Dispensationalism, Israel and the Church*, ed. Craig Blaising and Darrell L. Block (Grand Rapid: Zondervan, 1992), pp. 127-55.

[23]E.g,. Caragounis, *Ephesian Mysterion*, pp. 140-41.

[24]Caragounis, *Ephesian* Mysterion, p. 139 (cf. pp. 140-41). The *syn* prefix in Eph 3:6 is certainly compatible with this view: "the Gentiles are *fellow heirs* [synklēronoma] and fellow members of the body [syssōma], and fellow partakers [symmetocha] of the promise." See also O'Brien, *Ephesians*, p. 236; Frank Thielman, "Ephesians," in G. K. Beale and D. A. Carson, *Commentary on the New Testament Use of the Old Testament* (Grand Rapids: Baker, 2007), p. 819; Lincoln, *Ephesians*, p. 181; Bockmuehl, *Revelation and Mystery*, p. 202; Seyoon Kim, *The Origin of Paul's Gospel*, WUNT 4 (Tübingen: Mohr Siebeck, 1981; repr., Grand Rapids: Eerdmans, 1981), p. 23; G. W. Barker, "Mystery," in *ISBE* 3:454.

Israel. Finally, Ephesians 2:12 claims that in the Old Testament Gentiles were "separate from Christ." But how could this be said to be true of Gentiles in the Old Testament before Christ had even come? In the light of Romans 9:4-5, this refers to "covenants" and "promises" to Israel in connection to the ultimate coming of "the Christ." Now, Ephesians 3:6 says that those covenants and promises have begun fulfillment in Christ, and Gentiles are now "fellow partakers of the [fulfilled] promise in Christ Jesus." Thus, according to these scholars, Ephesians 2:11-22 is the revealed mystery that Gentiles are participating in Israel and her fulfilled promises, and Ephesians 3:3-13 is simply a further reflection on that truth.

Therefore, though this view merits consideration, and is true as far as it goes, it has Ephesians 3:6 being a mere repetition and making the new statement about what Ephesians 2:11-22 has said about the Jew-Gentile relationship. This view comes up short, however, in that it does not *make sense of several explicit Old Testament references where it is prophesied that Gentiles will, indeed, become part of true Israel in the end time* (Ps 87:4-6; Is 11:9-10; 14:1-2; 49:6; 51:4-6; 60:1-16; Jer 3:17; Zeph 3:9-10). In other words, what is "new" about the revelation in Ephesians 3:6 that Gentiles constitute true Israel? Why would Paul even receive such a revelation if the Old Testament explicitly (and often) made such a claim? This point is enforced by noticing Paul's explicit language saying just the opposite (!): "which [the mystery of Christ] in other generations was <u>not made known to the sons of men</u> as now it has been revealed."[25] Paul's point, as we saw above, is that this doctrine is simply not found with any clarity in the Old Testament. Therefore, the unveiled mystery in Ephesians 3 does not *primarily*

---

[25]Caragounis argues that the adverb *hōs* ("as") should be best understood as expressing a comparative of degree (*Ephesian* Mysterion, p. 102). In other words, the Old Testament prophets had indeed *some* insight into the unveiled mystery that was disclosed to Paul. Others, though, argue that the *hōs* is absolute and that the Old Testament writers did not have any inkling of this doctrine (Thielman, "Ephesians," pp. 818-19). The former view is to be preferred for two reasons: (1) we have seen throughout this project that the New Testament's conception of mystery as it pertains to a specific idea (kingdom, messiahship, etc.) does not envision a radical break from the Old Testament's prophetic view of that notion. Like planted seeds blooming into a magificent tree, these disclosed mysteries in the New Testament have their origins in the Old Testament; some continuity indeed exists between the Testaments, while the fulfillment is nevertheless surprising from the Old Testament vantage point. (2) The Old Testament and Judaism predict the end-time conversion of Gentiles. The Gentiles were to embrace certain nationalistic distinctives (circumcision, food laws, etc.). These prophecies are not discarded in the New Testament but are applied typologically to Christ. Christ, as true Israel, fulfills them. When Gentiles possess faith in Christ, they too fulfill these prophecies. It is the way in which the Gentiles fulfill these Old Testament expectations and become part of true Israel that constitutes the "newness" of the revealed mystery, as we will argue further directly below.

concern the equality between Jews and Gentiles (though, as we have seen, that is essential to understanding the mystery!) as the Old Testament makes clear.

Rather, the third view of the mystery primarily concerns *the way in which* Gentiles become part of true Israel in the latter days. What is then the precise content of the mystery in Ephesians 3:6? The most specific answer is that *Gentiles in the period known as the "latter days" are no longer required to obey Israel's national customs and outward signs required by the law to become true Israelites.* Let us quote Ephesians 3:6, the content of the mystery, once more: "the Gentiles are fellow heirs and fellow members of the body, and fellow partakers of the promise in Christ Jesus through the gospel." It is of great importance to highlight *how* Paul places these two groups on equal footing. The mystery is not that these two groups are merely one community, since that had already been clearly prophesied in the Old Testament; rather, they are one *in Christ* (*Messiah*), who as the Israelite messianic king represents true Israel (as did Israelite kings in the Old Testament), so that they are part of true Israel. Perhaps we could put it like this: according to the Old Testament and Judaism, Gentiles became members of *true* Israel through their adherence to Torah (e.g., Rahab, Ruth, Uriah). They were to conform to Israelite culture in all aspects of life by taking on national distinctives such as circumcision, food laws and honoring Sabbath rest, which were required by Israel's law.

The Old Testament also prophesied that when Gentiles would become Israelites in the latter days, they also would adhere to the same nationalistic tags that identified a person as an Israelite (e.g., Is 56:3-8; 66:18-21; Zech 14:16-19; see excursus 6.1 for a survey of this theme in the Old Testament and Judaism). Surprisingly, Paul claims that Gentiles, together with Jewish believers, have now become *true* Israelites through faith in Christ, the embodiment of true Israel,[26] without having to identify themselves with the various nationalistic distinctives formerly required by Israel's law. *Simply put, the mystery comprises how Gentiles become true Israelites in the end-time without taking on the covenantal markers of Israel, which formerly they were required to do to be considered Israelites according to the Old Testament perspective.* The only marker that is now required for one to be considered a true Israelite is identification with Christ, and this is true also for "fellow" ethnic Jewish believers, so that the way ethnic Jews become true Israelites is part of the mystery. Nevertheless, the focus of the mystery is on how Gentiles become end-time Israel, since Ephesians 3:6 reflects this emphasis:

---

[26]Cf. Gene Wiley, "'Mystery' in the New Testament," *GTJ* 6 (1985): 356.

"[the mystery is] that Gentiles are fellow heirs . . . in Christ Jesus" (this thrust is reinforced with the antithetical parallelism of Eph 3:6 with Eph 2:12). Since Christ's identification as true Israel is the key presupposition in understanding the mystery in Ephesians 3, we will quickly summarize this concept.

Christ as true Israel as the key presupposition. That Christ functions as true Israel is a crucial presupposition here in understanding the mystery of Ephesians 3.[27] Though Paul does not explicitly mention this notion, as he does in Galatians 3:16 (Chris is the "seed" of Abraham), it functions as the backbone of this entire discussion. Already in the Old Testament, Isaiah 49:3 affirms that the messianic servant was to be true Israel: "you are My Servant Israel." Those who place their faith in Christ, whether Jew or Gentile, are identified with him as true, end-time Israel, just as those who are identified with Christ as Abraham's seed in Galatians 3:16 are then considered to be part of that Israelite seed in Galatians 3:29.

A broader biblical theology of Jesus as true Israel is appropriate here as background to Jesus as a representative of true Israel. Jesus' titles "Son of Man" and "Son of God" reflect respectively both the Old Testament figures of Adam and Israel. Israel and its patriarchs were given the same commission as Adam in Genesis 1:26-28. Consequently, it is not unwarranted to understand Israel as a corporate Adam who had failed in its "Garden of Eden," in much the same way as its primal father had failed in the first garden. In this respect, it is understandable that one reason why Jesus is called "Son of God" is that this was a name for the first Adam (Lk 3:38; cf. Gen 5:1-3 in relation to Gen 1:26-28) and for Israel (Ex 4:22; Hos 11:1), who was also called a "firstborn" (Ex 4:22; Jer 31:9). The Messiah was also prophesied to be a "firstborn" (Ps 89:27). Likewise, the expression "Son of Man" from Daniel 7:13 refers to end-time Israel and its representative king as the son of Adam who is sovereign over beasts. Thus God had designed that the nation of Israel to be a corporate national Adam who was to represent what true humanity should be like (see, e.g., Deut 4:6-8). Consequently, for the church to be the beginning of true end-time Israel is to begin to be identified with the original purposes of Adam, true humanity, and the Daniel 7 "Son of Man" prophecy, which Christ has fulfilled. This discussion of Adam in Genesis 1:28 and the Son of Man from Daniel 7 is in fact relevant to Ephesians, since we have seen that part of the mystery in Ephesians 1 is linked

---

[27]For an extended discussion of Christ's role as true, end-time Israel and its relationship to Eph 3, see G. K. Beale, *A New Testament Biblical Theology: The Unfolding of the Old Testament in the New* (Grand Rapids: Baker Academic, 2011), pp. 651-56 (and more broadly see pp. 657-749).

to allusions to Adam (from Ps 8:6, developing Gen 1:26-28, in Eph 1:22) and to the Son of Man's rule (from Dan 7:13-14, 27 in Eph 1:20-21).

Therefore, it is important to maintain that the church in Ephesians 3:6, and elsewhere in the New Testament, is not merely like Israel but actually is Israel. This is most in keeping with the original purposes of Israel itself and why the Old Testament prophesies that in the latter days Gentiles would become a part of Israel and not merely be redeemed people who retain the name "Gentiles" and coexist alongside as a separate people from redeemed ethnic Israel. These Old Testament prophecies did not envision that Gentile converts to Israel would have their complete Gentile identity erased (in keeping with the past examples of Rahab, Ruth and Uriah), but neither did these prophecies foresee that redeemed Gentiles would exist alongside Israel but not be part of Israel because of their Gentile ethnic identity. Rather, Gentiles in the latter days were expected to be identified with Israel and Israel's God, in keeping with those previously converted Gentiles in the Old Testament epoch.

Once we understand Christ's role as true Israel and the Gentiles' relationship to him, we can better grasp the main content of the unveiled mystery here in Ephesians 3. Christ's identity as true, end-time Israel explains Paul's reasoning. It was not fully revealed in the Old Testament that Gentiles would become part of true Israel by faith alone *without* adhering to Israel's nationalistic identification tags of the law. The revealed mystery is that Gentiles can become true Israel only by identifying by faith with Christ, the true Israel, and not having to identify with the nationalistic marks of an Israelite of the old epoch (whether that be circumcision, Sabbath laws, dietary laws, etc.). Christ's identity as true Israel is the key to the mystery: Gentiles identify with him, not Israel's law, to become true Israelites. Gentiles do not have to move to geographical Israel to become Israelites; they only have to move to Jesus to become true Israelites. Though it is true that a part of the mystery likely includes ethnic Jews also becoming latter-day Israel by identifying with Christ and not with the old distinguishing signs of the law, the focus of the mystery is the manner by which Gentiles join true Israel. With this in mind, we will now examine an allusion to Daniel 2 that is line with our conclusions.

Gentile identification with the Messiah as true Israel in light of Daniel 2:28. Paul claims in Ephesians 3 that the converted Gentiles, together with a remnant of Jewish believers, are now no longer required to embrace the old Israelite nationalistic identification tags required by the law. But how can Gentiles and Jews become part of true Israel without adopting the law's nationalistic signs that mark out true Israelites? The most plausible answer, as we argued above, is that Jesus the Messiah is true Israel, and since there is only one Messiah, there can only be one people of God.[28] Christ is now the only "tag" with which one needs to be identified. This is why Ephesians 2:15-18 speaks of Christ's death uniting Jew and Gentile into "one new man," "one body" that exists in the sphere of "one Spirit." This "one new man" and "one body" are none other than the body of Christ, the Messiah: Jew and Gentile are one because they are now incorporated and identified with Christ, the Israelite Messiah who represents them. Gentiles can be "fellow heirs and fellow members of the body and fellow partakers of the promises in Christ Jesus" along with Jewish Christians because the promises and inheritance of true, end-time Israel has been inaugurated in Christ, the Israelite king who represents all true Israelites, whether ethnic Jew or Gentile.

It was partially hidden in the Old Testament that when the Messiah would come, the theocracy of Israel would be so completely reconstituted that it would continue only as the new organism of the Messiah (Jesus), the true Israel.[29] In Christ, Jews and Gentiles would be fused together on a footing of complete equality through corporate identification in the Israelite king, Jesus, and not by identifying with Israel's old covenant signs.[30]

An allusion in Ephesians 3 to the book of Daniel reinforces our contention that the Gentiles became full-blown participants in the end-time Israelite kingdom through Christ. The expression "by revelation there was made known to me the mystery" (*kata apokalypsin egnōristhē moi to mystērion*) in Ephesians 3:3 alludes to Daniel 2:28 (Theodotion; see table 6.2).

---

[28]For an extended discussion of the Gentiles' relationship to Jesus as true Israel, see Beale, *New Testament Biblical Theology*, pp. 873-78.

[29]Note again the *hōs* in Eph 3:5 noting degree and not absolute hiddenness.

[30]So similarly William Hendriksen, *New Testament Commentary: Exposition of Ephesians* (Grand Rapids: Baker, 1967), pp. 153-55, whose comments have helped to clarify our own conclusion, though he is not clear about whether Christ is the "new organism" or the church. Cf. F. F. Bruce, *The Epistles to the Colossians, to Philemon, and to the Ephesians* (Grand Rapids: Eerdmans, 1984), p. 314, who says the mystery is that the complete lack of discrimination between Jew and Gentile was not foreseen. Saucy, "Church as the Mystery," pp. 149-51, says that a secondary nuance of the Eph 3 mystery indicates unanticipated fulfillment in the sense that Gentiles are being saved though Israel's salvation is being set aside for the most part, and in the sense that the Old Testament expected only one age of fulfillment, but Ephesians pictures two such ages. We do not find the first notion present in Eph 3, though the second may be included to some degree, since we have seen it as part of the mystery in our discussion of Matthew 13 (see chap. 3 above), and the concept of already-and-not-yet end-time fulfillment permeates Ephesians (see footnote 30 below). Nevertheless, this temporal two age notion is not the focus of the mystery in Eph 3.

Table 6.2

Daniel 2:28 (Theodotion)	Ephesians 3:3
"There is a God in heaven revealing mysteries, and he has made known to King Nabouchodonosor [apokalyptōn mystēria kai egnōrisen tō basileî] what must happen at the end of days."	"By revelation there was made known to me the mystery" (kata apokalypsin egnōristhē moi to mystērion)

What added significance could the Daniel background contribute to what we have concluded thus far about the unveiled mystery? As in Daniel 2, in parallelism with Daniel 7 (where the stone is parallel to the Son of Man),[31] the Ephesian mystery concerns the Messiah establishing Israel's kingdom following his defeat of evil rulers in the end time (as we saw in Eph 1:9-10, 20-22; cf. also Eph 3:5, 10 ["now"]; cf. Gal 4:4).[32] It is likely that the establishment of the kingdom in Daniel 2 includes Gentiles who are incorporated into the worldwide kingdom. The reason for this is that the stone that demolished the colossus representing opposing evil kingdom is said subsequently to have "become a great mountain" and "filled the whole earth" (Dan 2:35). The stone, representing God's kingdom, rules over the entire earth. Would this not include ruling over Gentiles who submit to this rule? We know from other Old Testament prophecies that not all Gentiles will be judged at the eschaton but some will trust in God and submit willingly to his rule (e.g., Is 2:2-4; 11:10, 12). That this to some degree is included in the image of God's kingdom filling the earth is apparent from the parallel in Daniel 7:13-14, where the Son of Man's eternal, eschatological kingdom and dominion focus on "all the people, nations, and men of every tongue . . . [who] serve him."

---

[31]Note also that 4 Ezra 13:1-11 very closely associates the Dan 7 Son of Man with the stone of Dan 2 in portraying the defeat of the enemy nations: e.g., see 4 Ezra 13:6: "he [the Son of Man] carved out for himself a great mountain, and flew up upon it."

[32]That the mystery in Eph 3 is clearly developing the mystery mentioned in Eph 1 is apparent from noticing the parallel wording between Eph 1:9-10 and 3:9-10, which also show both being concerned with the mystery as an aspect of inaugurated eschatology:

Table 6.3 (from footnote 32)

Ephesians 1:9-10	Ephesians 3:9-10
"Having made known the mystery . . . with a view to a household management of the fullness of the times" (gnōrisas hēmin to mystērion . . . eis oikonomian tou plērōmatos tōn kairōn)	"A household management of the mystery which has been hidden from the ages . . . in order that it should be made known now" (oikonomia tou mystēriou tou apokekrymmenou apo tōn aiōnōn . . . hina gnōristhē nyn)

Thus Paul alluded to the "mystery" of Daniel 2:28, since he not only wants to refer to the mystery of the inaguration of the prophesied kingdom but may also desire to draw out that element of the end-time kingdom that includes Gentiles.[33]

In this light, the divulged mystery in Ephesians 3 explains the new entrance requirements for anyone (Jew or Gentile) becoming citizens of the Israelite kingdom prophesied in Daniel 2: *submission only to and identification only with Jesus the Israelite king, not submission to and identification only with the ethnic identification marks of the Mosaic law.* The kingdom of Israel is at issue here, because of the background of Daniel 2 and the references to "in Messiah [Israel's anointed king] Jesus" and "fellow heirs [*synklēronoma*] . . . in Christ Jesus" in Ephesians 3:6, which are expanded in Ephesians 5:5 by reference to having "an inheritance [*klēronomian*] in the kingdom of Christ."[34] That the subject of Gentiles being now related to Israel is in mind in Ephesians 3:6 is also apparent from Ephesians 2:12, as we also argued in an earlier section of this chapter, where Gentiles who do not believe are viewed as separated from the following three realities set up in synonymous parallelism: (1) "without Christ," (2) "alienated from the commonwealth of Israel," and (3) "strangers of the covenants of promise."[35] As we have noted, the relation of Ephesians 3:6 to Ephesians 2:12 also shows that the Gentiles are the focus of the mystery, though the way ethnic Jews become true Israel probably is included in the mystery.

But how does the mystery in Ephesians 3 relate to the Old Testament's and Judaism's portrayal of Gentiles becoming Israelites in the latter days by actually moving geographically to Israel and taking on specific nationalistic marks required by the law? Is this not complete discontinuity between Paul and the Old Testament and Jewish thinking on this issue? Several considerations point in the direction that the revealed Ephesians 3 mystery is not absolutely new but a clear manifestation of something found, albeit faintly, in the Old Testament:

1. The Servant in Isaiah 49:3 is an individual servant who sums the nation

---

[33]We are grateful to a paper by Ochang Kwon which has called our attention to the possible Gentile notion contained in Daniel 2's kingdom ("A Biblical Theology of Ephesians," New Testament Theology Seminar at Westminster Theological Seminary, January 2014).

[34]The Gentiles can be considered part of true Israel, since the Is 57:19 prophecy of Israel's restoration is applied to and seen to be fulfilled in Gentiles (Eph 2:17), and that they can be seen as a part of Israel's inaugurated end-time temple in Eph 2:20-22.

[35]The cumulative force of the argument in this section points in the opposite direction of Saucy, "Church as the Mystery," pp. 127-55, who contends, among other things, that the "mystery" has nothing to do with Gentiles becoming a part of true Israel.

Israel up in himself ("You are my Servant Israel in whom I will show my glory").
He accomplishes the commission from God that corporate Israel failed to
perform. This is the same Servant who dies on behalf of the nation (Isaiah 53).
Then, from Isaiah 54:17 onward, faithful Israelites are for the first time in the
book of Isaiah called God's "servants." The apparent reason for this is that their
identity is to be found in the individual messianic Servant.[36] They are now true
Israelite "servants" because they are identified by faith with the individual
Servant. The Servant is now their main identification tag. Recall that both Jews
and Gentiles were the direct objects of the Servant Israel's mission in Isaiah
49:1-8. We know Paul was quite aware of the context of Isaiah 49:1-8 (Acts 13:47;
2 Cor 6:2), so it may not be unreasonable to conclude that one of the contributing reasons why Jewish and Gentile Christians in Ephesians 3 are not required to preserve the nationalistic identification signs of the law is that the
Messiah functions as true Israel, the main tag of the new covenant community.
We have argued above that Christ, as true Israel, is crucial to understanding the
mystery—the one to whom the law pointed all along (e.g., Rom 10:4; Col 2:3).
Thus this revealed mystery may be Paul's understanding of the implications of
Isaiah's messianic Servant being the summation of true Israel. Those who
belong to latter-day Israel, Jesus the messianic Servant, no longer need any
outward identifying marks except their identification with Jesus, the true Israel.
Thus the significance of Isaiah 49 and the following chapters may lie as a presupposition underlying Paul's view of the mystery in Ephesians 3.

    2. There are other considerations suggesting that there were anticipations of
the revealed mystery of Ephesians 3 in the Old Testament. Isaiah 56:3-5 affirms
that in the eschatological future "eunuchs" may participate in temple worship,
something they were excluded from by the law under the old covenant (e.g.,
see Lev 21:20; Deut 23:1). Furthermore, in the same passage (Is 56:3, 6), Gentile
"foreigners" not only can be a part of temple worship (which was true of Gentile
converts under the old covenant) but also can be priests who "minister" in the
temple, a notion to which Isaiah 66:19-21 also attests (on which see the excursus
below). According to the law, only ethnic Israelite descendants from Aaron and
the Levites were eligible to be priests. Though it is true that Isaiah 56 still portrays "eunuchs" and "foreigners" keeping part of the Mosaic law (see our discussion of Isaiah 56 in the excursus below), nevertheless, this passage reveals a

---

[36]We are indebted to Daniel J. Brendsel, "'Isaiah Saw His Glory': The Use of Isaiah 52–53 in John 12,"
    (PhD diss., Wheaton College Graduate School, 2013), pp. 77-82, for this idea in Isaiah.

loosening of the law's requirements for "eunuchs" and Gentile "foreigners" in the end time. Indeed, the ethnic requirement that priests come only from the tribe of Levi is erased, so the removal of this barrier means that even Gentiles can become priests.

In this respect, significant to observe is the citation of Isaiah 57:19 in Ephesians 2:17 about Jews and Gentiles being restored in Christ and the directly following reference to Jews and Gentiles forming one temple built on Christ, the apostles, and prophets (Eph 2:19-22). This observation suggests that the temple prophecy about Gentiles in Isaiah 56 lies within Paul's peripheral vision and may anticipate his discussion of the mystery in Ephesians 3.

3. An additional Old Testament passage that suggests that Gentiles would not have to obey the law in the latter days is Genesis 15:6, where Abraham, before being circumcised, is said to believe God, "and it was reckoned to him as righteousness." Thus Abraham was said to have a faith leading to justification *before* he took on the nationalistic distinguishing sign of circumcision. This also would appear to anticipate the notion that Gentiles in the eschaton would be able to have faith, be justified and be a member of the new Israel without abiding by the nationalistic signs of old Israel. Indeed, Genesis 17:5 directly links Abraham and Gentiles by saying that Abraham was to be a "Father of a multitude of nations." That this is a valid inference from the example of Abraham is made explicit by Paul in Romans 4:1-5, 9-17. There Paul quotes Genesis 15:6, where Abraham is justified by faith before he receives the sign of circumcision. As such, Abraham is said to be "the father of all who believe without being circumcised, that righteousness might be reckoned to them" (Rom 4:11; cf. further Rom 4:12-17). Paul also adduces Genesis 17:5 as part of his argument that Abraham's example anticipates Gentiles becoming part of the latter-day covenant community without adhering to Israel's old law.

4. One last example from the Old Testament may be relevant to discuss here. Noah was to take on the ark both clean and unclean animals (Gen 7:2, 8). After the flood, when he left the ark, "Noah built an altar to the Lord, and took of every clean animal and of every clean bird and offered burnt offerings on the altar" (Gen 8:20). Yet in Genesis 9:3 God abolishes the clean-unclean distinctions when he says to Noah, "every moving thing that is alive shall be food for you; I give all to you." Thus during the brief ark period God instituted that there be clean and unclean animals, the former for sacrifices to God. Some scholars see this as anticipating or as the root of later Israel's unclean-and-clean animal

laws, which were crucial for distinguishing which animals were "clean" for the sacrificial system and which humans were "clean" and "unclean" for temple worship (humans defiled by unclean animals had to offer a sacrifice for the cleansing).[37] The instituting of and then doing away with the Noahic unclean-and-clean animal distinctions in what looked to be the beginning of the new creation directly after the flood (respectively in Gen 7:2, 8; 9:3) may anticipate another, indeed irreversible, new creational age in which the same distinctions of the Mosaic law are abolished for God's new creational people (the notion that Christ and the church are part of a new creational epoch is attested by many scholars).[38] At least one Old Testament scholar even sees this Noahic circumstance as an anticipation of Peter's vision in Acts 10, where God reveals to him a vision in which the clean-and-unclean animal distinctions are abolished for Jewish and Gentile Christians.[39]

Therefore, those who believe that the revealed mystery in Ephesians 3 has absolutely no antecedents in the Old Testament need to reckon with the above Old Testament anticipations of members of eschatological Israel not being bound by the external identity markers of old Israel's law.[40] We believe that these are anticipations to one degree or another and that they point to the revealed mystery in Ephesians 3 being not completely new but a major clarification of what was already implicit in the Old Testament. This is why Paul uses *hōs* to qualify the mystery in Ephesians 3:4-6. It was something that had been faintly revealed in the Old Testament and now radically clarified in the New Testament.

Consequently, the best approach to the revealed mystery of Ephesians 3 Jesus sums up in himself all that true Israel was to be, both in terms of his faithful obedience but also in terms of being the true temple, of being truly clean (not cleansed by Israel's clean and unclean food laws), the true circumcision, the true Sabbath (rest is found only in Christ), the beginning fulfillment of the promises of the worldwide extension of Israel's land, and so on. All of these end-time promises find their typological fulfillment in Christ, the true

---

[37]Meredith G. Kline, *Kingdom Prologue* (Overland Park, KS: Two Age Press, 2000), pp. 254-56; Gordon J. Wenham, *Genesis 1-15*, Word Biblical Commentary (Waco, TX: Word, 1987), pp. 176-77, 189; cf. John H. Walton, *Genesis*, NIVAC (Grand Rapids: Zondervan, 2001), p. 313, who says the unclean-clean animal distinction in relation to sacrifice is not an "innovation first instituted at Sinai but established already at the time of Noah."

[38]E.g., see Beale, *New Testament Biblical Theology*.

[39]Kline, *Kingdom Prologue*, pp. 254-56.

[40]E.g., in addition to others cited earlier who support this view, see also Sigurd Grindheim, "What the Old Testament Prophets Did Not Know: The Mystery of the Church in Eph 3,2-13," *Biblica* 84 (2003): 531-53.

Israel (see Gal 3:16; Rev 2:12). If it is correct to understand these realities to have their typological fulfillment in Christ (which we believe can be substantiated),[41] then we have the correct answer to why Paul can say that Gentiles, together with Jews, can become true Israelites by submitting to and identifying with Christ as true Israel rather than by submitting to and identifying with the nationalistic distinctives of Israel's land and her law. This is the content of the unveiled mystery. Thus, to become true Israel one now moves to Jesus, not to the geographical region of Israel in the Middle East.

MARITAL MYSTERY IN EPHESIANS 5

After sketching cosmic and ethnic unity in Christ, we now move to Paul's discussion of marital unity. The content of the mystery in Ephesians 5:30-31 turns on the use of Genesis 2:24. The disclosed mystery in Ephesians 5 continues to be a source of debate, partly because of its relationship to the Genesis 2:24 quotation and Paul's seemingly difficult interpretation. Its difficulty lies also in the unending commentary and secondary literature dedicated to Ephesians 5:22-33. Evaluating this use of mystery requires us to examine first the immediate and larger canonical Old Testament context of Genesis 2:24. After we have briefly investigated the Old Testament context of this quotation, we will return to Ephesians 5 and attempt to understand Paul's use of Genesis 2:24 in light of its Old Testament context.

Immediate context. The revealed mystery occurs in the midst of what is labeled a "household code" (see Eph 5:22–6:9; so also Col 3:18–4:4). The designation "household code" refers to a Greco-Roman social understanding of the ancient family structure that entails proper relationships between the members of the family household order. Scholars often find strong conceptual links between the Greco-Roman household codes and those found in Ephesians 5–6 and Colossians 3–4. What must be kept in mind, however, is the code's relationship to the end-time people of God as a new creational community. The household code is intimately bound up with the gospel and believers' relationship to it (Eph 5:1-21). In this respect, Ephesians 1:10 says that

---

[41]On which see Leonhard Goppelt, *Typos: The Typological Interpretation of the Old Testament in the New,* trans. Donald H. Madvig (Grand Rapids: Eerdmans, 1982); David L. Baker, "Typology and the Christian Use of the Old Testament," *SJT* 29 (1976): 137-57; G. P. Hugenberger, "Introductory Notes on Typology," in *The Right Doctrine from the Wrong Texts?* ed. G. K. Beale (Grand Rapids: Baker, 1994), pp. 331-41; P. Fairbain, *The Typology of Scripture* (New York: T & T Clark, 1876); on many of these ideas, see Beale, *New Testament Biblical Theology.*

Christ's "summing up of all things" was for a household management at the "fullness of the times." Accordingly, Christ has come to restore the household of creation as a "household manager." In addition to restoring people groups in the cosmic household, Christ has come also to put back together the fragmented relationships of individual family households: husbands and wives, parents and children, and slaves and masters. We will now turn to Paul's discussion concerning the restored relationship between a husband and a wife.

> Wives, *be subject* to your own husbands, as to the Lord. For the husband is the head of the wife, as Christ also is the head of the church, He Himself *being* the Savior of the body. But as the church is subject to Christ, so also the wives *ought to be* to their husbands in everything. Husbands, love your wives, just as Christ also loved the church and gave Himself up for her, so that He might sanctify her, having cleansed her by the washing of water with the word, that He might present to Himself the church in all her glory, having no spot or wrinkle or any such thing; but that she would be holy and blameless. So husbands ought also to love their own wives as their own bodies. He who loves his own wife loves himself; for no one ever hated his own flesh, but nourishes and cherishes it, just as Christ also *does* the church, because we are members of His body. For this reason a man shall leave his father and mother and shall be joined to his wife, and the two shall become one flesh. This mystery is great; but I am speaking with reference to Christ and the church. Nevertheless, each individual among you also is to love his own wife even as himself, and the wife must *see to it* that she respects her husband. (Eph 5:22-33)

After detailing the responsibilities of the wife (Eph 5:22-24), Paul progresses to the responsibilities of the husband (Eph 5:25-33). The mandate in Ephesians 5:25 for husbands to love their spouses is undergirded by a comparison to Christ and the church. Husbands are to love their wives just as Christ loves the church. Paul then spends the next few verses elaborating on Christ's selfless love toward the church (Eph 5:25b-27). In Ephesians 5:28, another comparison is made between the husband's love for his wife: self-love. Paul then quotes Genesis 2:24 in Ephesians 5:31 to support the notion that the church finds its unity in Christ. Paul says that this unified relationship of Christ with the church is a "mystery" (Eph 5:32). Ephesians 5:33 summarizes Ephesians 5:22-32 by restating briefly the responsibilities of the husband and the wife. Now that we have looked at the New Testament context, we will turn to the immediate and broader Old Testament context of Genesis 2:24.

The context of Genesis 2:24. God creates Adam in Genesis 2:7 and furnishes him with the "breath of life." Adam is charged with the mandate to "cultivate" and "keep" the Garden of Eden (Gen 2:15). In Genesis 2:18, God says: "It is not good for the man to be alone; I will make him a helper suitable for him." A few verses later God creates the man's partner, Eve: "The LORD God fashioned into a woman the rib which he had taken from the man, and brought her to the man." On God presenting the woman to him, Adam poetically declares,

> This is now bone of my bones,
> And flesh of my flesh;
> She shall be called Woman,
> Because she was taken out of Man. (Gen 2:23)

We then arrive at our verse, and the narrator comments, "<u>For this reason</u> [*'al-kēn*] a man shall leave his father and his mother, and be joined to his wife; and they shall become one flesh." The logic of Genesis 2:23-24 is the following: woman is man's intimate partner and companion, so much so that they are a unity (Gen 2:23); therefore (*'al-kēn*), marriage is the ultimate expression of this creational relationship (Gen 2:24).

We will briefly make a few observations regarding Genesis 2:24.[42] First, the union between Adam and Eve is the climax of the Genesis 1–2 narrative, particularly Genesis 2:18-24. Adam is the pinnacle of the created order, since he is in God's image (Gen 1:26-27; 2:7). Nevertheless, as such he yet remains incomplete. All the animals have partners and function harmoniously except Adam (Gen 2:19-20). It is not until the woman is created and the primeval couple "married" (Gen 2:24) that all of creation reaches a point of completion; it is only within the context of marriage that the first man and woman achieve relational balance and union.

Second, in addition to the primeval couple's marriage being the climax of Genesis 1–2, *Genesis 2:24 is the fountainhead of Israel's conception of marriage and serves as the paradigmatic expression of marriage.* Indeed, Genesis 2:24 is so foundational that any discussion or portrayal of marriage in the Old Testament and New Testament is invariably dependent on it. Gordon Hugenberger likewise affirms this paradigmatic nature of marriage in Genesis 2:24 and a

---

[42]We found many of our initial observations of Gen 2:24 are confirmed in Gordon P. Hugenberger, *Marriage as a Covenant: Biblical Law and Ethics as Developed from Malachi,* VTSup 52 (Boston: Brill, 1994; repr., Grand Rapids: Baker, 1998), pp. 151-67.

number of texts are adduced to support this conclusion.[43] He observes that Genesis 2:24 contains "generalized language" (instead of "Adam" and "Eve," Gen 2:24 reads "man" and "wife") so that this verse can be applied throughout Israel's existence. The Genesis 2:24 passage is picked up and repeated throughout the canon.

The most explicit Old Testament allusion to Genesis 2:24 probably occurs in Malachi 2:15, but the syntax of this text is notoriously difficult to grasp.[44] Nevertheless, Malachi 2:15a probably ought to be read as the following: "<u>Has not the Lord made the two of you one?</u> You belong to him in body and spirit" (TNIV; see also ESV, ASV, NJB). If this rendering is correct, it is likely that Genesis 2:24 is in mind.[45]

Third, not only does the primeval couple's marriage serve as the climax of the Genesis 1–2 narrative and constitute the foundation of Israelite marriage, but it also should be viewed as a covenant between man and woman.[46] Though the term *covenant* is not found in Genesis 2, the concept is present there. Hugenberger persuasively makes this point in his work *Marriage as a Covenant*. He recognizes that "the language of 'leave' and 'cleave' appears intended to stress the necessity of a radical change, not of domicile, but of one's preeminent loyalty—a husband is to transfer to his wife the primary familial loyalty which he owed to his parents."[47] The act of Adam and Eve becoming "one flesh" does not primarily refer to sexual union but a "bond which is founded on a love commitment which exceeds even filiation" (see Mal 2:14).[48]

Fourth, and most importantly, marriage in the Old Testament is analogous to God's covenant with Israel. Throughout the Old Testament, the Lord's relationship to Israel is often metaphorically portrayed as a marriage between a husband and a wife. A few key verbs that are found in Genesis 2:24 occur

---

[43]Hugenberger, *Marriage as a Covenant*, pp. 153-56.

[44]Ibid., pp. 125-51.

[45]In addition to Mal 2:15, four quotations of Gen 2:24 are even found in the New Testament: Mt 19:4-6, Mk 10:7, 1 Cor 6:16 and Eph 5:31. Clearly, Gen 2:24 plays a large role even from an intertextual and canonical standpoint.

[46]Some scholars who see Adam and Eve's marriage as covenantal are: Victor Hamilton, *The Book of Genesis: Chapters 1–17*, NICOT (Grand Rapids: Eerdmans, 1990), p. 181; Richard M. Davidson, *Flame of Yahweh: Sexuality in the Old Testament* (Peabody: Hendrickson, 2007), pp. 44-46; David Instone-Brewer, *Divorce and Remarriage in the Bible: The Social and Literary Context* (Grand Rapids: Eerdmans, 2002), pp. 1-19; John K. Tarwater, "The Covenantal Nature of Marriage in the Order of Creation in Genesis 1 and 2" (PhD diss., Southeastern Baptist Theological Seminary, 2002).

[47]Hugenberger, *Marriage as a Covenant*, pp. 159-60.

[48]Ibid., p. 162.

elsewhere in covenantal texts with God and Israel,[49] and possibly may echo Genesis 2:24. Deuteronomy 31:16-17 may be using the key verb "forsake" (*ʿzb*) in an ironic fashion: "these people will soon prostitute themselves to the foreign gods of the land they are entering. They will forsake me [*waʿăzābanî*] and break the covenant I made with them. And in that day I will become angry with them and forsake them [*waʿăzābtîm*]; I will hide my face from them" (NIV; cf. Deut 29:25). Instead of "forsaking" their idols and cleaving to the Lord, Israel "forsook" the Lord. Therefore, the Lord will "forsake" them. The verb "cling" (*dbq*) also occurs in a few interesting contexts. In Deuteronomy 10:20, "You shall fear the LORD your God; you shall serve him and cling [*tidbāq*] to him, and you shall swear by his name." A few chapters later, this same theme is repeated: "You shall follow the LORD your God and fear him; and you shall keep his commandments, listen to his voice, serve him, and cling [*tidbāqûn*] to him" (Deut 13:4; cf. Deut 4:4; 11:22; 30:20; *Jub.* 1.23-24).

The most explicit application of Genesis 2:24 in the Old Testament, as we have seen above, is found in Mal 2:15: "Has not the Lord made the two of you one? You belong to him in body and spirit. And why has he made you one? Because he was seeking godly offspring. So be on your guard, and do not be unfaithful to the wife of your youth" (TNIV). Here the prophet Malachi in his third disputation addresses various concerns with the post-exilic community. The land is polluted because of Israel's unfaithfulness to the covenant, particularly by their committing divorce and perfidy. The prophet conceives of marriage as a "covenant" (Mal 2:14), and thus admonishes the people to regard it as such.

Conceptually, the metaphor of God taking Israel as his wife permeates the Old Testament, particularly the prophetic corpus.[50] Weinfeld claims that a marital relationship between God and Israel already exists in the Pentateuch.[51] Sinai, the founding moment of Israel, may even be viewed as a "marriage" between the Lord and Israel (cf. Hos 13:5; Ezek 20:9).[52] A few suggest that the

---

[49]In *L.A.E.* 32.15, the narrator comments, "Not unjustly did God take from you the rib of the first-formed, knowing that from his [Adam's] rib Israel would be born." Here Israel is organically related to the union between Adam and Eve.

[50]On the marital relationship between God and Israel, see, e.g., Davidson, *Flame of Yahweh*, pp. 113-17; Instone-Brewer, *Divorce and Remarriage*, pp. 34-58; Raymond C. Ortlund, Jr., *Whoredom: God's Unfaithful Wife in Biblical Theology*, NSBT (Grand Rapids: Eerdmans, 1996).

[51]Moshe Weinfeld, *Deuteronomy and the Deuteronomic School* (Oxford: Clarendon, 1972), pp. 81-82n6; see also Moshe Weinfeld, "Berit—Covenant vs. Obligation," *Bib* 56 (1975): 120-28 (esp. p. 125).

[52]J. K. Hoffmeier, "Moses," in *ISBE* 3:419; George A. Knight, *Hosea: Introduction and Commentary* (London: SCM Press, 1960), pp. 22-25; Seock-Tae Sohn, *The Divine Election of Israel* (Grand Rapids: Eerdmans, 1991), pp. 40-44.

notion of God being "jealous" for Israel and the natural corollary of Israel "playing the harlot" also bear this out.[53] The Lord is jealous for Israel because he has entered into a marriage contract with her (Ex 34:14; cf., e.g., Deut 4:24; 5:9; 6:15; 32:16, 21; 1 Kings 14:22). Elsewhere in the Old Testament, this metaphor of adultery against the Lord appears in greater detail (e.g., Is 54:6; 50:1-3; 62:5; Jer 2:29–3:25; Hos 1–3; Amos 7:17).

In conclusion, the Old Testament conception of marriage properly understood finds its roots in Genesis 2:24. The Israelites were to hearken back to Adam and Eve's marriage in the garden as the fountainhead of all Israelite marriage. Genesis 2:24 is the paradigm of the Israelite model of marriage. Since the primeval couple's marriage was the template for future marriages, we must keep Genesis 2:24 in mind when we study the marriage metaphor between the Lord and Israel. Just as Adam made a covenant with his wife, Eve, the Lord made a covenant with his wife, Israel. Israel was to model her behavior after Eve and remain faithful to her Adamic husband, the Lord. With the Old Testament context of Genesis 2:24 in mind, we will now return to Ephesians 5:31-32.

The content of the mystery. Paul cites the LXX of Genesis 2:24[54] about man and woman becoming "one flesh," and claims that "this mystery is great [*to mystērion touto mega estin*],[55] but I am speaking with reference to Christ and the Church" (Eph 5:32). That mystery is here called "great" is unique in the New Testament; nowhere else is mystery labeled as such.[56]

Scholars have yet to reach a consensus regarding the precise content of the unveiled mystery in Ephesians 5:32. The views fall generally into five categories:

---

[53]Davidson, *Flame of Yahweh*, pp. 113-14; Instone-Brewer, *Divorce and Remarriage*, p. 34.

[54]Paul makes only few changes to the Greek Old Testament of Gen 2:24. At the beginning of the verse, the Septuagint reads *heneken toutou* ("because of this" or "therefore"), whereas Eph 5:31 has *anti toutou* ("for this reason"). A few scholars have made much of this change. Moritz, for example, thinks that this change reflects Paul's logical digression, thus downplaying the significance of the quotation (*Profound Mystery*, p. 135). It is best, however, to recognize that Paul's use of the Old Testament occurs not as a digression but as the crucial basis for the unified relationship of Christ with the church. The change probably reflects Paul's attempt to weave the quotation into the overall logical flow of the text (O'Brien, *Ephesians*, p. 429).

[55]Scholars disagree as to how to render the clause *to mystērion touto mega estin*. There are two possible renderings: "this is a great mystery" (TNIV; KJV; NRSV) and "this mystery is great" (ESV; NET; ASV). O'Brien, *Ephesians*, p. 430n284, rightly notes that the latter rendering highlights the gravity of the mystery. On the other hand, the former translation underscores the inscrutability of the mystery. For further discussion of this syntactical problem, see Sampley, 'One Flesh,' pp. 86-87; and Moritz, *Profound Mystery*, pp. 142-43.

[56]1 Tim 3:16 is close ("great is the mystery of godliness"). The closest we have to this occurrence outside of 1 Tim 3:16 stems from the pseudepigraphical *LAE* [*Apocalypse*] (21.1; 34.1).

1. The "sacrament" of marriage. Roman Catholic theologians often advocate this view, yet it is the least likely option. Nowhere in the biblical or Jewish literature does *mystery* possess a sacramental sense.[57]

2. It primarily concerns the mysterious relationship between a man and a woman. Moritz is representative of this position.[58]

3. *Mystery* strictly refers to the intimate relationship between Christ and the church and not to an exposition of Genesis 2:24.[59] Like the first two views above, this view also overlooks the significance of the Genesis 2:24 quotation. That is, according to these views, the revealed mystery is not Paul's *interpretation* of Genesis 2:24, rather, *mystery* is only being applied in some way to marriage.

4. Paul discovers a typological relationship between Christ and the church in his exegesis of Genesis 2:24,[60] but his interpretation is generally at odds with the original meaning of Genesis 2:24. This view is much more concerned with the use of Genesis 2:24 and Paul's strained exegesis of it. But is this really the case? Does Paul's hermeneutic violate the meaning of Genesis 2:24? If the verse is viewed narrowly, only within the context of Genesis 2, then such a conclusion could seem to be warranted.

5. Our view is closest to view number 4 here in that we do believe that the divulged mystery is grounded in Paul's exegesis of Genesis 2:24, but his exegesis is not *entirely* "new" or so creative that it contravenes the meaning of Genesis 2:24, as view number 4 affirms. We also disagree with the first three views in that we believe that Genesis 2:24 and its immediate and broader context play a crucial role in the revealed mystery.

---

[57]See the critique by Andreas J. Köstenberger, "The Mystery of Christ and the Church: Head and Body, 'One Flesh,'" *TJ* 12 (1991): 86-87.

[58]Moritz, *Profound Mystery*, pp. 144-45.

[59]E.g., Köstenberger, "Mystery of Christ," pp. 91-92; J. Cambier, "Le grand mystère concernant le Christ et son Église: Éphésiens 5,22-33," *Bib* 47 (1966): 43-90; Hoehner, *Ephesians*, pp. 777-78; Lincoln, *Ephesians*, p. 381.

[60]Bruce, *Ephesians*, pp. 394-95; Bockmuehl, *Revelation and Mystery*, p. 204; Kim, *Origin of Paul's Gospel*, p. 78n1; Günther Bornkamm, "μυστήριον, μυέω," in *TDNT* 4:823; C. Brown, "Secret," in *NIDNTT* 3:505 (501-11); R. Brown, *Semitic Background*, pp. 65-66; Joseph Coppens, "'Mystery' in the Theology of Saint Paul and Its Parallels at Qumran," in *Paul and Qumran: Studies in New Testament Exegesis*, ed. Jerome Murphy-O'Connor (Chicago: Priority, 1968), pp. 146-47. Though Thielman, "Ephesians," p. 828, does not use the terms *pesher* or "inspired exegesis," he nevertheless states that "he [Paul] believed that God had revealed to him an allegorical application of the statement in Genesis."

If Genesis 2:24 is rightly understood in both its immediate and broader Old Testament context, then Paul's interpretative approach is much more in line with a natural reading of the Old Testament text. It is important for our view that three observations be maintained in understanding Paul's interpretation of Genesis 2:24. First, as we argued earlier, Genesis 2:24 is the model for the Israelite conception of marriage in the Old Testament. Therefore, when marriage is significantly discussed in the Old Testament, Genesis 2:24 is conceptually in mind to one degree or another.

Second, it would appear plausible that marriage, for which Genesis 2:24 is foundational, is metaphorically applied in the Old Testament to God and his past dealings with Israel and to his future, consummative marriage to Israel in the end time. A few prominent Old Testament texts employ the marriage metaphor to God's restoration of Israel in the latter days (Is 61:10; 62:2-5; *4 Ezra* 10).[61]

Third, therefore, in light of the preceding point, it may be concluded that *to some degree* the Genesis 2:24 template for human marriage serves as a as background for and a pointer to the marriage between God and Israel in the Old Testament itself, including God's end-time marriage relationship with Israel in the latter days.

Though the relationship of these three observations is interpretative, as suming their correctness, once they are brought to bear on this discussion Paul's application of Scripture makes sense. *The only major interpretative leap by Paul, it would appear, is the application of the Lord's relationship with Israel to Christ's relationship with the church. Christ becomes identified with the Lord and the church is identified with the true end-time Israel.* But these identifications are not interpretative obstacles too big to hurdle, since both these two notions are already anticipated in the Old Testament itself and, indeed, have already been found in Paul, as well as the preceding sections of Ephesians.[62]

The strongest piece of evidence for this conclusion is found in the immediate context of Ephesians 5. Some commentators have suggested that the Old Testament background to Christ's relationship to the church in Ephesians 5 is the relationship between the Lord and Israel. O'Brien is explicit in this regard: "The

---

[61]Is 62:4b-5 says, for example, "The Lord delights in you, / And *to Him* your land will be married. / For *as* a young man marries a virgin, / So your sons will marry you; / And *as* the bridegroom rejoices over the bride, / So your God will rejoice over you." This is noteworthy since it predicts a final, consummate marriage between God and Israel.

[62]For the latter, see our study above in this chapter on Eph 1 and Eph 3; see also Eph 2:17; 4:8; 5:14, where Christ is identified with Old Testament passages that describe Israel's God.

imagery from the Old Testament about God's relationship to Israel stands behind this use of the marriage analogy."[63] In the Old Testament, as we have seen, Israel is the Lord's bride. In the same way, Paul claims that the church is Christ's "body" (Eph 5:23) and his bride: "Christ loved the church and gave Himself up for her, that He might sanctify her . . . that He might present to Himself the church in all her glory" (Eph 5:25-27). Strengthening this suggestion is that Ephesians 5:26 is an allusion to Ezekiel 16:9 (see table 6.4).[64] As we saw above, Ezekiel 16 speaks of God rescuing Israel from abandonment and marrying her, a notion that corresponds to Christ's marriage to the church. Both passages also even mention the cleansing of the bride with "water."

Table 6.4

Ezekiel 16:9	Ephesians 5:26
"Then I bathed you with water [*en hydati*], washed off your blood from you and anointed you with oil."	"So that He might sanctify her, having cleansed her by the washing of water [*hydatos*] with the word."

Though Paul has already established the marriage relationship in the previous context on firm grounds (Eph 5:23-29), he finally reveals in Ephesians 5:31-32 (the Gen 2:24 quotation and the "mystery") that this relationship was actually anticipated in the primeval couple's marriage. *The revealed mystery in Ephesians 5 therefore refers to Paul's perception that Adam and Eve's union in marriage typologically corresponds to Christ and the church.* The Old Testament contains historical patterns that foreshadow or anticipate corresponding events at a later time period (i.e., the "latter days"). The nation Israel, its kings, prophets, priests and its significant redemptive episodes composed the essential ingredients of this sacred history. It is within this framework where Adam and Eve's marriage plays a prominent role. Paul views Adam and Eve's marriage in Genesis 2:24 (and all subsequent marriages in the pre–New Testament epoch) to foreshadow Christ's marriage to the church. What facilitated this typology was the Lord's marriage relationship to Israel, which itself was linked to Genesis 2:24 and which was also typological of Christ and the church,

---

[63]O'Brien, *Ephesians*, p. 420. Cf. Sampley, *'One Flesh,'* p. 49, who claims, "A definite relationship of dependence existed between Ephesians and the YHWH-Israel hieros gamos [sacred marriage] of Ezekiel and Song of Songs. Ezekiel and Song of Songs show greatest affinity to Ephesians in their emphasis on the bride, the betrothal of the bride and related washing in water" (our brackets).

[64]Several commentators affirm this allusion to Ezek 16:9 in Eph 5:26: e.g., O'Brien, *Ephesians*, p. 422; Thielman, "Ephesians," p. 826.

as the quotation of Ezekiel 16 demonstrates. Paul's interpretative under-standing of Genesis 2:24 therefore is not strained but in accordance with an established Old Testament pattern.[65]

We can even take this one step further and notice Paul's view of Christ in this regard. We noted above the correspondence between God's relationship with Israel and Christ's present relationship with the church. Paul here ex-plicitly identifies Christ with God,[66] as he does throughout the epistle (Eph 2:17; 4:8; 5:14).

What is "new" about the revealed mystery? We have seen just above that Adam and Eve's marriage in Genesis 2:24 points to God's marriage to Israel in later Old Testament history and to the consummative marriage to him in the end time (Is 61:10; 62:4-5). It was partially hidden in the Old Testament that God's relationship with Israel would be later applied to a single figure, the latter-day Messiah and true Israel. The natural implication of Paul's use of the quo-tation is Christ being identified with God and the church as the true, end-time Israel. This was embedded implicitly in the Old Testament, since as we have seen, Christ's identity with God and end-time Gentiles' identity with end-time Israel is to be found in the Old Testament itself, but there is no explicit identi-fication of the coming Messiah as a husband who would marry end-time Israel. This, however, is a biblical-theological deduction that could have been made by an astute Israelite interpreter, but Paul makes it explicit.

Thus, it is important to recognize *continuity* and some *discontinuity* between the two testaments in Paul's use of *mystery*. His understanding of the disclosed mystery is not a radically new doctrine, but a teaching that, while surprising, finds its roots in the Old Testament. We saw how Adam and Eve's marriage

---

[65]O'Brien is right to note that the application of marriage to the Christ-church relationship has its antecedents in the Old Testament. He claims, "At one level, then, Paul's teaching on marriage is grounded in the Old Testament, while at another level the church's marriage to Christ is prefigured in Adam and Eve" (*Ephesians*, p. 435). Thus, he is right to see that Gen 2:24 is typological of Christ and the church, and he begins to go in the right direction in relating this to the mystery, but he does so vaguely; he does not integrate Gen 2:24 directly enough into the definition of mystery, not at-tempting to show how Gen 2:24 functions in its immediate and wider canonical context in explicit connection to understanding the mystery.

[66]Köstenberger, "Mystery of Christ," p. 89, concedes that if Paul understood Gen 2:24 to be a type of Christ and the church, it should be categorized as a "retrospective typology." That is, the type is only seen *after* the event, which, in this case, is the union between Christ and the church. The shortcom-ing of this view is that it fails to note how Gen 2:24 in its Old Testament canonical context already functions to some degree as the foundation of the metaphor for the relationship between the Lord and Israel.

relationship is viewed as a template that is picked up and reused conceptually throughout the Old Testament, especially when it is applied to God and Israel. It is precisely at this point where the seeds of the Ephesian mystery are sown. These same seeds finally blossom in the New Testament when Paul applies this notion to Christ and the church.[67]

THE MYSTERY OF THE GOSPEL IN EPHESIANS 6

We find the last occurrence of the unveiled mystery in Ephesians 6:18-19:

> With all prayer and petition pray at all times in the Spirit, and with this in view, be on the alert with all perseverance and petition for all the saints, and *pray* on my behalf, that utterance may be given to me in the opening of my mouth, to make known with boldness the <u>mystery of the gospel.</u>

This occurrence appears in Paul's final section of admonition in which he requests that the church be a prayerful community (Eph 6:18-20). In Ephesians 6:18, he asks that his audience "pray at all times in the Spirit" and remain vigilant and sober minded. Finally, in Ephesians 6:19 Paul specifies how they ought to pray for his personal ministry. The apostle requests that the church pray that he will "make known with boldness the mystery of the gospel" (Eph 6:19). To put it another way, the church is to pray that Paul will spread the "mystery of the gospel" to others, even unbelievers. This is the only occurrence in the New Testament where we have the precise phrase "mystery of the gospel" (*to mystērion tou euangeliou*; cf. 1 Tim 3:9, 16).

Colossians 4:3 is similar on a number of levels with regard to our current passage (see table 6.5). In both passages, Paul asks that his audiences pray for his ministry and remain vigilant. They both mention that Paul is imprisoned for the sake of the gospel. Like Ephesians, Colossians 4:3 further specifies the object of prayer—the opportunity for Paul to spread the "mystery of Christ." Since both contexts are nearly identical (and may share a textual relationship), the "mystery of Christ" in Colossians 4:3 seems to be synonymous with the "mystery of the gospel" in Ephesians 6:19. It is likely that the notion of mystery in Colossians 4:3 and Ephesians 6:19 is so tightly bound up with Christ and his work that it has become nearly synonymous with the gospel.

---

[67]The Dead Sea Scrolls display a remarkable similarity to Paul here in Eph 5. To our knowledge, it is the only occurrence outside of Paul where Gen 2:24 is paired with "mystery." 4Q416 2 III, 15-21 (= 4Q418 9–10) and 4Q416 2 IV, 1-5 (= 4Q418 10; 4Q418a 18) form one complete text that encourages readers to conduct themselves in light of the revealed mystery.

Table 6.5

Colossians 4:2-3	Ephesians 6:18-20
"Devote yourselves to <u>prayer, keeping alert</u> in it with an *attitude of* thanksgiving; <u>praying</u> at the same time for us as well, that God will open up to us a door for the word, so that we may speak forth the <u>mystery of Christ, for which I have also been imprisoned</u>; that I may make it clear in the way I ought to speak."	"With all <u>prayer</u> and petition <u>pray</u> at all times in the Spirit, and with this in view, <u>be on the alert</u> with all perseverance and petition for all the saints, and *pray* on my behalf, that utterance may be given to me in the opening of my mouth, to make known with boldness <u>the mystery of the gospel, for which I am an ambassador in chains</u>; that in *proclaiming* it I may speak boldly, as I ought to speak."

The centrality of the gospel, that is, the death and resurrection of Christ and their implications, formulates a fundamentally new phenomenon. Though anticipated and prophesied in the Old Testament (e.g., Rom 1:2; 16:25-26; 1 Cor 15:3-4), the gospel contains new elements. For example, as we have already seen in our discussion of 1 Corinthians 1–2, the crucifixion is labeled a mystery because it was not as clear in the Old Testament that the Messiah would suffer and conquer *in the midst of* death and defeat. Also, that not all the righteous but the Messiah alone would first be resurrected is also a mystery. The Old Testament foretells of a resurrection of *all the righteous* but not of solely the Messiah.[68] These two cardinal truths, absolutely central to the gospel, should be understood as revealed mysteries.

Another dimension of the "mystery of the gospel" is its relationship to events occurring in the "latter days." One salient characteristic of mystery is its end-time connotations. The book of Daniel and early Judaism make this point. The mystery of the gospel concerns God's eschatological actions in Christ and the splitting of the ages.[69]

These aspects of the "mystery of the gospel" would appear to be included to one degree or another in the thickly packed meaning of Ephesians 6:19.

CONCLUSION

We have attempted to demonstrate the significance of the disclosed mystery in the book of Ephesians by not only studying how the term *mystery* functions throughout the book but also by evaluating the concept in light of the Old

---

[68]See pp. 289-91, for further discussion of this theme.

[69]For a helpful discussion on the relation between eschatology, Paul's gospel, and mystery, see Herman Ridderbos, *Paul: An Outline of His Theology*, trans. John Richard de Witt (Grand Rapids: Eerdmans, 1977), pp. 49-53.

Testament. Being deeply rooted in the Old Testament, Paul's teaching in Ephesians is saturated with Old Testament allusions and quotations. Yet, Paul presents his audience with startling "new revelations," albeit anchored in the Old Testament. It is this "newness" in relation to continuity with the Old Testament that we have attempted to tease out in this chapter.

Paul in Ephesians 1 pleads with his audience to grasp the "mystery of His [God's] will." We observed three aspects of this unveiled mystery: the scope, instrumentation and result of Christ's cosmic rule. The scope of the mystery is Christ's rule over the cosmos. The Old Testament and Judaism often speak of the Messiah's rule over the pagan nations on earth, but they do not explicitly speak of the Messiah reigning over the heavenly realm of the cosmos; that prerogative is reserved for God and him alone, though there are some hints that the Messiah's rule would extend even into heaven (e.g., Dan 7:13-14 in relation especially to Dan 10:20-21). The instrumentation of Christ's rule pertains to his death as the means to achieving his rule. Lastly, and the main focus of the mystery in Ephesians 1:9, the result of Christ's rule includes the cosmic unity of "all things" in Christ, whether spiritual or physical. All has come under the domain and rule of the Messiah; Christ "sums up" these estranged entities.

One concrete application of the "mystery of his will" (Eph 1:9) is the unity that Jews and Gentiles enjoy in Christ, which is described in Ephesians 3. Though most commentators contend that the mystery in Ephesians 3 entails the equality between Jews and Gentiles, we argued that it includes the *manner* in which these two groups become one as true Israel, namely, through Christ. The Old Testament and early Judaism seem to describe the end-time conversion of the Gentiles as necessitating that they embrace nationalistic tags that demarcate the covenant community from the surrounding nations (e.g., circumcision, food laws, Sabbath). Gentiles would thus be nearly indistinguishable from their Jewish counterparts, since they would become part of Israel in a similar way that Rahab and Ruth did. The mystery that was revealed to Paul, however, is that Gentiles are no longer required to take on the covenantal identification tags of Judaism, which were required by the law. By attaching themselves by faith to Christ—who is true Israel and the only identification tag for being a true Israelite—they become part of the covenant community of latter-day Israel. It simply was not as clear in the Old Testament that when the Messiah would come the theocracy of Israel would be so completely reconstituted that it would continue only as the new organism of the Messiah, the true

Israel of God, who represents those identified with him by faith.

The marital mystery is like the first few occurrences of the term in that it deals once more with the theme of unity. The nature of the revealed mystery in Ephesians 5 is organically tied to Genesis 2:24 in that it draws threads from that earlier passage. Paul reads Genesis 2:24 and surmises that the text is indeed speaking of the union between Christ and the church. Once we interpreted Genesis 2:24 in its immediate and broad Old Testament context, Paul's use of Scripture, though somewhat creative, is not out of line with the original meaning of Genesis 2:24 and its reverberations elsewhere in the Old Testament.

Finally, Paul, in Ephesians 6:19, employs the phrase "mystery of the gospel" to describe how the gospel, that is, the death and resurrection of Christ in establishing his rule, is a new phenomenon and contains some new elements. The centrality of suffering in the inaugurated rule of the Messiah, the resurrection of only *one* righteous Israelite, and the already-and-not-yet nature of the kingdom, though subtly anticipated in the Old Testament, are all new latter-day revelations, which are presumably included to one extent or another in the thick content of the mystery in Ephesians 6:19, though there these things are not explicitly mentioned.

EXCURSUS 6.1: END-TIME CONVERSION OF THE GENTILES IN THE OLD TESTAMENT AND JUDAISM

We will now attempt to make a thumbnail sketch of the end-time conversion of Gentiles to the Israelite faith according to the Old Testament and Judaism in order to lay out clearly the Old Testament expectation of Gentile salvation in the end-time and the contrast with Paul's mystery in Ephesians 3. Scholars have spent much time studying proselytization in early and later Judaism but not with respect to the Gentiles' *latter-day conversion*.[70] That the Gentiles would be restored to God as a result of Israel's end-time restoration and become united to them is clear from a number of Old Testament texts (e.g., Ps 87:4-6;

---

[70]See, for example, Shaye J. D. Cohen, "Crossing Boundary and Becoming a Jew," *HTR* 82 (1989): 13-33; John P. Dickson, *Mission-Commitment in Ancient Judaism and in the Pauline Communities: The Shape, Extent, and Background of Early Christian Mission*, WUNT 159 (Tübingen: Mohr Siebeck, 2003), pp. 15-19; John G. Gager, *The Origins of Anti-Semitism: Attitudes Toward Judaism in Pagan and Christian Antiquity* (New York: Oxford University Press, 1985), 59-66; Scot McKnight, *A Light Among the Gentiles: Jewish Missionary Activity in the Second Temple Period* (Minneapolis: Fortress, 1991).

Is 11:9-10; 14:1-2; 19:18-25; 25:6-10; 42:1-9; 49:6; 51:4-6; 60:1-16; Jer 3:17; Zeph 3:9-10; Zech 2:11). Scholars often term this notion as the "eschatological pilgrimage" of the Gentiles.[71] Yet we are more concerned with the *manner* in which Gentiles become part of God's eschatologically redeemed people group. The converted nations were, it seems, to be nearly indistinguishable from the Israelite in the latter days, as was the case with converted Gentiles in the Old Testament epoch (like Ruth and Uriah).

Though some doubt that the Gentiles were required to take on external nationalistic signs in the latter days,[72] the following texts seemingly state that conversion to the Israelite faith was required and accompanied by external covenantal signs. However, we ought to keep in mind one thought as we briefly survey the following texts—the lack of overwhelming, explicit evidence. The Gentiles becoming Jewish proselytes in the end time is a practice hinted at in a few Old Testament texts, but it is not prominent nor is it discussed at great length. All that we have are a few enigmatic texts scattered here and there in the prophetic corpus and the precedent of how Gentiles would convert to Israel's religion in the Old Testament period.

End-time conversion of the Gentiles in the Old Testament. The book of Isaiah contains some of the more noteworthy references to the Gentiles embracing covenantal markers in the latter days. Isaiah 56:3-8 envisions a future time when Gentiles will become part of true Israel in the latter days.[73]

> Let not the foreigner who has joined himself to the LORD say,
> "The LORD will surely separate me from His people."
> Nor let the eunuch say, "Behold, I am a dry tree."

---

[71]See Joachim Jeremias, *Jesus' Promise to the Nations*, SBT 24 (London: SCM Press, 1958), pp. 55-73. Jeremias's study is particularly seminal in this regard. He identifies five characteristics of the eschatological pilgrimage of the Gentiles: the epiphany of God, the call of God, the journey of the Gentiles, worship at the world sanctuary, and the messianic banquet on the world-mountain (pp. 57-59). For other surveys of this theme, see also James P. Ware, *The Mission of the Church in Paul's Letter to the Philippians in the Context of Ancient Judaism,* NovTSup 120 (Boston: Brill, 2005), pp. 57-91; Michael F. Bird, *Jesus and the Origins of the Gentile Mission,* LNTS 331 (New York: T & T Clark, 2006), pp. 26-29.

[72]E.g., Terence L. Donaldson, "Proselytes or 'Righteous Gentiles'? The Status of Gentiles in Eschatological Pilgrimage Patterns of Thought," *JSP* 7 (1990): 12.

[73]Note also Is 2:2-3, wherein Isaiah refers to an expectation when God will one day reveal "instruction" to the Gentiles (Is 42:4; 51:4), and all the nations will stream to Jerusalem in the latter days; they are to learn divine instruction and participate with Israel in worshiping Yahweh (see the parallel in Mic 4:1-3). See also the Targums of Is 2:3 and Mic 4:1-3. The *Midrash Rabbah* likewise claims, "The Torah will go forth from Zion; as it says, *For out of Zion shall go forth the Torah* (Isa. II, 3)" (Lev 24:4).

For thus says the LORD,

"To the eunuchs who keep My sabbaths,
And choose what pleases Me,
And hold fast My covenant,
To them I will give in My house and within My walls a memorial,
And a name better than that of sons and daughters;
I will give them an everlasting name which will not be cut off.

Also the foreigners who join themselves to the LORD,
To minister to Him, and to love the name of the LORD,
To be His servants, every one who keeps from profaning the sabbath
And holds fast My covenant;
Even those I will bring to My holy mountain
And make them joyful in My house of prayer.
Their burnt offerings and their sacrifices will be acceptable on My altar;
For My house will be called a house of prayer for all the peoples."
The LORD God, who gathers the dispersed of Israel, declares,
"Yet *others* I will gather to them, to those *already* gathered."

That this vision refers to an end-time era is clear from several indicators. The Gentiles will receive a "name better than that of sons and daughters," that is, "an everlasting name" (Is 56:5). Elsewhere in Isaiah, this slogan refers to God's new creational act whereby he creates a new people group (Is 62:2).[74] In addition, God's promise to "bring [them] to my holy mountain" is the same eschatological event of Isaiah 2:3 and is repeated in several other texts (Zech 2:11; 8:20-23). This means that Gentiles would have to move geographically to the land of Israel in order to be able to participate in the Israelite community of the latter days. Finally, Isaiah 56:8, though extraordinarily difficult to nuance, seems to refer to a future "gathering" of Gentiles: "I will gather still others [Gentiles] to them [Jewish exiles] besides those already gathered [Jewish proselytes]" (NIV).

Isaiah 56 targets two particular classes of people who will be able to serve in God's end-time temple. The first class is a general "foreigner" (lit., "son of a foreigner": *ben-hannēkār*), who was traditionally forbidden to participate in covenantal obligations and responsibilities, such as Passover (Ex 12:43, 45) or actively participate in the Israelite community's worship in the temple (Deut 23:3). In addition to the "foreigner," the "eunuch" (*sārîs*) is also mentioned as

---

[74]See also G. K. Beale, *The Book of Revelation: A Commentary on the Greek Text*, NIGTC (Grand Rapids: Eerdmans, 1999), pp. 254-55.

fully participating in this latter-day gathering. Like the foreigner, the eunuch was forbidden to participate in the assembly of Israel's worship in the temple (Deut 23:1).[75] Here, however, the eunuch is granted full access to the Israelite community, especially temple worship, and is deemed an equal member. For our purposes, we need to highlight the *way in which the Gentiles participate in the end-time people of God.*

Isaiah 56:3 mentions that the foreigner "has joined himself to the LORD" and then Isaiah 56:6 further describes how the foreigner does so. Foreigners "minister to Him [the LORD]," "love the name of the LORD," and, importantly, "keep from profaning the Sabbath." The last description is the most telling in that the foreigners are required to maintain one of the most distinctive features of the covenant community—keeping the Sabbath (e.g., Ex 20:8-11; 31:14-16; Lev 23:3, 11, 15). The same conduct is required of the eunuch in Isaiah 56:4-5: "to the eunuchs who keep My sabbaths . . . to them I will give in My house and within My walls a memorial" and a new name. Childs suggests that the conditions which the eunuch meets "are simply the norms appropriate to a life lived under torah."[76] Keeping the Sabbath is not required to enter the covenant yet it is a requirement of covenant membership in the eschaton, by which also the Gentile foreigners were to abide.

In addition to covenant keeping, the "foreigners" and "eunuchs" are expected to offer sacrifices at the temple: "Even those I will bring to My holy mountain and make them joyful in My house of prayer. Their burnt offerings and their sacrifices will be acceptable on My altar" (Is 56:7). Apparently, at the end of the latter-day pilgrimage (see Is 2:2-3; Mic 4:1-2), Gentiles will bring sacrifices to the temple, an act of obedience to Israel's law that further separates the covenant community from the pagan nations. The Gentiles are also to serve in the temple as Israelite priests: "Also the foreigners who join themselves to the LORD, to minister to him . . . in My house of prayer" will offer "burnt offerings and their sacrifices" (Is 56:6-7).

Isaiah 66:18-21 provides another example describing the manner in which Gentiles become part of God's eschatological community, especially becoming qualified as priests for temple worship:

---

[75]Though it is possible that Deut 23:1, 3 forbids these people from becoming a part of the Israelite community in general.

[76]Brevard S. Childs, *Isaiah*, OTL (Louisville: Westminster John Knox, 2000), p. 458; cf. John Oswalt, *The Book of Isaiah Chapters 40-66*, NICOT (Grand Rapids: Eerdmans, 1998), p. 460.

For I know their works and their thoughts; the time is coming to gather all nations and tongues. And they shall come and see My glory. I will set a sign among them and will send survivors from them to the nations: Tarshish, Put, Lud, Meshech, Tubal and Javan, to the distant coastlands that have neither heard My fame nor seen My glory. And they will declare My glory among the nations. Then they shall bring all your brethren [i.e., who are Gentiles] from all the nations as a grain offering to the LORD, on horses, in chariots, in litters, on mules and on camels, to My holy mountain Jerusalem," says the LORD, "just as the sons of Israel bring their grain offering in a clean vessel to the house of the LORD. "I will also take some of them [Gentiles] for priests *and* for Levites," says the LORD.

This passage is notoriously difficult to interpret, since there is some ambiguity about the identity of "them" in Isaiah 66:19. It most likely refers to faithful Jews who have begun to experience restoration. The following verse then mentions their missionary efforts of restored Jews to the Gentiles, who become "brethren" to the restored Jews. Though it is not entirely clear to whom the "brethren" refers, in the immediate context the term probably should be identified with the Gentiles from the surrounding nations. Nowhere in all of Isaiah or in the prophets is there any mention of Israelites restoring other Israelites (though Isaiah does envision an "individual Israel" restoring the remnant of Israel, e.g., Is 49:2-6; 53). If we are correct, we can then interpretatively paraphrase Isaiah 66:20 in the following manner: "Then they, the restored Jews, shall bring all your brethren, the Gentiles, from all the nations as a grain offering to the LORD" (Is 66:20a). Again, as in Isaiah 2:2-3; 56:7, Gentiles are becoming Israelites, in part by moving geographically to Israel.

We can finally grasp the meaning of Isaiah 66:21. These "brethren" of Isaiah 66:20 are Gentile converts, some of whom God will make as priests over Israel: "I will also take some of them [the Gentiles] for priests *and* for Levites" (Is 66:21). God selects some Gentiles and Jews to function, astonishingly, *as priests and Levites* in his end-time temple, which would be a development of Isaiah 56:3-8, where this idea is explicit. This is another of the various ways to indicate that the nations become identified as Israelites in the latter days.[77]

---

[77]On the debate over whether or not this passage views Gentiles as those who will become "priests and . . . Levites," see Beale, *New Testament Biblical Theology*, pp. 660-62. The commentary on Is 66:21 in the *Midrash on the Psalms* is noteworthy in this regard: "Out of the heathen who will bring Israel to the King Messiah, God will single out any one of priestly, or Levitical, or Israelitish origin, for of them also will I take means that God will take priests and Levites not only out of the children of Israel that are brought, but also out of the nations that bring the children of Israel" (*Midr. Ps.* 68.6).

Though we have seen earlier that Isaiah 56 and 66 show a slackening of the Mosaic law for people in the latter days, these passages also reveal that parts of that law will be kept.

The final passage is drawn from Zechariah 14:16-19:

> Then it will come about that any who are left of all the nations that went against Jerusalem will go up from year to year to worship the King, the LORD of hosts, and to celebrate the Feast of Booths. And it will be that whichever of the families of the earth does not go up to Jerusalem to worship the King, the LORD of hosts, there will be no rain on them. And if the family of Egypt does not go up or enter, then no *rain will fall* on them; it will be the plague with which the LORD smites the nations who do not go up to celebrate the Feast of Booths. This will be the punishment of Egypt, and the punishment of all the nations who do not go up to celebrate the Feast of Booths.

Here the surviving Gentiles of Zechariah 14:1-15 will "go up to [the location of] Jerusalem" and will worship the Lord in Jerusalem and will "celebrate the Feast of Booths." Not only will the Gentiles join with the Jews in their worship of Yahweh, they will also participate in the celebration of certain Jewish festivals, particularly the Feast of Booths. The Feast of Booths is of particular interest to our study. According to Leviticus 23:40-43 the feast was to last seven days annually. Only Israelites were to celebrate this feast: "all the native-born in Israel shall live in booths" (Lev 23:43; cf. Deut 16:13-16). The purpose of this celebration was to rehearse Israel's deliverance from Egypt, when they lived in "booths" in the wilderness. It was a time of meditation and reflection on God's forgiveness and gracious election. This feast publically indicated that Israel was God's chosen nation, set apart from all other nations. In Zechariah 14, "all the nations" celebrate this identical feast. Indeed, if a particular nation refuses to participate, then God will judge them by withholding rain: "If the family of Egypt does not go up or enter, then no rain *will fall* on them. . . . This will be the punishment of all the nations who do not go up to celebrate the Feast of Booths" (Zech 14:18-19).

The above survey of various Old Testament passages seems to indicate that restored Gentiles in the eschaton will join themselves to Israel by taking on the covenantal badges or signs of Israel's law—external indicators that demarcate them as part of God's chosen people group. Isaiah 56:3-8 claims that Gentiles will "hold fast to the covenant" and "keep the sabbaths." We have seen repeatedly that moving to the location of Israel was a presupposition for Gentiles to become eschatological Israelites. We have also seen repeatedly that Gentiles would serve as priests in the temple. Finally, Gentiles, according to Zechariah 14:16-19, will participate in the celebration of the Feast of Booths. All of these examples indicate that the Old Testament perspective is that Gentiles in the eschaton were required to take on external covenantal badges of Israel's law that identified them as true Israelites in order for them to become true Israelites.

Other relevant passages in the Old Testament likewise predict the conversion of the Gentiles. Most of them show that Gentiles had to move to geographical Israel in order to be considered to be true end-time Israelites. Though they do not focus on the manner in which Gentiles become part of the covenant community (as the previous texts do), they readily *anticipate a time when Gentiles will become true Israelites, especially by moving geographically to Israel.* The following is a brief survey of some of the more relevant texts (see also Is 19:18-25; Zech 2:11; 8:22-23; 9:6-7).[78]

Isaiah 49 is among the clearest statements in the Old Testament that in the latter days the Messiah would sum up true Israel in himself, and this is related to Gentiles:

> He said to Me, "You are My Servant, Israel,
> In Whom I will show My glory."
> But I said, "I have toiled in vain,
> I have spent My strength for nothing and vanity;
> Yet surely the justice *due* to Me is with the LORD,
> And My reward with My God."
>
> And now says the LORD, who formed Me from the womb to be His Servant,
> To bring Jacob back to Him, so that Israel might be gathered to Him
> (For I am honored in the sight of the LORD,
> And My God is My strength),
> He says, "It is too small a thing that You should be My Servant
> To raise up the tribes of Jacob and to restore the preserved ones of Israel;
> I will also make You a light of the nations
> So that My salvation may reach to the end of the earth." (Is 49:3-6)

Here the Servant is called "Israel": "And He [the LORD] said to me, 'You are My Servant, Israel, in Whom I will show My glory'" (Is 49:3). And his latter-day

---

[78]For more detailed interaction with these Old Testament texts and others, see Beale, *New Testament Biblical Theology*, pp. 651-68.

mission is "to raise up the tribes of Jacob and to restore the preserved ones of Israel" (Is 49:6). The Servant in Isaiah 49:3 is best understood to be an individual messianic Servant who would restore the remnant of Israel. One individual sums up and represents the actions of "the many."[79]

But how is the notion of the messianic Servant summing up true Israel relevant to Gentiles becoming true Israel in the eschaton? Since this Servant was to be the summation of true Israel, all who wanted to identify with true Israel, whether Jew or Gentile, must identify with him (which is the implication of Isaiah 53). Though the Old Testament never makes this connection explicit between the individual true Israel, the Servant (or Israel's end-time king) and Gentiles who identify with him, it appears to be implicit or an implication. We have discussed in the preceding section that Isaiah 2:2-3; 56:3-8; 66:21 also portray Gentiles becoming part of true, end-time Israel partly by moving to the geographical region of Israel. Other Isaiah texts describe the nations making pilgrimage to Israel's land in the latter days (Is 49:22-23; 60:4-12). Such incoming Gentiles would need to make obeisance not only to Israelites in general but, in the light of the context in Isaiah 49–53, presumably also to the one who sums up all Israel in himself.

Psalm 87 speaks of Gentiles being "born" in Zion in the eschaton, inheriting the status of native-born Israelites:

> His foundation is in the holy mountains.
> The LORD loves the gates of Zion
> More than all the *other* dwelling places of Jacob.
> Glorious things are spoken of you,
> O city of God.
> "I shall mention Rahab and Babylon among those who know Me;
> Behold, Philistia and Tyre with Ethiopia:
> 'This one was born there.'"
> But of Zion it shall be said, "This one and that one were born in her";
> And the Most High Himself will establish her.
> The LORD will count when He registers the peoples,
> "This one was born there."
> Then those who sing as well as those who play the flutes *shall say*,
> "All my springs *of joy* are in you." (Ps 87:1-7)

The "glorious things" spoken of "Zion," the "city of God" (Ps 87:2-3), entail

---

[79]Cf. Dan 7:13-27, where the "Son of Man" functions as and represents true Israel.

Gentile nations having been "born there" (Ps 87:4). The reference to "there" in Psalm 87:4, where the nations are born, refers to "Zion" and the "city of God" in Psalm 87:2-3. In Psalm 87:6 the clause "the LORD will count when He registers the peoples" refers to a final, end-time accounting of the Gentile peoples who "know Him" (Ps 87:4) and who are considered true end-time Israelites because they have been "born there" (Ps 87:6b) in "Zion" (Ps 87:2, 5), the "city of God" (Ps 87:3). Thus, people who have their national and ethnic origins among Gentile nations will be deemed true latter-day Israelites or true citizens of Zion.

Likewise Ezekiel 47, also mentioned briefly above, understands that at the final restoration of Israel, Gentiles will be considered to be part of the nation.

> "So you shall divide this land among yourselves according to the tribes of Israel. You shall divide it by lot for an inheritance among yourselves and among the aliens who stay in your midst, who bring forth sons in your midst. And they shall be to you as the native-born among the sons of Israel; they shall be allotted an inheritance with you among the tribes of Israel. And in the tribe with which the alien stays, there you shall give *him* his inheritance," declares the LORD GOD. (Ezek 47:21-23)

Gentile "aliens" are reckoned here as a constitutive part of the nation Israel. The nation is commanded to "divide this land among yourselves according to the tribes of Israel (which included giving the "alien" an "inheritance") since these aliens were to be considered "as the native-born among the sons of Israel." It is possible that since Ezekiel 47:22 says that the sons of the alien were to be considered "as" (or "like") native-born Israelites, the Gentiles were not considered to be *genuine* Israelites. However, the best context for understanding this is the precedent of how Gentiles became converts to the faith of Israel in the Old Testament epoch.

When people—such as a remnant of the Egyptians who went with Israel out of Egypt (Ex 12:38, 48-51), or Rahab (Josh 6:25; cf. Mt 1:5), or Ruth (Ruth 1:16; 4:10; cf. Mt 1:5)—converted to the faith of Israel, they were considered members of the nation of Israel, *just as much as was a native-born Israelite*. The same is likely the case here in Ezekiel 47. According to the principle that "the last things will be like the first things," the eschatological condition of the "alien" in Ezekiel 47:22 ("and they [aliens] will be unto you as a native [*wĕhāyû lākem kĕᵓezrāḥ*] among the sons of Israel") appears to echo the condition of the alien at the very inception of Israel's history according to Exodus 12:48 ("and he [the alien] will

be as a native [*wĕhāyâ kĕ'ezrāḥ*] of the land"). Ezekiel 47:22-23 is introduced by
the statement "You shall divide this land among yourselves according to the
tribes of Israel" (Ezek 47:21). Then these verses describe members of the tribes
of Israel to be ethnic Israelites, and those who are nonethnic members of the
tribes are also mentioned and are also considered to be true tribal members,
since they get an inheritance of part of Israel's land just like the native born do.[80]

End-time Gentile conversion in early Judaism. Like the Old Testament,
not many texts exist in Judaism that explicitly address the *manner* in which
Gentiles become part of true Israel in the end time. Several texts do mention
the inclusion of the Gentiles (e.g., Tob 14:5-6; 13:13; *T. Zeb.* 9.8; *Jos. Asen.* 15.6;
Pss. Sol. 17.29-34), yet they lack clarity about how this conversion is accomplished. Nevertheless, a few texts seem to indicate that Gentiles will not only
join Israel in the latter days but will also externally look like Israelites and
behave accordingly.[81]

> No longer will the unclean foot of Greeks revel around your land but they will
> have a mind in their breasts that conforms to your laws. (*Sib. Or.* 5.264-66; cf.
> 1.383-384, first to second century A.D.)

> And then all islands and cities will say, "How much the Immortal loves those
> men! . . . They will bring forth from their mouths a delightful utterance in hymns,
> "Come, let us fall on the ground and entreat the immortal king, the great eternal
> God. Let us send to the Temple, since he alone is sovereign and let us all ponder
> the Law of the Most High God." (*Sib. Or.* 3:710-719, first century B.C.)

These two texts from *Sibylline Oracles* speak of the nations embracing Torah.
The first passage expresses the hope that the "Greeks" will "conform to your
laws." This is made even more explicit in book three. There the Gentiles or the
"islands and cities" entreat the Lord by coming to his temple (cf. Is 2:2; Mic 4:2)
and "pondering the Law of the Most High God" (7.10-19). The word here for
"pondering" (*phrazō*) occurs a few other times in the *Sibylline Oracles*. In 14.273,
the word means something to the effect of "telling" or "relating": "When he
gathers many oracles from islands which declare [*phrazomenoi*] to strangers
battle and grievous strife" (cf. *T. Sol.* 6:8). The word also occurs in 14.300-301,

---

[80]Note also Isaiah's prophecy that Jews will bring Gentiles from the surrounding nations back to
Jerusalem, where they will become part of true Israel and some of them will even function as Levitical priests (Is 66:19-21).

[81]See also *1 En.* 10.21: "And all the children of the people will become righteous, and all nations shall
worship and bless me; and they will all prostrate themselves to me" (cf. also 90.6-42).

though it is probably closer to our text in 7.19: "When three children win Olympian victories, even if he tells those who <u>ponder</u> [*phrazōsi*] to purify first the famous oracles." In the light of these two uses elsewhere in the *Sibylline Oracles*, the word in line 7.19 probably denotes "meditating upon" or "thinking about."[82] The point is significant in that the nations are regarded as not only following the law of the Most High but also contemplating and, perhaps, studying it. The theme is made explicit in *2 En.* 48.6-7 [J]: "You must hand over the books to your children, and throughout all your generations, <and to (your) relatives> and among all nations who are discerning so that they may fear God, and so that they may accept them" (cf. *2 En.* 33.9).[83]

Perhaps one of the most explicit references to Gentiles converting to Judaism is found in Philo's *De vita Mosis* (first century B.C. to first century A.D.). This passage is not overtly focused on the latter days, but it is framed in such a way that Philo looks forward to a future time period when the nations will convert to Judaism.

> In this way those admirable, and incomparable, and most desirable laws were made known to all people, whether private individuals or kings, and this too at a period when the nation had not been prosperous for a long time. And it is generally the case that a cloud is thrown over the affairs of those who are not flourishing, so that but little is known of them; and then, if they make any fresh start and begin to improve, how great is the increase of their renown and glory? I think that in that case every nation, abandoning <u>all their own individual customs</u> [*ta idia kai polla chairein*], and utterly disregarding <u>their national laws</u> [*tois patriois hekastous*], would change and come over to the honour of such a people only; for their laws shining in connection with, and simultaneously with, the prosperity of the nation, will obscure all others, just as the rising sun obscures the stars.[84] (*Mos.* 2:43-44)

Philo claims that "every nation" will "abandon all their own individual customs." This obviously includes behavior such as idolatry and general wickedness, yet it may even have in mind national badges or distinctive customs (*tois patriois hekastous*). For example, in *De Iosepho* 1.202 Philo likewise claims, "And the

---

[82]Liddell & Scott point out that the verb *phrazō* in middle/passive voice means "*to indicate to oneself,* i.e. *to think* or *muse upon, consider, ponder, debate*" (1958).

[83]For the general theme of Gentiles embracing Torah, see Wis 18:4; *T. Benj.* 11.2–3; cf. *T. Levi* 4.2-5; 18:3-9; *T. Jud.* 24.6; *T. Zeb.* 9.8; *T. Naph.* 8.3-4; *T. Benj.* 10.9.

[84]Translation of Philo in this section is from C. D. Young, *The Works of Philo* (Peabody, MA: Hendrickson, 1993).

manner of their entertainment was to each party in accordance with their national customs [*ta patria hekastois*], since Joseph thought it wrong to overturn ancient laws." Again in *Legatio ad Gaium* 1.153: "They were aware of the attention which he paid to every thing, and of the very exceeding care which he took that the national laws and customs [*tōn par' hekastois patriōn*] prevailing in each nation should be confirmed and preserved" (cf. *Somn.* 2.78). *Life of Moses* 2.43-44 therefore highlights the notion that the nations will forsake their own national pride, manifested in various laws, regulations, feasts and so on, and adopt Israel's national distinctives. In other words, the nations are trading one set of distinctives for another set of distinctives. Ware likewise comments on this passage: "Just as he [Philo] understood the pagan adoption of Jewish customs as a proleptic anticipation of the universal sway of the law of Moses in the time of fulfillment, so Philo understood present-day proselytes as in some sense foreshadowing or *anticipating the time when all nations would become proselytes to Judaism*."[85]

Conclusion. To summarize, we have learned that the Old Testament and some parts of early Judaism expected that the Gentiles would (1) become part of *true* Israel in the latter-days and (2) would embrace Israelite nationalistic distinctives, making them virtually indistinguishable from native Israelites. They would become eschatological Israelites presumably in the same way as Gentiles in the past did (Egyptians coming out with Israel at the time of the exodus, Rahab, Ruth, etc.), by moving to geographical Israel and taking on the nationalistic identification tags of the law. This is why, as we argued in Ephesians 3, that it is a mystery that Gentiles can become true Israelites *without* identifying with the nationalistic tags of Israel's old law.

---

[85]Ware, *Mission of the Church*, p. 142. See also Peder Borgen, "Proselytes, Conquest, and Mission" in *Recruitment, Conquest, and Conflict,* ed. Peder Borgen, Vernon K. Robbins and David B. Gowler (Atlanta: Scholars, 1998), p. 65.

7

THE USE OF *MYSTERY*
IN COLOSSIANS

◆ ▨ ◆

PAUL'S LETTER TO THE EPHESIANS CLOSELY RESEMBLES the book of
Colossians so much that some have labeled them the "twin epistles." One point
of contact between the two letters lies in Paul's use of the term *mystery*. Our
previous investigation into the book of Ephesians yielded several conclusions.
Paul encourages the church at Ephesus to grasp the "mystery of His [God's] will"
(Eph 1:9). We sketched three aspects of this mystery: the scope, instrumentation and results of Christ's cosmic rule. The result of Christ's cosmic rule
entails the unity of "all things" in him.

The second use of *mystery* in Ephesians is a subcategory of the first: unity
between two formerly estranged people groups. Many scholars argue that the
revealed mystery in Ephesians 3 entails the equality between Jews and Gentiles,
but we contended that the mystery includes the manner in which these two
groups stand on equal footing.

The Old Testament predicts that in the latter days the Gentiles will come to
Israel and will obey the covenant stipulations by adopting physical, nationalistic tags that separate the Israelite community from the surrounding nations
(e.g., circumcision, food laws). According to Old Testament prophecy, when
Gentiles would eventually adopt these stipulations, they would migrate to
Israel and become nearly indistinguishable from their Jewish counterparts.
When the New Testament addresses this issue in light of Christ's inauguration
of the latter days, the fulfillment of the nations' conversion has undergone
some transformation. The apostle Paul, for example, argues that Gentiles are
no longer mandated to obey these covenant stipulations, because they have

placed their faith in Christ, who is true Israel. When the Gentiles are united to Christ, they become part of the end-time community of Israel.

A third use of mystery refers to the nature of the unity of Christ and the church, especially as this is understood through marriage. A final use of mystery in Ephesians refers to the nature of the gospel itself. The book of Colossians continues the Ephesians' theme of Gentiles becoming part of latter-day Israel, as Paul links the concept of mystery to the conversion of the nations. Perhaps the greatest difficulty in determining the significance and content of *mystery* in Colossians is teasing out Paul's brief comments on the matter. It is not surprising to find very little scholarly commentary on mystery in the letter to the Colossians.

If the revealed mystery is not explicitly defined, then how are we to proceed? As we have done throughout this project, we find it critical to ascertain and evaluate Old Testament allusions that are linked to mystery. Often Paul will employ an Old Testament quotation or allusion in conjunction with mystery, and, in doing so, subtly disclose the content of the revealed mystery.

A cursory examination of the letter to the Colossians suggests that the church at Colossae struggled with their understanding of Christ and their identity in him; the church apparently became involved in pagan and Jewish practices to overcome some sort of spiritual oppression. Now that Christ has come, how do the Colossians relate to the Mosaic law? In addition, the Colossians had a weakened view of Christ's rule. Is Christ truly sovereign over all things, both spiritual and physical? How is the church at Colossae to understand their identity in light of Christ's cosmic rule?

We will first attempt to unpack the meaning of mystery in Colossians 1:26-27 and then relate it to an allusion to Daniel 2, where the end-time kingdom is largely in view. As some commentators have noted, the book of Daniel is important for understanding the mystery here in the epistle to the Colossians. For example, Clinton Arnold states, "Paul's concept of mystery should be interpreted on the basis of the use of 'mystery' (רָז) in the book of Daniel."[1] This theme continues on into the divulged mystery of Colossians 2:2, where Paul states in the following context that God has "raised up" Christ (Col 2:12), "disposed of" the evil powers and kingdoms, brought about victory in Christ (Col 2:15), and installed his eternal kingdom in Christ (Col 3:1). Finally, in Colos-

---

[1]C. E. Arnold, *The Colossian Syncretisim: The Interface Between Christianity and Folk Belief at Colossae*, WUNT 77 (Tübingen: Mohr Siebeck, 1995; repr., Grand Rapids: Baker, 1996), p. 271.

sians 4:3, Paul was imprisoned for preaching the "mystery of Christ," and he remains imprisoned because of the proclamation of this revelation.

Kingdom, Gentiles and the Unveiled Mystery of Christ in Colossians 1:26-27

Immediate context. Colossians 1:23-29 is largely concerned with Paul's relationship to the gospel and his role in its promulgation:

> If indeed you continue in the faith firmly established and steadfast, and not moved away from the hope of the gospel that you have heard, which was proclaimed in all creation under heaven, and of which I, Paul, was made a minister. Now I rejoice in my sufferings for your sake, and in my flesh I do my share on behalf of His body, which is the church, in filling up what is lacking in Christ's afflictions. Of *this church* I was made a minister according to the stewardship from God bestowed on me for your benefit, so that I might fully carry out the *preaching of* the word of God, *that is,* the mystery which has been hidden from the *past* ages and generations, but has now been manifested to His saints, to whom God willed to make known what is the riches of the glory of this mystery among the Gentiles, which is Christ in you, the hope of glory. We proclaim Him, admonishing every man and teaching every man with all wisdom, so that we may present every man complete in Christ. For this purpose also I labor, striving according to His power, which mightily works within me.

The thrust of this section is that Paul endures great personal suffering for the sake of converting unbelievers (particularly the Gentiles) and ministering to those who have become Christians. Colossians 1:24 is notoriously difficult to understand, but it probably refers to some extent to Paul living a lifestyle in keeping with the cross (cf. 2 Cor 4:7-12; 12:9-10). That is, the apostle embodies the paradox of the cross—strength in weakness, victory in defeat and wisdom in foolishness. Paul's apostleship is then highlighted in Colossians 1:25: "Of this church I was made a minister according to the stewardship from God bestowed on me for your benefit, so that I might fully carry out the preaching of the word of God." The unveiled mystery in Colossians 1:26 follows on the heels of this statement and further clarifies the phrase "word of God." In Paul's clarification of the "word of God," he furnishes a good, thumbnail definition of mystery: "the mystery which has been hidden from the *past* ages and generations, but has now been manifested to his saints." By defining the revealed mystery in Colossians 1:26, Paul draws attention to its content in the following verse. Colossians

1:27a unpacks in more detail the nature of the audience or "the saints" ("to whom God willed to make known what is the riches of the glory"). Finally, in Colossians 1:27b the apostle discloses the content of the disclosed mystery: "this mystery among the Gentiles, which is Christ in you, the hope of glory."

The reconstitution of the kingdom. Commentators are reticent to describe the content of the revealed mystery in 1:26-27 with any specificity, and those that do make an attempt prefer to define it broadly as the person of Christ or, generally, the gospel.[2] It is certainly the case that the word *mystery* (*mystērion*) can indeed refer to God's salvation in Christ, which the gospel encapsulates (e.g., Eph 6:19). But is that the case in Colossians 1:26-27? Determining the content of the mystery, as we have seen throughout this project, requires sensitivity to the immediate context, including Old Testament allusions and quotations in that context.

We are immediately presented with a number of important syntactical problems in Colossians 1:27. Syntactically, it is difficult to ascertain what the phrase "among the Gentiles/nations" (*en tois ethnesin*) modifies. Does the phrase modify the infinitive "to make known" (*gnōrisai;* TNIV, HCSB) or the phrase "this mystery" (*mystēriou toutou;* NASB, NRSV, ASV, NJB, NET)?[3] If the prepositional phrase modifies "this mystery," then the emphasis falls on the significance of the mystery as it relates to "the Gentiles."[4] That is, the mystery largely entails how the Gentiles are part of the mystery. If, on the other hand, it modifies "to make known," as several commentators and translations suggest, Paul is highlighting the *proclamation* of the mystery "among" or "to the Gentiles."

The former rendering, though it does not betray the precise content of *mystery,* underscores the significance of the mystery *as it relates to* the Gentiles. It would lend further credence to the view that the revealed mystery concerns, to a large extent, a truth about the Gentiles. The latter construction places emphasis not so much on the Gentiles being part of the mystery but the extent to which the mystery has been heralded—the unveiled mystery has reached *even* to the Gentiles. We, however, prefer the former rendering: the disclosed

---

[2]E.g., Eduard Lohse, *Colossians and Philemon,* Hermeneia (Philadelphia: Fortress, 1971), p. 76; cf. Douglas J. Moo, *The Letters to the Colossians and Philemon,* PNTC (Grand Rapids: Eerdmans, 2008), pp. 158-59.

[3]A good case can also be made for the phrase to modify "what is the riches of the glory." See Murray J. Harris, *Colossians and Philemon,* EGGNT (Nashville: B & H Academic, 2010), p. 64.

[4]See J. B. Lightfoot, *St. Paul's Epistles to the Colossians and Philemon,* 4th ed. (Peabody, MA: Hendrickson, 1995), p. 169.

mystery concerns the Gentiles.[5] If we are correct in our construal of Colossians 1:27, the first part of the verse could be rephrased as follows: "to whom God willed to make known what is the riches of the glory of this mystery [as it is demonstrated] among the Gentiles."

Now that we have tried to arrive at a better understanding of the syntax of Colossians 1:27, we can probe the content of the mystery by paying attention to Paul's use of the Old Testament. We have seen that the word "mystery" (*to mystērion*) in the LXX (*rāz* in the MT) with a prophetic and eschatological sense occurs in the Old Testament only in Daniel 2 (Dan 2:18-19, 28-30, 47; *mystery* also occurs in Dan 4:6 [MT] with reference to the hidden interpretation of the king's prophetic dream that Daniel makes known to him, though this dream does not concern explicit eschatological issues). There the revelation of the "mystery" refers to the *hidden* interpretation of the king's dream, the content of which was a giant statue that represented four world kingdoms. A rock is cut out without hands, smashes the statue, grows into a mountain and fills the earth. The rock is interpreted to represent God's kingdom, which will defeat the evil kingdoms of the world in the end time. The primary focus of the meaning of the dream was that in the end times God would destroy the kingdom of evil and establish his own eternal kingdom (Dan 2:44-45).

We have also observed that *mystery* (*to mystērion*) occurs twenty-eight times in the New Testament. A feature noticeable in many of the occurrences is that the word usually is directly linked with Old Testament quotations or allusions (sometimes from the book of Daniel itself). In almost all of these cases, at least, *mystery* appears in order to indicate two things: (1) that Old Testament prophecy is beginning to be fulfilled and (2) that this fulfillment is unexpected from the former Old Testament vantage point. With respect to this last point, it is apparent that various New Testament authors are understanding Old Testament texts in the light of the Christ event and under the

---

[5]What perhaps may tip the scales in favor of the former rendering ("this mystery [demonstrated] among the Gentiles") is the relative pronoun "whom" at the beginning of Col 1:27. As is quite evident, Col 1:26 largely focuses on those who have been privileged to receive the mystery, namely, the believers (Jewish and Gentile Christians): "the mystery . . . has now been manifested to his saints." The antecedent of the pronoun "whom" (*hois*) of v. 27 is the saints (*tois hagiois*) in v. 26 and specifies the group who has received the mystery: "to whom [*hois*] God willed to make known . . . this mystery." In other words, to affirm that "among the Gentiles" modifies the infinitive "to make known" renders the phrase somewhat redundant, since Paul has already specified that Gentiles are among the recipients of the mystery in Col 1:26 and in his use of "whom" in Col 1:27 which repeats reference to the recipients (i.e., Jewish and Gentile believers). See Moo, *Colossians and Philemon*, pp. 157-58, for reasons for preferring the latter rendering of seeing "mystery" as a modifier of "make known."

guidance of the Spirit, which result in new interpretative developments though still consistent with the Old Testament idea. Thus, though Daniel may not always be in mind in all of these uses, the notion of an eschatological prophecy needing further inspired interpretation is. While such a notion appears not always to be directly allusive to Daniel 2, this idea of "mystery" probably had its ultimate origin there.

How do these uses of "mystery" in Daniel and especially elsewhere in the New Testament relate to those in Colossians 1? The wording of the "mystery" phraseology in Colossians 1:26-27 appears to be based on the verses in Daniel 2.[6]

Table 7.1

Daniel 2 (Old Greek; authors' trans.)	Colossians 1:26-27 (authors' trans.)
"The mystery [mystērion] was revealed . . . [the one] giving wisdom [sophian] to the wise and knowledge to ones knowing understanding [synesin]" (vv. 19-21); "he makes known . . . the hidden things [apokrypha]" (v. 22); "The one revealing mysteries and he made known [mystēria, egnōrisen]" (v. 28; so virtually identically v. 29 and similarly v. 30, while the following mss. of the Theodotionic tradition read "he made known this mystery [egnōrisen to touto mystērion]": 230; the same phrase without touto is read in mss. 106 and 584 of A and in the Armenian). The Old Greek differs somewhat with Theodotion.	"The hidden mystery [to mystērion to apokekrymmenon] . . . manifested to his saints to whom God willed to make known [gnōrisai] what is the richness of the glory of this mystery [mystēriou]" (for some of these text comparisons, see H. Hübner, Vetus Testamentum in Novo 2 [Göttingen: Vandenhoeck & Ruprecht, 1997], p. 530). In addition to these parallels, note the use of "wisdom [sophia]" and "understanding [synesin]" in direct relation to "mystery" in Col 2:2-3 and Eph 3:3-10.

The above underlined lexical combinations are found only in Daniel 2, Ephesians 3:3, 9, and Colossians 1-2. And, as in Ephesians 3, so also here the wording expresses eschatological realities likewise in line with the end-time focus of the Daniel 2 "mystery" (e.g., Dan 2:28-29, 44-45).[7] Daniel concerns the establishment of the eschatological kingdom, and Ephesians and Colossians focus on the end-time messianic king (*christos*) and the "mystery" revolving around him. The explicit identification of the "mystery" in Colossians 1:27 as "*Christ in you [the Gentiles]*," and the similar identification of the "mystery" as Christ in Colossians 2:2, point to the same kind of mystery as in Ephesians 3: Jews and

---

[6]The following discussion of the allusions to Dan 2 and Prov 3 in this chapter is based on G. K. Beale, "Colossians" in Commentary on the New Testament Use of the Old Testament, ed. G. K. Beale and D. A. Carson (Grand Rapids: Baker Academic, 2007), pp. 858-60.

[7]See Jean-Noël Aletti, *Saint Paul Épitre Aux Colossiens*, Études Bibliques no. 20 (Paris: J. Gabalda, 1993), pp. 156-57, who sees Daniel 2 broadly as the background for "mystery" in Col 1:27-27; cf. Michael Wolter, *Der Brief an die Kolosser; Der Brief Philemon*, Ökumenischer Taschenkommentar zum Neuen Testament Band 12 (Gütersloh: Gütersloher Verl.-Haus Mohn/Würzburg: Echter-Verl, 1993), p. 104, who understands "mystery" here generally against the background of Jewish apocalyptic and Qumran.

Gentiles are fused together on a footing of complete equality by means of corporate identification in Jesus the Messiah, the true Israel: they are in Christ, and Christ is in them (presumably through the Spirit). This is a "mysterious" fulfillment of Daniel's prophecy because it was not clear in the Old Testament that Israel's theocratic kingdom would be so thoroughly transformed that it would find its continuation only in the sphere of the end-time, Israelite, messianic king himself.[8] This may well have been hinted at by the four-kingdom parallel in Daniel 7, where the Son of Man's reign replaces the image of the stone of Daniel 2. There in Daniel 7, the Son of Man represents the saints of Israel, so that what is true of him is true of them and vice versa.[9] This link between the Daniel 2 stone and the Daniel 7 Son of Man is explicitly made by *4 Ezra* 13:3-7, where the Daniel 7 Son of Man figure "carved out for himself a great mountain [grown from a stone] and flew up upon it."

But how could the idea of "Christ" as the messianic Israelite king being "among the Gentiles" (Col 1:27) be part of this mystery? How do the Gentiles in relation to Christ play a role in the Old Testament mystery? Keeping in mind that Colossians 1:26-27 alludes specifically to the Daniel 2 mystery, the climactic interpretation of that mystery in Daniel 2:34-35, 44-45 is the stone (representing God's end-time Israelite kingdom) that smashes the statue (representing the evil world kingdoms). After the stone annihilates the statue, "the stone . . . became a great mountain and filled the whole earth" (Dan 2:35). As we argued in the Ephesians 3 discussion, one surmises that throughout the earth will be at least a remnant of Gentiles not part of the evil kingdoms that were just destroyed, who will be restored and become part of eschatological Israel's kingdom and experience salvific restoration (to which the Old Tes-

---

[8]In Ephesians, Jew and Gentile are one because they are now incorporated and identified with the risen Messiah (which is also clear from comparing Eph 1:20-21 with Eph 2:5-6). Gentiles can be "fellow-inheritors and fellow-members of the body and fellow-partakers of the promises in Christ Jesus" along with Jewish Christians (see the contrast of these three ideas in Eph 2:12) because the promises and inheritance of Israel have been inaugurated in Messiah, the Israelite king who represents all true Israelites. Christ's resurrection has launched the beginning of the new creation, wherein there can be no nationalistic distinctions. Some commentators have seen the mystery consisting of complete equality, but as far as we can determine none have recognized that the basis for such equality lies in the one resurrected person "Christ Jesus" *as the true Israel*, since there can be no distinguishing marks in him but only unity. The same notion from the parallel in Ephesians carries over to Col 1:26-27, where also believers' unity with Christ, the Israelite king, is highlighted (Col 1:27; 2:10-13, 19-20; 3:1-4). For fuller discussion of this conclusion and of the use of Daniel's "mystery" in Ephesians 3, see pp. 159-73.

[9]See further Beale, *New Testament Biblical Theology*, pp. 393-96.

tament elsewhere testifies, e.g., Is 2:1-4; 11:1-13; 49:6, 22-23; Zech 2:11; 8:22-23). Daniel 7:14, part of the parallel to Daniel 2, makes explicit what is implicit in image of the stone-mountain filling the earth: "to him [the Son of Man] was given dominion, glory and a kingdom, that all peoples, nations, and tongues might serve him. His dominion is an everlasting dominion . . ." Accordingly, Daniel 2 and 7 express the idea that Israel's end-time kingdom would include Gentiles as part of this kingdom. The emphasis on Christ being "among the Gentiles" in Colossians 1:27 is likely not coincidental but draws out more clearly what was implied in the stone filling the entire world in Daniel 2.[10] Colossians is a clarification of what was not so clear in Daniel 2, that is, was a mystery, though the parallel in Daniel 7 clarifies Daniel 2 to some degree. In fact, Daniel 7:14 could be echoed in Christ being "the hope of glory" at the end of Colossians 1:27, since it is one of only two passages in the Septuagint where a messianic figure is said to have "glory" in the midst of a kingdom composed not only of Jews but also of Gentiles.[11]

While this is a specific part of the revelation of the Daniel 2 mystery, we have seen that the idea of the Gentiles becoming part of Israel's and the Son of Man's kingdom is found elsewhere in Daniel and Isaiah. The core of the mystery is to be found elsewhere. Colossians 2:16-23 is parallel with Ephesians 2:14-18, the latter of which underscores that Christ's coming did away with the former ethnic markers of God's people and replaced them with Christ, which is key to understanding the mystery of Ephesians 3. Colossians 2:16-23 emphasizes the same thing, where the Mosaic laws pertaining to "food or drink or Jewish festivals or new moons or Sabbath days" are no longer binding because they must now be seen as only "shadows" pointing toward Christ, who is the eschatological "substance" of these things. The parallel passage to Ephesians 2:13-18 in Colossians 2 defines the "decrees" (*dogma*) of Ephesians 2:15 that Christ abolished as the external nationalistic expressions of the law: food, drink festivals, new moons or Sabbaths (see Col 2:15-17, 20-21). Col. 2:20-21 even refers to these "decrees" with the verbal form of dogma: "[why] <u>do you submit yourself to decrees</u> [*dogmatizō*]—do not handle, do not taste, do not touch, which things

---

[10]A former student, Ochang Kwon, drew our attention to this view of Daniel 2 in a paper on the nature of the "mystery" in Ephesians 3 ("A Biblical Theology of Ephesians," Westminster Theological Seminary, January 2014).

[11]The only other passage is Is 49:3, 5, where the messianic servant is glorified by God in his task of restoration, which includes Gentiles (Is 49:6). In Num 24:8 (LXX) and Ps 8:5 a messianic figure is said to have "glory" but not in direct connection to Gentiles.

are all destined for perishing with the consuming, according to the commandments and doctrines of men."

Accordingly, believers have "died with Messiah" to these things that were so
important to Israel's old world but no longer are crucial for membership in
God's true end-time people and kingdom (Col 2:20-22). While, as we have seen,
Gentile salvation in the latter days was a clear prophetic expectation, it would
have been assumed that they would come to the land of Israel and convert to
the faith of Israel, which would include taking on the nationalistic signs (circumcision, etc.) of becoming an Israelite. Ephesians 3 and Colossians 1-2 reveal that
it was formerly a mystery that Gentiles could become a part of latter-day Israel
by not submitting to the identification marks of the old theocracy but only
submitting to and having the Messiah as their sole identification. Thus the
Colossians' "mystery" indicates inaugurated fulfillment not only of the Daniel
2 kingdom prophecy but of the general prophetic expectation about how Gentiles would become part of the saved people of God and his kingdom in the end
time. In addition, we have seen that the mystery also includes the notion that
Israel's prophesied kingdom would be so thoroughly renovated that it would
find its ongoing existence only in the sphere of the latter-day, Israelite messianic
king himself and, of course, subsequently all those who identify with him.

Was this revealed mystery something that was completely hidden in Daniel
and the Old Testament, or was it partly revealed? Colossians 1:26 might seem
to indicate that it was entirely hidden: "the mystery which has been hidden
from the *past* ages and generations, but now has been manifested to his saints."
It is best, however, to see this as parallel to Ephesians 3:4-5, where "the mystery
of Christ . . . in other generations was not made known to the sons of men, as
[*hōs*] it has now been revealed to his holy apostles and prophets." The *hōs*
before "now" indicates that Ephesians views the revelation of the mystery
there as one of degree. The content of the mystery was evident partly in the
Old Testament, but "now" it is fully revealed. There is no reason not to see the
same partial-to-full revelation in Colossians 1:26, especially since we have seen
that the inclusion of the Gentiles in verse 27 was something partly revealed in
Daniel 2. In fact, we have seen in an earlier chapter that even in Daniel 2 and
Daniel 4 Daniel's revealed interpretation of the mystery about Nebuchadnezzar was a clarification or fuller revelation of something about which the
king had some partial knowledge. But what does not appear to have been revealed at all is how Gentiles become members of the end-time Israelite

kingdom through identification with the Messiah and not the nationalistic tags of the law. However, even this may have arisen from some seed-like ideas in the Old Testament.[12]

The mention of "now" (*nyn*) in contrast to former "ages and generations" indicates that the revelation of the mystery is part of the inauguration of the latter days. Paul elsewhere uses "now" (*nyn*) with an inaugurated end-time sense (Rom 8:18; 13:11-12; 2 Cor 6:2; 2 Thess 2:6[13]). The above-mentioned parallel with Ephesians 3:5, as well as Ephesians 3:9, and its use of "now" is significant since the word in Ephesians 3:5, 9 is developing an inaugurated sense of "the fullness of the times" from Ephesians 1:10, which is the time when the "mystery" there was "made known" (cf. Eph 1:9; see also Rom 16:25-26, where both "now" and "mystery" occur, for a virtually identical notion in parallel with Eph 3:5, 9). This use of "now" continues the "now" (*nyni*) in Colossians 1:22, where "reconciliation" is part of the commencement of the latter days.

---

[12]While the revealed mystery that Gentiles become members of the latter-day kingdom of Israel by identification with the Messiah and not the nationalistic tags of the law was not verbalized in the Old Testament, it does not seem to be absolutely unanticipated. The revelation may have grown from the notion that the Old Testament views the messianic servant to be one who summed faithful Israel in himself (e.g., Is 49:3). Even from the Old Testament perspective (e.g., from Isaiah's vantage point) all those who would be redeemed in the eschaton would have not only have to trust in the servant's redemptive work (Isaiah 53) but also identify with the servant. This would appear to be the reason that, after Isaiah 53, for the first time in the book faithful Israelites corporately are repeatedly referred to as "servants" (11x), presumably because they identify with the servant. One could surmise then that the messianic servant is the key eschatological marker of being a true Israelite. Paul then plausibly develops this further and sees that Gentiles do not have to take on the nationalistic identity markers of Israel's law to become true Israelites but only have to identify with the key identity marker of the Messiah, Jesus. This makes even more sense when it is seen that Paul sees Jesus as typologically fulfilling that to which the identity markers of Israel's law ultimately pointed: i.e., he represents the epitome of the wisdom of the law (Col 2:3), he is the true temple (Col 1:19), the true circumcision (Col 2:11-12), the true Sabbath (Col 2:16-17) and everything to which the dietary laws truly pointed. Some of these developments by Paul even are intimated in the Old Testament itself. For example, I have noted above in this section that the "stone" of Daniel 2 is parallel to the "Son of Man" in Daniel 7, which means that the "kingdom" of Daniel 2 (which is interpreted in Dan 2:44-45 to be what the "stone" represented) is to be identified with the Son of Man. But I have argued elsewhere that the stone represented not only the kingdom of Israel but its end-time temple (see G. K. Beale, *The Temple and the Church's Mission* [Downers Grove, IL: InterVarsity Press, 2004], pp. 144-53). If that is the case, the Son of Man is not only seen to be the king who represents Israel's kingdom (which is also apparent by comparing Dan 7:13 with Dan 7:17-27) but also is essentially identified with its temple. Therefore, in Daniel 7 to be a true Israelite one must identify with the Son of Man, the representative of true Israel. Furthermore, in the chapter on Ephesians above, we have suggested other Old Testament anticipations of a lessening of the law's of restricitons on Gentiles in the latter days (e.g., see Is 56:6-7; 66:18-21; Rom 4; Gen 7-9).

[13]See other inaugurated eschatological uses elsewhere of "now" (*nyn* and *nyni*) in Paul on the comment on "now" in Col 1:22 above. See further Beale, *A New Testament Biblical Theology,* pp. 480-83.

Daniel 2 and the Mystery of God in Colossians 2:1-4

We need not look much further in our search for mystery, as the next one occurs in Colossians 2:1-4:

> For I want you to know how great a struggle I have on your behalf and for those who are at Laodicea, and for all those who have not personally seen my face, that their hearts may be encouraged, having been knit together in love, and *attaining* to all the wealth that comes from the full assurance of understanding, *resulting* in a true knowledge of God's mystery, *that is,* Christ *Himself,* in whom are hidden all the treasures of wisdom and knowledge. I say this so that no one will delude you with persuasive argument.

Paul relates to the church at Colossae that he desires for them and others "who have not seen" him to understand how strenuously he ministers on their behalf (Col 2:1). In Colossians 2:2, the apostle discloses the purpose of his struggle, but the specific logical movement of the verse is not readily discernable. Whatever the precise flow of Paul's thought may be, the last purpose statement of Colossians 2:2 receives some if not all of the emphasis as the main point of Colossians 2:1-2: "<u>that</u> their hearts may be encouraged, being knit together in love . . . resulting in a true <u>knowledge of God's mystery, which is Christ</u>."[14] Paul, in other words, labors diligently so that the congregation at Colossae and other churches may grasp "God's mystery."

The revealed mystery is then further described in Colossians 2:2 as "Christ."[15] Apparently, the unveiled mystery is so focused on Christ that Paul can simply label it as "Christ." Immediately, the reader can conclude that whatever the precise content of *mystery* may be, it must be related to and centered on Christ. Colossians 2:3 describes Christ in more detail and offers us further insight into the mystery: "in whom are hidden all the treasures of wisdom and knowledge." This description of Christ fits admirably into our previous study of mystery in the preceding chapters. As we will see below, Paul alludes to two Old Testament

---

[14]The last few words of Col 2:2b (*tou theou, Christou*) contain a host of textual variants. But the reading *tou theou, Christou* should still be deemed original. Externally, the phrase garners early support (P[46] B Hilary Pelagius Ps-Jerome), and internally the rather abrupt phrase, *tou theou, Christou,* explains all the existing variants—see Bruce M. Metzger, *A Textual Commentary on the Greek New Testament,* 2nd ed. (Stuttgart: Deutsche Bibelgesellshaft, 1998), p. 555. Thus, as the majority of commentators and translations suggest, the reading *tou theou, Christou* is to be preferred.

[15]Note here the genitive of apposition ("the mystery of God, *namely* Christ"). Syntactically, *Christou* ("Christ") may be governed by the word *theou* ("of God"), but it is far more cogent to pair *Christou* ("Christ") with *mystēriou* ("mystery"; NASB, ESV, NIV, ASV, NRSV).

texts, Daniel 2 and Proverbs 2, integrating them into the content of *mystery*.

Colossians 2:3 explains that in Christ, who is the "mystery" (Col 2:2), are hidden all the treasures of wisdom and knowledge. We have already seen that the "mystery" has its background in Daniel 2. The same Daniel 2 background continues here but, as we will see, is supplemented by Proverbs:

Table 7.2

Daniel 2 (Theodotian [NETS])	Colossians 2:2-3 (authors' trans.)
"The <u>mystery</u> [*mystērion*] was revealed . . . [the one] giving <u>wisdom</u> [*sophian*] to the wise and knowledge to ones knowing <u>understanding</u> [*synesin*]" (vv. 19-21); "he makes known <u>the hidden things</u> [*apokrypha*]" (v. 22).	"Unto all the richness of the full assurance of <u>understanding</u> [*syneseōs*], unto a knowledge of the <u>mystery</u> [*mystēriou*] of God, which is Christ, in whom are <u>hidden</u> [*apokryphoi*] all the treasures of <u>wisdom</u> [*sophias*] and knowledge."

Thus the idea of the inauguration of the prophesied Daniel 2 kingdom continues from Colossians 1:26-27 here. Not only believing Jews but also Gentiles are a part of this kingdom. It is best, however, to see the Daniel 2 allusion now merged with Proverbs 2:3-6 and leading Paul to focus on the latter text in verse 3:

Table 7.3

Proverbs 2:3-6	Colossians 2:2-3
"For if you should call upon <u>wisdom</u> [*sophian*], utter your voice for <u>understanding</u> [*synesei*], and if . . . you should search for her as <u>treasures</u> [*thēsaurous*] [in place of "treasures" in Prov. 2:4, Sym. and Theod. read hidden things (*ta apokrypha*)], then you will <u>understand</u> [*synēseis*] . . . and find the <u>knowledge</u> [*epignōsin*] of God. For the Lord gives <u>wisdom</u> [*sophian*], and from his presence is <u>knowledge</u> [*gnōsis*] and <u>understanding</u> [*synesis*]."	"Unto all the richness of the full assurance of <u>understanding</u> [*syneseōs*], unto a <u>knowledge</u> [*epignōsin*] of the mystery, which is Christ, in whom are <u>hidden</u> [*apokryphoi*] all the <u>treasures</u> [*thēsauroi*] of <u>wisdom</u> [*sophias*] and <u>knowledge</u> [*gnōseōs*]." (For some of these text comparisons, see Hübner, *Vetus Testamentum in Novo* 2, pp. 532, 534.)

Though "wisdom (*sophia*)" and "understanding (*synēsis*)" (and occasionally even the additional word "knowledge [*gnōsis*]") occur together throughout the LXX, all of the unique word combinations in table 7.3 are found only in Proverbs 2 and Colossians 2. Furthermore, the validity of the Proverbs reference is to be seen in the prior emphasis on Christ as epitomizing true "wisdom" in Colossians 1:15-17 (many commentators see Prov 8:22-31 as part of the possible background in Col 1:15-17).[16] That identification rises to the surface again here. It may

---

[16]Cf. Wolter, *Der Brief an die Kolosser; Der Brief Philemon*, pp. 111-12, who sees Paul's "treasures of wisdom" to be reflective of a common metaphor used for "wisdom" in early Judaism, though he

even be that the preceding description of the "mystery" in Colossians 1:26 anticipates the clearer reference to the "mystery" as "wisdom" here, since "mystery" and "wisdom" occur so closely together in Daniel 2:19-21 (Theod.): compare the loose link between "mystery" in Colossians 1:26-27 and "wisdom" in Colossians 1:28, and compare "the mystery hidden from the ages [*apo tōn aiōnōn*]."

Believers are able to have genuine "knowledge of the mystery of God, which is Christ," because it has been revealed to them (Col 1:26-27; 2:2). Since Christ is the true fount of "wisdom and knowledge" (Col 2:3), the saints also share in such understanding by virtue of their identification and union with him (likewise see Col 2:3-8). Whereas the Torah was the epitome of "wisdom" in the Old Testament epoch, Messiah is now the grandest expression of divine "wisdom." In this light, Torah was the typological precursor of the fullest expression of "wisdom," which has come in the person of the Messiah. This very much relates to our discussion on Colossians 1:26-27, where we concluded that the focus of the revealed mystery was on how Gentiles become members of the later-day Israelite kingdom through identification with the Messiah and not the nationalistic tags of the law. Colossians 2:2-3 clarifies further why this is the case: Jesus Christ is what Israel's old law pointed to, so that he is the fullest expression of the law's revelation and wisdom. Consequently, membership in the new covenant community must come by identifying with Jesus "in whom are hid all the treasures of wisdom and knowledge."

This fits well with our conclusions about the use of *mystery* in Ephesians 3 and in Colossians 1:26-27. There we saw that the essence of the mystery was that in the end time Gentiles are no longer required to obey Israel's national customs and outward signs required by the law to become true Israelites. Simply put, the only marker that is now required for an ethnic Jew or Gentile to be considered a true Israelite is to identify with Christ. Christ sums up true Israel and the full wisdom of Israel's law in himself (for the latter, see Rom 10:4). Colossians 2:2-3 refers to Israel's law (Torah) as "wisdom." Since all the "wisdom" of the Old Testament law is found "in Christ," all those, whether Jews or Gentiles, who are unified with Christ have him as their ultimate marker and do not need to take on the nationalistic markers demanded by Israel's law in the Old Testament.

---

includes Prov 2:3 among the list of references he adduces; some commentators see a parallel to Is 45:3 ("I will give you dark treasures [*thēsaurous*], hidden [*apokryphous*] invisible things I will open to you"), but the Proverbs passage is much closer in wording.

Is there any inkling in the Old Testament that the Messiah could become the zenith point and sum total of wisdom expressed in God's law? If so, it is certainly not clear, though we suggested earlier in this chapter that the Isaianic servant who represents end-time Israel may have some bearing on this issue. There may also be a faint precedent in early Judaism, where wisdom was not only personified but *appears* sometimes even to represent an independent being existing in God's presence. At the least, Judaism personified God's attributes such as wisdom to explain how a transcendent God related to a fallen world. Early Judaism itself was probably elaborating on such texts as Proverbs 8:24-31, which refer to the law and personify it as God's wisdom, which existed along with God at the inception of creation. Paul may have been influenced by Judaism to interpret Old Testament wisdom in a similar way but to apply it to Christ as true wisdom, or he may merely have done something similar on his own.[17] What was a personification in the Old Testament and Jewish tradition becomes personally incarnate in Christ. Another way to put this is that the Old Testament law as the epitome of wisdom was typological of Christ.

IMPRISONED FOR THE MYSTERY OF CHRIST IN COLOSSIANS 4:3

Immediate context. Colossians 4:1-6 continues the segment begun at Colossians 3:5, which explains the new creational living of believers based on their identification with Christ's death and resurrection (Col 3:1-4).

> Masters, grant to your slaves justice and fairness, knowing that you too have a Master in heaven.
>
> Devote yourselves to prayer, keeping alert in it with *an attitude of* thanksgiving; praying at the same time for us as well, that God will open up to us a door for the word, so that we may speak forth the mystery of Christ, for which I have also been imprisoned; that I may make it clear in the way I ought to speak.
>
> Conduct yourselves with wisdom toward outsiders, making the most of the opportunity. Let your speech always be with grace, as *though* seasoned with salt, so that you will know how you should respond to each person. (Col 4:1-6)

Colossians 4:2-6 is a concluding subsection of Colossians 3:5–4:6, which is tied to Paul's concern for the gospel message to be communicated to nonbelievers. Paul asks the Colossian congregation to pray earnestly for their own lives and his (Col 4:2). Specifically, when the Colossians pray for Paul, they are to ask

---

[17]For a summary of the Old Testament and Jewish background for Paul's understanding of Christ as wisdom in Col 1:15-17, see Moo, *Colossians*, pp. 111-13, 118-20.

that God would open a "door for the word" (Col 4:3a). This opportunity will allow Paul to "declare the mystery of Christ." Here the "mystery of Christ" appears to be synonymous with the "word" or "message" (NIV). In other words, Paul pleads with the Colossians that they pray for the proclamation of the disclosed mystery. According to Colossians 4:3b, Paul was imprisoned for preaching the "mystery of Christ": "for which I have also been imprisoned."[18] Paul's personal insight betrays the significance of the "mystery of Christ" and the urgency of his request; he remains imprisoned because of the proclamation of this unveiled mystery.

Content of the mystery. Paul drops two hints, subtly disclosing the content of the revealed mystery in Colossians 4:3. The first is the phrase "mystery of Christ." In all likelihood, the content of *mystery* in Colossians 4:3 closely resembles the unveiled mystery in Colossians 1:26-27 and Colossians 2:2. In each case, as we have seen, Christ plays a central role:

> That is, the mystery which has been hidden from the *past* ages and generations, but has now been manifested to his saints, to whom God willed to make known what is the riches of the glory of this mystery among the Gentiles, which is Christ in you, the hope of glory. (Col 1:26-27)

> That their hearts may be encouraged, having been knit together in love, and *attaining* to all the wealth that comes from the full assurance of understanding, resulting in a true knowledge of God's mystery, *that is,* Christ *Himself*. (Col 2:2)

The revealed mystery thus plays a pivotal role in the fulfillment of the long-awaited kingdom of God, as it denotes the reconstitution of the kingdom in the person of Christ and the saints' identification with him. It even indicates the initial fulfillment not only of the end-time kingdom but of the general prophetic expectation about how Gentiles would become part of the covenant people of God in the end time.[19]

In Colossians 4:3, Paul uses the phrase "mystery of Christ," a phrase found only one other time in the New Testament: "When you read you can understand my insight into the mystery of Christ" (Eph 3:4). The apostle claims that he is imprisoned on account of the divulged mystery (Col 4:3). Paul may have authored Colossians from his first Roman imprisonment (see Acts 28:16-31);

---

[18]It is likely that the antecedent of the neuter relative pronoun "which" [*ho*] refers back to the neuter noun *mystērion* ("mystery").

[19]So also O'Brien, *Colossians*, p. 239.

however, determining the provenance of Colossians is fraught with difficulties, so our conclusions must remain tenuous.[20] Wherever he was, Paul states that he was imprisoned because of the "mystery of Christ": "that we may proclaim the mystery of Christ, <u>for which</u> I am in chains."[21] The prepositional phrase "for which" may mean that Paul is *currently* suffering for the sake of the mystery or that he was *originally* imprisoned in Rome because of the "mystery of Christ."[22] Whatever the precise meaning may be, it is important to note that Paul views the "mystery of Christ" as integral to his ministry and his imprisonment.[23] Why does Paul place so much emphasis on this mystery, particularly as it relates to his career as an apostle? The answer, we believe, lies in the revealed mystery in Colossians 1:26-27 and Colossians 2:2.

The significance of this revelation is consistent with what we know of Paul's missionary activity among the Gentiles. The book of Acts describes in three separate accounts Paul's conversion and commissioning on the Damascus road (Acts 9:1-43; 22:1-21; 26:9-19). All three passages highlight Christ's commission to Paul to preach the gospel to the Gentiles (cf. Acts 13:44-47; Is 49:6). One significant detail that makes Paul's ministry unique is *his conviction to preach a Torah-free gospel to the Gentiles.* The Gentiles, Paul says, become full members of the covenant community only through faith in Christ (Gal 3:29). This is precisely the teaching Paul deems an unveiled mystery in Ephesians and Colossians and considers to be absolutely central to his ministry. Some of the persecution that Paul endured at the hands of Judaizers stems from this conviction. This explains why Paul requests prayer in Colossians 4:2-4 and perhaps part of

---

[20]The authorship and provenance of Colossians continues to be a matter of great debate (see Moo, *Colossians*, pp. 28-41). Some advocate Pauline authorship but deny the book's provenance in Rome (e.g., N. T. Wright, *The Epistles of Paul to the Colossians and Philemon: An Introduction and Commentary,* TNCC [Grand Rapids: Eerdmans, 1986], pp. 37-42). We, though, affirm Pauline authorship and its provenance in Rome.

[21]Bockmuehl makes an intriguing observation regarding Col 4:2: "Paul speaks here of a *demonstration* of the 'mystery of Christ' by way of his own bonds. He proposes a manifestation of the *theologia crucis* in his own person, as it were" (*Revelation and Mystery*, p. 192). Paul may very well have this in mind, especially in light of Col 1:24. Our only reservation is that Paul does not explicitly employ here other terms that are often found with the concept of the *theologia crucis* ("theology of the cross"), such as *glory, wisdom, rule,* etc.

[22]Lk 23:25 uses the preposition *dia* in a similar fashion to Col 4:3: "He [Barabbas] was one who had been thrown into prison <u>for</u> [*dia*] an insurrection made in the city, and for murder."

[23]Eph 6:19-20, a parallel passage to Col 4:2-4, further explains, "*pray* on my behalf, that utterance may be given to me in the opening of my mouth, to make known with boldness the mystery of the gospel, <u>for which</u> [*hyper hou*] I am an ambassador in chains; that in *proclaiming* it I may speak boldly, as I ought to speak."

the reason that led him to be imprisoned. (Jews sometimes reported Christians to the Gentile authorities as not being a sect of Judaism and therefore not under the protective umbrella of Judaism, which Rome had exempted from obligation to worship the emperor.)[24]

Conclusion

Paul's allusion to Daniel's narrative provides insight into the content of the mystery in Colossians 1:26-27. The allusion to Daniel 2 coupled with the mention of the "Messiah" leads us to the conclusion that the end-time kingdom plays an integral role in Colossians 1:26-27. It was partially hidden in the Old Testament that Israel's theocratic kingdom would be so thoroughly transformed that it would find its continuation only in the sphere of the end-time, Israelite, messianic king himself.

Adding an additional layer to the notion of the developed understanding of the latter-day kingdom is Paul's conviction that Jews and Gentiles are one in Christ. But it is still more than that. The term *mystery* can entail different, though organically related, topics. The same phenomenon occurs here in Colossians 1:26-27. The mystery partly concerns the theocratic kingdom as reconstituted in Christ, whereas the other aspect of the mystery pertains to the relationship between Jews and Gentiles. The Jew-Gentile relationship is not at odds with the reconstitution of the kingdom, since Jews and Gentiles comprise the eschatological kingdom in Christ without having to identify with the nationalistic covenantal badges of old Israel.

In Colossians 2:2-3, Paul makes the staggering claim that in Christ "are hidden all the treasures of wisdom and knowledge." Christ is the true "wisdom and knowledge" of God, and believers, because of their identification with him, share in such understanding. Previously the Torah was the epitome of God's wisdom, but now Christ is the fullest expression.

In Colossians 4:3, Paul requests prayer that he may have an opportunity to proclaim the mystery that pertains to Christ. The apostle even claims that he is imprisoned on account of the unveiled mystery, as he views the "mystery of Christ" to be integral to his ministry and his imprisonment. Since Gentiles become part of end-time Israel through faith alone, his message is obviously a stumbling block to a Jewish audience, which could be the reason for his imprisonment.

---

[24]See Lightfoot, *Colossians*, p. 231 (also cited in Garland, *Colossians*, p. 272).

8

THE USE OF *MYSTERY* IN 2 THESSALONIANS

◆ ▨ ◆

THE LAST TWO CHAPTERS LARGELY FOCUSED ON the nature of Gentile conversion in the latter days. We argued that according to the Old Testament, at the time of the Gentiles' end-time conversion, they were prophesied to adopt Israelite laws that distinguished them from the pagan nations (e.g., food laws, Sabbath, circumcision). The apostle Paul, however, claims that God revealed to him that the Gentiles were not required to do so, because they have joined themselves to Christ, the embodiment of true Israel. Christ is the only distinguishing mark for true Israel, since he represents true Israel and sums the wisdom of the law up in himself. It is no coincidence that Paul needed to address this theme in these two epistles, as this issue would be hotly contested in the nascent church (cf. Acts 15; Galatians).

Another aspect of mystery found in Ephesians and Colossians is the establishment of God's end-time kingdom in Christ. Paul argues that Israel's prophesied theocratic kingdom finds the locus of its fulfillment and continuation in the sphere of the end-time, Israelite, messianic king himself and those whom he represented. It was partially hidden in the Old Testament (Dan 2) that end-time saints would be represented to such an extent by union with the Messiah and in this manner would participate in his end-time kingdom by coreigning with him.[1]

Paul's conception of mystery in 2 Thessalonians continues this discussion of the end-time kingdom, but with an emphasis on a few negative

---

[1]See the further elaboration of this in the section "The Reconstitution of the Kingdom" on pp. 166-73 above.

traits. With the establishment of God's eternal kingdom comes the surprising end-time presence of Israel's antagonist. The book of Daniel warns that in the "latter days" an evil figure will arrive on the scene directly before the coming of Israel's kingdom, and this end-time opponent will come against Israel, bringing about large-scale deception and persecution within the covenant community.

In a culture preoccupied with the Bible's conception of the "end times," the "antichrist" and the "tribulation" are explosive issues. When will the antichrist arrive on the scene? Is it strictly a future phenomenon? These issues come to a head here in 2 Thessalonians as Paul writes to the church at Thessalonica about their faulty understanding of the end times. Crucial to understanding this issue is the meaning of the "mystery of lawlessness" in 2 Thessalonians 2:7.

We will briefly examine the immediate context of 2 Thessalonians 2:7 and its allusion to the final vision of the book of Daniel.

IMMEDIATE CONTEXT

> Now we request you, brethren, with regard to the coming of our Lord Jesus Christ and our gathering together to Him, that you not be quickly shaken from your composure or be disturbed either by a spirit or a message or a letter as if from us, to the effect that the day of the Lord has come. Let no one in any way deceive you, for *it will not come* unless the apostasy comes first, and the man of lawlessness is revealed, the son of destruction, who opposes and exalts himself above every so-called god or object of worship, so that he takes his seat in the temple of God, displaying himself as being God. Do you not remember that while I was still with you, I was telling you these things? And you know what restrains him now, so that in his time he will be revealed. For the mystery of lawlessness is already at work; only he who now restrains *will do* so until he is taken out of the way. (2 Thess 2:1-7)

Paul most likely used 2 Thessalonians to correct the Thessalonians' aberrant view of eschatology because they did not completely understand his teaching in 1 Thessalonians. In 1 Thessalonians Paul corrects those who have set up timetables for Christ's return, explaining why the Thessalonians appear lethargic (1 Thess 5:12-14). In order to curb their idle behavior, Paul thus warns them that the Day of the Lord is imminent: "For you yourselves know full well that the day of the Lord will come just like a thief in the night. While they are saying, 'Peace and safety!' then destruction will come upon them suddenly like labor pains upon a woman with child, and they will not escape. But you, brethren, are not in darkness, that the day would overtake you like a thief" (1 Thess 5:2-4). By the time we read 2 Thessalonians, such imminence has been overly developed: the Thessalonians believe that Christ's final coming has already arrived in some invisible, spiritual manner. Paul must now correct an aberrant view of eschatology once more and explain why the Day of the Lord has *not* already consummately occurred.

Second Thessalonians 1 begins with Paul giving thanks for the Thessalonians' spiritual growth and perseverance in the midst of intense persecution (2 Thess 1:3-4). God promises to punish those who inflict harm on the Thessalonians at Christ's coming (2 Thess 1:5-9). Believers will be vindicated and unbelievers will be judged. Paul, therefore, prays that the Thessalonians would continue on in their faith, so that they might be "considered worthy" (2 Thess 1:5, 11-12).

The next section explains one way in which the Thessalonians are to persevere in their faith. In 2 Thessalonians 2:1-12, Paul exhorts the Thessalonian community not to be deceived about the timing of the "day of the Lord." Apparently, false teachers proclaimed that the final coming of Christ and the resurrection have already arrived. In 2 Thessalonians 2:2 Paul says, "[Do] not become easily unsettled or alarmed by the teaching allegedly from us—whether by a prophecy or by word of mouth or by letter—asserting that the day of the Lord has already come. Don't let anyone deceive you in any way" (2 Thess 2:2-3a TNIV).[2] These false teachers claim that the final resurrection had occurred and that, therefore, Christ had already come finally to raise his people to glory (cf. 1 Cor 15:12-24; 2 Tim 2:16-18; 2 Pet 3:3-13).

Paul contradicts this false teaching by claiming that two events must come to fruition before Christ's return: "Let no one in any way deceive you, for it will not come unless the <u>apostasy</u> comes first, and the <u>man of lawlessness</u> is revealed, the son of destruction."[3] The "apostasy" probably refers to those within the covenant community who fall away from the faith,[4] and the "man of

---

[2]See G. K. Beale, *1-2 Thessalonians*, IVPNTC (Downers Grove, IL: InterVarsity Press, 2003), 199-203.
[3]Tension exists between 1 Thess 5:1-8 and 2 Thess 2:1-4. The former passage claims that Christ's coming is imminent and without signs, whereas the latter affirms that two signs will precede that event. See ibid., pp. 198-203, for a discussion of this difficult issue and a suggested resolution.
[4]Beale, *1–2 Thessalonians*, pp. 204-6.

lawlessness"[5] is the latter-day opponent of Israel—the "antichrist."[6] Since neither of these two events has occurred in their fullness, Christ's return remains an event to occur in the future.

Paul expounds on the "man of lawlessness" in 2 Thessalonians 2:4. He states emphatically that a third reason they should not be deceived about this is because what Paul has just told them is not new information. Paul had repeatedly told them about the coming apostasy and antichrist: "Do you not remember that when I was with you I was telling you these things?" (2 Thess 2:5). These verses (2 Thess 2:3-4) constitute a reminder of what the Thessalonians already knew. The implication of the reminder is that Paul has perceived that the readers were becoming vulnerable to false teaching because they were in the process of forgetting the truth he had already taught them. They were "dumbing themselves down" by not reminding themselves of these crucial facts about the future.

In 2 Thessalonians 2:6, Paul says there is another item the Thessalonians have known: that the reason this devilish figure has not yet appeared in history is because there is one who "restrains him now, so that in his [the lawless one's] time he will be revealed." Then surprisingly in 2 Thessalonians 2:7, Paul explains that the "mystery of lawlessness"[7] is "already at work." It is not until "the restrainer" withdraws that the end-time oppressor of Israel will be physically manifested.[8] The main point of this section is in 2 Thessalonians 2:3 ("let no one in any way

---

[5]Several texts (A D F G Ψ 𝔐 lat sy; Ir[lat] Eus) read "man of sin" (*anthrōpos tēs hamartias*) instead of "man of lawlessness" (*anthrōpos tēs anomias*). It is likely that scribes altered the far more common term "sin" for the less common "lawlessness" (the noun *anomia* occurs 6 times in the Pauline corpus, whereas *hamartia* occurs approximately 64 times). Moreover, 2 Thess 2:7 appears to presuppose the man of "lawlessness" in 2 Thess 2:3 (see Beale, *1–2 Thessalonians*, pp. 204-5n2:3, and Bruce Metzger, *A Textual Commentary on the Greek New Testament*, 2nd ed. (Stuttgart: Deutsche Bibelgesellschaft, 1998), p. 567.

[6]Within the New Testament, the term *antichrist* (*antichristos*) appears only in the Johannine epistles (1 Jn 2:18, 22; 4:3; 2 Jn 7).

[7]It is likely that *anomias* is a genitive of quality—"mystery characterized by lawlessness" (BDF § 165).

[8]Commentators are divided as to the precise identity of "the restrainer." Complicating matters is the neuter gender in 2 Thess 2:6 (*to katechon*), whereas the masculine gender is found in 2 Thess 2:7 (*ho katechōn*). In addition, 2 Thess 2:7b is notoriously difficult to translate. The general options for the identity of the restrainer are the following: the Roman Empire; a nonspecific empire; the Jewish nation; Satan or one of his agents; the influence of false teachers within the local church; God or the Spirit; and the gospel as heralded by an angel. We opt for the last view: an angel represents God's sovereignty in making the heralding of the gospel effective by prevailing over the devil's influence, especially the devil's desire to bring about the "man of lawlessness" into history, when that evil figure will be able temporarily to suppress the growth of the gospel through persecution and deception (see Mt 16:18; Rev 20:1-9). For a discussion of this problem, see Beale, *1–2 Thessalonians*, pp. 213-18.

deceive you"), which is supported by all the other verses around it. Second Thessalonians 2:8-10 proceeds to speak of the demise of this eschatological figure and his cooperation with Satan: "Then that lawless one will be revealed whom the Lord will slay with the breath of his mouth and bring to an end by the appearance of his coming" (2 Thess 2:8). The figure will bring about a great deception within the covenant community and among those on the outside (2 Thess 2:10-12). Individuals who succumb to the deception and "take pleasure in wickedness" are on the receiving end of God's judgment (2 Thess 2:12).

But Paul is thankful that God has elected the Thessalonian community and is maintaining sound doctrine, the latter of which is due to the protection that election affords, so that the "elect" are not deceived (2 Thess 2:13). Yet the readers must continue to live holy lives and keep the gospel free from corruption. It is of utmost importance that they not abandon apostolic tradition but seek to preserve it: "Brethren, stand firm and hold to the traditions which you were taught, whether by word of mouth or by letter from us," thereby encouraging them to remain faithful to the gospel (2 Thess 2:15).

DANIEL 11–12 AND THE "MAN OF LAWLESSNESS"

The expression "man of lawlessness" in 2 Thessalonians 2:3 recalls Daniel 11:29-36; 12:10 (LXX, Theodotion).[9] Commentators are in general agreement that part of the description of this "man of lawlessness" in 2 Thessalonians 2:3-4 alludes to Daniel 11 (see table 8.1).[10]

The final section of Daniel (Dan 10–12) constitutes Daniel's final vision. Those who have insight will further illuminate "the many" and be refined during a time of affliction (Dan 11:33-35). In Daniel 12:1, a great persecution

---

[9]Some suggest that Is 57:3 stands behind the expression "man <u>of lawlessness</u> [*tēs anomias*], <u>the son</u> [*ho huios*] of destruction" in 2 Thess 2:3: "But come here, you <u>sons of a sorceress</u> [*huioi anomoi*], offspring of an adulterer and a prostitute." Psalm 89:22 (88:23 LXX) is also listed as a possibility: "The enemy will not deceive him, nor the <u>son of wickedness</u> [*huios anomias*] afflict him." See Gordon D. Fee, *The First and Second Letters to the Thessalonians*, NICNT (Grand Rapids: Eerdmans, 2009); and Jeffrey A. D. Weima, "1–2 Thessalonians," in G. K. Beale and D. A. Carson, *Commentary on the New Testament Use of the Old Testament* (Grand Rapids: Baker, 2007), p. 887. Though these texts could be slightly echoed here, it is more likely that Paul focuses on the book of Daniel and alludes to it, especially, Daniel 12:10. Not only is the language closer to Paul's words (note the repetition of "lawless"), but close thematic connections to the book of Daniel are also apparent.

[10]E.g., C. A. Wanamaker, *The Epistles to the Thessalonians*, NIGTC (Grand Rapids: Eerdmans, 1990), pp. 245-46; O. Betz, 'Der Katechon,' NTS 9 (1963): 282-84; F. F. Bruce, *1 & 2 Thessalonians*, WBC 45 (Dallas, TX: Word, 1982), p. 168; I. H. Marshall, *1 and 2 Thessalonians*, NCBC (Grand Rapids: Eerdmans, 1983), pp. 190-91.

will set in—"a time of distress such as never occurred." But in the midst of this tribulation, a remnant will remain and "be rescued" (Dan 12:1). They will eventually be resurrected, and those who have understanding will "shine brightly" (Dan 12:2-4). The end-time events in Daniel 11–12 largely comprise the rise and fall of kings and the antagonism of Antiochus IV (the Seleucid king) and a latter-day opponent (Dan 11:36-45). It is not entirely clear whether or not Antiochus IV should be identified with the figure in Daniel 11:36-45. At the very least, Antiochus IV certainly functions as a precursor to or type of this antagonist.

Table 8.1

Daniel 11:31, 36; 12:10	2 Thessalonians 2:3-4
"Forces from him will arise, desecrate the sanctuary fortress, and do away with the regular sacrifice . . . they will set up the abomination of desolation" (Dan 11:31).	"And the man of lawlessness [*anthrōpos tēs anomias*] is revealed, the son of destruction, who opposes and exalts himself above every so-called god or object of worship, so that he takes his seat in the temple of God, displaying himself as being God."
"He will exalt and magnify himself above every god and will speak monstrous things against the God of gods" (Dan 11:36).	
"Let many choose and be made white and be refined and the lawless act lawlessly [*anomēsōsin anomoi*]. And the lawless [*anomoi*] will not understand, and the intelligent will understand" (Dan 12:10 LXX Theodotion).	

In the immediate context of Daniel 11:36-45, a final opponent of God besieges the covenant community. Daniel 11:36, to which Paul directly alludes in 2 Thessalonians 2:3-4, characterizes the opponent in stunning terms: "Then the king will do as he pleases, and he will exalt and magnify himself above every god and will speak monstrous things against the God of gods; and he will prosper until the indignation is finished, for that which is decreed will be done" (cf. Dan 2:8, 11, 25; 8:9-12; Is 14:12-14). We learn that this figure will commit great blasphemy by "exalting and magnifying himself above every god." In other words, he places himself on a pedestal above God. Not only does this opponent promote himself above God, he also disparages God by "speaking monstrous things against the God of gods." Paul is asserting in 2 Thessalonians 2:4 that, while this has not yet happened, it will assuredly come to pass at some point in the future, immediately preceding the final coming of Christ.

In addition, the end-time attack on Israel prophesied by Daniel manifests itself in two ways. First, an opponent will persecute righteous Israelites. Daniel 11:31 says, "Forces from him will arise, desecrate the sanctuary fortress, and do away with the regular sacrifice. And they will set up the abomination of desolation." Here the latter-day opponent will wage war against the temple precinct and defile it by "setting up the abomination of desolation." Daniel 11:33-35 further describes the attack against the "wise" within the covenant community: "Those who have insight among the people . . . will fall by sword and by flame, by captivity and by plunder for many days" (Dan 11:33). The righteous nevertheless will persevere under pressure (Dan 11:32), though they will "fall" and be "refined" and "purified" (Dan 11:36).

In addition to persecution, there is a second way that Daniel's predicted end-time attack on Israel will be manifested. Israel's latter-day enemy will deceive some within the covenant community by enticing speech. His deception will be accompanied with "smooth words," resulting in some "forsaking" the "holy covenant" (Dan 11:30). His influence also extends to those "who act wickedly toward the covenant" to become even more "godless" themselves (Dan 11:32), to compromise, and to foster deception and further compromise among others. Daniel 11:34 claims that "many will join with them [the faithful] in hypocrisy," claiming to be faithful but who are not.

Daniel 12:10 generally describes the conduct of two groups in the latter days: "Many will be purged, purified and refined, but the wicked will act wickedly; and none of the wicked will understand, but those who have insight will understand." The righteous Israelites will have great discernment in understanding God's actions. From the outside, it seems as though the wicked have the upper hand, especially in light of grave persecution. But those who have insight into God's plan (the "wise") will grasp the significance of the end-time turmoil. God has decreed that the wicked become increasingly hostile to those within the covenant community, resulting in the faithful being "purged, purified and refined." On the other hand, the wicked or the "lawless ones" have apparently been deceived by the end-time opponent (so Dan 11:29-34). These "lawless ones" spiral into greater wickedness and deception: "the wicked will act wickedly" (Dan 12:10).[11] This lawless behavior is directly linked, if not partly explained,

---

[11]Dan 11:32 (LXX, Theodotion) also includes the theme of "lawlessness"; however, Theodotion's translation differs in that it replaces the end-time opponent with a group of "lawless ones": "And those who are lawless [*hoi anomountes*] will introduce a covenant by means of slipperiness" (NETS).

by "the time of the removal of the perpetual sacrifice, when the abomination of desolation shall be set up."

When Paul cites Daniel 11:31, 36; 12:10 in 2 Thessalonians 2:3-4, he likely has the wider context of Daniel 11:31–12:10 in his mind. He claims that these things will surely come to pass in the future through the individual "man of lawlessness" (2 Thess 2:4). The book of Daniel elaborates in some detail on this great oppressor of Israel (see also the surveys of this theme elsewhere in Daniel, early Judaism and the New Testament in excususes 8.1-3). Foremost is the end-time context of the antagonist. The key passages are contextualized with "latter days" (Dan 10:14), "days yet future" (Dan 10:14) and "time of the end" (Dan 8:17). In other words, this character will arrive on the scene when the "latter days" dawn in Israel's history. The end-time opponent will also commit grave blasphemy by exalting himself above God (Dan 11:36).[12] The figure will be marked by primarily two characteristics: (1) he will wage war against Israel on a number of fronts (Dan 7:25; 8:24; 9:26; 11:31, 33-35); and (2) he will deceive many within the covenant community (though not the remnant or the "wise") and will further delude the wicked (Dan 8:25; 9:27; 11:30, 32, 34; 12:10).[13]

CONTENT OF THE MYSTERY

In light of our brief analysis of the allusion to Daniel, we can now understand Paul's admonitions in 2 Thessalonians 2:1-7 more deeply. As mentioned above, Paul corrects the church's confusion over the second coming of Christ. He makes it clear that Christ's final coming has not yet occurred, since that day will be preceded by two events—"apostasy" and the unveiling of the "man of lawlessness" (2 Thess 2:3).[14]

Though Paul claims in 2 Thessalonians 2:3 that Daniel's "man of lawlessness" has not yet arrived, alarmingly there is a sense in which the end-time oppressor is already on the scene. This suggestion explains the language in 2 Thessalonians 2:7: "The mystery [mystērion][15] of lawlessness is already at work [ēdē ener-

---

[12]Antiochus had coins minted with the title BASILEOS ANTIOCHOU THEOU EPIPHANOUS ("King Antiochus, the Manifestation of God"); so Martin Hengel, *Judaism and Hellenism: Studies in their Encounter in Palestine during the Early Hellenistic Period* (Philadelphia: Fortress, 1974), 1:285; cited in John J. Collins, *Daniel*, Hermeneia (Minneapolis: Fortress, 1993), p. 386.

[13]See excursus 8.1, "The Book of Daniel and Israel's Latter-Day Antagonist," and excursus 8.3, "The End-Time Opponent in Early Judaism."

[14]On the "man of lawlessness," see Craig S. Keener, *The Gospel of Matthew: A Socio-Rhetorical Commentary* (Grand Rapids: Eerdmans, 2009), pp. 570-71.

[15]Some translations incorrectly render *mystērion* as "secret power" (TNIV) or "hidden power" (NET).

geitai]." It is important to maintain the continuity of subject matter between these two verses (2 Thess 2:3, 7). In 2 Thessalonians 2:3 Paul mentions the future coming of the "man of <u>lawlessness</u>," and in 2 Thessalonians 2:7 he further describes this same figure but in terms of its present existence. Second Thessalonians 2:7 does not refer to a general form of wickedness and persecution, as some presume, but a specific end-time deception and persecution that ought to be attributed to Israel's long-awaited antagonist. The end-time persecutor in Daniel was to appear to the covenant community in his full bodily presence, yet Paul argues that the antagonist is nevertheless surprisingly "already at work" in the community, though he is not bodily present.

We noted above that the book of Daniel mentions twice how Israel's antagonist will desecrate the sanctuary:

> Forces from him will arise, desecrate the sanctuary fortress, and do away with the regular sacrifice. And they will <u>set up the abomination of desolation</u>. (Dan 11:31)

> From the time that the regular sacrifice is abolished and <u>the abomination of desolation is set up</u>, *there will be* 1,290 days. (Dan 12:11)

These two texts describe the end-time oppressor entering Israel's temple precinct and defiling the sanctuary, actions initially fulfilled by Antiochus IV in 167 B.C. With this in mind, Paul says in 2 Thessalonians 2:4 that the antichrist will "take his seat in the temple of God." Though heavily debated among scholars, it is likely that the "temple" (*naos*) here does not refer to a rebuilt, physical temple in Jerusalem sometime in the future. Rather, "temple" (*naos*) refers to the community of believers, the church.[16] In other words, the antichrist will assume a position of authority in the church and thereby promulgate widespread deception. This event predicted in 2 Thessalonians 2:3-4 will be a fulfillment of the tyrant "setting up" the "abomination of desolation" in the temple.[17]

The revealed mystery is that the prophecy of Daniel is beginning unex-

---

Instead, the term ought to be translated as "mystery" (NASB, ESV, NRSV, ASV). This not only preserves the Danielic background of the term as it is typically translated there, it also maintains the continuity between the usages of the term throughout the New Testament, where also it is typically rendered as "mystery."

[16]See 1 Cor 3:16-17; 2 Cor 6:16; Eph 2:19-21; 1 Pet 2:4-7; Rev 3:12; 21:22.

[17]For discussion of other identifications of the temple in 2 Thess 2:4 and for further argument in favor of the position taken here, see G. K. Beale, *The Temple and the Church's Mission*, NSBT 17 (Downers Grove, IL: InterVarsity Press, 2004), pp. 274-92.

pectedly because the latter-day foe has not yet come in bodily form, yet he is already inspiring his "lawless" works of deception and persecution. Commentators appear to be somewhat in line with this suggestion. F. F. Bruce, for example, says, "at present it ['mystery of lawlessness'] works beneath the surface but when the due time comes for its disclosure it will find its embodiment in the manifested 'man of lawlessness.'"[18]

Daniel's prophecies of an end-time oppressor of Israel have been inaugurated and are coming to fruition in the first century, though the final end of history has not yet come. The full meaning of Daniel's prophecy was partially hidden, because *the latter-day foe had not yet come in bodily form, as expected by Daniel, yet in his invisible spiritual presence he is already inspiring his "lawless" works of deception. His deceiving activity comes through the agency of his allies, the false teachers, which Daniel had also predicted would come in conjunction with the end-time opponent's coming.*

As with the majority of New Testament uses of *mystery* (*mystērion*) that we have seen so far, the one here in 2 Thessalonians 2:7 is likewise joined to an Old Testament reference (Dan 11 in 2 Thess 2:4). Such a placement is not surprising, since we saw in chapter one above that the "latter-day" use of *mystery* occurs repeatedly. In this respect, Paul is taking the end-time "mystery" reference from Daniel 2 and applying it to Daniel 11; he is saying that Daniel's predictions of the antichrist and his emissaries in Daniel 11 are part of the eschatological "mystery" of Daniel 2. And, as we have also observed elsewhere in the New Testament, the word *mystery,* when linked to Old Testament references, is typically used to indicate that prophecy is beginning fulfillment but in an unexpected manner in comparison to the way Old Testament readers might have expected these prophecies to be fulfilled.

The consummation of the fulfillment of this Daniel prophecy will occur when this evil figure comes in incarnate form, directly preceding the final coming of Christ (2 Thess 2:3-4, 8-12). Thus Daniel's prophecy will be fulfilled literally in its "already-and-not-yet" dimensions, but the inaugurated timing of the fulfillment and the way it begins fulfillment is initially unexpected and thus a revealed mystery. Therefore, the reason Paul uses the word *mystery* in 2 Thes-

---

[18]Bruce, *1 & 2 Thessalonians,* p. 170; see also, for example, Wanamaker, *Epistles to the Thessalonians,* p. 255; Markus Bockmuehl, *Revelation and Mystery in Ancient Judaism and Pauline Christianity,* WUNT 36 (Tübingen: Mohr Siebeck, 1990; repr., Grand Rapids: Eerdmans, 1997), pp. 197-98; Günther Bornkamm, "μυστήριον, μυέω," in *TDNT* 4:823.

salonians 2:7 is that he understands the antichrist prophecy from Daniel to be beginning fulfillment in the Thessalonian church in an enigmatic manner and not as clearly foreseen by Daniel. Daniel's readers would have expected the end-time opponent's deceptive allies to appear at the same time of his own bodily appearance, which would be visible to all eyes (he would "exalt and magnify himself"). In fact, however, Paul says in the inaugurated phase of the fulfillment of this prophecy, only the false teachers will appear, without the expected personal *bodily* presence of the antichrist. Nevertheless, the antichrist was already present spiritually and at work in the covenant community through his deceivers.

This was still in literal fulfillment of Daniel's prophecy about the eschatological enemy's coming, since his physical coming would include also his spiritual presence (the two would not be distinguished from the prophetic perspective). The part of the prophecy about his physical presence would not be fulfilled until the very end, but the part about his spiritual presence was beginning fulfillment. The personal spirit of the lawless one is already present and operating through the false prophets. In this respect we can refer to the "corporate" man of lawlessness. As an individual, and even though not yet bodily present, this end-time fiend infuses his emissaries with his spirit, so that they will do his will; he is accordingly their representative and they are his representatives on earth until he comes in person. (This is the reverse of Christ as a corporate person: he represents Christians and inspires them to do his will by his Holy Spirit, even though he is not on earth but in heaven.) Just as believers represent the "body of Christ" on earth, so unbelieving false teachers in the church represent the body of the antichrist on earth. This is strikingly similar to 1 John 4:3, which says that false teachers were manifesting "the spirit of the Antichrist, of which you have heard that it is coming, and now it is already in the world."

Some might doubt that Daniel's end-time opponent is in mind, since he was prophesied there not only to deceive but to persecute. Clearly, it is deception and not persecution that is in mind in 2 Thessalonians 2, but persecution is explicitly in view in 2 Thessalonians 1:4-6 and 2 Thessalonians 3:1-3.[19] Thus Paul

---

[19]In 2 Thess 3, Paul comes the closest to claiming forthrightly that present persecution is linked to the influence of the antichrist: "Pray for us that . . . we will be rescued from <u>perverse and evil men</u>; for not all have faith. But the Lord is faithful, and he will strengthen and protect you from <u>the evil one</u>" (2 Thess 3:1-3). One item worthy of note in this passage is the following: Paul draws a tight connection between the "evil one" and the "perverse and evil men." This relationship is nearly

may well have in mind secondarily that the persecution that the Thessalonians are described as going through in 2 Thessalonians 1 and 2 Thessalonians 3 is linked to the work of the man of lawlessness.

Permanent Hiddenness

Throughout this book we have taken note of a phenomenon that we have labeled "permanent hiddenness."[20] That is, there is an ongoing state of hiddenness that accompanies mystery, which will never be removed for intractable nonbelievers. Believers, since they are indwelt with the revelatory Spirit (1 Cor 2:6-16), are able to perceive and understand the content of the revealed mystery. Unbelievers, on the other hand, do not possess the Spirit and are therefore unable to grasp the salvific implications of God's revealed wisdom. Though Paul does not explicitly identify this particular characteristic in the immediate context of 2 Thessalonians 2, this notion may be implicit. Evidently the Thessalonians misunderstood Paul's teaching on Christ's second coming (1 Thess 4–5), so Paul has to remind them once more of what will precede his return. But he makes it plain that the antichrist is "working" in their midst (2 Thess 2:7). A few verses later, Paul admonishes the church constantly to be thankful that God has sanctified them through *the Spirit* and "faith in the truth." It is likely that Paul's instruction on eschatology (2 Thess 2:3-12) is bound to the "truth" mentioned in 2 Thessalonians 2:13. The Thessalonian community must maintain a correct view of the second coming and the events leading up to it. Second Thessalonians 2:7 delineates how the "mystery of lawlessness" plays a key role in the unfolding of those events. In other words, the Thessalonian believers, Paul says, ought to be on constant alert for the pervasive influence of the invisible and corporate antichrist. His deception is largely "presently hidden" from unbelievers, which includes the false teachers (who were professing Christians) in the midst of the Thessalonian church (see 2 Thess 2:3!), and this deception will continue until the consummation of the

---

identical to the relationship between the "man of lawlessness" and Satan in 2 Thess 2:8-9: "Then that lawless one will be revealed . . . that is, the one whose coming is in accord with the activity of Satan, with all power and signs and false wonders." Here the antichrist is nearly viewed as Satan's representative ("in accord with the activity of Satan"). In the same way, Paul asks prayer that he and his companions be protected or "rescued" from "perverse and evil men" (2 Thess 3:2) and then quickly progresses to the protection from the "evil one" that God grants to the Thessalonians. It is likely that the "perverse and evil men" are under the same demonic influence as the antichrist and thus perform his nefarious task to persecute the covenant community.

[20]See discussion on pp. 60-66 above.

age, as 2 Thessalonians 2:8-12 says: "the lawless one will be revealed [at the very end] . . . with all the deception of wickedness for those who perish, because they did not receive the love of the truth . . . For this reason God will send upon them a deluding influence so that they will believe what is false." Yet the mystery is revealed to the believing Thessalonians who must remain sober minded (1 Thess 5:6), in order that they might perceive the "mystery of lawlessness." Best agrees, "Will the Thessalonians see the mystery of rebellion active in the work of heretics who mislead them with false teaching or in their harassment by the Jews or their fellow-countrymen (1 Th. 2.14) or in a 'holy war' waged in the supernatural sphere?"[21]

Conclusion

Paul warns the Thessalonians that two events will precede Christ's return—the great "apostasy" and the revelation of the "man of lawlessness" (2 Thess 2:3). By alluding to the book of Daniel in 2 Thessalonians 2:3-4, Paul suggests that Daniel's prophecies of the latter-day tyrant will come to fruition in the "man of lawlessness" whose arrival will immediately precede Christ's final coming. The apostle Paul, like the book of Daniel and early Judaism, claims that the "man of lawlessness" will commit blasphemy, persecute the church and bring about great deception within the covenant community. Yet Paul goes on to make a staggering claim: this latter-day antagonist presently exists invisibly and corporately in the false teachers and persecutors of the church: "the mystery of lawlessness is already at work" (2 Thess 2:7). Daniel's prophecies of an end-time oppressor of Israel have been inaugurated and are coming to fruition in the first century, though the final end of history has not yet come. The prophecy of Daniel 11 is beginning unexpectedly, indeed "mysteriously," because the latter-day foe has not yet come in bodily form, as expected by Daniel, yet he is personally fulfilling the prophecy in his spiritual presence by already inspiring his "lawless" works of deception and persecution. His deceiving activity comes through the agency of his allies, the false teachers, which Daniel had also predicted would come in conjunction with the end-time opponent. The end-time deceiver of Israel will appear in a physical, incarnate form directly preceding Christ's final coming (2 Thess 2:3-4). At this time, the spiritual will be combined with the physical being of the antichrist. It was partially hidden in the book of

---

[21]Best, *Thessalonians*, p. 293; cf. Bockmuehl, *Revelation and Mystery*, p. 198.

Daniel that this two-staged arrival of the antichrist would take place. Paul, therefore, deems this a "mystery."

Second Thessalonians 2:7 is parallel to 1 John 2:18, which also alludes to Daniel's prophecy (see excursus 8.2): "Children, it is the last hour; and just as you heard that antichrist is coming, even now many antichrists have appeared; from this we know that it is the last hour."[22] John also sees that the prophesied antichrist has begun to come unexpectedly but will also come in a consummate way at the very end of time.

In the light of this staggering conclusion, the church must remain vigilant and committed to the truth of the gospel in the face of persecution and rampant false teaching. Even though the antichrist is not yet present in bodily form, he is nevertheless present in spirit and working through the false teachers, so that the deceptions of the great tribulation to be worked through the antichrist are already present in the first-century church itself and will be until the final coming of Christ. Accordingly, Daniel's prophecies about the end-time opponent begin to take place in the first century and will be consummated at Christ's final coming.

Some Christians today think that, since the antichrist is not yet here physically and the future great tribulation has not yet started, then they cannot be affected by his deceptive activity. Christians living during the church age, however, should not think that they are immune from the deceptions of the antichrist to come in the great tribulation, since in fact the antichrist has already begun to manifest himself. This is also an indication that the great tribulation itself has also commenced. The final fulfillment of this end-time tribulation will intensify the persecution and deception that is already happening during the church age. That is, whereas the persecutions and deceptions inspired by the antichrist during the church age are selective and do not affect every church in every place (though all churches are threatened by these things), in the consummated phase of the eschatological tribulation such persecutions and deceptions will be universal (as 2 Thess 2:3-4 suggests, and Rev 11:7; 20:7-9 attest).

The only thing that could protect the Thessalonians from deception in Paul's time and believers in our own time is to remember vigilantly the Word of God. This is evident from recalling that Paul says this is what they should "remember"

---

[22]Likewise 1 Jn 4:3: "And every spirit that does not confess Jesus is not from God; this is the spirit of the antichrist, of which you have heard that it is coming, and now it is already in the world."

(2 Thess 2:6) and "stand firm" in and "hold to" (2 Thess 2:15), so that they and we can obtain "eternal comfort and good hope by grace" (2 Thess 2:16). In the following context of 2 Thessalonians 2:8-12, Paul tells the Thessalonians that if they are not deceived by the false teaching of the antichrist now, they will not be judged with the antichrist and his deceived followers later, at the final judgment. The church in Thessalonica, says Paul, ought to continue to maintain sound teaching that they learned through him (including this teaching about the antichrist in 2 Thess 2:1-12) and his associates. Persevering in the truthfulness of the gospel will prevent the antichrist's influence through false teaching. And crucial to this perseverance is to realize how Paul is explaining that the prophecy from Daniel 11 is beginning fulfillment as a revealed mystery.

EXCURSUS 8.1: THE BOOK OF DANIEL AND ISRAEL'S LATTER-DAY ANTAGONIST

Though a few Old Testament passages may allude to a similar figure,[23] by far the most detailed account of an end-time enemy is found in the book of Daniel:

> As for the ten horns, out of this kingdom ten kings will arise; and another will arise after them, and he will be different from the previous ones and will subdue three kings. He will speak out against the Most High and wear down the saints of the Highest One, and he will intend to make alterations in times and in law; and they will be given into his hand for a time, times, and half a time. (Dan 7:24-25; cf. Dan 7:7-12)

> Out of one of them came forth a rather small horn which grew exceedingly great toward the south, toward the east, and toward the Beautiful *Land*. It grew up to the host of heaven and caused some of the host and some of the stars to fall to the earth, and it trampled them down. It even magnified *itself* to be equal with the Commander of the host; and it removed the regular sacrifice from him, and the place of his sanctuary was thrown down. And on account of transgression the host will be given over to the *horn* along with the regular sacrifice; and it will fling truth to the ground and perform *its will* and prosper. . . .

> In the latter period of their rule,
> When the transgressors have run *their course*,

---

[23]E.g., Deut 13:1-11; Ezek 28:2; Zech 11:15-17. See the discussion in G. W. Lorein, *The Antichrist Theme in the Intertestamental Period*, JSPSup 44 (New York: T & T Clark, 2003), pp. 30-42; Kim Riddlebarger, *The Man of Sin: Uncovering the Truth About the Antichrist* (Grand Rapids: Baker, 2006), pp. 37-60.

A king will arise,

Insolent and skilled in intrigue.

His power will be mighty, but not by his *own* power,

And he will destroy to an extraordinary degree

And prosper and perform *his will*;

He will destroy mighty men and the holy people.

And through his shrewdness

He will cause deceit to succeed by his influence;

And he will magnify *himself* in his heart,

And he will destroy many while *they are* at ease.

He will even oppose the Prince of princes,

But he will be broken without human agency. (Dan 8:9-12, 23-25;
    see also 9:26-27)

Though we think it likely, it is not entirely clear that each vision in Daniel 7–12 speaks of the *same* fiendish character. They do describe a persecutor and deceiver who will arise and oppress Israel, but it is difficult to determine whether or not each passage focuses on an identical figure. Some figures may be typological precursors of an end-time antichrist and others may refer directly to this end-time figure himself. In any case, the New Testament focuses on the persecuting and deceiving figure of each of these passages, which constituted the central background for the New Testament doctrine of Israel's latter-day antagonist.

These above-cited passages from Daniel 7–9 reinforce our previous conclusions about the prophecies of Daniel 11–12 and their already-and-not-yet fulfillment in 2 Thessalonians 2. Each text mentions the ferocious attack of the antagonist against Israel: he will "wear down the saints" (Dan 7:25)[24] and "destroy mighty men and the holy people" (Dan 8:24). Great deception, according to these texts, will also mark the opponent's dealings: "he will make alterations in times and in law" (Dan 7:25) and "through his shrewdness he will cause deceit to succeed" (Dan 8:25).

Many commentators view the end-time opponent mentioned in Daniel 7, 8, 9, 11, as referring to the Greek king, Antiochus IV (see 1 Macc 1:48-50; 2:15). While this remains possible in some cases, we ought to note that Antiochus IV

---

[24]Several LXX/Theodotion manuscripts and versions, as well as some Fathers, replace "wear out" (LXX *kataribō* and Theodotion *palaioō* = Aramaic *ybl*ˀ) with "deceive" (*planaō*), so that the end-time opponent is portrayed as "deceiving" the saints here (36-770 C´ 26 46´ 239 410 590 Aeth Arab Arm Hippol. Polychr.).

was only the initial fulfillment of these prophecies and that Daniel anticipates another, even graver, end-time opponent that will bring increased oppression to God's people. Daniel's language concerning this opponent, according to many scholars, is "telescoped." That is, near and far fulfillment have been compressed into a single event. The initial or near fulfillment concerns Antiochus IV and the far fulfillment looks forward to *the* "man of lawlessness."[25]

EXCURSUS 8.2: OTHER NEW TESTAMENT REFERENCES TO THE ANTICHRIST

In addition to Paul's teaching in 2 Thessalonians, the antichrist plays a prominent role in the Gospels and early Christianity.[26] In the Olivet Discourse, Jesus discusses an end-time figure who will deceive and bring about the destruction of many.[27]

> For many will come in My name, saying, "I am the Christ [*ho christos*]," and will mislead many. (Mt 24:5; par. Mk 13:6; Lk 21:8)

> Many false prophets will arise and will mislead many. Because lawlessness [*tēn anomian*] is increased, most people's love will grow cold. (Mt 24:11-12)

> Then if anyone says to you, "Behold, here is the Christ," or "There *He is*," do not believe *him*. For false Christs and false prophets will arise and will show great signs and wonders, so as to mislead, if possible, even the elect. Behold, I have told you in advance. So if they say to you, "Behold, he is in the wilderness," do not go out, or, "Behold, he is in the inner rooms," do not believe *them*. (Mt 24:23-26; par. Mk 13:21-22)

These passages reinforce our previous conclusions about the nature of the end-time opponent. Jesus envisions an antichrist figure(s) that will deceive Israel

---

[25]See also Tremper Longman, *Daniel* (Grand Rapids: Zondervan, 1999), pp. 280-83; Riddlebarger, *Man of Sin*, pp. 68-75; G. B. Caird, *The Language and Imagery of the Bible* (Philadelphia: Westminster Press, 1980), pp. 262-63; Anthony A. Hoekema, *The Bible and the Future* (Grand Rapids: Eerdmans, 1979), p. 156; Joyce G. Baldwin, *Daniel,* TOTC (Downers Grove, IL: InterVarsity Press, 1978), pp. 199-201.

[26]See also Rev 13:1-8; 17:7-8; 19:19-20. For a survey of this theme in the early church, see L. J. Lietaert Peerbolte, *The Antecedents of Antichrist: A Traditio-Historical Study of the Earliest Christian Views on Eschatological Opponents,* JSJSup 49 (Boston: Brill, 1996), pp. 63-220; Paul Hanley Furfey, "The Mystery of Iniquity" *CBQ* 8 (1946): 179-91.

[27]*The Apocalypse of Elijah* (first to fourth century A.D.), partly under the influence of Mt 24 and 2 Thess 2:3, includes both deception (3.1, 5-18; 4.15) and persecution (1.10; 4.2, 7-10; cf. *Apoc. Pet.* 2; *Didache* 16.3-4).

preceding the destruction of the temple in A.D. 70.[28] His influence will be a sign
that Israel's destruction is near. In Matthew 24:5, the oppressor will be characterized by deception, claiming to be the Messiah (*ho christos*), and, therefore,
upsetting the faith of "many." Matthew 24:11-12 may even allude to the emissaries of the antichrist, since they, like the end-time antagonist, will "mislead
many" (Mt 24:5). This text is strikingly relevant to our argument in its mention
of the "increase" of "lawlessness" (*tēn anomian*). Matthew 24:12 may even have
Daniel 12:10 in mind ("the <u>lawless</u> act <u>lawlessly</u>. And the <u>lawless</u> will not understand") and is remarkably similar to our texts in 2 Thessalonians 2:3 ("man <u>of</u>
<u>lawlessness</u> [*anomias*]") and 2 Thessalonians 2:7 ("mystery of <u>lawlessness</u>
[*anomias*]").

Jesus thus also refers to the same prophecy from Daniel to which Paul is
referring (see Mt 24:4-5, 10-13, 23-26). Just as *the main point in 2 Thessalonians
2:1-7 is on "do not be deceived" (2 Thess 2:3),* the main point of the Matthew 24
passage is that no one should mislead Jesus' followers about his second coming
(Mt 24:3-4). Jesus predicts that before he comes, many antichrists will indeed
come. He is focusing not on the final coming of one antichrist but on the
coming into the church of many antichrists who are the semi-fulfillments and
forerunners of the final predicted opponent of God (Mt 24:5, 10-15, 24). These
are the same false prophets to which 2 Thessalonians is referring (and, as we
will see, 1 Jn 2:18 is also referring). Jesus even says in Matthew 7:21-23 that those
who were regarded as teachers of the church will be judged as false teachers at
the final judgment. Note that Jesus refers to them as those who practiced "lawlessness" (*anomia*), the same word used in 2 Thessalonians 2:7 in the phrase
"the mystery of lawlessness."

Paul is saying in 2 Thessalonians 2:1-7 that even now the false teachers that
have been prophesied by Daniel and Jesus (e.g., Mt 24:4-5, 23-24) are with us,
and therefore the end-time "great tribulation" has begun in part! The prophecy
of the "apostasy" and coming of "the man of lawlessness" has started to be
fulfilled, and accordingly the two stage already-and-not-yet fulfillment is a
revelation of a mystery, as we discussed earlier.

In light of a saturation of allusions to Daniel in the Olivet discourse, it appears that Jesus develops the prophecy of Daniel's latter-day opponent.[29] For

---

[28]See Hoekema, *Bible and the Future*, pp. 148-49, 156.
[29]On which see further L. Hartman, *Prophecy Interpreted: The Formation of Some Jewish Apocalyptic
Texts and of the Eschatological Discourse Mark 13 par,* ConBNT 1 (Lund: Gleerup, 1966), pp. 145-77.

example, Matthew 24:15 and Matthew 24:21 respectively quote the famous "abomination of desolation" and "great tribulation" passages from Daniel 9 and Daniel 12.

Perhaps the most detailed discussion of the antichrist appears in 1 John 2:18-23. Whereas Jesus' primary focus in the Olivet Discourse is on the relationship between the antichrist(s) and the coming destruction of the temple, John highlights the inauguration of the latter-day deceiver as it pertains to heresy within the local church:

> Children, it is the last hour; and just as you heard that <u>antichrist</u> is coming, even <u>now many antichrists have appeared</u>; from this we know that it is <u>the last hour</u>. They went out from us, but they were not *really* of us; for if they had been of us, they would have remained with us; but *they went out,* so that it would be shown that they all are not of us. But you have an anointing from the Holy One, and you all know. I have not written to you because you do not know the truth, but because you do know it, and because no lie is of the truth. Who is the liar but the one who denies that Jesus is the Christ? This is the <u>antichrist</u>, the one who denies the Father and the Son. Whoever denies the Son does not have the Father; the one who confesses the Son has the Father also.

This passage appears to depend on Jesus' prediction of "antichrists" in the Olivet Discourse and the discussion of the "man of lawlessness" in 2 Thessalonians 2. John says that his audience "heard" about the antichrist's arrival (1 Jn 2:18), suggesting that the audience was familiar with a circulating oral form of the expectations in the Synoptics and 2 Thessalonians 2.

John's words echo much of what we saw in the book of Daniel and in 2 Thessalonians 2:7. First, John claims that the coming of an antichrist(s) signals the inauguration of the "last hour." The phrase "last hour," found here, as well as the end-time "hour" in John's Gospel (Jn 4:21, 23; 12:23; 16:25, 32; 17:1), stems from the book of Daniel (Dan 8:17, 19; 11:6, 35, 40; 12:1).[30] Now that the church is aware that the "latter days" or the "last hour" has begun, they are to remain sober minded and be on heightened alert for deceivers in the church, as Daniel prophesied long ago.

Second, the church can be confident that the "last hour" has been inaugurated because the end-time enemy has arrived on the scene corporately through

---

[30]Cf., e.g., Dan 11:13, 20, 27, 29, 35. See Stefanos Mihalios, *The Danielic Eschatological Hour in the Johannine Literature,* LNTS 436 (New York: T & T Clark, 2011) and G. K. Beale, "The Eschatological Hour in 1 John 2:18 in the Light of Its Daniel Background," *Biblica* 92 (2011): 231-54.

the false teachers: "even <u>now</u> many <u>antichrists</u> have appeared." As we noted earlier, John's words in 1 John 2:18 are remarkably similar to Paul's in 2 Thessalonians 2:7: "the mystery of lawlessness <u>is already at work</u>." Like 2 Thessalonians 2, John claims that the end-time opponent of Israel is present in the local congregations, though not physically but spiritually and corporately. This is especially highlighted in 1 John 4:3 where John says that false teachers were manifesting "the *spirit* of the antichrist, of which you have heard that it is coming, and now it is already in the world." John, though, does not label this a "mystery," but perhaps the force of "now" in 1 John 2:18 comes close to this notion.

Finally, as we have repeatedly observed in this chapter, the antichrist is marked by two characteristics in the book of Daniel—persecution and deception. Here John highlights the latter. First John 1:22 describes in some detail the falsehood that the "antichrists" were proclaiming: "Who is the liar but the one who denies that Jesus is the Christ? This is the antichrist, the one who denies the Father and the Son." The majority of commentators are convinced that these "antichrists" or false teachers "denied that Jesus is the Christ" by espousing the view that Christ was not fully human.

This description of the already-and-not-yet antichrist from 1 John is virtually identical to that of 2 Thessalonians 2:3-7.

EXCURSUS 8.3: THE END-TIME OPPONENT IN EARLY JUDAISM

The "man of lawlessness" is part of a broader expectation in early Judaism, which envisioned an opponent(s) of faithful Israel.[31] Restricting ourselves to an end-time opponent(s) that antagonizes Israel allows us to manage a considerable amount of material. Two examples, from 2 Baruch 39 and Martyrdom and Ascension of Isaiah 4, are generally representative. Both draw heavily from the book of Daniel in their portrayal of the oppressor:[32]

---

[31]See, for example, Lorein, *Antichrist Theme.*

[32]Cf. *4 Ezra* 12.22-30; 11.29-35 (first century A.D.). For the influence of Daniel in *4 Ezra and 2 Baruch,* see G. K. Beale, *The Use of Daniel in Jewish Apocalyptic Literature and in the Revelation of St. John* (Lanham, MD: University Press of America, 1984), pp. 112-29, 144-53. On the role of Daniel in *Martyrdom and Ascension of Isaiah,* see Richard Bauckham, *The Climax of Prophecy: Studies on the Book of Revelation* (New York: T & T Clark, 1993), pp. 425-27. This section from the *Martyrdom and Ascension of Isaiah* is probably a Christian interpolation, which has built on an earlier Jewish literary core or was added to it, on which cf. M. A. Knibb, "Martyrdom and Ascension of Isaiah," in J. H. Charlesworth, *The Old Testament Pseudepigrapha 2* (Garden City, NY: Doubleday, 1985), pp. 147-49. We include the *Martyrdom of Isaiah* passage here, since it likely builds on early Jewish expectations.

After that a fourth kingdom arises whose power is harsher and more evil than those which were before it, and it will reign a multitude of times like the trees on the plain, and it will rule the times and exalt itself more than the cedars of Lebanon. And the truth will hide itself in this and all who are polluted with unrighteousness will flee to it like the evil beasts flee and creep into the forest. (2 *Bar.* 39.5-6)

Beliar will descend, the great angel, the king of the world, which he has ruled ever since it existed. He will descend from his firmament in the form of a man, a king of iniquity, a murderer of his mother—this is the king of this world—and will persecute the plant which the twelve apostles of the Beloved will have planted; some of the twelve will be given into his hand. This angel, Beliar, will come in the form of that king, and with him will come all the powers of this world . . . he will act and speak like the Beloved, and will say, "I am the Lord, and before me there was no one." And all men in the world will believe him. They will sacrifice to him and will serve him, saying, "This is the Lord, and besides him there is no other." And the majority of those who have associated together to receive the Beloved he will turn aside after him. And the power of his miracles will be in every city and district, and he will set up his image before him in every city. And he will rule for three years and seven months and twenty-seven days. (*Mart. Ascen. Isa.* 4.2-12)[33]

Second Baruch, in recalling the "fourth kingdom" of Daniel 2:40-43; 7:23-25, expects that this kingdom will rule over all others and with it "the truth will hide itself." That is, not only will this latter-day kingdom oppress the righteous, it will also bring about a great deception on the land. The *Martyrdom and Ascension of Isaiah*, a second-century B.C. to fourth-century A.D. text, once again mentions Beliar and that he will arrive "in the form of a man." He will persecute the twelve apostles and blaspheme God by claiming, "I am the Lord, and before me there was no one" (v. 7). This is strikingly similar to Daniel 11:36: "he will exalt and magnify himself above every god and will speak monstrous things against the God of gods." In addition to persecution and blasphemy, the antagonist will delude the community ("those . . . he will turn aside after him") into believing that he himself is divine. This is clear from verse 8: "They will sacrifice to him and will serve him, saying, 'This is the Lord, and besides him there is no other.'"[34]

---

[33]Dating the *Martyrdom and Ascension of Isaiah* is difficult since the book contains distinctively Jewish and Christian sections. 4:2-12 appears to integrate both Jewish and Christian elements but with an eye on the narrative of Daniel.

[34]For further discussion of Israel's end-time antagonist, see 4Q169 3–4 III, 1-3, 1QpHab II, 5-8,

These Jewish texts together with others express the following notions of the expectation of the end-time opponent of God's people: (1) either implicitly or explicitly, these passages maintain that the tyrant will arrive "in the latter days" or "at the end of time." One of the chief characteristics of the period known as the latter days, therefore, is the advent of Israel's antagonist. (2) This end-time opponent will bring about persecution on a grand scale. Those who do not submit to his teachings and rule will be punished. (3) Coinciding with persecution are false teaching and great apostasy. The latter-day ruler will be the fountainhead of deception and falsehood. Many will be misled who in turn will deceive others. (4) One falsehood, perhaps central to the teaching, will be the opponent's utter claim to divinity. This false assertion by the antagonist appears explicitly in only a few texts but could be implicit throughout.

CD-A I, 11–21, 1QM XIV, 9-15, 1QM XVI, 11-16, XVII, 8-9, *Sib. Or.* 2.165-69; 5:361-70, *2 Bar.* 39.5-6, and *Mart. Ascen. Isa.* 4.2-12. See also Beale, "Eschatological Hour."

9

THE USE OF *MYSTERY*
IN 1 TIMOTHY

◆ ▨ ◆

PAUL'S DISCUSSION OF MYSTERY IN 2 Thessalonians 2:7 refers to the surprising presence of the end-time antichrist: the apostle proclaims, "the mystery of lawlessness is already at work." Here the antichrist is labeled the "mystery of lawlessness," who is surreptitiously deceiving and persecuting the church. On the one hand, the antichrist is present spiritually through his emissaries, the false teachers in the local congregation. On the other, the antichrist will one day arrive consummately and physically immediately preceding Christ's final return. False doctrine and persecution are pervasive in the early church, two indications that the man of lawlessness or the antichrist is a present reality.

We now turn to a passage that is very much related to our discussion of the mysterious presence of the antichrist. Paul attempts to ward off false teaching by divulging to Timothy the "mystery of godliness" in 1 Timothy 3. Though only spanning a few lines, the hymn of 1 Timothy 3:16 encapsulates the heart of the gospel. If Timothy and the church at Ephesus commit themselves to the fidelity of the gospel as summarized in the "mystery of godliness," then they will ward off the deceptive practices of the antichrist.

Surveys of the use of *mystery* in the New Testament rarely focus on the two expressions "mystery of faith" and the "mystery of godliness" in 1 Timothy. Günther Bornkamm, for example, penned an overall helpful survey of *mystery* but only relegates a few sentences to its occurrence in 1 Timothy 3.[1] Markus Bockmuehl's discussion on the matter, one of the longest to date, spans roughly

---

[1]Günther Bornkamm, "μυστήριον, μυέω," in *TDNT* 4:822.

four pages.[2] This present chapter is an attempt to redress the lack of investigation of the revealed mystery in 1 Timothy 3.

Commentators are right to relate the content of the hymn of 1 Timothy 3:16 with the notion of mystery, and nearly all are content to affirm that the unveiled mystery encompasses Christ's life, death and resurrection, yet they fail to recognize what precisely in the hymn constitutes a "new revelation." Though the Old Testament anticipated Christ and his work, some aspects were not fully revealed to the Old Testament authors. Approaching 1 Timothy 3:16 from this vantage point sets us on the right path and forces us to ask fresh questions about the hymn.

IMMEDIATE CONTEXT

In 1 Timothy 3:1-16, Paul writes:

> It is a trustworthy statement: if any man aspires to the office of overseer, it is a fine work he desires *to do.* An overseer, then, must be above reproach, the husband of one wife, temperate, prudent, respectable, hospitable, able to teach, not addicted to wine or pugnacious, but gentle, peaceable, free from the love of money. *He must be* one who manages his own household well, keeping his children under control with all dignity (but if a man does not know how to manage his own household, how will he take care of the church of God?), *and* not a new convert, so that he will not become conceited and fall into the condemnation incurred by the devil. And he must have a good reputation with those outside *the church,* so that he will not fall into reproach and the snare of the devil. Deacons likewise *must be* men of dignity, not double-tongued, or addicted to much wine or fond of sordid gain, *but* holding to the mystery of the faith with a clear conscience. These men must also first be tested; then let them serve as deacons if they are beyond reproach. Women *must* likewise *be* dignified, not malicious gossips, but temperate, faithful in all things. Deacons must be husbands of *only* one wife, *and* good managers of *their* children and their own households. For those who have served well as deacons obtain for themselves a high standing and great confidence in the faith that is in Christ Jesus. I am writing these things to you, hoping to come to you before long; but in case I am delayed, *I write* so that you will know how one ought to conduct himself in the household of God, which is the church of the living God, the pillar and support of the truth. By common confession, great is the mystery of godliness:

---

[2]Markus Bockmuehl, *Revelation and Mystery in Ancient Judaism and Pauline Christianity,* WUNT 36 (Tübingen: Mohr Siebeck, 1990; repr., Grand Rapids: Eerdmans, 1997), pp. 210-14.

He who was revealed in the flesh,
Was vindicated in the Spirit,
Seen by angels,
Proclaimed among the nations,
Believed on in the world,
Taken up in glory. (1 Tim 3:1-16)

Paul exhorts his "son" Timothy to remain firm in his devotion to the gospel (1 Tim 1:2). Not only must Timothy live in accordance with the gospel, Timothy ought to ensure that the local church(es) at Ephesus do so as well. Adherence to the gospel, Paul claims, manifests itself in a variety of ways. First Timothy 1 is largely devoted to Timothy weeding out false teaching and heresy in the church. For example, Paul commands him in 1 Timothy 1:3b-4, "Instruct certain men not to teach strange doctrines, nor to pay attention to myths and endless genealogies." In 1 Timothy 1:12-16, Paul uses himself as an example of one who "acted ignorantly in unbelief," yet God was merciful to him. Hymenaeus and Alexander are two further examples of those who fail to persevere in sound doctrine (1 Tim 1:19-20). False teaching is a theme that recurs throughout the epistle (1 Tim 4:1-3, 7; 5:13-15; 6:3-5, 20-21).

Moving from rooting out false teaching to other practical matters, Paul reminds Timothy that the church must be filled with believers who are characterized by prayer: "I urge that entreaties *and* prayers, petitions *and* thanksgivings, be made on behalf of all men" (1 Tim 2:1; cf. 1 Tim 2:8). The next section, 1 Timothy 2:9-15, concerns the role of women in the church. A woman's dress, Paul argues, is indicative of her character and heart condition (1 Tim 2:9-10). Moreover, the apostle claims that women are not to "teach or exercise authority over a man" (1 Tim 2:12). His admonition is grounded in the pre-fall condition of Adam and Eve (1 Tim 2:13-14).

In 1 Timothy 3 Paul lists the requirements of "overseers" and deacons. The office of an "overseer" is identical with that of an "elder" (cf. Tit 1:5-7). First Timothy 3:1-7 has the office of an elder in mind, whereas 1 Timothy 3:8-13 concerns deacons. With respect to both offices, Paul issues a series of ethical requirements. The requirements for an elder touch on virtually every part of life: conduct within the church (1 Tim 3:2, 6), at home (1 Tim 3:2, 4-5) and "outside" the church (1 Tim 3:7).

Much of what is said concerning an elder is applied to deacons in verses 8-13, save one notable detail: elders must be "able to teach" (1 Tim 3:2). Paul says that deacons are to be dignified or "worthy of respect" (1 Tim 3:8 NIV), then goes on to list qualities that are *not* part of a dignified way of life: "not double-tongued, or addicted to much wine or fond of sordid gain" (1 Tim 3:8b). In contrast, the following verse outlines how deacons are to pursue a life of dignity: "holding to the mystery of the faith [*echontas to mystērion tēs pisteōs*] with a clear conscience" (1 Tim 3:9).

Just as men are to be dignified (1 Tim 3:8), so are the women (i.e., wives of male deacons or perhaps deaconesses): "Women must likewise be dignified" (1 Tim 3:11). The next two verses (1 Tim 3:12-13) return to listing the requirements for deacons; they too must be upright in character and godly. Paul ends this section with one of his central purposes in penning this letter: "*I write* so that you will know how one ought to conduct himself in the household of God" (1 Tim 3:15). It is probable that Paul has in mind in these final verses the entire congregation and not simply elders and deacons. Nevertheless, 1 Timothy 3:16 contains a hymn that Paul describes as a revealed mystery: "By common confession, great is the mystery of godliness [*to tēs eusebeias mystērion*]: He who was revealed in the flesh, was vindicated in the Spirit, seen by angels, proclaimed among the nations, believed on in the world, taken up in glory."

MYSTERIES OF FAITH AND GODLINESS

Since both occurrences of "mystery" (*mystērion*; 1 Tim 3:9, 16) probably refer to the identical content, it is best to interpret them together. The meaning of "mystery of faith" (*mystērion tēs pisteōs*) in 1 Timothy 3:9 is not readily apparent.[3] In the immediate context, Paul likely has in mind a revelation that concerns a specific article of faith or belief.

Yet in what way is the revealed mystery related to faith? Fortunately, Paul gives us a few clues. The first clue stems from his use of the common verb "to hold" or "to have" (*echō*). Though found often in the Pauline corpus, this verb occurs in the context of maintaining sound doctrine (or lack thereof). First

---

[3]The precise use of the genitive *pisteōs* ("of faith") is also seemingly ambiguous. The top two candidates are a descriptive genitive and a genitive of reference. The former is far more common, yet less specific; the phrase would thus be rendered as "faithful mystery," but this is an awkward rendering. Perhaps a better use is the genitive of reference. If this use is in mind, then we could construe the phrase as "the mystery with reference to faith" or "the mystery with respect to faith." Does "faith" describe mystery or is faith the referent? The latter fits much better in the immediate context and is consonant with the second occurrence of mystery in 1 Tim 3:16. This particular use of the genitive limits the referent of mystery. In other words, mystery is specifically applied to the concept of "faith" or belief.

Timothy 1:19 closely resembles our text: "<u>keeping</u> [*echōn*] faith and a good conscience, which some have rejected and suffered shipwreck in regard to their faith."[4] Not only is "to have" linked to "faith" but also Paul includes the reference to a "good" or "clear conscience." In the immediate context, Paul encourages Timothy to persevere and "fight the battle well." Timothy must not succumb to outside pressure but "hold on to faith." Hymenaeus and Alexander are cited as negative examples of those who have "rejected" the "faith." Faith in 1 Timothy 1:19; 3:9, in other words, does not primarily refer to a believer's response to the gospel, as is sometimes the case (e.g., Rom 1:17), but the summation of Christian tradition or *teaching.*[5] If we are correct in assuming that the "mystery of faith" refers to some aspect of Christian doctrine or teaching, then what specifically does Paul have in mind? Fortunately, the second occurrence of mystery is explicitly related to an early Christian hymn in 3:16.

First Timothy 3:16 begins with a rare adverb (*homologoumenōs*) and is often rendered "by common confession" (NASB) or "without any doubt" (NRSV).[6] This adverb contains both positive and negative elements.[7] On the one hand, it refers to an agreement reached by all parties. On the other hand, the adverb contains a negative nuance by referring to something that is undeniable. In other words, the word denotes something that is unquestionably truthful or certain. But to what does the adverb refer? In the immediate context, the most likely referent is the following clause: "great is the mystery of godliness" (*mega estin to tēs eusebeias mystērion*). Paul therefore claims that the "mystery of godliness" is undeniably "great." A near equivalent of Paul's claim occurs in Ephesians 5:32: "<u>this mystery is great</u>, but I am speaking with reference to Christ and the church." In our discussion of Ephesians 5:32, we suggested that the mystery constitutes Paul's insight into Genesis 2:24 that the original couple typologically corresponds to Christ and the church. This insight into Genesis 2, according to Paul, is "great." Here the apostle also describes mystery as "great" but takes it one step further, prefacing it with the adverb "by common confession." The significance of this adverb and the description that the revealed

---

[4]2 Tim 1:13 is similar: "<u>Retain</u> the standard of sound words which you have heard from me, in the faith and love which are in Christ Jesus." The opposite of holding to sound doctrine is holding to false doctrine (2 Tim 3:5; see also 1 Tim 4:1; 6:10; 2 Tim 2:18).

[5]See also BDAG, p. 820. The NIV is on the right track when renders the phrase *mystērion tēs pisteōs* ("mystery of faith") as "deep truths of the faith."

[6]See 4 Macc 6:31; 7:16; 16:1.

[7]George W. Knight, *The Pastoral Epistles,* NIGTC (Grand Rapids: Eerdmans, 1992), p. 182.

mystery is "great" should not be overlooked; by describing mystery in this way, Paul prepares the reader for a climactic revelation.

The apostle describes the second occurrence of the revealed mystery as "the mystery of godliness" (*to tēs eusebeias mystērion*). The modifier, "godliness," is most peculiar.[8] Like the previous genitive, syntactically related to mystery (*mystērion tēs pisteōs*, 1 Tim 3:9), "of godliness" (*eusebeias*) is probably a genitive of reference—"a mystery with reference to godliness." We surmised in 1 Timothy 3:9 that "faith" largely encompasses a body of teaching or Christian doctrine. Thus, the "mystery of faith" is a revelation that largely concerns a body of Christian teaching.[9] Here "godliness," a common word in the Pastorals, ought to be understood in its normal sense as "piety" or "devotion" (e.g., 1 Tim 2:2; 4:7-8; 6:3, 5). The mystery, in other words, bears on the Christian experience (cf. NRSV). These are not two different mysteries but a single mystery that wholly encompasses the Christian experience—worship and knowledge.[10] As we will see below, the content of *mystery* in 1 Timothy 3:9, 16 pertains to a hymn. Yet this hymn is not simply a theological exercise but a summary of doctrine that transforms the Christian life, leading to a godlier existence.

THE HYMN

After the mystery is described as "undeniably great," Paul proceeds to delineate the precise content of the revealed mystery.[11] The hymn is rich and pregnant with meaning. Like panning in a streambed filled with gold, the more we sift through each line, the more theological nuggets we uncover. Though the hymn cited in 1 Timothy 3:16 is theologically rich, it presents a variety of problems on a number of different fronts, and, in order for us to determine the precise content of the unveiled mystery, we must attempt to answer a few difficult problems.

1. He who was revealed in the flesh (*hos ephanerōthē en sarki*)

---

[8]Apparently, *Diogn.* 4:6 contains the closest use of mystery to that of 1 Tim 3:16: "But as for the mystery of the Christian's own religion [*to de tēs idias autōn theosebeias mystērion*], do not expect to be able to learn this from man." We were made aware of this text by Andrew Y. Lau, *Manifest in Flesh: Epiphany Christology of the Pastoral Epistles*, WUNT 86 (Tübingen: Mohr Siebeck, 1996), p. 91.

[9]G. W. Barker, "Mystery," in *ISBE* 3:454; Raymond Brown, *The Semitic Background of the Term "Mystery" in the New Testament*, BS 21 (Philadelphia: Fortress, 1968), p. 67.

[10]Cf. Philip H. Towner, *The Goal of Our Instruction: The Structure of Theology and Ethics in the Pastoral Epistles*, JSNTSup 34 (Sheffield: Sheffield Academic, 1989), p. 88.

[11]The majority of translations are right to add a colon after the phrase "mystery of godliness" (e.g., NASB, TNIV, ESV, NRSV), thus drawing not only a close relationship between mystery and the hymn but also the precise content of mystery.

2. Was vindicated in the Spirit (*edikaiōthē en pneumati*)

3. Seen by angels (*ōphthē angelois*)

4. Proclaimed among the nations (*ekērychthē en ethnesin*)

5. Believed on in the world (*episteuthē en kosmō*)

6. Taken up in glory (*anelēmphthē en doxē*)

The hymn focuses exclusively on the person of Christ, covering a wide array of topics. Due to the constraints of this project, we are unable to tease out each component in great detail.[12] We will only investigate the hymn's more prominent features. Our goal is to determine what aspects of Christ and his work are "new," bearing in mind the Old Testament and early Jewish background.

Many debate the origin of the hymn. Was it penned by Paul (which we hold) or did it arise from an early Christian community? Whatever the case may be, answering these questions, though important, are not our immediate concern and do not make any interpretive difference. As it stands, the hymn is tied to the context of 1 Timothy 3, and that is of upmost importance for our purposes. We will first examine an important textual variant and then examine the hymn's form. We will then be in a better position to understand more fully the meaning of this theologically rich passage.

Textual variant. Immediately on venturing into the terrain of the hymn, a textual problem confronts us. The first word of the hymn *who* (*hos*) is disputed ("<u>who</u> was revealed in the flesh"). Because this textual problem alters the meaning of the passage, we must briefly evaluate the variant. Externally, the textual support for "who" (*hos*) is definitely stronger than the two other possibilities of "that" (or "which," *ho*) and "God" (*theos*).[13] Evaluating the internal evidence is slightly more complex. Two key principles that are often employed when evaluating a variant are: (1) What variant is the most difficult

---

[12]See Jerome D. Quinn and William C. Wacker, *The First and Second Letters to Timothy: A New Translation and Commentary*, ECC (Grand Rapids: Eerdmans, 2000), pp. 317-48, for an in-depth analysis of the origin, background, form and content of the hymn.

[13]The external manuscript support for "who" (*hos*) is as follows: ℵ* A* C* F G 33 365; Did Epiph Cyril Jerome. The early and somewhat broad support, particularly the quality mss. of ℵ* A*, makes this reading very likely. The second variant, and perhaps the most intriguing one, reads "God" (*theos*) instead of "who" (*hos*). The support for this reading is broader than the first variant and is composed of later manuscripts (some of which are of correctors of important manuscripts): ℵᶜ Aᶜ C² D² Ψ 1739 1881 𝔐 vgᵐˢ. Lastly, and least likely, a few manuscripts read "that" or "which" (*ho*): D* itᵃʳ, ᵇ, ᵈ, ᶠ, ᵍ, ᵐᵒⁿ, ° vg. From the perspective of external manuscript considerations, and especially the early support of ℵ* A*, the scales are clearly tipped in favor of the variant "who" (*hos*).

(copyists often attempted to smooth out difficulties)? (2) What variant can best explain the other variants? The presence of the relative pronoun "that" or "which" (*ho*) was likely a scribe's attempt to change the relative pronoun from masculine to neuter in order to harmonize it with the neuter gender of the preceding noun *mystery*. The variant of the neuter *ho* is possible but its scant manuscript support renders it improbable. In addition, the different masculine gender of *hos* in comparison with the neuter *mystērion* makes this reading more preferable since it is more difficult than the reading with the harmonized *ho* ("that," "which").

On the other hand, the variant "God" (*theos*) presents a more viable option. Metzger suggests that this reading may have arisen because of the confusion between the uncial script "who" (OC) and the shorthand for "God" (ΘC).[14] While possible, this variant is probably unlikely because of its lack of quality manuscript support in comparison to "who" (*hos*). So the question remains, why would the variant of "God" (*theos*) arise? Contextually, "God" makes very good sense in the immediate context: "great is the mystery of godliness: God was revealed in the flesh." If this reading were original, the mystery would be explicit: new, end-time revelation from the Old Testament concerns God becoming human. Yet it is quite possible that a scribe merely made explicit what is implicit.[15] The reading "God" (*theos*) is more theologically precise and removes the ambiguity of "who" (*hos*), thus showing the marks of a later scribal interpretation. Thus, Metzger also rightly points out that the reading "God" (*theos*) presupposes "who" (*hos*), whether the scribal change was accidental (confusing the uncial script "who" [OC] with the shorthand for "God" [ΘC]) or intentional (interpreting what "who" meant).[16] As we will argue below, the immediate context suggests that the mystery pertains to various aspects of the incarnation. Therefore, in light of the aforementioned points, "who" (*hos*) ought to be viewed as the original reading.[17] Line 1 of the hymn thus should thus read as follows: "He <u>who</u> was revealed in the flesh."

The form of the hymn. Determining the form of the hymn is not simply an exercise in exegesis but influences our understanding of it and particularly the

---

[14]Bruce M. Metzger, *A Textual Commentary on the Greek New Testament,* 2nd ed. (New York: United Bible Societies, 1994), p. 574.

[15]Ibid.

[16]Ibid.

[17]Commentators (e.g., Knight, *Pastoral Epistles*, p. 182) and translations (e.g., NASB, NRSV, HCSB, NJB, TNIV, ESV, NET) by far prefer the reading *hos* ("who").

content of the revealed mystery. The form reveals which lines ought to be paired and thus interpreted together.[18] A few scholars suggest that all six lines are generally independent of one another; these commentators view the lines falling into a chronological sequence.[19] Though attractive on many fronts, the lines of the hymn appear to be far tighter than these scholars admit and the sequence of the lines are somewhat strained.[20]

Today, however, many commentators contend that the hymn ought to be arranged in three smaller sections.[21]

1. He who was revealed in the flesh,

2. Was vindicated in the Spirit,

3. Seen by angels,

4. Proclaimed among the nations,

5. Believed on in the world,

6. Taken up in glory.

According to Kelly, each section or couplet contains an antithesis: flesh/Spirit (lines 1-2), angels/nations (lines 3-4), world/glory (lines 5-6).[22] He argues that the first two lines concern the incarnation and the resurrection; the second concerns Christ's manifestation to angels and his proclamation to the nations; the third pertains to the reception of Christ in the world and heaven. Kelly's argument is persuasive and makes good sense of the form and content. Capitalizing on Kelly's view that the hymn consists of three couplets, several others observe that each couplet has a "spatial" contrast.[23] By spatial, we mean the contrast between the old age or "earth" and the new creation or "heaven":

---

[18]The following discussion of the hymn's form is largely indebted to Robert Gundry's fine essay on this passage: Robert H. Gundry, "The Form, Meaning and Background of the Hymn Quoted in 1 Timothy 3:16," in *Apostolic History and the Gospel: Biblical and Historical Essays Presented to F. F. Bruce,* ed. W. Ward Gasque and Ralph P. Martin (Exeter: Paternoster, 1970), pp. 203-22.

[19]E.g., C. K. Barrett, *The Pastoral Epistles* (Oxford: Clarendon, 1963), pp. 64-66.

[20]E.g., line 4 ("proclaimed among the nations") is understood as the apostolic proclamation during Jesus' earthly ministry. The Gospels certainly suggest that Jesus' kingdom message has indeed come to the Gentiles (e.g., Mk 7:24-30), but line 4 suggests that this proclamation has occurred on a much wider scale—something that the book of Acts and Paul make clear.

[21]E.g., Lau, *Manifest in Flesh,* p. 91; I. H. Marshall, *The Pastoral Epistles,* ICC (New York: T & T Clark, 1999), p. 500.

[22]J. N. D. Kelly, *The Pastoral Epistles* (London: Black, 1963), pp. 71-77.

[23]Martin Dibelius and Hans Conzelmann, *The Pastoral Epistles,* trans. Philip Buttolph and Adela Yarbro, Hermeneia (Philadelphia: Fortress, 1972), pp. 61-63.

a earthly ("flesh")

b heavenly ("spirit")

b heavenly ("angels")

a earthly ("nations")

a earthly ("world")

b heavenly ("glory")

The contrast between these polarities bears further reflection, as we will offer below.

The content of the hymn. Having achieved more clarity about the organization of the hymn, we are now on much more solid ground to interpret it. We will proceed to study a few lines in some detail, with the aim to grasp further the revealed mystery in 1 Timothy 3. The majority of commentators agree that the unveiled mystery in 1 Timothy 3:16 constitutes Christ's incarnation, life and ministry, death, and resurrection.[24] Can the revealed mystery be nuanced with more precision?

Our brief evaluation of this passage is a bit different from contemporary scholarship in that we are attempting to determine what is "new" about the hymn. Since the hymn exclusively focuses on Christ as the long-awaited Messiah, we are generally able to narrow our search to those texts that predict the coming Messiah and determine whether or not this hymn offers any unanticipated matters of fulfillment.

The first line of the hymn is perhaps the most theologically pregnant: "he who was revealed in the flesh." Even though the subject of the verb "was revealed" is "who," the verb indirectly remains tied to the central noun *mystery* (*mystērion*) only two words earlier. On two other occasions in the New Testament, mystery is found in conjunction with the verb "to reveal" (*phaneroō*): "according to the revelation of the mystery which has been kept secret for long ages past, but now is manifested" (Rom 16:25b-26); "the mystery which has been hidden from the *past* ages and generations, but has now been manifested to his saints" (Col 1:26; cf. 1 Cor 4:5). It is therefore perhaps not a matter of coincidence that Paul chooses this verb to describe the incarnation. For the event of the incarnation was itself an end-time revelation. In other words, Paul

---

[24]E.g., Lau, *Manifest in Flesh*, p. 91; Dibelius and Conzelmann, *Pastoral Epistles*, p. 61; Brown, *Semitic Background*, p. 68; H. Krämer, "μυστήριον," in *EDNT* 2:448; C. Brown, "Secret," in *NIDNTT* 3:505; Bockmuehl, *Revelation and Mystery*, p. 212.

received a revelation or mystery about an event that itself was a revelation.

Though a few suggest that line one refers to the crucifixion or a post-resurrection appearance, the majority of commentators are in agreement that the
first line of the hymn concerns the incarnation.[25] The textual variant "God"
(*theos*), though not original, is perhaps the earliest commentary on this clause.
By substituting "God" (*theos*) for "who" (*hos*), the scribe removed any ambiguity in the text and explicitly made this a reference to the incarnation. But
even without the variant, a strong case can be made for an incarnational interpretation. The verb "to reveal" (*phaneroō*) is slightly ambiguous and can either
mean to "make visible" in the sense of becoming manifest or to "reveal" or
"disclose." As we noted above, the latter sense is paired with revelation—"the
mystery . . . has now been manifested" (Col 1:26). Yet in the immediate context
of 1 Timothy 3:16, the verb may also have the former sense in mind: Christ was
made visible or was made manifest publicly. Given the highly stylized and
poetic nature of this hymn, it would not be impossible for a single word to have
a few related layers of meaning.[26]

Elsewhere in the New Testament this verb is applied to Christ with this sense:
"When Christ, who is our life, is <u>revealed</u>, then you also will be revealed with
Him in glory" (Col 3:4).[27] Adding further proof that the first line does indeed
describe the incarnation is the prepositional phrase "in the flesh" (*en sarki*) that
modifies the verb. The phrase tells us *how* Christ was publicly visible—"in the
flesh"—and underscores Christ's humanity, particularly his existence in the old
age (see below). John 1:14 is not a far cry from Paul's assertion here in 1 Timothy
3: "And the Word became <u>flesh,</u> and dwelt among us, and we saw his glory, glory
as of the only begotten from the Father" (cf. Rom 1:3-4). In other words, Paul
poetically concludes that God became man in bodily form in the person of
Christ.[28] Several pieces of evidence in the apostolic fathers increase the likelihood that line one of 1 Timothy 3:16 speaks of Christ's incarnation, as they use
nearly identical language to articulate this idea.[29] The statement that Christ was

---

[25]See, for example, Gundry, "Form, Meaning and Background," p. 209; Marshall, *Pastoral Epistles*, p.
524; Gordon D. Fee, *1 and 2 Timothy, Titus,* NIBC (Peabody, MA: Hendrickson, 1988), p. 93; C.K.
Barrett, *The Pastoral Epistles* (Oxford: Clarendon, 1963), p. 65; See Lau, *Manifest in Flesh,* pp. 92-99,
who interacts with other viewpoints but agrees that the clause indeed refers to the incarnation.
[26]Lau, *Manifest in Flesh,* pp. 92-93, argues that *phaneroō* may have this twofold meaning in the present passage; cf. Quinn and Wacker, *1-2 Timothy,* p. 332.
[27]See Jn 1:31; 21:1, 14; Col 3:4; 2 Tim 1:10; 1 Pet 5:4; 1 Jn 1:2; 2:28; 3:2, 5, 8.
[28]Note here the NIV's translation of the clause in 1 Tim 3:16: "He appeared in a body."
[29]See Ign. *Eph.* 19.3; *Magn.* 8.2; *2 Clem.* 14.2; *Barn.* 5.6, 9; 6.7, 9, 14; 12.10; 14.5; *Diogn.* 11.2.

"revealed in the flesh" also presupposes his existence prior to being "revealed," which further points to his revelation as a divine being.

CONTENT OF THE MYSTERY

Like a diamond with all of its facets, several of the hymn's lines reflect various aspects of Christ's deity and preexistence.[30] The incarnation undergirds and is presupposed throughout the entirety of the hymn. As we will soon see, language that is often used for God is applied to the incarnate Christ. Reading the hymn in light of the unveiled mystery, some light is shed on the significance of the hymn. We must continually ask ourselves what is "new" in light of the Old Testament. Lines four and five are fine examples of new, end-time revelations. Line four reads, "[he was] proclaimed among the nations."

The Old Testament often makes reference to God's redemptive works being made known throughout the nations. A sample of texts readily makes this point:

> That Your way may be known on the earth,
> Your salvation among all nations. (Ps 67:2)

> The LORD has made known His salvation;
> He has revealed His righteousness in the sight of the nations. (Ps 98:2)

> He says, "It is too small a thing that You should be My Servant
> To raise up the tribes of Jacob and to restore the preserved ones of Israel;
> I will also make You a light of the nations
> So that My salvation may reach to the end of the earth." (Is 49:6; cf. Is 52:10)

Psalm 67 and Psalm 98 similarly describe the Lord's work or "salvation" being proclaimed to the "nations." In other words, not only will the Lord bring salvation to the nations, resulting in the conversion of many Gentiles, he will also make his redemptive work known to all people groups. Isaiah 49:6 and other similar texts[31] are pertinent in that there the Servant is the means by which the Lord restores the righteous remnant within Israel and brings salvation to the nations. Yet in the hymn of 1 Timothy 3:16, the center of gravity has shifted from the Lord's actions being declared to the nations to *Christ himself* being made known to the nations. This subtle shift makes much sense given the divine status and prerogative of Christ. The incarnate Christ is now being identified with the Lord; what is true of God is true of Christ. The Old Testament,

---

[30]See Lau, *Manifest in Flesh*, pp. 98-99.
[31]E.g., Is 42:1-9; 50:4-9; 52:13–53:12.

however, *does not explicitly describe the Messiah as being the very object of proc-lamation to the nations.* The Messiah is instrumental in proclaiming the works of the Lord but never does he become the object of proclamation. Such proc-lamation is reserved for God alone.

This same line of interpretation extends to line five: "[he was] believed on in the world." One of the most salient themes of the Old Testament is the command to trust or believe in God and his promises. Trusting in the Lord happens on an individual and corporate level. God promised Abraham that he would be the forefather of a mighty nation and that this people group would eventually bring God's glory to the nations. God would fulfill his promise to Abraham in unforeseen and unanticipated ways. Yet Israel refused to trust in the Lord's power and promises in the midst of trying circumstances. Not only was the nation to believe in the Lord, individuals that comprised the nation were also to trust him personally. Each Israelite was responsible to trust in God's pro-vision and his promise of salvation. The following texts, positive and negative, are representative of both of these aspects.[32]

> Then he [Abraham] <u>believed</u> in the LORD; and He reckoned it to him as
> righteousness. (Gen 15:6)

> Then they despised the pleasant land;
> They did not <u>believe</u> in His word. (Ps 106:24)

> "You are My witnesses," declares the LORD,
> "And My servant whom I have chosen,
> So that you may know and <u>believe</u> Me
> And understand that I am He.
> Before Me there was no God formed,
> And there will be none after Me. (Is 43:10)

We have tapped into a central theme of the Old Testament, and these texts belong to a much larger swath of passages. When we turn to the hymn in 1 Timothy 3, we quickly recognize a significant difference. The Old Testament unequivocally makes clear that Israel, and humanity in general for that matter, must rely on and trust solely in God as he has revealed himself through his promises and redemption. But in 1 Timothy 3:16, *Christ* is the veritable object of faith and trust: "[he was] believed on in the world." The Old Testament ap-

---

[32]See also, e.g., Deut 1:32; 2 Chron 14:11; Ps 4:5; 9:10; 31:6; 31:14; 40:4; 115:9-11; Is 26:4; 31:1; 36:7.

pears to refrain from describing the Messiah in these terms.[33] Like line four, line five draws attention to a "new revelation." That is, part of the revealed mystery here is that *Christ functions as God and is now the object of personal faith and trust*.[34] Was this revelation only partially hidden in the Old Testament and Judaism or was it fully hidden?

The Old Testament prophesies that a coming Messiah would usher in God's eternal kingdom in the "latter days" by vanquishing Israel's enemies (e.g., Gen 49, Num 24). But does the Old Testament anticipate that the end-time Messiah would be a divine, preexistent being? The Old Testament, on a few occasions, contains a few texts that may suggest some inkling of messianic preexistence and thus messianic deity. These texts are notoriously enigmatic, and scholars predictably offer a variety of interpretations. The first text is from Micah 5:2 (5:1 MT, LXX):

> But as for you, Bethlehem Ephrathah,
> *Too* little to be among the clans of Judah,
> From you One will go forth for Me to be ruler in Israel.
> His goings forth are from long ago [*miqqedem*],
> From the days of eternity [or "of old" = *ôlām*].

This text appears to be describing the origin of the end-time Messiah, both his geographic origin (Bethlehem) and his temporal origin ("long ago, from the days of eternity"). The temporal expressions, however, may refer to the Messiah's continuity with the line of David in that the reference may be to the prophecies of the end-time ruler that began from the beginning of Israel's existence as a nation (Gen 49:9-12; Num 24:15-19), as many contend; or the phrases may refer to a time period well before King David. The Hebrew text of

---

[33]Even line three may have an Old Testament background that is applied to Christ. Lau postulates that the verb "was seen" recalls Old Testament theophany texts (*Manifest in Flesh*, pp. 103-4, 198-201; cf. Gundry, "Form, Meaning and Background," p. 221). He is not the only scholar to highlight the verb "to see" as it pertains to significant theophanic texts—e.g., Wilhelm Michaelis, "ὁράω," in *TDNT*, 5:331-33. The verb "to see" (*horaō*) is particularly prominent in the Pentateuch, where without exception all occurrences are found in conjunction with Yahweh manifesting himself to Israel and the patriarchs. Genesis 12:7a, for example, says: "The Lord appeared to Abram" (see Gen 17:1; 18:1; 22:14; 26:2, 24; 35:9; 48:3). Another noteworthy passage is Ex 16:10b: "Behold, the glory of the Lord appeared in the cloud" (see Lev 9:23; Num 14:10; 16:19, 42; 20:6). If this is the case, then this further supports our conclusion that this hymn includes several items that align the person of Christ with the Lord. To suggest that Christ has "appeared" like the Lord appeared to Israel in the Old Testament heightens the christological significance of the hymn.

[34]See also Jn 11:27; 20:31; Acts 11:17; 24:24; Rom 3:22; Gal 2:16, 20; 3:22; Phil 1:29; 3:9; Col 1:4; 2:5.

"long ago" can refer to both scenarios,[35] whereas the latter phrase "from the days of eternity" clearly concerns an ancient time period, such as Israel's exodus or the time of Moses.[36] The Old Testament Greek translation of Micah 5:2 reads: "and his goings forth were from the beginning [*ap' archēs*], <u>even</u> from the days of eternity [*ex hēmerōn aiōnos*]." The Greek translators may have clarified the ambiguity of the Hebrew text's "from long ago" with "from the beginning." Does this refer to a period well before Israel's history, or does it refer to the very beginning of Israel's history at the Exodus? Perhaps the former is preferable, since the actual wording of both the Hebrew and Greek Old Testament is not that the prophecy of this messianic figure stems from an early period but that his actual "goings forth" as an existent being are from an early time. If this is not an overly literalistic reading, then the phrase *mîmê ʿôlām* in Hebrew and the phrase *ex hēmerōn aiōnos* in Greek would best be rendered "from the days of eternity,"[37] in the sense of before creation. Nevertheless, this text remains a bit enigmatic.

Isaiah 9:6 is another text that continues to be a source of debate, yet the passage is highly relevant for our discussion:

> For a child will be born to us, a son will be given to us;
> And the government will rest on His shoulders;
> <u>And His name will be called Wonderful Counselor, Mighty God,</u>
> <u>Eternal Father, Prince of Peace.</u>

The person described here is certainly the end-time Messiah. The question remains, however, whether or not Isaiah describes the figure in purely royal categories. A full discussion of this problem is beyond the scope of this project, so we can only provide a cursory explanation. Isaiah 9 describes the arrival of an individual who will bring about Israel's redemption and the establishment of God's eternal reign. The series of divine labels that are attached to this figure in Isaiah 9:6b are staggering: "Wonderful Counselor, Mighty God, Eternal Father, Prince of Peace." Though a number of commentators disagree, the most natural way of reading this text appears to be that the messianic figure is en-

---

[35]For those texts that describe an ancient time period (Israel coming out of captivity, King David, etc.), see Neh 12:46, Ps 77:5, 11; 143:5, and Is 46:10, and for those texts which describe God as existing as a preexistent being, see Hab 1:12 and Ps 74:12.

[36]See, for example, Is 63:9, 11, Amos 9:11, Micah 7:14, and Mal 3:4.

[37]Sometimes the Hebrew word *ʿôlām* may connote a long time ago in history or an "eternal" or never-ending period.

dowed with divine qualities, qualities that belong to God alone.[38] The implication of these titles is clear: the end-time Messiah will be a divine figure of
some sort. John Oswalt comments on the titles of this verse: "The titles underscore the ultimate deity of this child-deliverer. Although some commentators
have expended a great deal of energy attempting to make these titles appear
normal, they are not."[39]

In the end, it is probably best to view the Old Testament's conception of a
preexistent, end-time Messiah to be somewhat ambiguous.[40] We are given a faint
yet legitimate expectation of this particular aspect. Unlike the latter-day Messiah's
prerogative to rule, his preexistence is not developed in much detail; we only have
a few texts that could point in this direction. Perhaps we could put these texts on
a trajectory of sorts, the end of which is a full-blown development of the doctrine
of preexistence and deity of the Messiah as seen in the New Testament.[41] Thus,
there appear to be some revelatory anticipations of a divine Messiah (above all
in Isaiah 9), so that the mystery about the divine Christ in lines four and five of
the 1 Timothy 3:16 hymn was one that was mostly hidden in the Old Testament,
though not without some glimmers of light on it.[42]

---

[38]The LXX steers clear of any divine title that is attributed to the messianic figure in its translation of
Is 9:6b: "His name is called the Messenger of great counsel: for I will bring peace upon the princes,
and health to him" (L. C. L. Brenton, trans., *The Septuagint Version of the Old Testament* [London:
S. Bagster and Sons, 1844]). The Targum, the Aramaic translation of the Hebrew text, likewise affirms the messianic nature of Is 9:6 but rejects the notion of a divine individual: "*The prophet said
to the house of David*, For to us a child is born, to us a son is given; and *he will accept the law* upon
himself to keep it, and his name will be called *before the* Wonderful Counselor, *the* Mighty God,
existing forever, "The messiah *in whose days* peace *will increase upon us*."

[39]John Oswalt, *The Book of Isaiah: Chapters 1-39*, NICOT (Grand Rapids: Eerdmans, 1986), p. 246.

[40]A few other texts that may contain overtones of messianic preexistence are Ps 110 and Dan 7. See
William Horbury, *Messianism Among Jews and Christians: Twelve Biblical and Historical Studies*
(London: T & T Clark, 2003), pp. 58-63, for further discussion of this issue and the Jewish expecta-
tion of a preexistent figure.

[41]See the excursus on "Origins of Christ's Divinity" for further discussion of the origins of Jesus' deity
in the New Testament and its bearing on the mystery in 1 Timothy 3.

[42]1 Enoch presents a "Son of Man" figure as preexistent: "he [the Son of Man] was concealed in the
presence of (the Lord of the Spirits) <u>prior to the creation of the world, and for eternity</u>" (*1 En.* 48.6).
This text and others like it (cf. *1 En.* 62.7-9) cast this Son of Man figure as existing before creation.
Perhaps 1 Enoch developed this notion by understanding that the Son of Man in Dan 7:13 was a
divine being (according to the OG and implied by "coming with clouds," which elsewhere is a
portrayal of God) who first had a heavenly existence before coming to earth to reign. Though this
preexistent figure is not largely developed in the Old Testament or Judaism, there exists some general precedents for this notion. For further discussion of how Judaism in general and early Christianity developed a preexistent notion of the coming end-time ruler (Son of Man, Son of God, Messiah, Lord), see Simon J. Gathercole, *The Preexistent Son: Recovering the Christologies of Matthew,
Mark and Luke* (Grand Rapids: Eerdmans, 2006).

CHRIST'S RESURRECTION AS THE BEGINNING OF THE NEW CREATION

The hymn not only presents Christ as a divine being who receives the divine prerogative of being the object of proclamation and trust, it also describes Christ as the beginning of a new age. This last characteristic, though subtle, is evident in lines one and two:

> He who was revealed in the flesh (*hos ephanerōthē en sarki*),
> Was vindicated in the Spirit (*edikaiōthē en pneumati*)

Paul sets forth the common polarity of "flesh" and "Spirit," but this polarity in 1 Timothy 3:16 may refer to Christ in his resurrection body of the new creation or new age. The closest New Testament counterpart to this couplet occurs in 1 Corinthians 15:35-57, so it may be best to use that chapter as an interpretative grid in our discussion of 1 Timothy 3:16. The presence of the revealed mystery in both passages lends even further evidence that both texts are remarkably similar. In our discussion of mystery in 1 Corinthians 15, we surmised that the unveiled mystery in 1 Corinthians 15:51-52 is the transformation of believers from the natural body to the spiritual body. According to 1 Corinthians 15:45 Christ, through the instrumentality of the Spirit, is the one who transforms the body from one physical realm to another. In the hymn of 1 Timothy 3, Paul likely has these themes in mind, but Paul's focus here is solely on the transformation of Christ's old-age body into the transformed body of the new age.

Line one, as we argued above, probably pertains to the incarnation. Christ was visibly and publicly "manifested in the flesh." We noted that the prepositional phrase "in the flesh" connotes the manner in which Christ was made known. That is, he became human or was "in the flesh." But the key word *flesh* may also refer to a redemptive-historical mode of existence.[43] Often the term *flesh* (*sarx*) concerns individuals who identify with the "old age" (e.g., Rom 8:4-5, 12-13; 2 Cor 1:17; 5:16; 10:2-3)—an age that falls under the auspices of the original Adam. In contrast to being identified with the old age, those who are "in the Spirit" participate in the "new age" (e.g., Rom 8:1-16; Gal 5:16-18, 22, 25). Christ's life, and especially his death and resurrection, inaugurated the new age. By claiming that Christ was "revealed in the flesh," Paul refers to Christ's mode of existence in the old age or the epoch under the domination of the original Adam (though not sinful). Conversely, when the apostle says that Christ was "vindicated by the Spirit," Christ's new-creational existence is at the forefront.

---

[43]See also Towner, *Goal of Our Instruction*, p. 91.

Even the clause "vindicated by the Spirit"[44] most likely describes Christ's resurrection when the Spirit transformed Christ's body from one form of existence that belongs to the old age to another—one that belongs to the new age. The Spirit is often portrayed as the giver of latter-day life.[45] Geerhardus Vos argues along these lines in his discussion of Romans 1:3-4, where he observes that "flesh" and "Spirit" refer to two ages: "the resurrection [the work of the "Spirit"] is characteristic of the beginning of a new order of things, as sarkic ["fleshly"] birth is characteristic of an older order of things."[46]

In addition to a temporal polarity (an old age body and a new age body), Paul introduces a spatial distinction (heaven and earth). We mentioned above regarding the hymn's form that each couplet reflects a spatial polarity:

a earthly ("flesh")
b heavenly ("spirit")

b heavenly ("angels")
a earthly ("nations")

a earthly ("world")
b heavenly ("glory")

The significance of this observation ought to be applied thoroughly to lines one and two: Christ's earthly body differs from his new creational one. God became flesh in the person of Jesus, but his body had not been transformed into a body fit for the new heavens and earth. The earthly form of existence is simply not fit for that new creational environment.

Likewise in 1 Corinthians 15, Paul takes up this precise topic, setting forth two sets of polarities: spatial and temporal. What is implicit in the hymn of

---

[44]Not only does the Spirit fashion Christ with a new, eschatological body, he also "justifies" or "vindicates" (*dikaioō*) Christ (cf. Rom 1:4). In other words, at the resurrection the Spirit was instrumental in God vindicating the Son or deeming him as just or righteous. Throughout Jesus' career, the world cast aspersions and considered Jesus to be in the wrong. But at the resurrection, God, through the Spirit's power, publicly declared that Jesus was in the right and that the world's guilty verdict declared over him was wrong.

[45]E.g., "But if the Spirit of him who raised Jesus from the dead dwells in you, he who raised Christ Jesus from the dead will also give life to your mortal bodies through his Spirit who dwells in you" (Rom 8:11); "The letter kills, but the Spirit gives life" (2 Cor 3:6); "For if a law had been given which was able to impart life, then righteousness would indeed have been based on law" (Gal 3:21); "so that He might bring us to God, having been put to death in the flesh, but made alive by the Spirit" (1 Pet 3:18).

[46]Geerhardus Vos, *Redemptive History and Biblical Interpretation: The Shorter Writings of Geerhardus Vos,* ed. Richard B. Gaffin Jr. (Phillipsburg, NJ: P & R, 2001), p. 105.

1 Timothy 3 becomes explicit in 1 Corinthians 15. There Paul distinguishes between "natural" and "spiritual" bodies: "It is sown a <u>natural</u> [*psychikon*] body,
it is raised a <u>spiritual</u> [*pneumatikon*] *body*. If there is a <u>natural</u> [*psychikon*] body,
there is also a <u>spiritual</u> [*pneumatikon*] body. . . . However, <u>the spiritual</u> [*to
pneumatikon*] is not first, but <u>the natural</u> [*to psychikon*]; then <u>the spiritual</u> [*to
pneumatikon*]" (1 Cor 15:44, 46). These two bodies refer to two types of existence: earthly and heavenly.[47]

Returning to our present concern in 1 Timothy 3, our brief discussion of
1 Corinthians 15 aids us in our pursuit of determining the significance of the
first two lines of the hymn. It was not obvious from the Old Testament and
early Judaism that the Messiah (or believers for that matter) was to undergo
a transformation into a new creational existence. As we concluded in our
discussion of mystery in 1 Corinthians 15,[48] Judaism expected the righteous
Israelites to be refashioned into the image of the first Adam—to recapture
what he had lost. But Paul, while not using the language of "old Adam" and
"last Adam" in the 1 Timothy 3 passage, makes clear that Christ's and believers' bodies will go beyond the "image" of those living in the old age
and will be fashioned in accordance with a body fit only for the new heavens
and earth.

One might surmise that the Old Testament prophecies of Israel's resurrection implied such a transformation, but this was not explicit. Accordingly
we can say that this aspect of the revealed mystery was mostly hidden in the
Old Testament and revealed in the New. In addition, recalling our initial explanation of the mystery in lines four and five of the hymn as Christ proclaimed
as deity to the nations of the world, it was also partially hidden in the Old
Testament that the Messiah would first become identified *with God in a body
that was identified with the old age, which would then be transformed into a
new-creational, incorruptible body.*

Part of the mystery in the hymn—particularly in lines one and two—is
therefore the nature of Christ's resurrected body. It is a new, latter-day revelation given to Paul that *Christ's resurrected existence would not assume the*

---

[47]The adjective "natural" (*psychikos*) is roughly synonymous with "flesh" (*sarx*) in 1 Tim 3:16, as they
    both refer to the fallen realm of existence. For an extended discussion of earthly and heavenly po-
    larities, see Benjamin L. Gladd, *Revealing the* Mysterion: *The Use of Mystery in Daniel and Second
    Temple Judaism with Its Bearing on First Corinthians,* BZNW 160 (Berlin: Walter de Gruyter, 2008),
    pp. 245-60.
[48]See pp. 129-36 above.

body of the old earthly existence but would be fashioned after a new body far
more glorious.

Conclusion

As the majority of commentators agree, the hymn in 1 Timothy 3:16 constitutes
the content of the *mystery*. We saw that the incarnation is absolutely central to
the general thrust of the hymn. Christ's divinity is mentioned in line one ("he
who was revealed in the flesh"), but we suggest that his divine being is at the core
of the hymn. Like spokes protruding from the center of a wheel, several lines of
the hymn are linked to Christ's divine nature. We illustrated this notion in lines
four and five. Line four describes Christ as being "proclaimed among the nations." Our suggestion is that the Old Testament portrays God in his redemptive
work as the object of proclamation (e.g., Ps 67:2; 98:2), whereas 1 Timothy 3:16
presents Christ as the object of proclamation. The center of gravity has shifted
from the Lord being declared to the nations to *Christ himself* being made known.
Line five also conceives of Christ in this capacity: "[he was] believed on in the
world." The Old Testament unequivocally makes clear that Israel, and humanity
in general for that matter, must rely on and trust solely in God as he has revealed
himself through his promises and redemption (e.g., Gen 15:6; Ex 14:31). But in
1 Timothy 3:16, Christ is the object of faith and trust. The Old Testament does
not explicitly ascribe that role to the Messiah, whereas Paul and the other New
Testament writers do so without hesitation. Though the Old Testament appears
to anticipate, to some degree, the arrival of a divine, preexistent messiah, this
doctrine was mostly hidden. It is as though the door remained barely cracked
open for later interpreters to return to these Old Testament texts and discover
that a "preexistent messiah" was indeed anticipated in the Old Testament.

Digging deeper into the content of the mystery, we also concluded that
Christ's new-creational state of existence is probably part of the unveiled
mystery in 1 Timothy 3:16. The emphasis on the spatial polarity of the hymn
between earth and heaven along with the contrast between "flesh" and "Spirit"
lend sufficient evidence to suggest that end-time transformation into an incorruptible new creation plays a role in lines one and two.

We have seen that one of Paul's main concerns in writing 1 Timothy was to
combat false teaching. Therefore, it appears that the role of mystery in 1 Timothy
3:16 is to combat heresy in the Ephesian community, as the hymn occupies a
central role in 1 Timothy. Some were teaching that the final resurrection of

believers had already occurred in spiritual form only and, therefore, there would be no physical resurrection. Therefore, part of the heresy was a denial of the saints' physical resurrection body. It would appear that Paul's emphasis in the hymn on Christ's physical resurrection body as part of a new age implicitly entailed that those identified with Christ would also experience a physical resurrection (cf. 2 Tim 1:10-11; 2:8-12, 19; 4:7-8, 18).[49] This would nullify the false teaching about the resurrection being only of a spiritual nature. Timothy and the church at Ephesus must hold firm to sound doctrine, at the heart of which is a robust view of Christ, his work as the divine Son of God and his resurrection. This was likely the same sort of heresy as 1 Corinthians 15, to which Paul gave virtually the same response (1 Cor 15:12-23) and which was likewise linked to his understanding of mystery (1 Cor 15:45-55).

EXCURSUS 9.1: THE ORIGINS OF CHRIST'S DIVINITY AND THE MYSTERY IN 1 TIMOTHY 3:16

The origins of Christ's divinity are some of the thorniest and most debated areas of New Testament research. The amount of work in this area has blossomed in recent years and is showing no signs of abating.[50] One's presuppositions concerning the general background of the New Testament and its development bear directly on this debated issue. Are the New Testament authors largely indebted to the Greco-Roman world and the pagan conception of divinization, a view that was early on promoted by the "history of religions school"?[51] This view has waned in recent years. On the other hand, many scholars contend that the Old Testament and early Judaism are the dominant background that has shaped the New Testament's Christology. Within this category, a number of views fall across the entire spectrum. Some opt for a developmental view that sees Christ's divinity as a later phenomenon in the New Testament,[52] whereas

---

[49]That the heresy about resurrection expressed in 2 Tim 2:17-18 is likely part of the heresy in 1 Timothy is apparent from linking "Hymenaeus" to false teaching in both epistles (1 Tim 1:19-20 and 2 Tim 2:17-18).

[50]For a general summary of various approaches, see Larry W. Hurtado, *How on Earth Did Jesus Become a God? Historical Questions About Earliest Devotion to Jesus* (Grand Rapids: Eerdmans, 2005), pp. 13-30.

[51]Wilhelm Bousset, *Kurios Christos: A History of the Belief in Christ from the Beginnings of Christianity to Irenaeus,* trans. J. E. Steely (Nashville: Abingdon, 1970).

[52]Maurice Casey, *From Jewish Prophet to Gentile God: The Origins and Development of New Testament Christology* (Cambridge: James Clarke, 1991); James. D. G. Dunn, *Unity and Diversity in the New Testament: An Inquiry into the Character of Earliest Christianity,* 3rd ed. (London: SCM Press, 2006), pp. 243-44.

others argue that such a perspective arose in earliest Christianity, indeed with Jesus' own self-proclamation. In addition, there is no consensus as to where Jesus' divinity is conceptually rooted in the Old Testament or early Judaism. Does the existence of angelic beings or exalted patriarchs serve as the backdrop?[53]

Richard Bauckham has cast light on this issue, arguing that Jesus fits marvelously into Jewish monotheism. He argues that, contrary to several scholars, the Old Testament and early Judaism leave no ambiguity between God and angels or exalted patriarchs; the relevant literature overwhelmingly makes no room for semidivine beings. Instead, Bauckham argues, the background to Jesus' divinity is rooted in Jewish monotheism—Christ is to be identified with the unique person of the Lord himself. He claims, "The key to the way in which Jewish monotheism and high Christology were compatible in the early Christian movement is not the claim that Jewish monotheism left room for ambiguous semi-divinities, but the recognition that its understanding of the unique identity of the one God left room for the inclusion of Jesus in that identity."[54]

If Bauckham is correct, the background for Christ's deity rests not in complex analyses of texts that describe angels or preeminent patriarchs but in passages that detail the Lord's unique character and deeds. Scouring the Old Testament and early Judaism for texts that describe Yahweh is not necessary given the ubiquity of his uniqueness and redemptive-historical deeds, which are found abundantly throughout the literature, both explicitly and implicitly. Bauckham also maintains that the Lord is set apart from all of creation in primarily two respects: only God *creates* and *rules* over the cosmos. Such prerogatives are reserved only for him alone.

The New Testament, especially the Gospels and Revelation, often attributes acts and characteristics to Christ that only God performs and possesses.[55] It

---

[53]Larry W. Hurtado, *Lord Jesus Christ: Devotion to Jesus in Earliest Christianity* (Grand Rapids: Eerdmans, 2003), pp. 27-53.

[54]Richard Bauckham, *Jesus and the God of Israel: God Crucified and Other Studies on the New Testament's Christology and Divine Identity* (Grand Rapids: Eerdmans, 2008), p. 20. Note also his earlier *God Crucified: Monotheism & Christology in the New Testament* (Grand Rapids: Eerdmans, 1998), most of which is reproduced in his later publication.

[55]For an example of this line of argumentation in the Gospels, see Rikki Watts, *Isaiah's New Exodus in Mark*. On this theme in Paul, see David B. Capes, *Old Testament Yahweh Texts in Paul's Christology*, WUNT 47 (Tübingen: Mohr Siebeck, 1992), and in Revelation, see G. K. Beale, *The Book of Revelation: A Commentary on the Greek Text*, NIGTC (Grand Rapids: Eerdmans, 1998), pp. 209-14. Bauckham, *Jesus and the God of Israel*, pp. 186-91, also furnishes a helpful list of Old Testament texts that refer to Yahweh but are applied to Christ in the Pauline literature.

is also not a matter of coincidence that the New Testament ascribes sovereign rule and creational authority to Christ.[56] By and large, the New Testament connects Jesus' life, mission and identity with that of Israel's God in the Old Testament. Nevertheless, we must readily admit that *the Old Testament and early Judaism did not develop the idea of the arrival of a divine, preexistent messiah.* That is, the Old Testament or Judaism did not clearly identify the Messiah's being or actions with that of the Lord. We are simply left with a few texts that may point us in that direction (e.g., Is 9). Such an idea in 1 Timothy 3:16 is, therefore, the revelation of a mystery *mostly* hidden in the Old Testament.

---

[56]For example, Col 1:15-16 includes both of these characteristics, "He [Christ] is the image of the invisible God, the firstborn of all creation. For by him all things were created" (cf. 1 Cor 10:26). A number of other passages in the New Testament speak of Christ's sovereign reign (e.g., Acts 2:36; 3:20; 5:42; 8:5; 1 Cor 15:24-28; Eph 1:20-23; Phil 2:6-11; Col 1:20, 1 Pet 3:22; Rev 5:11-14).

10

THE USE OF *MYSTERY*
IN REVELATION

THE GOSPEL TO WHICH PAUL EXHORTS TIMOTHY to remain committed is concretely unpacked in the hymn of 1 Timothy 3:16. The hymn, also labeled the "mystery of godliness," asserts the central role of Christ's incarnation in the gospel. Although the Old Testament implicitly foresees the arrival of a divine, preexistent messiah, this notion was mostly hidden and not developed.

Christ's new-creational bodily existence is likewise part of the mystery in the hymn of 1 Timothy 3:16. Paul's emphasis on the spatial polarity between earth and heaven along with the contrast between "flesh" and "Spirit" suggests that end-time transformation in the first few lines of that hymn also form part of the content of the mystery.

Having spent the last several chapters in the Pauline corpus, we will now explore Revelation's use of *mystery*. Whereas the hymn of 1 Timothy 3:16 focuses on the person of Christ, Revelation applies the term *mystery* to specific end-time events. Some argue that the use of *mystery* in Revelation differs from other occurrences in the New Testament. G. W. Barker, for example, is not alone when he declares, "The use of mystery in Revelation is generally of a different order from that found in Paul. Its employment is less deliberate and its meaning less precise."[1] Those who survey *mystery* in the New Testament generally have the greatest amount of difficulty articulating its content in Revelation. Such surveys tend to define the term in vague generalities. Though many commentators rightly recognize the Danielic background of *mystery* in Revelation, they fail to define the content of the revealed mystery. It is therefore

---

[1]G. W. Barker, "Mystery," in *ISBE* 3:454.

imperative that we analyze in some detail the immediate context of each oc-currence and examine relevant texts and themes.[2]

The book of Revelation, more than any other book in the New Testament, graphically depicts the events that transpire during the "latter days," a period of time that stretches from the first century to the final coming of Christ. One of the more remarkable features of Revelation is the recasting of Old Testament prophecies. Standing on the shoulders of the ancient prophets, John addresses Old Testament expectations and somewhat reworks them, giving us insight into how John sees both continuity and discontinuity between the Old Testament prophets and his own prophetic insight. Into what Old Testament events in particular does John give the reader more insight? How should the church respond to such deeper revelations or mysteries?

John uses the term *mystery* (*mystērion*) four times in his book: Revelation 1:20; 10:7; 17:5, 7. The presence of this technical word is not surprising given the end-time nature of the book and its indebtedness to the book of Daniel.[3]

THE MYSTERY OF THE SEVEN STARS IN REVELATION 1:20

Immediate context. The first occurrence of *mystery* is in Revelation 1:20.

> Therefore write the things which you have seen, and the things which are, and the things which will take place after these things. As for the mystery of the seven stars which you saw in My right hand, and the seven golden lampstands: the seven stars are the angels of the seven churches, and the seven lampstands are the seven churches. (Rev 1:19-20)

Revelation 1 divides neatly into three sections: Revelation 1:1-3, 4-8, 9-20. The first section (Rev 1:1-3), the introduction, demonstrates that John's visions were revealed for the purpose of bearing witness, which consequently results in great blessing. The main emphasis here is the blessing obtained from reading the book and hearing it read. Revelation 1:4-8 comprise the salutation in which John greets the churches on behalf of the sovereign Father, Spirit and Son, whose redemptive work results in the church's new status. The goal of this middle section constitutes God receiving all glory and honor (Rev 1:8) because

---

[2]This chapter is largely drawn from G. K. Beale, *The Book of Revelation: A Commentary on the Greek Text,* NIGTC (Grand Rapids: Eerdmans, 1998).

[3]See G. K. Beale, *The Use of Daniel in Jewish Apocalyptic Literature and in the Revelation of St. John* (Lanham, MD: University Press of America, 1984); G. K. Beale, *John's Use of the Old Testament in Revelation,* JSNTSup 166 (Sheffield: Sheffield Academic Press, 1998).

of Christ's and God's sovereign rule. The last section, Revelation 1:9-20, outlines John's commissioning to write to the churches, grounding this commission in Christ's theophanic presentation. As a result of his victory over death Christ is installed as cosmic judge, priest and ruler of the church.

The vision in Revelation 1:12-20 follows the typical pattern of visions in the Old Testament and Jewish apocalyptic literature: the initial vision (Rev 1:12-16) is followed by the seer's response, and then an interpretation of the vision is provided (Rev 1:17b-20). Many regard only Revelation 1:20 as the formal interpretation, but the interpretation of the vision actually begins with Revelation 1:17b ("Do not be afraid; I am the first and the last"). Revelation 1:17b-20 are in fact essential to the meaning of the whole passage, since they constitute the formal interpretative section.

The vision in Revelation 1:12-20 develops the themes of suffering, kingdom and priesthood previously found in Revelation 1:1-9. Christ is described in Revelation 1:12-16 as the end-time heavenly priest, end-time ruler and judge. The interpretative section reveals that his victory over death grants him these offices (cf. Rev 1:17b-18) and his kingship in this section primarily concerns his rule over the church. The overall function of the larger visionary section of Revelation 1:9-20 serves as a commission to John from the risen Christ to write the entire vision that he witnesses. The risen Christ commissions John in Revelation 1:10-11 and presents his divine credentials and redemptive work as a basis for the exhortation to take courage in fulfilling this commission (Rev 1:17). These credentials also justify Christ's authority in the commissioning of John (Rev 1:12-18). On the basis of this exhortation (Rev 1:17: "Do not be afraid") and his own authority, Christ reissues his commission in Revelation 1:19 and tells John once more to write down his visionary experience: "Write the things which you have seen, and the things which are, and the things which will take place after these things." With Revelation 1:20 consisting of the last portion of John's commission, Christ underscores the *nature* of the church's existence and its *role* in the end-time kingdom. In Revelation 1:20, Christ reveals that the stars and lampstands seen in the preceding vision are a "mystery" needing interpretation. The interpretation reveals two distinct characteristics of the church: the angels in heaven represent the earthly church, and the seven lampstands symbolize the church on earth, which also has its existence in heaven.

Content of the mystery. The content of the mystery in Revelation 1:20 is bound up with two symbols[4] and refers to the hidden meaning of the stars and lamp-stands that are interpreted as "angels and churches." Is "mystery" merely the uncovering of the symbolic meaning of the lampstands (= churches) and the stars (= angels)? Perhaps. However, we think more is involved. Why? Recall that so far, we have seen throughout the New Testament that "mystery" is directly connected to Old Testament prophecies and the use of the term *mystery* relates to these prophecies and often indicates that they have begun fulfillment in a somewhat unexpected manner. As we will see, the use of "mystery" in Revelation 1:20 is likely in line with the other uses in the New Testament that we have examined. Accordingly, as we will see, the term *mystērion* ("mystery") has been taken over from an Old Testament text (Dan 2) in Revelation 1:20. It appears that the purpose of using *mystery* is to emphasize the ironic nature of fulfillment and reversal of expectations. It also includes the unexpected, end-time fulfillment in the symbolism of the stars and lampstands. The unveiled mystery indicates that the earthly church (lampstands) and her heavenly angelic correspondence (stars) in Revelation 1:20 are part of the unexpected, initial fulfillment of not only the kingdom anticipated by Daniel 2 and Daniel 7, but also the temple prophecy of Zechariah 4. In other words, the revealed mystery in Revelation 1:20 weaves together two thematic threads: the church as the end-time temple and its participation in the latter-day kingdom as prophesied in Daniel.[5]

The lampstands as God's presence. This unusual "mysterious" form of the emerging eschatological temple in Revelation 1 beckons further elaboration. The first image John sees in Revelation 1:12 is that of the lampstands: "And having turned I saw seven golden lampstands." We noted above that the "seven lampstands" symbolize the church (Rev 1:20). Its general Old Testament background is located in Exodus 25, Exodus 37 and Numbers 8, but the image in Revelation 1 is more specifically drawn from Zechariah 4:2, 10.[6]

In its immediate context, the lampstand in Zechariah 4:2-6 with its seven

---

[4]See also H. Krämer, "μυστήριον," in *EDNT,* 2:449.

[5]Grant R. Osborne, *Revelation,* BECNT (Grand Rapids: Baker, 2002), p. 98, argues that mystery does not largely entail the meaning of the two symbols but the vision as a whole. Barker is imprecise when he says, "Mystery in Rev. 1:20 designates the nature and source of the revelation.... The material is parenetic and practical, not theological" ("Mystery," p. 454; cf. C. Brown, "Secret," in *NIDNTT,* 3:505). Raymond Brown similarly concludes that mystery "refers to something which has a special role in God's mysterious providence" in *The Semitic Background of the Term "Mystery" in the New Testament, BS* 21 (Philadelphia: Fortress, 1968), p. 36. Yet Brown fails to mention what he means by "something" here.

[6]For further discussion of Zech 4, see G. K. Beale, *The Temple and the Church's Mission,* NSBT 17 (Downers Grove, IL: InterVarsity Press, 2004), pp. 320-28.

lamps is figurative: "I [Zechariah] see, and behold, a lampstand all of gold with its bowl on the top of it, and its seven lamps on it with seven spouts belonging to each of the lamps which are on the top of it" (Zech 4:2). The lampstand, as part of the temple furniture, represents the whole temple that further symbolizes faithful Israel (cf. Zech 4:6-9). True Israel must live "not by [earthly] might nor by power, but by My [the LORD's] Spirit" (Zech 4:6). The lampstand stood in the presence of God, and its luminescence apparently symbolized God's glorious presence (see Num 8:1-4).[7]

Similarly the lamps on the lampstand in Zechariah 4:2-5 are interpreted in Zechariah 4:6 as symbolizing God's presence (or Spirit) that empowers Israel (the lampstand).[8] Such divine enabling will equip Israel to finish rebuilding the temple, despite intense opposition (Zech 4:6-9). In the same way true Israel, the church, derives its strength from the Spirit,[9] the divine presence, before God's throne in its stand against the world's opposition. Just as in Zechariah the beginning establishment of the physical temple faced opposition, so the spiritual beginning of the new temple faces opposition.[10] Revelation 11:4 underscores the idea of the lampstand representing God's presence with the church: "lampstands . . . stand before the Lord of the earth." Furthermore, the church has already been identified with the "temple of God" in Revelation 11:1-2,[11] so that the lampstand imagery of Revelation 11:4 is a further elaboration of this temple. Note also the opposition to the two witnesses as part of a living temple and lampstands (Rev 11:5-10).

Keeping in mind Zechariah 4 as the background of the lampstands in Revelation 1:20, the seven churches, portrayed as lampstands, constitute the beginning of the end-time temple.[12] Ultimately the church is identified with

---

[7]In Ex 25:30-31 the lampstand is mentioned directly after the "bread of Presence" (cf. Ex 40:4; 1 Kings 7:48-49).

[8]*Targ. Ps-Jon.* on Lev 24:2-4 directly links the dwelling of God's glory in Israel to the continued burning of the seven lamps on the lampstand. The Qumran Teacher of Righteousness affirms that, despite his opponents, he "will shine with a sevenfold light . . . for you are an everlasting light for me, and you have established my feet" (1QH 7.24-25). Likewise the continual burning of the lamps (the Spirit) on the seven lampstands (churches) will mean that the presence of Christ (the divine Ancient of Days in Rev 1:14) will be continually with the churches and protecting them spiritually.

[9]In Rev 1:4 and Rev 4:5 the seven lamps are identified as the Spirit, as in Zech 4 (see Rev 1:4).

[10]Note the first indication of opposition in Rev 1:9, which is developed in the letters (e.g., Rev 2:8-11, 13; 3:9-10) and throughout the book.

[11]See Beale, *Revelation*, pp. 556-71.

[12]Elsewhere early Christianity identifies the church as the temple of God: 1 Cor 3:16-17; 6:19; 2 Cor 6:16; Eph 2:21-22; 1 Pet 2:5; Ign., *Eph.* 9; 15.

Christ, whose resurrection founds the new temple (Jn 2:19-22; cf. Rev 21:22). The seven lamps empower the "lampstand" or the church to witness as a light to the world, so that the powers of evil would not prevail against God's glorious temple. Revelation 11:1-13 confirms that the lampstands represent the church as the true temple and the totality of the people of God witnessing in the period between Christ's resurrection and his final coming. The shift from one lampstand in Zechariah to seven in Revelation stresses not only that the letters in Revelation are intended for the church universal of the escalated end times, but also that true Israel is no longer limited to a nation but encompasses all peoples.

Yet what is the revealed mystery in Revelation 1:20 as it pertains to the church becoming the latter-day temple? *The new, spiritual temple of the church appears insignificant and weak and vulnerable to the world's opposition*, whereas parts of the Old Testament appeared to anticipate the latter-day temple to be a physical structure at the arrival of the Messiah and the new creation (see, e.g., Ezek 40-48; Hag 2:9).[13] But this revealed mystery is not completely new, since even Zechariah 4 portrayed the building of the temple to be a small enterprise facing huge odds. In addition, even in the Old Testament there are some passages that *appear* to foresee a nonphysical eschatological temple (e.g., Jer 3:16-17; Zech 1:16–2:13).[14] From the New Testament vantage point, some Old Testament prophecies appeared to predict a physical temple, while others seemed to expect a spiritual temple of God's special revelatory presence. Accordingly, the upshot is that the temple prophecies *seemed* not to be clearly consistent. The New Testament perspective clarifies the Old Testament picture. In other words, it was partially hidden in the Old Testament that the end-time temple would be fulfilled in a community of faithful believers that physically suffered great loss but were spiritually impregnable.

Tribulation and kingdom. The unveiled mystery in Revelation 1:20 not only concerns the church as the latter-day temple, but it also includes the nature of the kingdom in which the church participates. The ideas of "tribulation" and "kingdom," discussed separately in the Old Testament (especially in Dan 7), have been surprisingly merged into a unified, ironic concept in Revelation 1:9: "I, John, your brother and fellow partaker in the tribulation and kingdom and perseverance *which are* in Jesus." By persevering through tribulation believers

---

[13]Beale, *Temple and the Church's Mission*, pp. 123-67.

[14]It is also possible to understand the Ezek 40–48 temple prophecy to be predicting a nonphysical temple (see Beale, *Temple and Church's Mission*, pp. 335-64).

are exercising their rule in the invisible kingdom, which is the same thing that happened with Jesus (note the end of Rev 1:9: "*which are* in Jesus'"). We have seen this precise combination of themes in our discussion of the revealed mystery in Matthew and elsewhere. Jesus labels his teaching in Matthew's Gospel as "mysteries of the kingdom." It is called such because it was partially hidden in the Old Testament that the latter-day kingdom would be fulfilled in two stages or an already-and-not-yet manner. Jesus' teaching on the kingdom differs from the latter-day conception of the kingdom in the Old Testament and Judaism in that the beginning fulfillment of the kingdom and those within it coexist with pagan empires and wickedness.[15] The revealed mystery in 1 Corinthians 2 is the exalted, kingly Messiah affixed to the cross. While Jesus is suffering a shameful death on the cross, he is simultaneously the supreme ruler; he rules in the depths of defeat. Jesus is king at the very moment he is accursed. That this could be the case was not developed in the Old Testament.

It is therefore not surprising to discover this theme once more in connection with *mystery* in Revelation 1:20. Revelation 1:6 readily affirms the believers' citizenship in the end-time kingdom: "He has made us to be a <u>kingdom</u>, priests to his God and Father." Christ's death and resurrection (Rev 1:5) established a twofold office, not only for himself (Rev 1:13-18) but also for believers. Their identification with his resurrection and kingship (Rev 1:5a) means that they too have been resurrected and are currently coreigning with him: he is "the ruler of the kings of the earth . . . [so that] he made them a kingdom" (Rev 1:5-6). Believers enjoy participating in his kingdom and share his priestly office by virtue of their identification with his death and resurrection.

John goes on to describe *how* the saints participate in the kingdom: by persevering through tribulation (Rev 1:9). John and the churches currently reign together in Jesus' kingdom. Yet this is a kingdom unanticipated by the majority of the Jewish people. The exercise of rule in this kingdom begins and continues only as one faithfully endures tribulation. Faithful endurance through tribulation is the means by which one reigns in the present with Jesus. Believers are not mere subjects in Christ's kingdom: "fellow partaker" underscores the active involvement of saints not only in enduring tribulation, but also in reigning in the midst of tribulation. Such kingship will be intensified at death (e.g., Rev 2:10-11) and consummated at Jesus' final parousia (cf. Rev 21:1–22:5). This ironic

---

[15]On the theme of kingdom in the Old Testament and early Judaism, see pp. 75-83.

exercise of ruling and suffering is modeled by Christ, who revealed his veiled kingship on earth before his exaltation by enduring suffering and death in order to achieve his heavenly rule (cf. Rev 1:5). Just as Christ ruled in a veiled way through suffering, so do Christians.

Those reigning in the kingdom are at the same time experiencing tribulation. Indeed, ruling in the kingdom occurred partly by persevering through tribulation. Revelation 1:13-16, 20 shows the "Son of Man" in a *present* position of sovereignty among the weak and suffering churches (lampstands) of his kingdom, bringing into sharper focus the unexpected form in which the expected Daniel 7 kingdom has reached its initial fulfillment.

The book of Daniel, perhaps more than any other Old Testament book, demonstrates that the latter-day kingdom arrives *after* persecution and tribulation. Daniel 7, for example, expresses this notion in some detail.[16] In Daniel 7:24-25, a king will arise and "speak out against the Most High and wear down the saints." Daniel 7:26 mentions the end of the latter-day antagonist: "the court will sit *for judgment,* and his [the king's] dominion will be taken away, annihilated and destroyed forever." Once he has met his demise, the righteous Israelites will inherit this consummate kingdom: "the sovereignty, power and greatness of *all* the kingdoms under heaven will be handed over to the holy people of the Most High. His kingdom *will be* an everlasting kingdom, and all rulers will worship and obey him" (Dan 7:27). Similarly, Daniel 12:1-3 follows this same pattern—tribulation, judgment and then the arrival of the consummate blessing/kingdom:

> Now at that time Michael, the great prince who stands *guard* over the sons of your people, will arise. And there will be a time of distress such as never occurred since there was a nation until that time; and at that time your people, everyone who is found written in the book, will be rescued. Many of those who sleep in the dust of the ground will awake, these to everlasting life, but the others to disgrace *and* everlasting contempt. Those who have insight will shine brightly like the brightness of the expanse of heaven, and those who lead the many to righteousness, like the stars forever and ever.

Though Daniel anticipates the sequence of tribulation, judgment and installation

---

[16]Dan 2:31-45 also fits this pattern, though persecution of the righteous is not as explicit. In the vision, four kingdoms arise but the fourth kingdom is eventually destroyed by a "stone" (Dan 2:35, 44-45). Once the fourth kingdom is demolished, God will install a "kingdom that will never be destroyed" and "it will itself endure forever."

of God's eternal kingdom, the New Testament makes it clear that the latter-day tribulation and kingdom, as prophesied by Daniel, have coalesced and occur at the same time when the kingdom commences. This surprising turn of events is so dramatic that the New Testament writers often remind their congregations of this doctrine by exhorting them to continue on in their faith despite present suffering (e.g., Acts 14:22; Jn 16:33; Rom 5:3; 8:35; 12:12; 2 Cor 4:17). The end-time kingdom has dawned, albeit invisibly, so believers are constantly reminded to "walk by faith" and recognize that they are indeed part of the end-time kingdom despite their surroundings and suffering. Therefore, the unveiled mystery in Revelation 1:20 refers to this hidden form of the temple, along with the unusual form of the kingdom. The ironic form of the kingdom (ruling through suffering) was not fully revealed in the Old Testament,[17] but it occurs because of the already-and-not-yet fulfillment of the latter days. In this inaugurated stage, unexpected things occur (like ruling in the midst of suffering), but when the consummation arrives, then the Old Testament prophecies of tribulation first and then kingship will happen in just the order prophesied in the Old Testament.

Kingdom and temple are not two separate realities in this case, since the temple itself reflects the irony in the kingdom of God being present and empowered through tribulation on earth. Furthermore, the partial overlap of the temple with the kingdom is also apparent from recalling that the innermost part of the temple (the Holy of Holies) was considered to be the bottom part of the throne room of God, which extended into the invisible heavenly dimension.

It is possible that the "mystery" of Revelation 1:20 does not include the ironic form of the kingdom, since it is found so much earlier in Revelation 1:6, 9. However, the concept of the kingdom continues with Jesus' appearance as the kingly "Son of Man" (Rev 1:13) who also is portrayed as a sovereign judge and priest (Rev 1:14-16) and again as a sovereign king (possessing "the keys of death and Hades," in Rev 1:18), who rules over the weak and suffering churches in his kingdom. And the "mystery" of Revelation 1:20 is located squarely in the vision of Revelation 1:13-18.

The background of Daniel 2. As we have repeatedly noted in this project,

---

[17]For example, consider David: as a king, he was fleeing in the suffering of exile from his son, Absalom, though he was the very king of Israel at the time. This may be an adumbration of what happens in the New Testament with Christ and his people. Perhaps even more pertinently, Gen 3:15 speaks of an end-time figure who defeats Satan and yet suffers in the midst of that victory (i.e., he is "bruised" while winning the victory).

mystery is often found in conjunction with allusions to the book of Daniel. Revelation 1:20 is no exception, as Revelation 1:19-20 clearly alludes to Daniel 2. The conclusion of the Revelation 1 vision comes in Revelation 1:19-20 and may serve as a reintroduction to the book. The threefold indication in Revelation 1:19 of what John is to write may represent a further adaptation of Revelation 1:8b (cf. Rev 1:18a) or a commonly used phrase like it: "Write, therefore, what you have seen: both what is now and what will take place later." The third part of the formula reflects the wording of Revelation 1:1 and has been composed primarily of terminology from Daniel 2:28-29a (cf. Dan 2:45-47 LXX, Theodotion; see table 10.1).[18]

Table 10.1

Daniel 2:28-29 (Theodotion)	Revelation 1:19
"However, there is a God in heaven who reveals mysteries, and He has made known to King Nebuchadnezzar what will take place in the latter days [*ha dei genesthai ep' eschatōn tōn hēmerōn*]. This was your dream and the visions in your mind while on your bed. As for you, O king, while on your bed your thoughts turned to what would take place in the future [*ti dei genesthai meta tauta*]; and He who reveals mysteries has made known to you what will take place [*ha dei genesthai*]."	"Therefore write the things which you have seen, and the things which are, and the things which will take place after these things [*ha mellei genesthai meta tauta*]."

That *mystery* in Revelation 1:20 comes directly after this allusion to Daniel 2:28-29 in Revelation 1:19 and can hardly be accidental. The same phrases even appear in direct connection in Daniel 2:28-29. Since mystery occurs with an eschatological sense in Daniel, its appearance in Revelation 1:20 in an end-time context confirms its connection to the book of Daniel. Furthermore, since the Daniel 2 mystery is about the establishment of the kingdom, this further confirms our argument that part of the *mystery* in Revelation 1:20 concerns the beginning establishment of the kingdom. Perhaps the syntactical awkwardness of beginning Revelation 1:20 with the word *mystery* without any transitional

---

[18]Although *mellei* replaces *dei* in most manuscripts of verse 19, *dei* is present in ℵ* *pc* (*dei mellein*), 2050 *pc* latt (*dei*), C (*dei mellei*). Cf. Josephus, *Ant.* 10.210. The LXX of Dan 2:29, 45 reads *ep' eschatōn tōn hēmerōn* ("in the latter days"), while Theodotion has *meta tauta* ("after these things"), which are apparently synonymous renderings of *ʾaḥărē denâ*. These renderings in Theodotion appear to be references back to *ep' eschatōn tōn hēmerōn* in Dan 2:28, so that "after these things" is an eschatological expression. The same phenomenon is found in Acts 2:17, where Peter changes the *meta tauta* (*ʾaḥărē-kēn*, "after this") of Joel 3:1 (LXX) to *en tais eschatais hēmerais* ("in the latter days"). It appears the same thing happens also in Rev 1:19.

wording was designed to make it more easily recognized as a clear part of the larger Daniel 2 allusion which concludes Revelation 1:19.[19]

Revelation 1:20 and Matthew 13. In many ways, *mystery* in Revelation 1 closely resembles the use of the term in Matthew 13, inviting us to pursue the connection. Commentators are not immediately inclined to establish this relationship between Matthew 13 and Revelation 1, but the similarities appear not to be coincidental. Matthew 13 may very well serve as part of the background of Revelation 1:20 in light of the following parallels:

1. The revealed mystery in both Matthew 13 and Revelation 1–3 occurs after an initial parabolic portrayal and before the formal interpretation of that portrayal to indicate that the hidden meaning of the preceding parable will be unveiled (cf. Mt 13:11 and Rev 1:13-19, 19-20; Rev 2–3).

2. Both Matthew 13 and Revelation 1 connect *mystery* to an interpretation of the Old Testament (Is 6 in Matthew and several Old Testament allusions, including some from Is 44–49, in Rev 1:12-18).

3. The hearing formula at the conclusion of each of the letters in Revelation 2–3 (which are an extension in part of the vision in Rev 1:13-20) is dependent, at least in part, on the same formula in Matthew.[20] Only those who have "eyes to see" are able to grasp the mystery.

4. The term *mystery* in Matthew 13:11 and Revelation 1:19-20 alludes to Daniel 2:28-29, 45, where the word occurs also in reference to the prophetic vision conveyed through symbols and concerning the establishment of the end-time kingdom of God (Mt 13:11, 19; Rev 1:6, 9).

5. Matthew and Revelation claim that the prophesied messianic kingdom has begun fulfillment in an unexpected, even ironic manner.[21]

---

[19]The solecisms of Revelation have a similar function of making readers pause to recognize more easily Old Testament allusions. The plural *mystēria* ("mysteries") and *mystērion* ("mystery") following *ha dei genesthai* ("what must come to pass") in Dan 2:28-30, while *mystēria* ("mysteries") precedes the same phrase in Dan 2:28a. Brown, *Semitic Background*, p. 36, sees a "connection" between Rev 1:20a and Dan 2 because of the similarity of usage, and H. B. Swete, *The Apocalypse of St. John* (London: Macmillan, 1906), p. cxxxvii, has seen explicit allusion to the "mystery" of Dan 2:29 in Rev 1:20a, but neither see allusion to Dan 2:28-30, 45 in Rev 1:19c. The margin of Kilpatrick's edition of the Greek New Testament is the only source indicating allusion to Dan 2:29 in *both* Rev 1:19c and Rev 1:20a.

[20]E.g., cf. Rev 2:7 ("the one having an ear, let him hear") with Mt 13:9, 43 ("the one having ears, let him hear").

[21]Cf. Mt 13:19-23, and chap. 3 above, together with the analysis of George Eldon Ladd, *The Presence of the Future: The Eschatology of Biblical Realism* (Grand Rapids: Eerdmans, 1974), pp. 218-42, as well as Rev 1:9 and the analysis of Beale, *Use of Daniel*, pp. 176-77.

Particularly striking in comparison to Revelation 1 is this last observation about the "mysteries of the kingdom" in Matthew 13:11 (and par.), referring *both* to the hidden meaning of Jesus' parables and to their interpretation concerning the unexpected form of the kingdom. The parables especially highlight the unanticipated nature of the initial phase of the kingdom: Jesus' latter-day revelation or teaching on the kingdom differs from the end-time conception of the kingdom in the Old Testament and Judaism in that the kingdom and those within it coexist with pagan empires and wickedness, a teaching that is similar to the use of *mystery* in Revelation 1:20.

THE MYSTERY OF GOD IN REVELATION 10:7

Throughout this book we have seen *mystery* used in a number of different ways. Oftentimes the technical term refers to general themes such as kingdom, suffering or messianic expectations. On other occasions, the unveiled mystery is organically related to a specific text (e.g., Eph 5:30-31). Here in Revelation 10 *mystery* resembles the latter in that it has a specific passage in mind: Daniel 11:29–12:13. The prophecy from the book of Daniel concerns the persecution of God's people and the establishment of the eschatological kingdom. Revelation 10 assures the reader that this prophecy will come to pass, yet both the timing and the manner of the prophecy constitute the revealed mystery.

Immediate context. Revelation 10:1-7 says:

> I saw another strong angel coming down out of heaven, clothed with a cloud; and the rainbow was upon his head, and his face was like the sun, and his feet like pillars of fire; and he had in his hand a little book which was open. He placed his right foot on the sea and his left on the land; and he cried out with a loud voice, as when a lion roars; and when he had cried out, the seven peals of thunder uttered their voices. When the seven peals of thunder had spoken, I was about to write; and I heard a voice from heaven saying, "Seal up the things which the seven peals of thunder have spoken and do not write them." Then the angel whom I saw standing on the sea and on the land lifted up his right hand to heaven, and swore by Him who lives forever and ever, WHO CREATED HEAVEN AND THE THINGS IN IT, AND THE EARTH AND THE THINGS IN IT, AND THE SEA AND THE THINGS IN IT, that there will be delay no longer, but in the days of the voice of the seventh angel, when he is about to sound, then the mystery of God is finished, as He preached to His servants the prophets.

Revelation 10 is the introduction to the parenthesis in Revelation 11:1-13, and the main point of this introduction is the recommissioning of the seer for the prophetic task that he has already undertaken. The prophet's task is twofold: prophesy about the persevering witness of Christians, despite intense persecution, and about the destiny of those who react antagonistically to the believers' witness. Revelation 10 itself can be broken down into four sections on the basis of thematic shifts (Rev 10:1-2, 3-4, 5-7, 8-10).

Like the parenthesis in Revelation 7, Revelation 10–11 does not narrate future events following those of the preceding chapters (Rev 8–9) but covers the same period of time. According to Revelation 10:6-7 the sounding of the seventh trumpet will signal the time when there will be no further delay in the completion of God's plan for history. Beginning in Revelation 11:15 the seventh trumpet sounds, the eternal kingdom is established and the final judgment takes place.

The chapter opens (Rev 10:1-2) with the descent of an angel, symbolically portrayed as a divine being (garbed with a cloud, rainbow on his head, face as the sun, fiery feet, etc.) and should probably be identified with the divine Christ.[22] The angel possesses a "little book" in his hand (Rev 10:2) that may be identified in some way with the "book" in Revelation 5. A reasonable assumption is that the meaning of the scroll of Revelation 10 is generally the same as that of Revelation 5. The scroll in Revelation 5 was symbolic of God's plan of judgment and redemption that can be found in Revelation 1–11, if not the entirety of the book of Revelation. John is then told to "seal up" the "seven peals of thunder" (Rev 10:4). Though the contents of the "seven peals of thunder" are never disclosed, it is likely that they relate to God's coming judgment on the ungodly.

Revelation 10:5-7 describes the angel swearing an oath before God that alludes to an oath made by an angel in Daniel 12:7. The specifics of the oath come on the heels of a description of God as creator (Rev 10:6a): "there will be delay no longer, but in the days of the voice of the seventh angel, when he is about to sound, then the mystery of God is finished, as He preached to His servants the prophets" (Rev 10:6b-7). In Daniel 12:6 the prophet Daniel asks the angel, "How long will it be until the end of these wonders?" This question refers to future end-time events of tribulation, judgment of evildoers, the resurrection and the establishment of God's eternal kingdom.

The oath of Daniel 12:7 is the angel's answer to the question in the previous

---

[22]See Beale, *Revelation*, pp. 525-26.

verse: "that it would be for a time, times and half a time; and as soon as they finish shattering the power of the holy people, all these events will be completed." In contrast to Daniel, the angelic oath of Revelation 10:6 reads, "that time shall be no longer." This is not to be understood in a philosophical sense that there will be an abolition of time at the end of history, replaced by timelessness, as some contend. Instead, the phrase expresses primarily the idea that there is a predetermined time in the future when God's purposes for history will be completed.[23] The expression could be translated "there will be delay no longer."[24] The point is that when God has decided to terminate history, there will be no delay in doing so.

Content of the mystery. *Delay of consummate judgment.* Parallel wording between Revelation 10:6b-7 and Revelation 6:11 suggests that the revealed mystery in Revelation 10 concerns God's decree that the saints suffer, leading directly to the judgment of their persecutors (see table 10.2). In Revelation 6:10 the saints ask "how long" it will be before God brings judgment on their persecutors. The divine response in Revelation 6:11 is that the judgment and the saints' vindication will be for "yet a little time until" the preordained suffering of "their servants, even their brothers who are about to be killed even as themselves, should be fulfilled." Revelation 10:6-7 affirms that the final judgment will commence once all believers whom God has decreed to suffer fulfill their destiny.[25]

Table 10.2

Revelation 6:11	Revelation 10:6b-7
"And there was given to each of them [the martyrs] a white robe; and they were told that they should rest for <u>a little while longer, until</u> *the number* <u>of their fellow servants and their brethren who were to be killed even as they had been, would be completed also.</u>"	"<u>That there will be delay no longer,</u> but in the days of the voice of the seventh angel, <u>when</u> he is about to sound, then <u>the mystery of God is finished,</u> as He preached to his servants the prophets."

Apparently, from the saints' perspective who cry out "how long?" (Rev 6:10), the intervening time before final judgment has already been a long time, but from God's perspective it is brief (cf. 2 Pet 3:4-9 and Ps 90:4, 13). The length-

---

[23]See J. Barr, *Biblical Words for Time*, SBT 33 (London: SCM Press, 1962), p. 76.

[24]The verb *chronizō* has the meaning of delay in Hab 2:3, where the fulfillment of the prophetic vision "will not delay" when the appointed time should arrive for its execution (so likewise Mt 25:5; 24:48; Heb 10:37).

[25]Likewise M. Kiddle with M. K. Ross, *The Revelation of St. John*, MNTC (London: Hodder and Stoughton, 1940), pp. 172-73; cf. J. P. Heil, "The Fifth Seal (Rev 6,9-11) as a Key to Revelation," *Biblica* 74 (1993): 233-34, for a link with Rev 6:9-11.

ening of the interadvent period may well be included as a part of the unveiled mystery. According to Old Testament prophecy, the events of the eschatological time period apparently take place quickly and climactically, followed by the destruction of the cosmos and its re-creation. One would never have assumed that an unusually extended period would transpire between the coming of the Messiah and the final judgment of the wicked. *The new temporal perspective is unexpected and, therefore, a "mystery" from the Old Testament viewpoint.*[26] We have already observed such an understanding of the mystery in Matthew 13,[27] where the force of the parable of the tares of the field was that though the kingdom has begun the final judgment has been put off for an unknown yet unusually prolonged time.[28] The parable of the mustard seed, sandwiched between the telling and the explanation of the tares of the field in Matthew 13, also suggested that an unexpected period must transpire before the growth of the kingdom is completed.

The timing and manner of Daniel's prophecy. The more precise meaning of the phrase "there will be delay no longer" in Revelation 10:6 is given in the next verse (Rev 10:7), unpacking further how the meaning of the oath from Daniel is understood. The prophecy of Daniel 11:29–12:13[29] concerns various facets of the latter days, such as the suffering and persecution of God's people, God's destruction of the enemy, the saints' resurrection and the setting up of the kingdom. Daniel 12:7 claims that the judgment of Israel's persecutor (cf. Dan 11:32-45) will occur after the enemy "shatters" them. The prophetic events occur

---

[26]Commentators typically understand mystery here to refer to the consummate establishment of God's kingdom—e.g., Osborne, *Revelation*, p. 401; Galen W. Wiley, "A Study of Mystery in the New Testament," *GTJ* 6 (1985): 357; Günther Bornkamm, "μυστήριον, μυέω," in *TDNT*, 4:824; Brown, *Semitic Background*, p. 38. This observation is generally on target except that it lacks the explicit acknowledgement that it was unforeseen in the Old Testament that the kingdom would only be inaugurated initially and then consummated (though Ps 110:1 does suggest the likelihood of an inaugurated reign followed by its consummation, though one might assume from an Old Testament vantage point a short period between the beginning and ending of the rule in the psalm).

[27]See also our pertinent discussion of 1QpHab VII, 1-8 on pp. 49-51. There we noted that even though God spoke to the prophet Habakkuk concerning "what was going to happen in the last generation," he did not primarily divulge *when* "the consummation of the era" would occur because "the final age will be extended and go beyond all that the prophets say, because the mysteries of God are wonderful;" likewise, lines 9-14 affirm that "the final age is extended," which also is part of God's "mysteries." The repeated reference to "mysteries" in this passage is based on the repeated use of the term in Dan 2 (for this and other allusions to Daniel in column VII of 1QpHab see Beale, *Use of Daniel*, pp. 35-38).

[28]See pp. 66-73.

[29]Though Krämer, "μυστήριον," 2:449, is right to detect a Danielic background of the content of *mystery* here, he narrowly limits it to Dan 12:1-7.

prior to and result in the consummation of history. Daniel 12:7 says these prophetic events would occur during "a time, times, and half a time," after which God's prophetic plan would "be completed." The word "completed" (*etelesthē*) in Revelation 10:7 alludes to "will be completed" (*syntelesthēsetai*) of Daniel 12:7 (LXX, OG). Yet Daniel "could not understand" this prophecy fully (cf. Dan 12:7-8), so he asks the angel *how long* it would be until the prophecy would be fulfilled (Dan 12:6) and *how* (the "outcome of") it would be fulfilled (Dan 12:8). The angel relays to Daniel that he will not be able to understand these things because the full meaning of the prophecy was to be "concealed and sealed up until the end time," when finally it would be fulfilled and all would be revealed to the "wise" living at the end of time (Dan 12:9; so also Dan 8:26-27).

In contrast to the oath of Daniel 12, the angel's oath in Revelation 10 emphasizes *when* and *how* the prophecy will be completed (which is further described in Revelation 11). According to Revelation 10, the prophecy of Daniel 11:29–12:13 (concerning the persecution of God's people and the establishment of the eschatological kingdom) will be fulfilled, and history will come to an end when the seventh angel sounds his trumpet. The point of asserting that there will be no delay in Revelation 10:6 is to affirm that the consummation of God's redemptive plan for history, as prophesied by Daniel, will finally reach fulfillment. The clause "then the mystery of God is completed" in Revelation 10:7 further elaborates on the clause "time shall be no longer" in Revelation 10:6.[30]

Mystery as the unexpected timing of the fulfillment of Daniel's prophecy. John views the "times, time and half a time" of Daniel 12:7 as the interadvent age beginning from the time of Christ's resurrection to the final judgment.[31] This identification of the threefold time formula from Daniel is discernible from Revelation 12:4-6, where the period begins from the time of Christ's ascension and refers to the church's time of suffering (so also Dan 12:11-12). The same meaning is apparent for the equivalent phrase "forty-two months" in Revelation 13:5 that describes the time of the beast's blasphemous and persecuting activities. This is indicated by the combined references to (1) the dragon "making war with the rest of her [the woman's] seed" (Rev 12:17), (2) followed by reference to the beast's "fatal wound" (Rev 13:3) alluding to the promise in

---

[30]Note that *kai* in Rev 10:6 is not a mere conjunctive but a temporal consecutive, "then."

[31]See further on the use of the phrase and its equivalents in Rev 11:3; 12:6, 14; 13:5. In this respect, see elaboration by Beale, *Revelation*, pp. 565-68.

Genesis 3:15 that is initially fulfilled through Jesus' death and resurrection.[32] According to Revelation 13:14, Christ inflicts the beast with such a fatal blow at the cross. Apparently a "sword" was the instrument of the beast's "fatal wound"[33] (elsewhere in Revelation *sword* often signifies Jesus' judgment of his enemies).[34] In this light Jesus wields the sword which struck the beast in Revelation 13:14. One of the heads of the beast is depicted as "slain" because of Christ's death and resurrection, as Revelation 2:5, 10-12—in conjunction with Revelation 1:5 and Revelation 5:9—explicate. This is consistent with other New Testament testimony affirming that Christ's death and resurrection defeat the devil.[35] Simply put, the defeat in mind here is more likely the victory over the devil *at the cross* rather than some punishment of an evil historical figure (Nero or any infamous villain). Therefore, Revelation 10:6-7 describes the end of the period of the entire interadvent age of the church, the very end of history.

Thus mystery in Revelation 10:7 concerns the unexpected lengthening of the timing of the fulfillment of the Danielic prophecies.

Mystery as the manner of the fulfillment of Daniel's prophecy. Mystery in Revelation 10:7 not only involves the elongated, two-stage or staggered timing of the fulfillment of the Daniel prophecies (they have commenced fulfillment at Christ's death and resurrection and continue fulfillment), it also concerns the precise *manner* of their fulfillment. Daniel 12:7b foretells that the kingdom of evil will not be defeated until it finishes defeating "the power of the holy people," yet the angel in Revelation 10:7 explains that this prophecy is coming to pass in a mysterious, unforeseen manner. The broad context of Revelation 10 explains that the prophecy of God's defeat of the evil kingdom is being ironically fulfilled by this evil kingdom's apparent physical victory over the saints. Mirroring the

---

[32]See Swete, *Apocalypse*, p. 210. Cf. also Rom 16:20: "And the God of peace will soon crush Satan under your feet," which is presumably based on Jesus' prior defeat of the devil.

[33]Literally the Greek reads "plague [*plēgēn*] of death." Everywhere else in Revelation *plēgēn* (usually rendered "plague") is a punishment inflicted by God (so 11x plus the verb in 8:12).

[34]These judgments by Jesus are either in the present (Rev 1:16; 2:12, 16) or future (Rev 19:15, 21), though these passages employ the synonym *rhomphaia* ("sword") and not *machaira* ("sword" or "dagger"), as in Rev 13:14; cf. P. S. Minear, *I Saw a New Earth: An Introduction to the Visions of the Apocalypse* (Washington, DC: Corpus, 1968), pp. 252-54. The future judgment by Jesus in Rev 19 occurs at the very end of history as part of the final judgment. Therefore, more likely in mind in Rev 13:3 is Jesus' judgment of the beast (who is the earthly representative of the dragon) at the cross.

[35]For other references affirming that Christ's coming was designed to nullify the purposes of Satan, see Mt 12:28-29; Jn 12:31; 16:11; Acts 10:38; 2 Cor 4:4-6; Eph 6:10-18; 1 Jn 3:8; 4:4; 5:19. Compare also the end-time expectation of God's destruction of the devil and his designs in Is 27:1 (which, in fact, may be echoed in Rev 13:1); *T. Jud.* 25.3; *T. Levi* 18.12; *Ascen. Isa.* 7.9-12.

event of the crucifixion, God's people are already beginning to win spiritually in the midst of their physical defeat (Rev 14:4: they "follow the Lamb wherever he goes"). Their enemies are already beginning to lose spiritually in the midst of their apparent physical victory over God's people. Unbelievers begin to undergo unseen loss, since their persecuting activities begin to lay the basis for their ultimate punishment (e.g., see Rev 11:4-13). Such antagonistic actions also betray their allegiance to and identification with Satan, who has already begun to be judged at the cross and resurrection. They also already stand under this inaugurated judgment. "The persecution of the church is thus the secret weapon by which God intends to win his victory over the church's persecutors."[36]

The mysterious nature of the saints' victory is to be understood through the ironic manner in which Christ achieved victory through his apparent defeat by the same evil kingdom. But where in Revelation 10 is there any hint of such an ironic victory either of Christ or of the saints? The legitimacy of this comparison is based on the observation that Revelation 10 is parallel to Revelation 5 and ought to be interpreted accordingly, especially with respect to the "books" in each chapter. The similarities between these two chapters are so striking that a tight connection between the two scrolls is probable.[37]

In Revelation 5 Christ's death already commenced victory because he was a "faithful witness" resisting the spiritual defeat of compromise (Rev 1:5) and because he was accomplishing the redemption of his people by paying the penalty of their sin (so Rev 5:9-10; 1:5-6). Jesus' death was also a victory because it was an initial step leading to the resurrection (Rev 1:5; 5:5-8). Jesus' ironic victory in the midst of the defeat of death is pictured as a lion who has conquered by means of being "slain" as a lamb (Rev 5:5-6). And it is this ironic "lion-lamb" who then receives authority by "taking the book out of the right hand of Him who sat on the throne" (Rev 5:7). Likewise, Revelation 10 claims that those believing in Christ will follow in his footsteps. Their defeat is also an initial victory, since they are faithful witnesses withstanding the spiritual defeat of compromise and their death is a spiritual resurrection (cf. Rev 2:10-11). John represents the saints' ironic destiny by taking the "little book" out of the angel's hand (Rev 10:9-10).

---

[36]So G. B. Caird, *A Commentary on the Revelation of St. John the Divine* (New York: Harper and Row, 1966), p. 128, who also proposes a similar link with Dan 12.

[37]For a discussion comparing the two books, see Beale, *Revelation*, pp. 530-32. See also P. Prigent, *L'Apocalypse de Saint Jean*, CNT (Paris: Delachaux et Niestle, 1981), p. 151.

There remains one difference between the scrolls of Revelation 5 and here, but this difference further strengthens the interpretation involving irony just explained. The scroll in Revelation 5 is called a "scroll" (*biblion*), whereas in Revelation 10:2, 9-10 it is called a "little scroll" (*biblaridion*). The similarities between the scrolls together with this small difference connote that just as Christ has his book, so Christians have their "book," which is also symbolic of their purpose: *they are to reign ironically as Christ did by being imitators on a small scale of the great cosmic model of the cross.* And this may be why Christ, or perhaps his representative angel, is portrayed as a large, cosmic figure overshadowing the earth (Rev 10:5-6). Therefore, the little book is a new version of those same purposes symbolized by the Revelation 5 book insofar as they are to be accomplished by the people of God, the body of Christ.[38]

This understanding of the "mysterious" way in which the Daniel 12 prophecy is being fulfilled is pointed to not only by the parallels with Revelation 5 but by the following context of Revelation 11:1-13. In the immediate context of Revelation 11, the persecution and defeat of the witnessing church are the means leading to their resurrection and their enemies' defeat and judgment.[39] *Therefore, revelation of the mystery in Revelation 10:7 involves not only the idea that fulfillment of prophecy has begun in an unusual temporal way but also concerns the formerly hidden, even unexpected and ironic manner in which the prophecy of Daniel would be fulfilled.* Remember that for Daniel the *timing* and the *manner of fulfillment* of the prophecy was "concealed and sealed up until the end time," when finally it would be fulfilled and all would be revealed to the "wise" living at the end of time (Rev 12:9). Daniel himself did have some degree of partial understanding of the revelation in Daniel 10–12, which is one unit in the book of Daniel (see Dan 10:1, 11-14). Furthermore, there were probably some Old Testament hints that were part of the fertile ground from which these New Testament revelations about the ironic kingdom grew.

In this respect, recall our earlier repeated comments about some of these hints. King David fled from his son in the suffering of exile despite the fact that

---

[38]So Caird, *Revelation,* p. 126; cf. similarly C. Brütsch, *Die Offenbarung Jesu Christi I-II* (Zürich: Zwingli, 1970), pp. 401, 407-8; Prigent, *L'Apocalypse,* p. 152. See Beale, *Revelation,* pp. 530-32, for the idea that *biblaridion* means "little book" and not merely "book."

[39]The parallel between Rev 10:7 and Rev 6:11 (above) shows, at the least, that the content of the mystery in Rev 10 concerns God's overt decree that the saints suffer, which leads directly to the final judgment of their persecutors. In this respect, the phrase "the mystery of God is fulfilled" of Rev 10:7 is paralleled and interpreted by "[the suffering of God's people through which they persevere and which is their ironic victory] should be fulfilled" of Rev 6:11.

he was king of Israel at the time. This may be a foreshadowing of what happens in the New Testament with Christ, the son of David, and his people, who are reigning as kings in the very midst of suffering and persecution. We also mentioned earlier Genesis 3:15 which refers to a latter-day conqueror who defeats Satan and yet suffers in the midst of that victory (i.e., he is "bruised" while winning the victory). Mention may also be made of the "Son of Man" prophecy in Daniel 7, where the Son of Man corporately represents the saints, so that the two are identified together. The king there represents the people. What is interesting is that if the two are truly identified, then the prediction that the saints will suffer tribulation before gaining a kingdom (Dan 7:21-22) must likewise probably be true of the Son of Man, so that his suffering as a king may be implicitly prophesied in Daniel 7.[40] This last reference to Daniel is particularly relevant, since our discussion in this chapter is exclusively concerned with the Old Testament background of Daniel, especially Daniel 2, which is a parallel with Daniel 7.

MYSTERY AND BABYLON THE GREAT IN REVELATION 17:5, 7

We will now examine the final occurrence of *mystery* in Revelation.

Immediate context. Revelation 17:1-7 says:

> Then one of the seven angels who had the seven bowls came and spoke with me, saying, "Come here, I will show you the judgment of the great harlot who sits on many waters, with whom the kings of the earth committed *acts of* immorality, and those who dwell on the earth were made drunk with the wine of her immorality." And he carried me away in the Spirit into a wilderness; and I saw a woman sitting on a scarlet beast, full of blasphemous names, having seven heads and ten horns. The woman was clothed in purple and scarlet, and adorned with gold and precious stones and pearls, having in her hand a gold cup full of abominations and of the unclean things of her immorality, and on her forehead a name was written, a mystery, "BABYLON THE GREAT, THE MOTHER OF HARLOTS AND OF THE ABOMINATIONS OF THE EARTH." And I saw the woman drunk with the blood of the saints, and with the blood of the witnesses of Jesus. When I saw her, I wondered greatly. And the angel said to me, "Why do you wonder? I will tell you the mystery of the woman and of the beast that carries her, which has the seven heads and the ten horns.

---

[40]For elaboration of this argument, see G. K. Beale, *A New Testament Biblical Theology: The Unfolding of the Old Testament in the New* (Grand Rapids: Baker Academic, 2011), pp. 191-99; see also pp. 393-401.

Revelation 17:1–19:10 is a large interpretive review of the sixth and seventh bowls, which have foretold the judgment of Babylon. The larger literary unit of Revelation 17:1–19:4 is dominated by the judgment of the harlot. So much space is taken up with the beast in Revelation 17 because the woman's significance and power cannot be fully understood except in her relationship to the beast. Furthermore, Revelation 17 graphically describes the eventual demise of Babylon, though the fall of the beast and his allies is also mentioned. Revelation 18:1–19:4 then focuses solely on Babylon's demise itself, as a continuation of the vision begun in Revelation 17:3.

Revelation 17:1-2 portrays an angel telling John that he will show the seer "the judgment of the great harlot . . . with whom the kings of the earth committed *acts of* immorality" and from whom the nations became drunk "from the wine of her fornication." Revelation 17:4 pictures her riding on a scarlet beast, revealing her alliance and intimate relationship with the beast. Revelation 17:5 presents her garbed in majestic dress, holding a cup which is "full of abominations and the unclean things of her fornication." The kings' and the nations' acquiescence to the "fornication" refers not to literal immorality but figuratively to an acceptance of the religious and idolatrous demands of the ungodly earthly order. The economic interpretation of the nations' intoxicating passion and the kings' immoral desire for Babylon is clear from Revelation 18:3, 9-19. There the identical phrases for immorality and intoxication of Revelation 17:2 are equated with terms for economic prosperity. The nations' loyalty to Babylon lay in her ability to provide economic prosperity for them.

Immediately preceding the official title of the whore in Revelation 17:5, the term *mystery* is found once more: "on her forehead a name *was* written, a mystery [*mystērion*], 'BABYLON THE GREAT, THE MOTHER OF HARLOTS AND OF THE ABOMINATIONS OF THE EARTH.'" In the conclusion of Revelation 17:5 the woman, "Babylon the Great," is given an additional description: "the mother of the harlots and of the abominations of the earth."[41] As in Revelation 17:4, the combination of these two words "abomination" and "harlot" (i.e., one committing fornication) probably refers to idol worship, as they so often did in the Old Testament.[42] That she is "mother" of idolaters connotes her au-

---

[41]It matters little whether "mystery" here is actually part of the title itself or part of the introduction to the title together with "having been written." Either way it describes a hidden meaning of "Babylon the Great" that needs further revelatory interpretation.

[42]The terms "fornication" (*porneia*) and "to fornicate" (*porneuō*) elsewhere in the book are figurative expressions for idolatry (so Rev 2:14, 20-21; cf. Rev 9:21; see on Rev 14:8; 17:2). The plural "abom-

thoritative influence over and inspiration of the system of idolatry that was an integral part of economic involvement. She manifests herself throughout the ages in ungodly economic-religious institutions and facets of culture.

Content of the mystery. Some commentators have observed that the Babylonian whore is an explicit contrast to the woman-mother (Rev 12) and the Lamb's bride (Rev 19:7-8; 21:2, 10),[43] indicated by the following: (1) the strikingly identical verbal introductory vision formulas of Revelation 17:1 and Revelation 21:9-10, which is the first indication of an intention to contrast the two figures; (2) the Babylonian whore's transtemporal nature, since the faithful woman of Revelation 12, 19, 21 spans the church age;[44] (3) Babylon spawns faithless children in contrast to the woman who bears faithful seed; (4) the Babylonian harlot is ultimately motivated by Satan in contrast to the woman motivated by Christ, so that the whore has a religious side in addition to her economic focus.

The nature of the woman is revealed in greater detail in Revelation 17:5 by the name written on her forehead. Names written on "foreheads" in the book reveal the true character of people and their ultimate allegiance. For example, Revelation 14:1 reads, "with him [Christ] one hundred and forty-four thousand, having his name and the name of his Father written on their foreheads." Similarly Revelation 22:4: "they will see his face, and his name will be on their foreheads" (see Rev 7:3). Both in Revelation 14:1 and Revelation 22:4 God's name on the forehead means, at least, that the person is identified with the character of God. The same goes for Satan: "And he causes all, the small and the great, and the rich and the poor, and the free men and the slaves, to be given a mark on their right hand or on their forehead" (Rev 13:16; see also Rev 14:1; 22:4), which is the "number of his [the beast's] name."

In the same way, the "name having been written on the forehead" of the whore in Revelation 17:5 reveals her seductive and idolatrous character, further allying her with the beast. Those who corporately comprise the bride of the Lamb and have "his name on their foreheads" (Rev 22:4) are dramatically juxtaposed to the whore.

---

inations" (*bdelygmatōn*) in Rev 17:4 establishes beyond doubt the connection with an idolatrous influence, since this is one of the common words for idol or idolatrous sacrifice in the LXX (so *bdelygma*, "abomination," occurs at least 47 times out of an approximate 122 total uses).

[43]That a contrast is intended is evident from the strikingly identical introductory vision formulas of Rev 17:1 and Rev 21:9-10.

[44]Cf. A. F. Johnson, "Revelation," EBC 12 (Grand Rapids: Zondervan, 1981), p. 556.

The first part of the name is "Babylon the Great" (see also Rev 14:8), which alludes to Daniel 4:27 (Dan 4:30 Eng.): "The king [Nebuchadnezzar] reflected and said, 'Is this not <u>Babylon the great</u>, which I myself have built as a royal residence by the might of my power and for the glory of my majesty?'"[45] The name in Daniel 4 is part of Nebuchadnezzar's self-adulation for which he is soon judged. Likewise, end-time Babylon is on the verge of judgment for its pride and evil. The prefixing of "mystery" (*mystērion*) to the title confirms the Daniel background, since the term also occurs in Daniel 4:9 (LXX, Theodotion) as an introduction to the narration of Nebuchadnezzar's pride and subsequent judgment.

Furthermore, as we have seen, the term *mystery* occurs with an eschatological sense in the book of Daniel.[46] Likewise, in Revelation 17:5 the term also has definite end-time connotations, since the primary focus of the vision is the destruction of Babylon immediately preceding Christ's coming (cf. Rev 17:10-18). Indeed, the revealed mystery has already been used with end-time connotations in Revelation 1:20 and Revelation 10:7, and both of these texts explicitly refer to the mystery as something prophetic which will be (or is being) fulfilled according to God's word (cf. Rev 17:17).

In Revelation 17:7 the unveiled mystery refers to the hidden meaning of the symbolism of not only the woman but also the beast (see Rev 17:8-18). This is not merely referring to the fulfillment of end-time events, but the revealing of an unanticipated or ironic manner in which such events will unravel. In Revelation 1:20, mystery involves the unexpected way in which Daniel's prophecy about the establishment of Israel's latter day kingdom and temple would occur; Revelation 10:7 describes the ironic defeat of evil empires. We have also seen in both passages the ironic pattern of the eschatological kingdom being ironically fulfilled through the suffering of Christ and his people.[47]

Revelation 17:8-18 is also termed a "mystery" because *it reveals the unexpected way in which the kingdom of evil will begin to be defeated; it will turn against itself and start to self-destruct before Christ returns.*[48] The political side

---

[45]Brown, *Semitic Background*, p. 37, argues that the mystery here in Rev 17:5 alludes to *1 En.* 43:1-4; 60:10; 69:14 and *3 Bar.* 3. He admits that mystery in these texts has positive connotations, whereas Rev 17:5, 7 contains the opposite. The allusion to Dan 4:27 occurs in a narration, where Nebuchadnezzar's kingdom is on the verge of destruction.

[46]See pp. 41-43.

[47]E.g., Rev 1:5-6, 13-14, 20.

[48]G. Bornkamm, "μυστήριον," pp. 823-24, comes close to this interpretation when he says, "the beast and the woman are delivered up to destruction . . . they are already condemned to annihilation (Rev

of the evil system (the beast and his allies) will turn against the social-religious-economic side and destroy it. The Old Testament generally expected that God, or his Messiah, would decisively defeat the entire forces of evil at a climactic battle at the very end. It did not foresee in such detail the precise events leading up to the close of the age. Who could have expected that God would commence the defeat of the kingdom of evil at the end of history by making that kingdom divide and conquer itself?

Revelation 17:16-17 describes in some detail this end-time event of internal strife and defeat: "And the ten horns which you saw, and the beast, these will hate the harlot and will make her desolate and naked, and will eat her flesh and will burn her up with fire. For God has put it in their hearts to execute his purpose by having a common purpose, and by giving their kingdom to the beast, until the words of God will be fulfilled." The coalition of the "ten horns" and the beast forms first to destroy the harlot before attempting to destroy the Lamb (Rev 17:12-14). The portrayal of the harlot's desolation is sketched according to the outlines of the prophecy of apostate Jerusalem's judgment by God in Ezekiel 23:25-29, 47: "your survivors will be consumed by the fire . . . they will also strip you of your clothes . . . and they will deal with you in hatred . . . and leave you naked and bare. And the nakedness of your harlotries will be uncovered . . . and [they will] burn their houses with fire." Likewise, Ezekiel 16:37-41 prophesies against faithless Israel: "I will gather together all your lovers with whom you took pleasure . . . they will demolish your high places . . . and they will leave you naked . . . they will burn your houses with fire." Ezekiel 23:31-34 even portrays the harlot as having a cup in her hand and becoming drunk from drinking it, which is strikingly similar to Revelation 17:4. Though Ezekiel 23 is a picture of judgment, the similarity between the woman in Revelation 17 and Ezekiel is remarkable. The Ezekiel picture is even supplemented by similar Old Testament descriptions of Israel's coming judgment that prophesy that God "will strip her naked and . . . make her desolate" (Hos 2:3; cf. also Jer 10:25; 41:22 LXX; Mic 3:3).[49] But these passages from Ezekiel were fulfilled in Israel's judgment and subsequent exile in Babylon.

This imagery is reapplied in Revelation 17 to the desolation of the Babylonian harlot. Three metaphors may have been combined in the description:

17:8). Here then, with the disclosure of the hidden meaning of the Satanic power, the present manifestation is understood in terms of the future which destroys it."
[49]See also Nahum 3:4-5, 15 with reference to Nineveh.

Babylon's nakedness is exposed like that of a whore, she is devoured like a victim of a fierce beast, and she is burned like a city. The political side of the ungodly world system will turn against the heart of the social-economic-religious side and destroy it. How does this begin to happen? The political forces cause the multitudes ruled by Babylon to turn against this great city. The drying up of the Euphrates' waters in Revelation 16:12 may be a picture of how many of Babylon's religious and economic adherents throughout the world (also portrayed as "waters" here in Rev 17:15) become disloyal to it. "The kings of the earth" (Rev 17:16-18) dissuade many of Babylon's innumerable economic-religious followers from remaining loyal to her. The disenchantment with Babylon is a prelude to her judgment by the kings (described in Rev 17:16) and the final judgment itself. Likewise in Revelation 16:12 the invasion of kings follows the drying up of the waters.

According to Revelation 17:17, the beast and his allies will overthrow Babylon, "because" God will inspire them to do so. God will "put into their hearts to perform his purpose." The greater purpose of the coalition of the ten kings and the beast is to topple Babylon. Just as God ultimately causes the persecution of the saints throughout history (e.g., Rev 6:1-11; 13:5-10) and at the end of time (Ezek 38:4-13; Zech 14:2), so he will cause the political forces of evil to attack and destroy Babylon. God executes his will through the "hearts" of both the righteous and the unrighteous.

God inspires such activity so that "the words of God will be fulfilled."[50] This clause refers not only to the prophecy in Revelation 17, but also to the prophecy in Daniel 7. Likewise, the declaration in Revelation 10:7 that "the mystery of God is completed" refers to an unexpected form of Old Testament prophetic fulfillment, especially from the book of Daniel. Here the unexpected aspect of the fulfillment is that the kingdom of evil will unknowingly begin to destroy itself by battling against itself and destroying its own economic-religious foundation. At the end of history God will cause "Satan to rise up against himself and be divided so that he cannot stand but will have an end" (Mk 3:26).

Old Testament prophecy did not foresee in such detail the events leading up

---

[50]The clause *ho logos synetelesthē* ("the word was fulfilled") is used of the fulfillment of God's prophecy of Nebuchadnezzar's judgment (so Dan 4:33 Theodotion; LXX has *telesthēsetai*). Rev 17:17 is similar: *telesthēsontai hoi logoi* ("the words should be fulfilled"). The substitution of *telesthōsin* for *telesthēsontai* (so 1006 1611 1841 2030 𝔐ᵏ) is insignificant since the subjunctive could function like the future, as elsewhere in the Apocalypse. Later scribes, however, may have changed the subjunctive to future because the subjunctive seemed inappropriate in a context speaking of the future.

to the close of the age but only generally expected that God, or his Messiah, would decisively defeat all the forces of evil at a climactic battle at the very end. Daniel 2:41-43 *does* speak of the end-time kingdom of evil as "a divided kingdom," but what this means precisely is not clear, though it would appear to include some kind of internecine conflict. Daniel 11:40-43 indeed refers to evil nations fighting against one another, but Revelation 17 does not picture nations opposing one another or even engaging in civil war; rather, it envisions a unified world system in which the political-military side will turn against the social-religious-economic side, resulting in its destruction. It would have been unexpected from the Old Testament perspective that God would commence defeating the unified world kingdom of evil at history's end by making that kingdom divide within itself and fight itself, even before Christ appears to defeat it.

It could also be argued on the basis of Ezekiel 38:21, Haggai 2:22 and Zechariah 14:13 that eschatological civil war was clearly revealed in the Old Testament as part of the demise of evil and therefore should not be considered part of the revealed mystery (see Rev 17:17):

> "I will call for a sword against him on all My mountains," declares the Lord GOD. "Every man's sword will be against his brother." (Ezek 38:21)

> I will overthrow the thrones of kingdoms and destroy the power of the kingdoms of the nations; and I will overthrow the chariots and their riders, and the horses and their riders will go down, everyone by the sword of another. (Hag 2:22)

> It will come about in that day that a great panic from the LORD will fall on them; and they will seize one another's hand, and the hand of one will be lifted against the hand of another. (Zech 14:13)

These prophecies, however, refer simply to God's enemies "raising their sword [or hand] against one another." Contributing to the picture of war among former allies are the prophecies from Ezekiel 16:37-41 and Ezekiel 23:22-29, 47 that harlot Israel's illicit lovers (idolatrous nations) will turn against her and destroy her. Following the same pattern as Revelation 17:14-16, *4 Ezra* 13.30-38 predicts that there will be civil war among wicked nations and that they will then unite to "fight against" God's Son when he comes. Likely even the civil war that occurs throughout the ages anticipates the final, end-time civil war.

The details of prophesied civil war in the Old Testament are vague, and this is what Revelation 17 describes in more detail. Indeed, the evil kingdom's destruction of its own economic-religious power base that apparently does not attempt to defend itself in the attack is unforeseen and unexpected in the Old Testament.

The final civil war, according to Revelation 17:16-17, arrives on an escalated scale, since Babylon represents the universal economic-religious system throughout the earth.

CONCLUSION

One of the contributions to the study of mystery that we have attempted to make is the close relationship between the book of Daniel and the use of the term *mystery* in the New Testament. John's use of the term is no exception. The book of Revelation, more than any other New Testament book, is dependent on Daniel's narrative on many levels; all usages of the technical term *mystery* occur either in the midst of allusions to Daniel or are directly related to a Danielic passage. There is no need to rehearse these connections to Daniel once more; suffice it to say the book of Revelation is consonant with our previous investigations into the nature of mystery elsewhere in the New Testament. Revelation augments our analysis, lending further credence to the likelihood that the biblical conception of mystery is not rooted in a Greco-Roman context, as some have argued, but in the apocalyptic book of Daniel. This is obviously not surprising given the apocalyptic nature of Revelation. Moreover, throughout our study so far we have seen the concept of mystery tied to Daniel and other Old Testament passages. The book of Revelation also makes clear that *mystery* comes specifically from Daniel and is used in conjunction with *other* Danielic themes and passages. With the use of *mystery* in Revelation there is either an unexpected timing of fulfillment (Rev 10:7) or an unexpected manner of fulfillment (Rev 1:20; 10:7; 17:5, 7) for that which was apparently prophesied in Daniel. Nevertheless, we have seen that the revelation of the mystery is not completely new but has its roots in the Old Testament itself—for example, with the civil war idea in Revelation 17:5, 7. This further confirms what we have concluded in our earlier chapters.

John encourages the seven churches in Asia Minor to have a robust understanding of their position in Christ, to spread and persevere in the gospel, and to grasp the nature of God's redemptive work in the world despite present circumstances. Believers are commanded to see through the devil and the world's deceptive machinations. One salient way believers are to discern God's work, according to John, is to comprehend the mystery in Revelation. The unveiled mystery in Revelation 1:20 is bound up with two symbols and refers to the hidden meaning of the stars and lampstands that are interpreted respectively as "angels and churches." The term *mystery* highlights the ironic nature of the fulfillment and its reversal of expectations. It even includes the unexpected, end-time fulfillment in the symbolism of the stars and lampstands. Believers may be encouraged in their present state of persecution, for it is indicative of their participation in the kingdom. In Revelation 10:7 the revealed mystery has Daniel 11:29–12:13 in mind. This prophecy from Daniel concerns the persecution of God's people and the establishment of the eternal kingdom. Revelation 10 assures the reader that this prophecy will come to pass, yet both the timing and the manner of the prophecy constitute the revealed mystery. Those who hold fast to Christ must not lose heart but persevere in the midst of affliction. The wicked will be punished and the righteous vindicated and restored, as prophesied in Daniel 11–12. The last passage, Revelation 17:8-18, is also termed a "mystery," because it reveals the unexpected way in which the kingdom of evil will begin to be defeated: it will turn against itself and start to self-destruct before Christ returns. The political side of the evil system (the beast and his allies) will turn against the social-religious-economic side and destroy it.

11

MYSTERY WITHOUT *MYSTERY*
IN THE NEW TESTAMENT

◆ ▦ ◆

WE SAW IN THE LAST CHAPTER that the book of Revelation, following in the footsteps of other New Testament writers, makes use of the term *mystery* as it pertains to events within the "latter days." The unveiled mystery in Revelation 1:20 is bound up with two symbols and refers to the hidden meaning of the stars and lampstands that are interpreted respectively as "angels and churches." The term highlights the ironic nature of fulfillment and reversal of expectations. It even includes the unexpected, end-time fulfillment in the symbolism of the stars and lampstands. The revealed mystery in Revelation 10:7 recalls to mind Daniel 11:29–12:13. This prophecy from Daniel concerns the persecution of God's people and the establishment of the end-time kingdom. Revelation 10 assures the reader that this prophecy will come to pass, yet both the timing and the manner of the prophecy constitute the mystery. The last passage, Revelation 17, reveals the unexpected way in which the kingdom of evil will begin to be defeated: it will turn against itself and start to self-destruct before Christ returns. The political leadership of the evil system (the beast and his allies) will turn against its own religious-economic and social infrastructure and destroy it.

Up to this point, we have concerned ourselves with the explicit occurrences of *mystery* in the Old Testament, Judaism and the New Testament, but we will now briefly discuss other New Testament concepts that fit well within the category of revealed mystery. "Mysteries" or end-time revelations need not retain the specific word *mystery* (*mystērion*). For example, in our discussion of mystery in the book of Daniel, we attempted to show how the concept of mystery is present in Daniel 5 and Daniel 7–12, though these chapters omit the term precise term *mystery* (*rāz; mystērion*). In our analysis, we concluded that revealed wisdom in Daniel is characterized by a twofold structure: symbolic and interpretative revelation. Revelation has taken the form of dreams, writing, previous prophecy and visions. It would therefore be a mistake to separate any of these forms of revelation from one another, since each of these modes is an expression of God's revealed wisdom. Revelation, albeit in several mediums, such as dreams, writing and Old Testament Scripture, is partially hidden or encoded until a full interpretation has been provided. This variance and flexibility can also be applied to particular passages and themes in the New Testament. The purpose of this chapter is to survey, albeit briefly, several concepts that could be labeled a "mystery without *mystery*."

The New Testament possesses several relevant topics that fall into this category, but we will limit ourselves to some of the more prominent and significant ones. The scope of this project prohibits us from interacting with the following texts and themes at a deeply exegetical level, so our comments will be more synthetic and brief.

RESURRECTION

Resurrection in the Old Testament is often debated, and scholars differ on which Old Testament texts advance the notion of a resurrection.[1] Typically Job 19:26-27, Isaiah 25:7-8, 26:19, Ezekiel 36:26-35; 37:1-14 and Daniel 12:2-3 are suggested. Minimalists agree that only one explicit reference to resurrection indeed exists in the Old Testament: "Many of those who sleep in the dust of the ground will awake, these to everlasting life, but the others to disgrace *and* everlasting contempt. Those who have insight will shine brightly like the brightness of the expanse of heaven, and those who lead the many to righteousness, like the stars forever and ever" (Dan 12:2-3). The Old Testament affirms that the resurrection would occur at the very end of history, when the corruption of all creation would be ended and a new creation was commenced. The righteous individuals will be physically restored in the new creation, and the unrighteous will be consummately punished.

Though Judaism at this time was exceedingly diverse, many portions of it

---

[1]For a more thorough discussion of resurrection texts in the Old Testament and Judaism, see G. K. Beale, *A New Testament Biblical Theology: The Unfolding of the Old Testament in the New* (Grand Rapids: Baker Academic, 2011), pp. 228-34.

significantly developed the Old Testament concept of a resurrection. (e.g., *1 En.* 22:13; 62.15; *4 Ezra* 2.16; *2 Bar.* 44.12-15). These texts also wed the concept of a physical, corporate resurrection and the arrival of the new creation.

The New Testament places the resurrection at the core of its teachings (e.g., Mt 22:30; Lk 14:14; Rom 6:5; Phil 3:10-11; Rev 20:5). Unlike the Old Testament, the New Testament proposes a somewhat radical notion—the resurrection of the saints is staggered.[2] John 5:25 says, "an hour is coming and now is, when the dead shall hear the voice of the Son of God, and those who hear will live." The Daniel 12:2 prophecy of resurrection begins fulfillment in the first century, but only on a spiritual level. People are raised spiritually but not yet physically. Only a few verses later in John 5, however, Jesus refers to the consummate fulfillment physically of the same Daniel prophecy: "an hour is coming, in which all who are in the tombs will hear His voice, and will come forth; those who did the good *deeds,* to a resurrection of life, those who committed the evil *deeds* to a resurrection of judgment" (Jn 5:28-29). Both fulfillments are literal. The "spiritual" resurrection is just as "literal" as the physical, since Daniel's prophecy certainly included the resurrection of bodies together *with resurrected spirits!* The prophecy is not fulfilled all at once, since first the spiritual resurrection occurs followed later by the physical. Therefore, it is not the nature of fulfillment that has changed, but its timing. That is, the fulfillment of the spiritual and physical resurrections are not spiritualized nor allegorized but merely staggered. This two-stage temporal fulfillment is the revelation conceptually of an Old Testament mystery, since it was not clear in Daniel that there would be such a staggered fulfillment.

There is another way in which the Old Testament prophecy of the resurrection was fulfilled in a twofold manner: Jesus' own resurrection was the beginning fulfillment ("the first fruits") and the subsequent physical resurrection of all saints at the end of history is the final fulfillment (1 Cor 15:22-23). In light of both John 5 and 1 Corinthians 15, the predicted resurrection is actually fulfilled in three stages: (1) Christ's physical resurrection; (2) believers' spiritual resurrection; (3) believers' physical resurrection.

The Messiah is physically raised first, and then later his people are raised physically. Remembering that the Old Testament appeared to prophesy that all of God's people together were to be resurrected as part of one event (e.g., Dan

---

[2]This section has been adapted from G. K. Beale, *The Temple and the Church's Mission*, NSBT 17 (Downers Grove, IL: InterVarsity Press, 2004), pp. 381-82.

12:2-3), Paul views the prophecy of the end-time resurrection as beginning fulfillment in Christ's physical resurrection, which necessitates that the saints' subsequent physical resurrection had to happen (1 Cor 15).[3] In other words, the great event of the final resurrection had begun in Christ, but since that event was not completed in the resurrection of others, the completion of that prophesied event had to come at some point in the future.

The New Testament's conception of the resurrection, that is, the staggered nature of the event, could have legitimately been labeled a "mystery." The nature of the fulfillment of the resurrection prophecies occur just as prophesied (i.e., resurrection is both spiritual and physical) but the timing is what was not clear from the Old Testament perspective. As far as we can discern, neither the Old Testament nor Judaism *clearly* anticipated this unusual timing of the resurrection.[4] It may not be a coincidence that Paul labels the transformation of believers into the image of the last Adam a "mystery" in 1 Corinthians 15:51-52.

THE CHRISTOLOGICAL UNDERSTANDING OF THE OLD TESTAMENT

Perhaps one of the most remarkable ways in which the New Testament authors viewed the Old Testament is their conviction that the entire Old Testament pointed toward Christ.[5] They believed that the Old Testament in its entirety anticipated the person of Jesus, his life, death and resurrection. While it is true that belief in Christ led the New Testament writers to interpret the Old Testament christologically, they would certainly insist that the Old Testament can be rightly understood even by unbelieving Jews to anticipate a priest-king, a suffering servant-king, a new high priest, and so on.

For example, while Luke 24:45 says that the resurrected Christ "opened their [his followers'] minds so that they understood the Scriptures," he also says a

---

[3]The specific Old Testament resurrection prophecy in mind in 1 Cor 15:1-24 is not clear, though the reference to "raised on the third day according to the Scriptures" is thought by some commentators to allude either to Hos 6:1-3 (e.g., "He will raise us up on the third day") or to Jonah 1:17 ("Jonah was in the stomach of the fish three days and three nights"), which Jesus applied typologically to himself (Mt 12:39-41). In none of these passages is there any indication of a staggered resurrection.

[4]The limitations of space in this chapter have prevented us from investigating the various Old Testament and Jewish resurrection texts in enough depth to make any exegetical judgment about whether or not there is anything implicit pointing to a multiple-stage resurrection. Nevertheless, see excursus 11.1 ("Possible Old Testament Anticipations of a Two-Stage Resurrection") regarding passages which appear to refer to a two-stage giving of life to Adam and Eve, which could have formed part of the background for believers' two-stage resurrection (spiritual then physical) in the New Testament.

[5]This section has been adapted from G. K. Beale, "A Surrejoinder to Peter Enns," *Themelios* 32 (2007): 19-20.

little earlier, "O foolish men and slow of heart to believe in all that the prophets have spoken! Was it not necessary for the Christ [lit. *Messiah*] to suffer these things and to enter into his glory?" Then "beginning with Moses and with all the prophets, he explained to them the things concerning himself in all the Scriptures" (Lk 24:25-27). Thus Jesus holds his followers accountable *even before the time of the resurrection* for not understanding that the Old Testament foresaw this event.

Consequently, the apologetic of the New Testament writers is not only "believe in Christ and you will understand the Bible better," but it also indicates that even non-Christians can perceive from the Scriptures that the Messiah was to die and rise again.[6] This is why Luke says in Acts 17:11 that the Bereans to whom Paul and Silas were witnessing "were examining the Scriptures daily, to see whether these things were so." And Luke can also say that Alexander, who "was mighty in the Scriptures," though "acquainted only with the baptism of John," was "teaching accurately the things concerning Jesus," and then when he was taught about the rest of Jesus' ministry "more accurately," he was able to refute Jewish opponents by "demonstrating by the Scriptures that Jesus was the Christ [Messiah]" (Acts 18:24-28). Note that he had an "accurate" understanding of the Old Testament in relation to John's baptism (which includes his baptism of Jesus), but after receiving the full revelation about prophetic messianic fulfillment in Jesus, he was able to have a "more accurate" understanding.

These examples show that there can be both an accurate understanding of the Old Testament and then also a much greater understanding in the light of the progressive revelation about Jesus. It is the latter phenomenon where the revealed mystery plays a central role. In a very real sense, a complete or full meaning of large swaths of the Old Testament was partially and sometimes mostly "hidden" but now has been fully revealed, particularly as it relates to Christ. Romans 16:25-26 is applicable here: "Now to Him who is able to establish you according to my gospel and the preaching of Jesus Christ, according to the <u>revelation of the mystery</u> which has been kept secret for long ages past, but now is manifested, and <u>by the Scriptures of the prophets</u>." The close association between Paul's gospel and Christ, together with mystery and the Old Testament "Scriptures," makes it probable that the Old Testament speaks of Christ, the core of the gospel message, in "new" or unanticipated ways. The

---

[6] D. A. Carson, "Three More Books on the Bible: a Critical Review," *TJ* 27 (2006): 44.

incarnation of Christ, the embodiment of God's full revelation, sheds new light on the Old Testament, bringing about a fuller meaning of the prior revelation. The hidden-but-now-revealed notion of mystery is an important category for understanding the Old Testament. Full or complete meaning was "hidden" in the Old Testament but has now been "revealed" in light of Christ.

JESUS, THE TEMPLE AND THE NEW CREATION

One of the more dominant themes in the Gospels is Jesus' relationship to the temple. Perhaps the most startling and sweeping claim is Jesus' identification *as* the temple and not just the one who has authority over it: "The Jews then said to Him, 'What sign do You show us as your authority for doing these things?' Jesus answered them, 'Destroy this temple, and in three days I will raise it up.' The Jews then said, 'It took forty-six years to build this temple, and will You raise it up in three days?' But He was speaking of the temple of His body" (Jn 2:18-21).

Jesus' resurrection was the first great act of new creation, as explicitly testified to by Paul: "he died and rose again . . . so that if anyone is in Christ, that one is a new creation" (2 Cor 5:15, 17, our translation; so likewise Gal 6:15-16; Col 1:18; Rev 3:14, though the concept occurs throughout the New Testament). This is the best explanation, for example, of why the Gospels repeatedly refer to Christ as "destroying the [old] temple, and in three days raising it up" (Mt 26:61; 27:40; Mk 14:58; 15:29; Jn 2:20-21; cf. Acts 6:14). To call Christ the "temple" is merely another way of referring to him as the new creation, since the temple was symbolic of creation.[7]

According to Genesis 1, Adam's commission was to be carried out by him serving in the Edenic temple, managing it in an orderly manner and expanding its boundaries (Gen 1:28; 2:15). In fact, the reapplication of Adam's commission to Noah, the patriarchs, Israel and end-time Israel was inextricably linked to the beginning of building temples and expanding them (Gen 9:1, 7; 12:2-3; 26:4; 28:3; 47:27; Ex 1:7, etc.). Therefore, Christ initiates the building of a new temple, once again performing the duties that the first Adam and Israel failed in executing. At various points in the Gospels Christ indicates that the old temple is becoming obsolete and that he is replacing it with a new one.

Jesus is greater than the temple now because "God's presence is more man-

---

[7]This section has been adapted from Beale, *Temple and the Church's Mission*, pp. 176-78.

ifest in him than in the temple (cf. Matt. 12:6: 'But I say to you that something greater than the temple is here.'). On him, not on the temple, rests the 'Shekinah' glory"[8] in an even greater way than previously in the temple (echoing perhaps the prophecy in Hag 2:9: "the latter glory of this house will be greater than the former"). Therefore, not only is Jesus identified with the temple because he is assuming the role of the sacrificial system, but he is also now, instead of the temple, the unique place on earth where God's revelatory presence is located. God is manifesting his glorious presence in Jesus in a greater way than it was ever manifested in a physical temple structure.

The New Testament's explicit conviction that God's glorious presence residing in Jesus can be aptly labeled a "mystery." Parts of the Old Testament appeared to anticipate the latter-day temple to be a physical structure at the arrival of the Messiah and the new creation (e.g., Hag 2:9).[9] But even in the Old Testament there are some passages that appear to foresee a nonphysical eschatological temple of God's revelatory presence (e.g., Jer 3:16-17; Zech 1:16–2:13).[10] Accordingly, the Old Testament prophecies of the temple did not seem to be consistent. The New Testament perspective clarifies the Old Testament picture in that it reveals that the temple prophecies are fulfilled in a nonarchitectural manner in Christ and his people.

The Old Testament also describes the prominence of certain individuals who should or do participate in temple building projects (e.g., Adam, Solomon), but nowhere does God's presence dwell fully in any of these sanctuaries, at least to the extent that it does in Christ. The Old Testament does, however, anticipate God's presence dwelling in his people, true Israel (e.g., Jer 3:16), but not to the extent it does in Christ. In a very real way, God's presence is reconstituted in Christ, allowing those who are united in Christ to participate in God's heavenly glory. Moreover, since Christ is divine and lived a perfect, sinless life, God's glory resides in his Son in a unique and unanticipated manner. But while the Old Testament does have precedents for the end-time temple being nonarchitectural, there appears to be no clear evidence that one person, like the Messiah, was ever prophesied to be the initial fulfillment of that temple. But there is evidence in the Old Testament and early Judaism that the individual high

---

[8]R. A. Cole, *The New Temple* (London: Tyndale Press, 1950), p. 12.

[9]Beale, *Temple and the Church's Mission*, pp. 123-67.

[10]It is also possible to understand the Ezek 40–48 temple prophecy to be predicting a nonphysical temple (see Beale, *Temple and Church's Mission*, pp. 335-364).

priest's clothing symbolized and was a microcosm of the temple itself.[11] It is easy to see how the later individual Messiah as a priest could represent the temple itself, especially since priests were classic types of Christ (e.g., Heb 10:20, where the temple "veil" is said to represent Christ's "flesh"; and more commonly, Heb 9:11-28, where Christ is viewed as a priest offering his blood in the heavenly temple as the ultimate temple sacrifice). Neither the Old Testament nor Judaism appear to anticipate God initially fulfilling his promise to begin to recreate the cosmos in a single individual.

A natural corollary is Christ's new creational body. As hinted above, the concepts of the new creation and temple intertwine. The Old Testament looks forward to the day when the Lord will once again "create new heavens and a new earth" (Is 65:16; 66:22), but the New Testament radically suggests that the Lord has indeed fulfilled this promise, at least initially (2 Cor 5:15, 17). At Christ's resurrection, God has performed a new creational act in his Son. Christ's body is truly the "firstfruits" of the new heavens and earth (Rev 3:14). God's new creational act in Christ, from an Old Testament perspective, is certainly unusual. Neither the Old Testament nor Judaism appear to anticipate God initially fulfilling his promise to begin to re-create the cosmos in a single individual. But, again, the above discussion of the individual person of Christ as the temple may also shed some light here. For not only was the individual priest's clothing representative of the temple in the Old Testament, but, just as the temple itself was a symbol of the creation, so the individual priest's clothing was also representative of the creation.[12]

Accordingly, the individual Christ as the temple was also representative of the new creation and its beginning at his resurrection. So again there appears to be a possible precedent for an individual not only to represent the temple but also the new creation. How clearly this would have been understood is hard to say. The point, however, is that the revelation of the individual Christ as the beginning of the eschatological temple and new creation is the manifestation of a previous mystery that does not appear to have been completely hidden.

INAUGURATED ESCHATOLOGY

The Old Testament generally speaking expects the very end of history to follow a certain order. It employs the phrase "latter days" and similar terminology as

---

[11]See Beale, *Temple and Church's Mission*, pp. 39-48.
[12]Ibid., pp. 39-48.

a reference to a future time when: (1) a final, unsurpassed and incomparable period of tribulation for God's people will arrive, perpetrated by an end-time opponent who deceives and persecutes, in the face of which they will need wisdom not to compromise. Afterward they are (2) delivered, (3) resurrected, and their kingdom reestablished; (4) at this future time, God will rule on earth (5) through a coming Davidic king who will defeat all opposition and reign in peace in a new creation over both (6) the nations and (7) restored Israel, (8) with whom God will make a new covenant, (9) on whom God will bestow the Spirit and (10) among whom the temple will be rebuilt.[13]

The New Testament picks up on this language and repeatedly uses the precise phrase "latter days" and other expressions as found in the Old Testament prophecies (e.g., Jn 6:39-40; Acts 2:17; 1 Cor 10:11; Gal 4:4; 2 Pet 3:3). The eschatological nuance of the phrases is generally identical to that of the Old Testament, except for one notable difference: according to the New Testament the "latter days," as predicted by the Old Testament, are initially fulfilled with Christ's first advent, and their consummation will follow. Thus there is a two-stage fulfillment of the latter days of the Old Testament.

We must, however, qualify this statement. A few passages in the Old Testament do expect multiple stages of fulfillment. Psalm 110:1-4, for example, anticipates or predicts an inaugurated messianic reign followed by a consummate reign at some later time, though the interval between the two may well have seemed short from the Old Testament perspective.

All that the Old Testament foresaw would occur in the end times has begun already in the first century, continuing until the final coming of Christ. In other words, the Old Testament end-time expectations of the great tribulation, God's domination of the Gentiles, deliverance of Israel from oppressors, Israel's restoration, Israel's resurrection, the new covenant, the promised Spirit, the new creation, the new temple, a messianic king, and the establishment of God's kingdom, have been set in motion by Christ's death, resurrection and formation of the Christian church. Generally speaking, the already-and-not-yet framework of the New Testament was largely unexpected in the Old Testament. We mentioned above how the Old Testament may have anticipated an already-and-not-yet eschatology. However, for the most part, such an idea is not found in the Old Testament. Therefore, the *pervasiveness* of the already/not yet of the latter days

---

[13]Beale, *New Testament Biblical Theology*, p. 115. For a thorough discussion of this theme in the Old Testament and Judaism, see pp. 88-127.

and related concepts in the New Testament can be understood to be a mystery not easily found to be revealed to any clear degree in the Old Testament.

THE GOSPEL

Perhaps one of the best examples of unanticipated notions in the New Testament is the gospel itself. Once properly understood, the central teaching of the New Testament—Christ's life, death and resurrection—adequately falls into the category of mystery. It is probably appropriate to use terms such as *continuity* and *discontinuity* here. The gospel displays both of these characteristics. On the one hand, certain elements of the gospel are an understandable fulfillment of Old Testament expectations (e.g., verbal prophecies of the coming of a Messiah; e.g., that the Messiah would die for the sins of his people; see Is 53). In this sense, the gospel is in *continuity* with the Old Testament. On the other hand, the gospel, as we have seen, contains unusual or unexpected elements that are in *discontinuity* with the Old Testament (e.g., the timing of a two-stage resurrection).

The book of Romans, perhaps more than any other epistle, demonstrates this phenomenon. At the beginning of the book, Paul highlights those aspects of the gospel that are considered to be in continuity with the Old Testament (Rom 1:1-4):

> Paul, a bond-servant of Christ Jesus, called *as* an apostle, set apart for the gospel of God, which He promised beforehand through His prophets in the holy Scriptures, concerning His Son, who was born of a descendant of David according to the flesh, who was declared the Son of God with power by the resurrection from the dead, according to the Spirit of holiness, Jesus Christ our Lord.

The gospel was indeed anticipated in the Old Testament (Rom 1:2); its message centers on Jesus the Messiah (Rom 1:3); Christ, the long-awaited Messiah, would die for the sins of humanity and presently rules in heaven because of his resurrection (Rom 1:4); the gospel includes bringing the Gentiles into the people of God, true Israel (Rom 1:5). As we have seen throughout this project, many of these elements find their origin in the Old Testament. The Old Testament expects: (1) a messianic figure to rule over Israel and the nations, (2) the resurrection of the dead and (3) the eschatological restoration and inclusion of the Gentiles in true Israel. Granted, the manner in which these events are fulfilled differs from expectations, but Paul's point is clear: the Old Testament anticipates the gospel message. In a word, the gospel stands in continuity with Old Testament expectations.

Romans essentially begins and ends with a description of the gospel, forming a gospel bookend of sorts (see table 11.1). In light of the exact language and concepts, there can be no doubt that these two texts are organically related. That much is clear. What is of particular note is the difference between these two texts: the term *mystery* and related language are only found in Romans 16:25-26. Now perhaps Paul had mystery in mind in Romans 1:1-5, but did not feel it was necessary to mention. This may very well be the case. We think it more cogent, however, that the term was omitted from Romans 1:1-5 for a reason—the apostle wanted to stress the *continuity* of the gospel message there. Paul firmly roots his gospel in the Old Testament.

Table 11.1

Romans 1:1-2, 5	Romans 16:25-26
"Paul, a bond-servant of Christ Jesus, called as an apostle, set apart for the gospel [*euangelion*] of God, which he promised beforehand through His prophets [*prophētōn*] in the holy Scriptures [*graphais*], . . . through whom we have received grace and apostleship to bring about the obedience of faith [*eis hypakoēn pisteōs*] among all the Gentiles [*pasin tois ethnesin*] for His name's sake."	"Now to Him who is able to establish you according to my gospel [*euangelion*] and the preaching of Jesus Christ, according to the revelation of the mystery which has been kept secret for long ages past, but now is manifested, and by the Scriptures of the prophets [*graphōn prophētikōn*], according to the commandment of the eternal God, has been made known to all the nations [*panta ta ethnē*], leading to obedience of faith [*eis hypakoēn pisteōs*]."

Romans 16:25-26, though, does not share the same emphasis, despite nearly identical language. Paul's point rests more on the idea of *discontinuity* with the Old Testament: "according to the revelation of the mystery which has been kept secret for long ages past, but now is manifested, and by the Scriptures of the prophets" (Rom 16:26). It is not entirely clear why Paul decides to punctuate this theme of hiddenness (see, though, our previous discussion of this text),[14] but his emphasis is clear enough. The certain particulars or aspects of Paul's gospel were "kept secret," that is, the gospel contains unexpected elements in the way it is fulfilled (cf. Eph 6:19; Col 4:3). The manner in which some of the events are fulfilled appears to differ from Old Testament expectations.

We can, therefore, say that Paul's gospel is simultaneously continuous and discontinuous with the Old Testament. How these two concepts interrelate is

---

[14]See pp. 95-97 above.

difficult to determine, but Romans holds these two truths together without any breach of reason. D. A. Carson, in his essay on mystery, speaks to this precise topic of continuity and discontinuity:

> Paul feels no tension between these two stances because, as he understands them, there isn't any. And this is why the gospel itself, not to say some of its chief elements, can be simultaneously seen as something that has been (typologically) predicted and now fulfilled, and as something that has been hidden and has now been revealed. What starts off as almost intolerable paradox emerges as a coherent and interlocking web.[15]

Parsing out which elements stand in continuity and discontinuity with the Old Testament is notoriously difficult. We have attempted to tease out in this project some elements that are bound up with continuity and some with discontinuity between the Old and New Testament, but much more could be written. The upshot of this brief discussion of mystery and the gospel is the importance of mystery in the New Testament, even as it applies to the gospel. Even the core teaching of the New Testament about the life, death and resurrection of the Messiah, presupposes a grasp of the biblical conception of mystery, and without it much of our understanding is left incomplete.

CONCLUSION

The purpose of this brief chapter was to explore areas in the New Testament that can be viewed as a "mystery," though the technical term is lacking. Our sampling of topics is but the tip of the iceberg, and work in this area is still much needed. In our discussion of resurrection, we noticed that the New Testament conception of resurrection differs from the Old Testament in some respects. Instead of the resurrection occurring as one event, the New Testament describes the resurrection as a staggered event—first Christ and then the saints. Even the saints' resurrection falls into the same staggered phenomenon. The believers' spiritual resurrection at the moment of conversion precedes their physical resurrection later.

Concerning the christological understanding of the Old Testament, we observed that the New Testament authors uniquely interpreted the entire Old Testament in light of Christ. In a very real sense, a more complete or fuller

---

[15]D. A. Carson, "Mystery and Fulfillment," in *Justification and Variegated Nomism: Volume 2—The Paradoxes of Paul*, ed. D. A. Carson, Peter T. O'Brien and Mark A. Seifrid (Grand Rapids: Baker Academic, 2004), p. 427.

meaning of the Old Testament was "hidden" but now has been revealed, particularly as it relates to Christ.

The concept of mystery also applies to Jesus' relationship to the temple and new creation. The New Testament's explicit conviction that God's special revelatory, glorious presence resides in an individual, namely Jesus, is unusual given the Old Testament texts that pertain to Israel's latter-day temple. And the same is true about how the New Testament views the new creation to have begun in the one person, Jesus Christ. Yet even in these respects, we saw that while such things were mysterious from the Old Testament vantage point, there may nevertheless have been hints even about these things.

Mystery can also be applied to the topic of inaugurated eschatology. Generally speaking, the Old Testament prophesied that God would decisively act in various ways in the latter days, which would apparently occur all at once at the very end of history. The New Testament sees the latter days being fulfilled in a two-stage manner. Such a New Testament revelation appears not to have been anticipated in the Old Testament and therefore is a mystery, though Psalm 110:1-4 may be the one exception this.

Finally, the heart of the New Testament—the life, death and resurrection of Christ—should also be considered a revealed mystery. On the one hand, the gospel is the direct fulfillment of Old Testament expectations. On the other, the gospel displays certain characteristics that were hidden in the Old Testament. The gospel, in other words, stands in both continuity and discontinuity with the Old Testament. To pit one against the other is to go beyond the evidence, resulting in a distorted view of the gospel.

EXCURSUS 11.1: POSSIBLE OLD TESTAMENT ANTICIPATIONS OF A TWO-STAGE RESURRECTION[16]

The first possible hint of resurrection life in the Old Testament may be discernible in Genesis 1–3. The promise of death due to disobedience in Genesis 2:16-17 begins to be fulfilled in Genesis 3, when Adam and Eve disobey God's command. Death comes in an inaugurated manner: first the couple is separated from God, suggesting the beginning of spiritual death, which would be followed at a later point by physical death. This then was an inaugurated spiritual death to be consummated by physical death at some future point.

---

[16]This excursus is an adaptation of Beale, *New Testament Biblical Theology*, pp. 228-34; see also pp. 252-54 on Ezek 36–37.

The promise in Genesis 3:15 of the seed of the woman who would decisively defeat the serpent likely entails also an implicit reversal of his work that introduced death. It might not be unexpected that the reversal toward life might mirror the inaugurated and consummative aspect of the death. For example, the subsequent clothing by God (Gen 3:21) after Adam and Eve's primal sin indicates an inaugurated restoration of life in relation to God, so that the separation of inaugurated death has begun to be overcome in some unseen way (in spiritual life). The clothing symbolizes not only an inauguration of life but also the coming, consummative inheritance of life that Adam and Eve would receive at some point.[17] Indeed, significant research has revealed that clothing in the ancient Near East and in the Old Testament indicated an inheritance and also a change in status for the person or object being clothed, whether idols (as images of the gods), people in general, or kings and priests in particular. Kings especially were clothed in an investiture ceremony as a mark or sign of the new status of their royal authority. And since kings were often considered to be living images of their gods, their clothing probably was considered as part of a reflection of this image and their living reflection of it. Since Adam was to be a king-priest in fulfilling the mandate of Genesis 1:28, after his sin and initial restoration to life, his destiny was likely to receive clothing appropriate to his kingly office, of which God's clothing him with "garments of skin" was a symbolic down payment of a greater clothing to come. If this is on the right track, then it "suggests that the reason for mentioning Adam and Eve's nakedness at the end of Genesis 2 is to arouse in the reader an expectation of royal investiture in keeping with man's Genesis 1 status as the ruling 'image of God' on earth."[18] Thus, clothing is another way of speaking conceptually of life in its inaugurated and consummated form.

This clothing not only symbolizes a beginning restoration of life in relation to God but probably has to do with a reflection of God's glory,[19] all of which

---

[17]See further Beale, *New Testament Biblical Theology*, pp. 43-46, 438-42 for a consummative understanding, and pp. 452-55 for an inaugurated understanding. With respect to an understanding that Adam and his posterity would undergo a final resurrection, see *LAE* [Apocalypse] 13.2-3: "I [God] shall raise you [Adam] on the last day in the resurrection with every man of your seed"; *LAE* [Vita] 51.2: "at the end of times . . . all flesh . . . shall be raised."

[18]See William N. Wilder, "Illumination and Investiture: the Royal Significance of the Tree of Wisdom," *WTJ* 68 (2006): 66, on whose broader section on pp. 56-69 we have depended for the significance of investiture with clothing and clothing as symbolizing inheritance, and which we find compatible with our discussion of the significance of clothing in 1 Cor 15 (see pp. 132-34, 144-46; see also this section in Wilder for numerous secondary sources on which he partly depends for his discussion).

[19]Ibid., pp. 64-69, who shows the close association of clothing with glory in the ancient Near East and in the New Testament.

must entail a living relationship with God and will come fully at some future point. Thus, spiritual and physical death will be reversed at some point. The naming of Adam's wife "Eve ['Life'] because she was the mother of all *the* living" further points to this notion that the curse of death was in the process of being removed.

Thus, the revelation of a two-stage fulfillment of resurrection life appears not to be wholly unanticipated in the Old Testament, especially since Genesis 1–3 was repeatedly used throughout the New Testament to describe both inaugurated and consummative eschatology,[20] probably on the basis that God would "make the last things like the first things" (*Barn.* 6.13, which itself is likely an interpretative paraphrase of Is 41:22 ["tell *us* what things were of old, and we will apply *our* understanding, and we shall know what are the last and the future things"[21]]). For examples of how the Genesis 2–3 clothing language is applied to inaugurated and consummative resurrection realities, see respectively Colossians 3:9-10[22] and 1 Corinthians 15:45-54.[23]

Many understand Ezekiel's vision of the "valley of dry bones" and the bones being given flesh and being resurrected to be a metaphorical prediction merely of Israel's return from Babylonian exile. Even though Judaism typically understood this passage to be predicting the literal, physical resurrection of dead Israelite saints, that appears not to be the primary focus in Ezekiel itself. Nevertheless, while the prophecy is a metaphorical reference to return from exile, an actual idea of resurrection is likely included. Ezekiel 37:1-14 develops the reference to spiritual renewal to life in Ezekiel 36:26-27 at the time Israel is to be restored to her land (Ezek 36:26-35):

> "Moreover, I will give you a new heart and put a new spirit within you; and I will remove the heart of stone from your flesh and give you a heart of flesh. I will put My Spirit within you and cause you to walk in My statutes, and you will be careful to observe My ordinances. You will live in the land that I gave to your forefathers; so you will be My people, and I will be your God. Moreover, I will save you from all your uncleanness; and I will call for the grain and multiply it,

---

[20]See Beale, *New Testament Biblical Theology*, passim and see the scripture index on Gen 1-3. The discussion of Gen 1–3 in Beale, *New Testament Biblical Theology*, pp. 29-46, is generally supportive of a two-stage blessedness of Adam, the last stage of which is eschatologically consummative.

[21]See also Is 42:9; 43:18-19 (note that both Is 42:15 and Is 43:16-17 say the last things will be like the exodus of old).

[22]As discussed in Beale, *New Testament Biblical Theology*, pp. 452-55.

[23]As discussed in ibid., pp. 438-42.

and I will not bring a famine on you. I will multiply the fruit of the tree and the produce of the field, so that you will not receive again the disgrace of famine among the nations. Then you will remember your evil ways and your deeds that were not good, and you will loathe yourselves in your own sight for your iniquities and your abominations. I am not doing *this* for your sake," declares the Lord GOD, "let it be known to you. Be ashamed and confounded for your ways, O house of Israel!"

Thus says the Lord GOD, "On the day that I cleanse you from all your iniquities, I will cause the cities to be inhabited, and the waste places will be rebuilt. The desolate land will be cultivated instead of being a desolation in the sight of everyone who passes by. They will say, 'This desolate land has become like the garden of Eden; and the waste, desolate and ruined cities are fortified *and* inhabited.'"

"Living in the land" (Ezek 36:26) is a result of God "giving Israel a new heart and a new spirit" (Ezek 36:27) and putting his "Spirit within them" (Ezek 36:26). This refers to Israel returning to her land and being spiritually regenerated. That Ezekiel 37:1-14 refers to the same thing is signaled by the concluding phrase of this visionary section: "I will put My Spirit within you, and you will come to life, and I will place you on your own land," the first phrase a verbatim repetition of Ezekiel 36:27a and the last clause a paraphrased rendering of Ezekiel 36:28a ("and you will live in the land"). This parallelism with Ezekiel 36 indicates that the prophecy of Israel's resurrection in Ezekiel 37 does indicate new creation but in terms of *resurrection of the spirit*. And resurrection of the spirit is inextricably linked to resurrection of the body, the latter of which, as we observed above, is the way the majority of Judaism understood the Ezekiel 37 prophecy.[24] It does not appear that Ezekiel 37 speaks of resurrection of the body, though one could assume that when Israel's spirit was resurrected, their body would be resurrected at the same time. Nevertheless, there is enough ambiguity that a later stage of physical resurrection following the spiritual could possibly be in mind.

Together with Genesis 1–3, Ezekiel 36–37 might be another text that leaves room for a staggered notion of resurrection. Consequently, the revelation of a two-stage fulfillment of resurrection life may not have been completely unan-

---

[24]See also N. T. Wright, *The New Testament and the People of God*, COQG 1 (Minneapolis: Fortress, 1992), p. 332, who likewise sees that the Ezek 37 prophecy of Israel's resurrection as a metaphorical expression of Israel's return from exile included also the notion of a literal, physical resurrection from the dead.

ticipated in the Old Testament. If so, its revelation in the New Testament is a much fuller manifestation of a mystery that may have been only very faintly foreshadowed earlier but is not a radically new revelation without any possible precedents at all.

12

THE CHRISTIAN MYSTERY AND THE PAGAN MYSTERY RELIGIONS

◆ ▣ ◆

AFTER ADDRESSING THE EXPLICIT OCCURRENCES of *mystery* in the New Testament, we focused on how the *concept* of mystery is found throughout the New Testament writings. We noticed how the New Testament conception of the resurrection differs somewhat from the Old Testament. Whereas the Old Testament expects the resurrection to occur as one event, the New Testament portrays the resurrection as a staggered event—first Christ and then believers. Even how the New Testament writers interpret the Old Testament in light of Christ can also be deemed a mystery. The full meaning of Old Testament Scripture was "hidden" but now has been revealed, particularly as it relates to the person of Christ. The New Testament's explicit conviction that God's glorious presence resides in an individual, namely Jesus, is unusual given the Old Testament texts that pertain to Israel's latter-day temple. The same can be said about the new creation beginning fulfillment in the one person, Jesus Christ. This too is a mysterious doctrine. Mystery can also be applied to the New Testament conception of eschatology. Though the Old Testament prophesied that God would act decisively and consummately in the "latter days," the New Testament clearly states that end-time events were only initially fulfilled. Only at Christ's second coming will these events be consummately fulfilled. At the core of the New Testament stands the gospel—Christ's life, death and resurrection. Unequivocally, the New Testament plainly states that the gospel is the fulfillment of Old Testament prophecies and expectations, but the apostle Paul also claims that the gospel contains fresh elements, which he terms a "mystery." Nevertheless, there appear to be faint glimmers of light in the Old Testament about this mystery.

Throughout this project we have argued that the New Testament's conception of mystery is deeply indebted to the Old Testament and sometimes to early Judaism. While this is certainly the case, it remains possible that the word *mystery* (*mystērion*) and other related terms in the New Testament may be derived from the wider Greco-Roman world. We mentioned in our introduction that in the late nineteenth and early twentieth centuries many scholars in the history of religions school suggested that the New Testament (particularly Paul) was influenced significantly by several religious practices of the Greco-Roman culture—baptism, Eucharist, regeneration and so on.[1] Moreover, the term *mystery*, they claimed, also reflects a dependence on the current religious environment. The history-of-religions approach was eventually put to the test and did not survive the rigorous evaluation of the data. The majority of New Testament scholars are now convinced that the New Testament (and Paul) is largely dependent on the Old Testament and Judaism for the notion of "mystery," and our investigation into the use of mystery bears this out.

In this chapter we would like to explore the issue once more but from a slightly different angle. Is it possible that the New Testament's usage of mystery language could have originated from the Greco-Roman world?[2] How would a concept that is so readily connected to the Old Testament be derived from a pagan environment? If the relationship is not one of direct dependence, could the term still resonate with the ideas of a pagan religious context? Our aim is to probe this relationship and offer some initial conclusions. We must, however, keep in mind that this discussion ought to remain cautious, and our conclusions are tenuous at best. We simply lack sufficient evidence to link with great certainty the New Testament to the pagan mystery religions. Moreover, since the constraints of this project limit us from delving deeply into the pagan cults, our discussion will be abbreviated and presented synthetically.

We will focus the discussion on the mystery religions that were commonly practiced in many cities of the Roman Empire during the first century A.D. We are beset with several methodological problems, making this venture into the mystery religions notoriously difficult. Since the mystery religions are, naturally, secretive, we lack detailed accounts. The initiates swore under oath (and even

---

[1]E.g., Richard Reitzenstein, *Die hellenistischen Mysterienreligionen nach ihren Grundgedanken und Wirkungen*, 3rd ed. (Berlin: Teubner, 1927); H. A. A. Kennedy, *St. Paul and the Mystery-Religions* (London: Hodder and Stoughton, 1913).

[2]For a survey of *mystērion* ("mystery") in the Greco-Roman world, see Chrys C. Caragounis, *The Ephesian* Mysterion: *Meaning and Content*, ConBNT 8 (Lund: Gleerup, 1977), pp. 11-19.

under the threat of death) to never betray what transpired. Much of what we know depends on secondhand accounts, some of which are later than the first century A.D. We have to rely on various mediums such as art, inscriptions and letters in order to piece together a cohesive portrait of a local mystery religion. In addition, the mystery religions existed in a variety of locales and developed over time, sometimes borrowing from one another. They were often quite syncretistic, making it difficult to distill the unique traits or particulars. The mysteries of these cults involved worship of deities from Persia, Egypt, Anatolia, Syria and Greece. Despite all their complexities, we will attempt to describe how the biblical conception of mystery may relate to the pagan environment. We will first briefly explain what the mystery religions are, offer a few examples of them, and then compare and contrast the biblical mystery and the mystery religions.

BRIEF INTRODUCTION TO THE MYSTERY RELIGIONS

The ancient mystery religions are typically classified into two categories: local and universal. In the first century A.D. the vast majority of the ancient mysteries comprised local religions confined to a particular region. On the other hand, a few mystery religions, such as the cults of Dionysus and Isis, were spread across the Roman Empire.

Mystery religions by definition are private and reserved only for the "initiates" (*mystai*). This stands out in sharp relief against the public religions in which citizens openly worship. Mystery religions often feature public spectacles such as processions or dancing but are at their core a religion of private worship and experience. Scholars suggest that the word *mystery* (*mystērion*) is derived from the verb *to close* (*myeō*), thus explaining the secrecy of the rites. Several scholars recognize that *mystery/to close* (*mystērion/myeō*) may be taken in two ways.[3] (1) The initiates were required to remain silent, under oath, about what transpired during the mystery rites. They were, quite literally, to keep their mouths "closed."[4] (2) The second sense is metaphorical in that it refers to the "closed" nature of the initiates' eyes. As we will see below, part of the purpose of the rituals is to "open the eyes" of the initiates that they may behold and experience deep truths.

---

[3]Marvin W. Meyer, *The Ancient Mysteries: A Sourcebook of Sacred Texts* (Philadelphia: University of Pennsylvania Press, 1999), pp. 4-5.

[4]Inscribed on gold tablets found in the graves of males and females who participated in the mystery religions are titles, such as *mystai, symmystai, archimystai, neomystai, archaios mystēs*. Fritz Graf, *Ritual Texts for the Afterlife: Orpheus and the Bacchic Gold Tablets* (New York: Routledge, 2007).

Marvin Meyer defines mystery religions in the following way: "The mysteries were secret religious groups composed of individuals who decided, through personal choice, to be initiated into the profound realities of one deity or another . . . the mysteries emphasized an inwardness and privacy of worship within closed groups."[5] For all their variety, a common denominator exists between all the mystery religions—only the "initiated" are granted access to the cult's secrets.[6] At Eleusis, becoming an initiate typically involves degrees of initiation—the Lesser Mysteries, the Greater Mysteries, and the disclosure of sacred knowledge or *epopteia*. The initiate is responsible to complete each stage through a variety of purifications, culminating in *epopteia*, the unveiling of the mystery's innermost secrets.

According to the Eleusianian mysteries, initiates are privy to the following aspects: "things enacted" (*dromena*), "things said" (*legomena*) and "things shown" (*deiknymena*).[7] "Things said" consist of speaking or singing of the "deep truths of the gods."[8] In addition, "things shown" focus on the visual nature of the mystery, placing emphasis on the unveiling of sacred objects or beholding religious murals. "Things enacted," perhaps the most famous of the three, reflects the initiates' dramatic rehearsal of the myth. Often a mystery religion was based on a particular cult myth. It itself was not a secret but a well-known story about the gods. Bornkamm's description of the mystery religions reveals the importance of the "things enacted": "Mysteries are cultic rites in which the destinies of a god are portrayed by sacred actions before a circle of devotees in such a way as to give them a part in the fate of a god."[9]

We need to draw attention to one particular aspect of the mystery religions that may seem obvious yet may hold profound implications for determining

---

[5]Meyer, *Ancient Mysteries*, p. 4.

[6]Diodous Siculus (*Library of History* 49.5) relates the profound secrecy of the mystery religions: "Now the details of the initiatory rite are guarded among the matters not to be divulged and are communicated to the initiates alone," translation from C. H. Oldfather, *Diodorus of Sicily III*, LCL (Cambridge, MA: Harvard University Press, 1939). Philo even claims, "Now I bid ye, initiated men, who are purified, as to your ears, to receive these things, as mysteries which are really sacred, in your inmost souls; and reveal them not to anyone who is of the number of the uninitiated, but guard them as a sacred treasure" (*Cher.* 1.48; see *Leg.* 1.104; translation from C. D. Young, *The Works of Philo* [Peabody, MA: Hendrickson, 1993]). Philo famously attempts to merge Hellenism with Judaism in many respects, and it is quite evident in his discussion of the mystery religions. On a few occasions, as he does here, he likens Judaism to the mystery religions (e.g., *Leg.* 3.100; cf. *Spec.* 1.319).

[7]Everett Ferguson, *Backgrounds of Early Christianity*, 3rd ed. (Grand Rapids: Eerdmans, 2003), p. 252; Meyer, *Ancient Mysteries*, pp. 10-11.

[8]Meyer, *Ancient Mysteries*, p. 10.

[9]Günter Bornkamm, "μυστήριον, μυέω," in *TDNT* 4:803.

the relationship between the biblical conception of mystery and the mystery religions. With all that pertains to secret rites, *experience* still remains the chief aspect. Synesius (*Dio* 7) remarks, albeit negatively, about a Bacchic mystery religion. What is particularly important is that part of Aristotle's view of mystery religions is contained in the quotation: "For the sacred matter [contemplation] is not like attention belonging to knowledge.... On the contrary—to compare small and greater—it is like Aristotle's view that men being initiated have not a lesson to learn, but an experience to undergo and a condition into which they must be brought, while they are becoming fit (for revelation)."[10] This quotation is revealing in that it helps us put the mystery rites in proper perspective. The ultimate purpose of the mystery religions was to give the initiate a unique, even divine, experience.[11]

EXAMPLES OF MYSTERY RELIGIONS

As mentioned above, mystery religions exhibit incredible diversity, making it notoriously difficult to summarize with precision. It is therefore probably best simply to give a few examples of Greek mystery religions and then compare and contrast them with the biblical mystery. Eleusis is a notable town not far from Athens. The Eleusinian mystery cults pertained to the fertility myths of Demeter (the "Grain Mother") and Kore (the "Maiden"). The myth behind the celebration of the mystery stems from the *Homeric Hymn to Demeter*. According to the myth, Hades rapes Kore and snatches her and takes her to the underworld. She then becomes Hades' wife Persephone. Kore's mother Demeter ventures on a journey to the underworld to find her. Demeter's search is unfruitful, so she travels to Eleusis, where she nurses the son of the queen of Eleusis. Demeter places the young boy into a fire in order to burn off his mortality. The queen eventually discovered Demeter, so the Eleusinians constructed a temple in her honor. In return, Demeter teaches the royal family mystery rites to ensure immortality and great prosperity. Kore is eventually allowed to return from the underworld but, as a result of eating a pomegranate, she has to return

---

[10]Translation from A. Fitzgerald, *The Letters of Synesius of Cyrene* (New York: Oxford University Press, 1926).

[11]Meyer rightly adds, "While the ancient initiates may have been emotionally affected by the rituals and may have gained insight into the divine profundities through the *legomena*, *deiknymena* and *dromena*, they were not given instruction or taught doctrine in any traditional sense. Initiation was not classroom education, but an eye-opening experience that transcended earthly realties and mundane learning" (Meyer, *Ancient Mysteries*, p. 12).

annually to the underworld for four months. Her absence from Eleusis causes the crops to wither. The Eleusinian initiates thus celebrated Kore's descent to the underworld and return from it, which was depicted in the ritual as her dying and rising in conjunction with the harvest cycle.

Toward the end of the *Hymn*, Demeter instructs the royal house and the attendants in the mystery rites: "She [Demeter] went to the royal stewards . . . She showed the tendance [religious function] of the holy things and explicated the rites to them all . . . sacred rites, which it is forbidden to transgress, to inquire into, or to speak about." Here Demeter reveals to the family secrets that must remain as such. A few lines later, the narrator claims: "Blessed of earthbound men is he who <u>has seen</u> these things, but who dies without fulfilling the holy things . . . [and who] has no claim ever on such blessings, even when departed down to the moldy darkness" (lines 480-84).[12] Because of extreme secrecy,[13] we simply do not know what the rites entailed or what was said during the initiation.[14] Importantly, grasping the mystery rites is figuratively portrayed as "seeing," whereas the uninitiated are sentenced to "darkness." Clinton agrees when he comments on this passage: "Participation in the rites [of Eleusis] is characterized by *seeing*" (emphasis original).[15] This explains why initiates carried torches during nocturnal processions,[16] and why it was common for them to be blindfolded at the beginning of their initiation.[17]

The next mystery religion that we will briefly recount is the mysteries of Dionysus (Bacchus). Dionysus descended from Zeus and Semele. Unlike the god Zeus, Semele was a mortal and was beguiled by Hera, Zeus's wife, to ask

---

[12]Translation from David G. Rice and John E. Stambaugh, *Sources for the Study of Greek Religion*, SBLSBS 14 (Chico: Scholars, 1979).

[13]See Tertullian, *Against the Valentinians* 1.

[14]Clement of Alexandria, enigmatically, hints at some of the rites when he states, "And the following is the token of the Eleusinian mysteries: <u>I have fasted, I have drunk the cup; I have received from the box; having done, I put it into the basket, and out of the basket into the chest</u>" (*Exhortation to the Heathen* 2, in *The Writings of Clement of Alexandria*, trans. William Wilson [Edinburgh: T & T Clark, 1884]).

[15]Kevin Clinton, "The Mysteries of Demeter and Kore," in *A Companion to Greek Religion*, ed. Daniel Ogden (Malden, MA: Blackwell, 2007), p. 344. Note also Plutarch's description of the Eleusinian mysteries: "He who has succeeded in getting inside, and <u>has seen a great light</u>, as though a shrine were opened, adopts another bearing of silence and amazement." *Progress in Virtue* 10, in *Plutarch's Moralia*, vol. 1, trans. Frank C. Babbitt, Loeb Classical Library (Cambridge, MA: Harvard University Press, 1927).

[16]Aristophanes, *The Frogs* 312-13, 340-55, 445; Clement, *Exhortation to the Heathen* 2.

[17]Kevin Clinton, "Stages of Initiation in the Eleusinian and Samothracian Mysteries" in *Greek Mysteries: The Archaeology and Ritual of Ancient Greek Secret Cults*, ed. Michael B. Cosmopoulos (New York: Routledge, 2003), p. 50.

Zeus to display his deity in its fullness. The request killed Semele, leaving Zeus to care for the unborn child, Dionysus. Zeus kept Dionysus in his thigh until he was born. Once Dionysus came of age, he descended into Hades and rescued his mother Semele. Establishing his mystery rites throughout many regions, he imparted knowledge of winemaking and sexuality.[18]

It was believed that Dionysus was present in wine and in the raw flesh of animals. Celebrating mystery rites became so riotous and amorous that it led to the Roman senate's restrictions of portions of the Dionysiac rites and the abolition of shrines in the decree *Senatus Consultum de Bacchanalibus*. In *History of Rome*, Livy states, "From the time when the rites were held promiscuously, with men and women mixed together, and when the license offered by darkness had been added, no sort of crime, no kind of immorality, was left unattempted" (39.13).[19] Unlike other mystery religions, the Dionysiac mystery was not confined to a particular city or region but was spread throughout the empire (Livy, *History of Rome* 39.15). Naturally, its popularity in the empire translated into less secrecy, as even children were admitted into the Bacchic mysteries. Not only were the rites deemed less secret, the term *mystery* was applied more generally to their dancing and dramatic reenactments, both of which were performed publicly.[20]

As mentioned above, experience formed an integral aspect of the mystery religions, particularly in the Bacchic mysteries. Euripides appears to be hinting at this phenomenon when he says, "Blesséd are those who know the mysteries of god. Blesséd is he who hallows his life in the worship of god . . . who is one with those who belong to the holy body of god" (*Bacchae* 72-75).[21]

Though more open than the mysteries at Eleusis, the mysteries of Dionysus still maintained a level of secrecy toward outsiders; only those properly initiated were given access to the cult's innermost secrets. An example of this occurs in Euripides *Bacchae* 467-75:

---

[18]Euripides, *Bacchae* 15-19, says, "There I [Dionysus] taught my dances to the feet of the living men, establishing my mysteries and rites that I might be revealed on earth for what I am." *Euripides, vol. 5*, trans. William Arrowsmith (Chicago: University of Chicago Press, 1959).

[19]*Livy: Rome and the Mediterranean*, trans. Henry Bettenson (New York: Penguin, 1976).

[20]Ferguson, *Backgrounds of Early Christianity*, p. 263.

[21]Susan Guettel Cole agrees: "The first Bacchic experience is induced by willing participation in *teletai* and *orgia*, where the worshiper yields to union with Dionysus and achieves simultaneous spiritual community with the Bacchic group" (*thiaseutai psukhan*: Euripedes, *Bacchae*, 75). "Finding Dionysus" in *A Companion to Greek Religion*, ed. Daniel Ogden (Malden, MA: Blackwell, 2007), p. 330.

Dionysus: He gave me his rites.

Pentheus: What form do they take, these mysteries of yours?

Dionysus: It is forbidden to tell the uninitiated . . . our mysteries abhor an unbelieving man.

THE BIBLICAL MYSTERY AND THE MYSTERY RELIGIONS

Those who determined that the New Testament's conception of mystery, particularly Paul's, was deeply indebted to the pagan mystery religions were overly confident and going in the wrong direction. The biblical conception of mystery not only differs from the mystery religions, but also contradicts the pagan understanding of the term and concept in many ways. The following brief discussion attempts to bring together these two perspectives and offers some conclusions regarding their relationship.

In one respect, the closest the New Testament mystery resembles its pagan counterpart is in the phenomenon of secrecy or, to use biblical parlance, "hiddenness." In the pagan mystery religions, "mystery" (*mystērion*) largely entails knowledge and performance of secret rites to which only the initiates are privy. These "secrets" (*mystēria*) were revealed by the deity to humankind for a variety of purposes. And, above all, these secrets were to remain a secret from the outsiders. As mentioned above, our relative lack of knowledge of the mysteries stems from the sworn secrecy of the participants; the initiates took their secrets quite literally to the grave.

When we examine the "secret" or "hidden" nature of the biblical mystery, we discover a different phenomenon. When discussing hiddenness or "secrecy" in our survey of mystery in the previous chapters, we have differentiated two types: temporary and permanent hiddenness. The former, temporary hiddenness, differs vastly from the pagan conception of mystery. Arising out of the book of Daniel, the biblical mystery encompasses particular aspects of redemptive history, particularly events related to the "latter days" (e.g., the nature of the kingdom, Jesus as Son of Man and Messiah). This end-time dimension of mystery stands in stark contrast to the hiddenness of mystery in the pagan religions, which focuses on myths about deities and on personal experience of some mysterious reality. According to the notion of temporary hiddenness, a revelation is hidden from the believing community and later revealed to it or to a later generation of that community.

Permanent hiddenness, on the other hand, somewhat resembles the mystery religions. In the pagan mysteries, the sacred rites performed by the initiates were meant to be "hidden" or secretly guarded from outsiders—those who lacked initiation. In this way, the element of secrecy permeated the mystery religions, and the term *mystery (mystērion)* was used to refer to this aspect of secrecy. Though not as explicit or as common, the biblical mystery includes similar phenomena.[22] Throughout Daniel's narrative, mystery is largely veiled from Nebuchadnezzar (Dan 2; 4) in which he is unable to offer a complete interpretation of the dream and apparently never seems to grasp even the redemptive-historical significance for himself of Daniel's revelation about his dreams.[23] The Babylonian wise men are puzzled by Nebuchadnezzar's dreams. Compare Belshazzar's feeble attempt to interpret the writing on the wall by summoning his wisest advisors in Daniel 5. Qumran and other areas of Judaism also attest to this characteristic of permanent blindness to God's mysteries among the unbelieving, and its presence is also felt in the Synoptics and the Pauline corpus. Those without eyes to see—that is, hardened unbelievers— simply lack the ability ever to perceive mysteries (e.g., Mt 13:10-15 and par.; 1 Cor 2:6-9).

Conceptually the mystery religions and the biblical mystery overlap with respect to "permanent hiddenness." In both cases "mysteries" are unable to be grasped by "outsiders" or unbelievers. But herein seems to be the difference between the two: the mystery religions attempted to maintain absolute secrecy, whereas the New Testament encourages *all* individuals to understand the mystery, even though only those who have received God's Spirit can understand the mystery in its salvific fullness.[24]

In this vein, one of the greatest differences between the biblical and pagan conceptions of mystery pertains to the promulgation of the biblical mystery. In one sense, it was good for a mystery religion to flourish, to become more popular among the populace. This popularized deities and their myths, spawning more believers and worshipers. One need only study briefly the

---

[22]See pp. 60-64.

[23]In the Daniel 4 narrative, even after Nebuchadnezzar was judged for not heeding Daniel's revelation and returned to his senses and praised God, it is apparent that he did not become a true believer in Daniel's God. See G. K. Beale, *The Book of Revelation: A Commentary on the Greek Text,* NIGTC (Grand Rapids: Eerdmans, 1998), pp. 751-54.

[24]The New Testament explicitly states that only those who have the Spirit are able to grasp the mystery (e.g., 1 Cor 2:6-16), but this does not lessen the evangelistic thrust of the biblical mystery to the unbelieving who do not have the Spirit.

religion of Dionysus to grasp this concept. We even have evidence that certain celebrations of Dionysus were demonstrated publicly. Nevertheless, all mystery religions were to some degree private affairs designed to keep the general public at a distance. This explains why those desiring to become part of the cult had to become "initiated," a process that could take well over a year. The deeper the initiation, the greater the enlightenment of the cult's secret rites and rituals.

The biblical mystery could not be more different. Paul often speaks of his proclamation of mysteries to his audience and even asks prayer that he may continue to do so.[25] For example, 1 Corinthians 2:1 says, "When I came to you, brethren, I did not come with superiority of speech or of wisdom, proclaiming to you the mystery of God" (see also 1 Cor 15:51). And in Ephesians 6:19, Paul requests, "*Pray* on my behalf, that utterance may be given to me in the opening of my mouth, to make known with boldness the mystery of the gospel" (see Eph 3:10; Col 4:3). This characteristic plays no small role in the Pauline texts and differs markedly from the mystery religions. The pagan mysteries prided themselves on selectivity, secrecy and enigmatic rituals. In contrast, the early church was impassioned with a desire to tell all people about the mysteries God had revealed to them. Barker agrees with this assessment when he states, "The content of the Hellenistic mystery had to be carefully hidden lest it fall into unworthy hands. In the Christian mystery the revelation is freely proclaimed to the whole world, for even where it is most openly displayed it remains unknown apart from the grace of God."[26]

Another key characteristic of the pagan conception of mystery is the emphasis on experience. Through rituals, initiates looked for a special bond with one another and with the deity. As noted above, Aristotle's comments as presented by Synesius (*Dio* 7) are telling: "Men being initiated have not a lesson to learn, but an experience to undergo and a condition into which they must be brought, while they are becoming fit (for revelation)."[27] This explains why the mystery religions are filled with rituals, dances, singing, feasting and in some cases amorous behavior. What links each of these characteristics is the initiates'

---

[25]A. E. Harvey makes a similar observation when he states, "When, therefore, we find the same juxtaposition of 'mystery' and 'revealing' in Paul we may say that *mystērion* in this instance could not have carried any allusion to a Greek mystery-metaphor, and could have been understood only in terms of *raz*" from the Old Testament. "The Use of Mystery Language in the Bible," *JTS* 31 (1980): 330.
[26]G. W. Barker, "Mystery," in *ISBE* 3:452.
[27]Translation from Fitzgerald, *Letters of Synesius of Cyrene.*

desire to experience the deity in one form or another; they are seeking above all else a special bond with the divine.

The biblical mystery, on the other hand, again stands in contrast to this model. It would not be a stretch to claim that what experience is to the mystery religions, knowledge is to the biblical mystery. Central to mystery in the Old Testament and New Testament is *revealed knowledge*. Though the mystery religions use the term *mystery* in a variety of ways (rites, dancing, singing, etc.), revealed knowledge does indeed play a key role in their understanding of mystery.[28] The deities, it was conceived, revealed to mortal humans secret rites and rituals. The term *mystery* itself certainly captures this phenomenon. The biblical mystery, however, is even more concerned with revealed knowledge. This explains why words such as *reveal, make known* and the like are commonly associated with mystery in the book of Daniel and the New Testament. For example, "There is a God in heaven who reveals mysteries, and he has made known to King Nebuchadnezzar what will take place in the latter days" (Dan 2:28; cf. 2:19, 30); "your God is a God of gods and a Lord of kings and a revealer of mysteries, since you have been able to reveal this mystery" (Dan 2:47); "revelation of the mystery which has been kept secret for long ages past" (Rom 16:25); "by revelation there was made known to me the mystery" (Eph 3:3; cf. Eph 3:9-10; Col 1:26). Therefore, the primary role experience plays in the biblical mystery is the experience of the revelation of the mystery, which comes through the Spirit. Experience certainly plays a role in the biblical conception of mystery in that the believer's life and actions are to be affected by the knowledge of the mystery. There is thus a different emphasis on knowledge and experience between the pagan and biblical conceptions of mystery.

Not only does the *function* of revelation have a different emphasis in contrast to the concept of revelation in the pagan mysteries, but the *content* of the biblical mystery also serves as a contrast. The biblical conception of mystery is marked by its content; as we have briefly seen above, it is a revelation of the meaning of a historical event related to the latter days. The content of the mystery religions mostly concerns pagan rituals and knowledge about the myth of the deity or some truth about his existence. For example, in Euripides, *The Bacchae*, Dionysus tells of his trip to Asia Minor: "There I [Dionysus] taught my dances to the feet of living men, establishing mysteries and rites

---

[28]See, e.g., Arthur Darby Nock, "Mysterion," *HSCP* 60 (1951): 201-4.

that I might be revealed on earth for what I am: a god" (16-19).[29] As we have seen, since the pagan mysteries were marked by extreme secrecy, it remains difficult to determine the precise content of their rites. Nevertheless, we can readily surmise that, based on the available texts and the evidence from the church fathers, the mystery religions, at the core of which were myths, clearly lacked the historical rootedness and eschatological content that is so pervasive in the biblical mystery.

The biblical concept of mystery, as we have argued in this book and elsewhere, originates in the book of Daniel.[30] In our discussion of mystery in Daniel, we defined the term as an end-time revelation about an event(s) that was partially hidden but has now been fully revealed. The eschatological tenor of the Danielic mystery can hardly go unnoticed, as we attempted to connect the term with the arrival of the end-time kingdom throughout the book of Daniel (e.g., Dan 2; 4; 5). Early Judaism and the New Testament, often in dependence on Daniel, explicitly demonstrate that mystery concerns the unveiling of matters related to the "latter days." Matthew, for example, claims that the "mysteries of the kingdom" are the unique and unexpected arrival of the end-time kingdom as prophesied in the Old Testament (Mt 13 and par.). Even Paul's use of *mystery* coincides with these usages: he argues in 1 Corinthians 1–2 that the Messiah ruling in the midst of suffering constitutes the mystery. Rehearsing each occurrence of mystery is not necessary, but it ought to be readily apparent that the content of the biblical mystery differs greatly from the pagan mysteries. Eschatological and redemptive-historical content drives the former, whereas the latter is motivated by experience and ritual based on myth.

A Polemic Against the Pagan Mysteries?

In light of our brief discussion, it appears that the biblical mystery does not have much in common with the pagan mysteries. Those who argued early on that the New Testament is much indebted to the mystery religions seem to have succumbed to what scholars call "parallelomania"—that is, detecting extraneous and general parallels between two texts. Drawing mere general parallels, which often are superficial, is not sufficient enough to establish dependence.[31]

---

[29]Translation from *The Complete Greek Tragedies, Euripides V*, ed. Mark Griffith and Glenn W. Most, trans. William Arrowsmith (Chicago: University of Chicago Press, 2013).
[30]See pp. 29-43.
[31]S. Sandmel, "Parallelomania," *JBL* 81 (1962): 1-13.

Nevertheless, we must admit that the mystery religions flourished in the first century A.D., particularly in Asia Minor and Italy. In all likelihood, early Christianity brushed up against the pagan mysteries; we have ample evidence that the church fathers engaged the mystery religions. Some kind of a relationship between the New Testament and the mystery religions may well have existed to some degree, even if implicitly so.

Instead of contending that the New Testament's conception of mystery *originates* from the mystery religions, as many older New Testament scholars maintained, perhaps there remains another way of examining this relationship. Is it possible that the New Testament's conception of mystery functions as a polemic against the pagan mysteries, albeit subtly? For example, it may not be a coincidence that the mystery religions and the biblical mystery highlight grasping or "seeing" the mystery. Only the individual who has passed through the proper steps of initiation is enabled to comprehend deep "mysteries" in the Greek cults. Even the term *mystery* (*mystērion*) and the verb *to close* (*myeō*) suggest a metaphorical dimension of the pagan mysteries: the individual's eyes are "closed" or "shut" from the truth. Initiation into the mysteries largely entails the removal of such blindness. For example, we cited a relevant passage above from the *Homeric Hymn to Demeter*: "Blessed of earthbound men is he who <u>has seen</u> these things, but who dies without fulfilling the holy things . . . [and who] has no claim ever on such blessings, even when departed down to the moldy darkness" (lines 480-84).[32] Throughout this study, we have noticed a prominent pattern emerging in early Judaism and the New Testament: mystery is often found in conjunction with "seeing" and "hearing." This theme is so prevalent in the material that we have attempted to highlight it throughout this project. A text from a Jewish sect, for example, says, "For from the source of his knowledge he has disclosed his light, and my <u>eyes have observed</u> his wonders, and the light of my heart <u>the mystery of existence</u>" (1QS XI, 3). The prominence of this theme in the biblical and Jewish literature and the mystery religions deserves to be thoughtfully analyzed. In both some are enlightened but others remain in the dark. It may not be a matter of coincidence that the New Testament uses this language when discussing mysteries.

The apostle Paul spent decades evangelizing Gentiles in their pagan environment, and he must have engaged many who had knowledge of the mystery

---

[32]Translation from Rice and Stambaugh, *Greek Religion*.

religions. We know that Paul had knowledge of local religious customs (Acts 17:16-34), so it is probably not a stretch to surmise that he had some familiarity with the major mystery religions. The pagan mysteries not only existed in the same cities and at the same time that Paul ministered, but they also exercised a considerable amount of influence in the local culture to one degree or another.[33]

In 1 Corinthians 4:1, Paul claims that he is a "steward of God's mysteries." The force of that statement must be brought to bear on this discussion. Paul thought it necessary that he remain "faithful" (1 Cor 4:2) in the proclamation of mysteries to the Gentiles at Corinth (and elsewhere). Perhaps combating the false pagan mysteries was part of Paul's apostleship. Paul, in other words, could be claiming, "You have heard about the secret and pagan mysteries, but I am proclaiming the *true* mysteries of God." The worshipers and cult leaders of the mystery religions believed that their deities had revealed to them special mysteries, but the New Testament claims that only the God of the Bible has revealed true mysteries. Harvey seems to be pursuing this line of thought when he claims, "Even if all the instances of *mystērion* ["mystery"] can be 'explained' in terms of *raz* [the Aramaic word for "mystery" from Daniel], it does not follow that the writer did not intend, and the reader did not pick up, some echo of the Greek mystery-metaphor."[34] We therefore must reckon with the possibility that the biblical mystery may to some degree engage the local religious culture.[35] We only suggest this as a possible avenue to explore further, since the limits of the present work do not allow space for pursuing it here.

Articulating the relationship between the mystery religions and the biblical mystery in this manner, to our knowledge, has not yet been done in much detail. Room could remain for further studies attempting to tease out this delicate relationship. Instead of suggesting how the mystery religions shaped Paul's gospel, perhaps we need to determine how the biblical mystery addresses the pagan mysteries.

---

[33]See Michael B. Cosmopoulos, ed., *Greek Mysteries: The Archaeology and Rituals of Ancient Greek Secret Cults* (New York: Routledge, 2003).

[34]Harvey, "Mystery Language," p. 331.

[35]See also C. E. Arnold, *The Colossian Syncretisim: The Interface between Christianity and Folk Belief at Colossae*, WUNT 77 (Tübingen: Mohr Siebeck, 1995; repr., Grand Rapids: Baker, 1996), pp. 271-74, who suggests that Paul may be conducting a polemic against the local mystery religions in his use of the genuine mystery that derives ultimately from Daniel.

CONCLUSION

In this brief discussion of the mystery religions and their relationship to the biblical mystery, we have attempted to bring some fresh thoughts to the debate. Once we have properly grasped the biblical "mystery," we can then compare and contrast it with our knowledge of the pagan mysteries (what little we have). The mystery religions, though considerably diverse, are marked by extreme secrecy, whereby only the initiates are permitted access. The term *mystery* (*mystērion*) and the verb *to close* (*myeō*) may be taken literally and figuratively. We also noted the emphasis on experience. Certainly knowledge of myths, rituals and rites played a key role, but experience with the deity in some form or another was ultimately the goal. We then gave two examples of prominent mystery religions: the mysteries of Eleusis and Dionysus.

Comparing the biblical mystery and the pagan mystery proved helpful in that conceptually they do not have a lot in common. Perhaps the greatest positive parallel lies in their common emphasis on secrecy. The pagan mysteries underscore the need for absolute secrecy; mythical rituals and rites must remain sealed from outsiders. Somewhat similar is what we have termed "temporary hiddenness" concerning the biblical mystery. There is a sense in which "outsiders" or unbelievers cannot grasp the mystery apart from the Spirit's work. And then, under the influence of the Spirit, those who believe understand the revealed mystery. The biblical conception of mystery, however, has a strong public, evangelistic component in contrast to the pagan mystery cults. The apostles felt obligated to teach the divine mysteries to as many as would lend an ear. In addition, experiencing the deity through a variety of means is uppermost in mind in many of the pagan mysteries. The biblical mystery, however, places much more emphasis on *knowledge* about end-time events that had transpired with the coming of Christ and the Spirit. The apostles communicated certain eschatological truths, some truths that were hidden but now had been revealed to the church.

Finally, we argued that a relationship between the pagan religions and the biblical mystery could exist. We contend, though, that the biblical mystery is not in any way *dependent* on its pagan counterpart, but it might address and confront the pagan conception of mystery. Perhaps Paul uses *mystery* to correct the aberrant teaching of local religions from which some in his congregation converted. We will probably never know precisely how the biblical mystery intersects with the pagan idea, but the time is ripe to approach the problem from a different angle.

13

Conclusion

Writing a biblical theology on a particular topic naturally includes synthesis and categorization. When we approach the New Testament's use of *mystery* from a bird's eye view, we immediately begin to detect patterns and common denominators between texts. Scholars have mostly done this kind of work on linguistic level and to some degree on a synthetic level.[1] A central problem with previous analyses of *mystery* is that they are either too brief or restrictive. Rarely has anyone attempted a thorough and comprehensive study of the term. Partly this is due to project restraints (essays are often found in dictionaries), but most often authors choose to limit their research to one book (e.g., 1 Corinthians, Ephesians) or a corpus (Paul's writings). It is something of a rarity to synthesize the New Testament themes that touch on mystery from Matthew to Revelation. What follows here is our attempt to tie together seemingly disparate strings and offer some reflections of the material. Though some may disagree with our conclusions and synthesis, it cannot be denied that the New Testament contains remarkably similar patterns as it uses the term *mystery* and related concepts.

Once we sketch some of these patterns, we will then unpack the significance of mystery as it relates to the broader field of the use of the Old Testament in the New Testament. When the New Testament authors use the Old Testament in unusual or creative ways, do these same New Testament writers perceive that

---

[1]See, for example, D. Deden, "Le 'Mystère' paulinien," *ETL* 13 (1936): 405-42; Raymond Brown, *The Semitic Background of the Term "Mystery" in the New Testament*, BS 21 (Philadelphia: Fortress, 1968); Chrys Caragounis, *The Ephesian Mysterion: Meaning and Content*, ConBNT 8 (Lund: Gleerup, 1977); Markus Bockmuehl, *Revelation and Mystery in Ancient Judaism and Pauline Christianity*, WUNT 36 (Tübingen: Mohr Siebeck, 1990; repr., Grand Rapids: Eerdmans, 1997).

meaning in the Old Testament passage or are they creating a radically new idea that cannot be found in the Old Testament? Is there a complete discontinuity between what Old Testament authors meant and how New Testament writers use the same Old Testament texts? Or, even when the New Testament gives a surprising interpretation of an Old Testament passage, are there any roots, however small, in the Old Testament text that could have given rise to the New Testament development?

THE REVEALED MYSTERY OF THE OLD TESTAMENT AND THE PERSON OF CHRIST

With the exception of a few occurrences, the revealed mystery is in some form or another linked to Old Testament references and bound up with the person of Christ. The unveiled mystery according to the New Testament is inextricably tethered to Christ and his work. Drilling down a bit further, we discover that particular aspects of Christ's work are often repeated across the New Testament literature as they pertain to mystery. We will now recount how the person of Christ is wedded to several New Testament passages that we have discussed in this project and how this is related to the Old Testament.

We noted that Matthew portrays the nature of the kingdom as a mystery, and we concluded that this entails the surprising arrival of the already-and-not-yet end-time kingdom. Jesus' teaching is unique in that he claims the kingdom and those within it unexpectedly coexist with pagan empires and wickedness (Mt 13:11 and parallel). Strangely, the kingdom is mysteriously marked by suffering and death, not outwardly by victory and success. Not only does the nature of the kingdom function along these paradoxical lines, but so also does Jesus' ministry. All four Gospels, in some capacity, portray Jesus as a suffering Messiah. Jesus' ministry and destiny are bound up with and run parallel to the nature of his "mysterious" kingdom. In other words, Jesus embodies the mystery of the kingdom—the kingdom of God in its triumph and tribulation are principally fused together and expressed at the cross. We saw that the revelation of this mystery, while seemingly unexpected, had Old Testament roots, tiny though they may have been.

According to Romans, there are two stages of the fulfillment of Jewish and Gentile redemption, something not clearly foreseen by the Old Testament. The first stage was an initial salvation of Jews being the majority of the redeemed, followed by Gentiles. Within this first stage Christ plays a prominent role, as he is the beginning of Jewish restoration. During the second, longer stage the majority of the saved would be Gentiles, which would spark off a remnant of Jews being saved. This is a mystery because such an explicit chronological two-stage salvation cannot be found in the Old Testament. We saw how Deuteronomy 32:21 (quoted in Rom 10:19 and alluded to in Rom 11:11, 13-14) may play a role in the sequence of Israel's salvation. Paul read Deuteronomy 27–32 as broadly prophesying Israel's disobedience, hardening and judgment, with covenantal favor being given to the Gentiles, and Israel subsequently being provoked to jealousy by such Gentile favor, with all of this finally leading to Israel's redemption. Why was it a "mystery"? Because the notion of "Gentile first then Jew" is not as clearly expressed in Deuteronomy, and everywhere else in the Old Testament, Israel's salvation is the catalyst for Gentile salvation (e.g., Is 49:5-6).

In a sense, *mystery* in 1 Corinthians 1–2 picks up where Matthew leaves off: at the cross, Jesus executes his messianic reign while at the same time undergoing defeat and shame. First Corinthians 1–2 overwhelmingly focuses on God's hidden wisdom of the cross and how believers can grasp that truth. The idea of ruling in the very midst of defeat and weakness was virtually unknown in the Old Testament, though we saw that there are some hints about this idea. At the end of the epistle in 1 Corinthians 15:51, Paul relates a revealed mystery as it pertains to the believers' resurrection and their identification with Christ and his new creational body. What is this mystery in 1 Corinthians 15:51? What the Old Testament does not teach is that those living at the very end of time will also experience a bodily transformation into a new creational, resurrected being (perhaps the rapture of Enoch and Elijah implied such a thing). And it would seem to make sense that those saints living at the time of the final resurrection of the dead would also need for their bodies to undergo an everlasting transformation fit for living an eternal new creation. This Paul also brings out more clearly. Unlike the Old Testament, many pockets of Judaism portray the resurrection as transformation, particularly as a return to the pre-fall Adamic state. But Paul differs even from his Jewish counterparts in that he views the resurrection not as a return to Adam's pre-fall state but as a transformation into an escalated Adamic condition. The notion that the first Adam, in connection with other heightened blessings, would have experienced an escalated eschatological blessing of such a transformation may be hinted at in Genesis 1–3, but now Paul makes this explicit. Even in this occurrence of *mystery*, Paul's end-time revelation is anchored in the person of Christ and his resurrected state (see 1 Cor 15:45-50).

Ephesians highlights Christ's relationship to mystery probably more than any other New Testament book. We observed three aspects of mystery in Ephesians 1:9: the scope, manner and result of Christ's cosmic rule, which were not clearly foreseen in the Old Testament. The scope of the mystery is Christ's rule over the cosmos; the manner of Christ's rule pertains to his death as the means to achieving his rule; and the result of Christ's rule includes the cosmic unity of "all things" in Christ, whether spiritual or physical, which is the main focus of the mystery of Ephesians 1. The mystery in Ephesians 3 includes the manner in which these two groups become true Israel through Christ (Eph 3:3, 9). By attaching themselves to Christ, who is true Israel, Gentiles become part of the covenant community without needing to identify with the nationalistic tags of Israel's old law. Such an idea did not have any clear precedent in the Old Testament. The divulged mystery in Ephesians 5 is bound up with Genesis 2:24. Paul reads Genesis 2:24 and surmises that the text is speaking of the union between Christ and the church. We observed how Genesis 2:24 plays a pivotal role in the Israelite conception of marriage and the prominence of the marriage metaphor used to portray the relationship between God and Israel. The mystery in Ephesians 5 refers to Paul's perception that Adam and Eve's union in marriage typologically corresponds to the Messiah and the church. Such a typology was certainly not plainly understood from the perspective of Genesis 2:24 or anywhere else in the Old Testament.

In the book of Colossians we discovered a similar thread to that of Ephesians 3: Christ's rule and his relationship to Jews and Gentiles. The allusion to Daniel 2 coupled with the mention of the "Messiah" leads us to the conclusion that the mystery refers to Israel's theocratic kingdom that was thoroughly transformed in Christ, continuing only in the sphere of the end-time, Israelite messianic king himself. Another aspect of mystery in Colossians 1:26-27 pertains to the relationship between Jews and Gentiles. Since Gentiles have joined themselves to Christ, who is true Israel, they naturally participate in the covenant community through faith alone, which entails the same revealed mystery noted above in Ephesians 3.

In Colossians 2:2-3, Paul makes the staggering claim that in Christ "are hidden all the treasures of wisdom and knowledge." Once again Paul calls to mind Daniel 2, but in this particular instance he focuses on Daniel 2. This is a "mysterious" fulfillment of Daniel's prophecy because it was not as clear in the Old Testament nor especially in Daniel 2 that Israel's prophesied theocratic kingdom would find its fulfillment and continuation only in the sphere of the end-time, Israelite messianic king himself and those whom he represented (though the parallel in Daniel 7 may to some degree anticipate this reality). Furthermore, this idea may also have partial roots in the Old Testament, where Israelite kings represented the nation (that is, their actions were seen to be representative for the actions of the nation), which appears to be true of the coming messianic Servant himself (e.g., Is 49:1-6).

Also, part of the mystery in Colossians 2 is that while the epitome of God's revelation of wisdom in the Old Testament was the law, now the zenith of God's revelation in the new age is the Messiah himself, God's end-time wisdom. This is a notion not apparent from the Old Testament standpoint, though it may have a faint but nevertheless real precedent in early Judaism, where Wisdom was not only personified but *appears* sometimes even to represent an independent being next to God's side. At the least, Judaism personified God's attributes such as wisdom to explain how a transcendent God related to a fallen world. Early Judaism itself was likely interpreting such texts as Proverbs 8:24-31, which refers to the law and personifies it as God's wisdom, which existed along with God at the beginning of creation. Paul may have been influenced by Judaism to interpret Old Testament wisdom in a similar way but to apply it to Christ as true wisdom, or he may merely have done something similar independently.[2] What was a personification in the Old Testament Jewish tradition becomes personally incarnate in Christ. In this respect, Colossians 2:2-3 is likely developing the earlier portrayal of Christ as Wisdom in Colossians 1:15-17. Now believers do not have to identify with the nationalistic signs of Israel's law (the epitome of God's revelatory wisdom) to become members of God's new covenant community; they need only to identify with Jesus, the grandest revelation of divine wisdom.

Rounding out the Pauline corpus, the hymn in 1 Timothy 3:16 constitutes the content of the revealed mystery. Christ's incarnation and divinity are central to the general thrust of the hymn. The Old Testament and early Judaism did not develop in great detail the arrival of a divine, preexistent messiah. We are simply left with a few Old Testament texts that point us in that direction. But by and large, the New Testament connects Jesus' life, mission and identity with

---

[2]For a summary of the Old Testament and Jewish background for Paul's understanding of Christ as wisdom in Col 1:15-17, see Douglas J. Moo, *The Letters to the Colossians and Philemon,* PNTC (Grand Rapids: Eerdmans, 2008), pp. 111-13, 118-20.

that of Israel's God in the Old Testament. We also concluded that Christ's new-creational state of existence constitutes part of the unveiled mystery in 1 Timothy 3:16. The emphasis of the spatial polarity in the hymn between earth and heaven along with the contrast between "flesh" and "Spirit" lend sufficient evidence to suggest that end-time transformation plays a role in the hymn. It was not apparent in the Old Testament that the Messiah would first become identified with God in an old age body that would then be transformed into a new creational, incorruptible body.

Revelation uses *mystery* four times. The first (Rev 1:20) refers to the interpretation of the "stars" in Christ's hand and the lampstands among which he is walking. They are respectively angels and the churches. The churches as lampstands have become part of the end-time temple, though weak and apparently unstable, whereas the Old Testament predicted a huge architecturally stable temple. The mystery of Revelation 1:20 also includes the church as part of Christ's kingdom, despite the fact that they were suffering defeat while being in that kingdom. We argued that these unexpected realities of the church as the temple and part of the kingdom nevertheless had some implied antecedents in the Old Testament. Similarly, the mystery in Revelation 10:7 focused also on how the church overcomes its enemies through being defeated physically by those enemies. Both of these realities have their basis in Christ and how he became the temple and achieved his kingship. Finally, Revelation 17:5, 7 uses *mystery* to explain the coming defeat of Babylon the Great (the social-economic-religious aspect of the world) by her former political allies, something not apparent from the Old Testament perspective.

In light of this brief survey, it is clear that the majority of occurrences of *mystery* in the New Testament pertain to Christ in some form or another. The aforementioned themes related to mystery are not peripheral or secondary matters contained in the New Testament but are central to the basic message of the New Testament. This list includes the end-time kingdom, the rule of Christ, crucifixion, resurrection, the relationship between Jew and Gentile, and Christ's incarnation. The importance of the New Testament's conception of these themes is obvious, but what has previously gone relatively unnoticed is the relationship between mystery and Christ's person and work. Not only is mystery tethered to these themes, but Christ stands at the very center of their content.

In addition to their relationship with Christ, these salient concepts roughly fall into two categories—the arrival of the end-time kingdom and the unity between Jews and Gentiles. The unexpected nature of the kingdom, particularly as it relates to the crucifixion, is a theme that spans much of the New Testament, and we have seen this developed in the Synoptics, 1 Corinthians, Ephesians and Revelation. The sociological dimension of mystery—that is, the relationship between Jews and Gentiles—occupies a central role in Ephesians and Colossians. Perhaps we could synthesize the New Testament data (as it pertains to mystery) as follows: Now that Christ has come, God rules and reigns over the covenant community in an unanticipated manner. Unexpectedly, believers reign with Christ through suffering and death, just as he ironically reigned through suffering and death. On the other hand, Christ reconstituted how Jews and Gentiles relate to one another. Both groups have been brought together in Christ and enjoy complete access to the covenant community without adhering to the distinguishing signs of Israel's old law. Since Christ is true Israel, both parties are likewise deemed true Israel. All of these things, to say the least, were not transparent from an Old Testament viewpoint.

Perhaps the reason why these two themes, the latter-day kingdom and Jew and Gentile relations, are paired in a few instances (Ephesians, Colossians) is due to their natural theological overlap. Jews and Gentiles, as God's covenant community, fully participate in God's kingdom; both concepts are organically related. Jews and Gentiles are joined together in Christ and likewise participate in his paradoxical rule over the kingdom.

MYSTERY OF THE CROSS AND CRUCIFORM LIFESTYLE

On systematically working through each occurrence of *mystery* in the New Testament, another theme soon gained prominence in our investigation—ruling in the midst of suffering. Its popularity is evident in numerous texts, spanning many New Testament books and genres (Synoptics, Pauline literature, Revelation). Scholars have noticed the importance of this theme in the individual New Testament books, but few have attempted a synthesis,[3] and still fewer have correlated it with the concept of mystery.

We saw how according to Matthew Jesus uses the phrase "mysteries of the kingdom" as a reference to the paradoxical nature of the kingdom. According to the Old Testament and Judaism, one of the main tenants of the latter-day kingdom is the *consummate* establishment of God's kingdom preceded by the ultimate de-

---

[3]See, though, Michael Gorman, *Cruciformity: Paul's Narrative Spirituality of the Cross* (Grand Rapids: Eerdmans, 2001).

struction of unrighteousness and foreign oppression. The advent of the Messiah would signal the death knell of evil empires. Pagan kings and their kingdoms were to be destroyed or "crushed" (Dan 2:44), but Jesus claims that the advent of the Messiah and the latter-day kingdom does not translate into a complete annihilation of wickedness. Paradoxically, two realms coexist—those who belong to the kingdom and those who belong to the "evil one." The eschatological kingdom in a very real sense has begun through Jesus. Jesus' defeat of the devil during his wilderness temptation is nothing short of the beginning fulfillment of Old Testament promises that portray God annihilating Israel's enemy through his Messiah. The presence of the end-time kingdom mysteriously involves suffering, persecution and tribulation. The Old Testament seems to anticipate some form of overlap of suffering and kingdom (e.g., King David's experiences, the Son of Man and his suffering in Dan 7), but it was not clear how these two themes precisely relate.

This may be why Jesus spends a fair amount of energy discussing the inevitable persecution of kingdom citizens (e.g., Mt 5:10-11; 10:23). Importantly, Jesus' ministry and eventual death embody his teaching on the "mysteries of the kingdom." He too as messianic king was persecuted and eventually killed. Jesus embodied the overlap of the ages—the arrival of the kingdom and the simultaneous presence of tribulation—during his earthly ministry and then on the cross. He was king during his ministry of weakness and at the moment of suffering and death. The Synoptics encourage the reader to connect the dots by showing them how the fate of the Messiah is bound up with that of the kingdom. John, on the other hand, is far more explicit in this regard. In John's Gospel, the theme of being "lifted up" is a double entendre—it literally refers to the lifting up of Jesus on the cross and figuratively to his exaltation or "lifting up" (Jn 3:14; 8:28; 12:32).

Not until we arrive at 1 Corinthians is the cross explicitly labeled a revealed "mystery." According to 1 Corinthians 2, the unveiled mystery is the exalted, kingly Messiah affixed to the cross. While Jesus is suffering a shameful death on the cross, he is simultaneously the supreme ruler. Seyoon Kim agrees: "The cross is the ground of boasting for the Christian because it is the cross of the *Lord* . . . who has triumphed over the world and its rulers precisely on that cross. . . . The cross which is a sign of defeat and shame, foolishness and scandal for those who are perishing in the world, is a sign of triumph and boasting, wisdom and glory for those who are called."[4]

---

[4]Seyoon Kim, *The Origin of Paul's Gospel*, WUNT 4 (Tübingen: Mohr Siebeck, 1981; repr., Grand Rapids: Eerdmans, 1981), pp. 80-81.

The theme of power and victory in the midst of suffering—the mystery of the cross—is significant to Paul's theology and apostolic ministry. In a very real sense Paul too performed the mystery of the cross. Though the concept of divine power through human suffering pertaining to Paul's ministry is indeed found in much of the Pauline corpus, 2 Corinthians highlights this notion more pointedly than any other epistle. Unlike his opponents at Corinth, Paul attempts to justify his apostolic status by embracing and imitating Jesus' suffering on the cross, through which God expressed his power. Only true apostles conduct themselves in accordance with the wisdom of the cross (e.g., 2 Cor 4:10-11; 12:9).

Not only does the mystery of the cross extend from Jesus to Paul and the apostles, it carries over to all believers (we also saw this in Jesus' teaching). The book of Revelation is perhaps the most explicit in this regard. John, in Revelation 1:9, goes on to describe *how* the saints participate in the end-time kingdom: "I, John, your brother and fellow-partaker in the tribulation and kingdom and perseverance in Jesus." Mystery in Revelation 1:20 not only concerns the church as the latter-day temple, it also appears to include some reference to the nature of the kingdom in which the church participates. This ironic exercise of rule is modeled on that of Christ, who revealed his veiled kingship on earth before his exaltation by enduring suffering and death in order to achieve his heavenly rule (cf. Rev 1:5). Just as Christ ruled in a veiled way through suffering, so do Christians. ✓

HERMENEUTICAL IMPLICATIONS OF THE NEW TESTAMENT USE OF THE OLD TESTAMENT

In recent years, scholars have become much more aware of how the New Testament writers use the Old Testament. Despite an avalanche of books on the topic, scholars remain divided on key hermeneutical questions. Given the restraints of this final chapter, we are unable to survey the debate, but we can offer some insight into the discussion in light of this project.[5] One fascinating implication of this book is that it addresses a few key issues in this discussion. Though the current hermeneutical debate shows no sign of abating, perhaps

---

[5]For a survey of the debate, consult G. K. Beale, ed. *The Right Doctrine from the Wrong Texts?: Essays on the Use of the Old Testament in the New* (Grand Rapids: Baker, 1994) and G. K. Beale, *Handbook on the New Testament Use of the Old Testament: Exegesis and Interpretation* (Grand Rapids: Baker Academic, 2012).

our study of the New Testament's conception of mystery can contribute to a better understanding of the issues involved.

The "hiddenness" of meaning. The link between *mystery* and the use of particular Old Testament texts is crucial here, and a few scholars have made this connection. We have seen how Judaism weds these two concepts (e.g., 1QpHab VII, 1-8 [Hab 2:2]) and how the New Testament explicitly follows suit (e.g., Eph 5:31 [Gen 2:24]). But not only are these Old Testament quotations and allusions found in the immediate context of the unveiled mystery, they also more often than not contribute to the meaning of the revealed mystery.

A proper understanding of the use of *mystery* in Daniel is helpful in understanding the New Testament use of the Old Testament. The book of Daniel demonstrates that hiddenness is essential for mystery. The term *mystery* possesses various levels of hiddenness: "The king spoke to Daniel and said, 'Truly your God is the God of Gods and the Lord of kings, the only one who reveals hidden mysteries, because you are able to disclose this mystery'" (Dan 2:47, our translation). Throughout Daniel's narrative, mystery is veiled from Nebuchadnezzar (Dan 2; 4) so that he is unable to interpret the dream. The Babylonian wise men are also puzzled by Nebuchadnezzar's dreams. The same can be said for Daniel, who, despite his inspired ability in Daniel 2, 4, fails to understand his own revelations fully in Daniel 7–12. These examples illustrate the principle that mystery is veiled to some and revealed to others, setting a pattern for later usage of the term in the New Testament. In addition, the concept of mystery refers also to the hidden nature of God's end-time plan. Again, the book of Daniel addresses this specific theme: "There is a God in heaven who reveals mysteries, and he has made known to King Nebuchadnezzar what will take place in the latter days" (Dan 2:28). Here the interpretation of the revelation, partially veiled from Nebuchadnezzar, concerns particular latter-day events.

With a proper understanding of hiddenness in mind, we are now able to better understand how New Testament authors quote the Old Testament. The "hidden" meaning of Old Testament texts most likely falls under the latter category of temporary hiddenness about the latter days. The full meaning of the Old Testament text is hidden until a later point in time when the interpretation is revealed to and understood by those who believe. A good way to understand this idea is by comparing it to a unique retail gift card. Let us say that on the back of the card, there are several numbers, partially hidden or protected by a gray strip but not completely blotted out. Only the owner of the card is lawfully permitted to scratch off that strip, revealing clearly the series of numbers. Upon scratching off the strip, numbers do not magically appear out of thin air; instead, the code is partially hidden or latent, only to be revealed fully when the grey strip is removed. The consumer may have an idea of what the number is by studying the partially revealed parts of the numbers, but the scrambled numbers become fully visible to the consumer only when he or she completely scratches off the strip.

The *full* meaning of an Old Testament text is revealed in much the same way. Full or complete meaning is indeed actually "there" in the Old Testament text; it is simply partially "hidden" or latent, awaiting a later revelation, whereby the complete meaning of the text is revealed to the interpreter. This is precisely the model of the Danielic mystery. Take, for example, Nebuchadnezzar's dreams in Daniel 2:1; 4:13-18. God revealed both dreams to Nebuchadnezzar (the initial revelation), and then God gave Daniel an inspired revelation of those dreams (final revelation). The first revelation that God gave to Nebuchadnezzar was "hidden," and Daniel was furnished with the key that unlocked the symbolic dream. Within Nebuchadnezzar's *initial* dream, the meaning that the colossus symbolizes four subsequent kingdoms and their eventual destruction is already present. The meaning of the colossus was really "there" in the dream, albeit perhaps in a scrambled or unclear manner. It was not until Daniel unlocked the message that a complete understanding of the dreams was made known. We can apply this identical model to Daniel 5 with the enigmatic writing on the wall and to Daniel's visions in Daniel 7–12. Even Daniel needed the aid of an "interpreting angel" to unlock the meaning of the visions.

With the book of Daniel in mind, we can now push a bit deeper into Nebuchadnezzar's initial knowledge of his dream in Daniel 4, which may well serve as a paradigm for understanding the problem of continuity and discontinuity between Old and New Testament revelation. According to Daniel 4:4-5, Nebuchadnezzar has another revelatory dream, prompting him once again to summon the Babylonian diviners. In contrast to Daniel 2, Nebuchadnezzar divulges to them the content of his dream: "I related the dream to them, but they could not make its interpretation known to me" (Dan 4:7). After the Babylonian wise men fail to interpret the dream, the king then tells Daniel the content of the dream (Dan 4:8). When we examine the king's dream that he related to Daniel, we discover a few relevant, hermeneutical elements.

Nebuchadnezzar not only demonstrates knowledge of his dream to Daniel, but also a partial understanding of its interpretation. The dream details the story of an enormous tree that provided food for all the animals (Dan 4:10-12). But in Daniel 4:13, the dream shifts (note the introductory formula introducing an angelic interpreter) and an angelic messenger supplements the dream and gives a partial interpretation. When the angel communicates the destruction of the tree, he interprets the tree as a *person:*

> He shouted out and spoke as follows:
> "Chop down the tree and cut off _its_ branches,
> Strip off _its_ foliage and scatter _its_ fruit;
> Let the beasts flee from under _it_
> And the birds from _its_ branches.
> Yet leave the stump with _its_ roots in the ground,
> But with a band of iron and bronze *around* _it_
> In the new grass of the field;
> And let _him_ be drenched with the dew of heaven,
> And let _him_ share with the beasts in the grass of the earth.
> Let _his_ mind be changed from *that of a* man
> And let a beast's mind be given to _him_,
> And let seven periods of time pass over _him_." (Dan 4:14-16)

Within the initial dream report that Nebuchadnezzar receives, an angel interprets the tree as a royal figure. Though the Aramaic third person pronoun remains the same throughout this passage (masculine singular), the angel clearly interprets the tree as a prominent human figure in Daniel 4:15b-16.

Not only does the king have a symbolic dream which he can recount, but he also *receives a partial interpretation of what the symbols mean within the initial dream report*. Indeed, he may even have suspected that the dream was about him. In Daniel 4:5, Nebuchadnezzar states, "I saw a dream and it made me fearful; and *these* fantasies *as I lay* on my bed and the visions in my mind kept alarming me." It is possible to understand the king's fearful reaction to the dream strictly as an effect of the bizarre dream. On the other hand, it is also very possible that the king's behavior stems from *his intuition that the dream may apply to him*. Nebuchadnezzar's dream in Daniel 4 comes on the heels of his dream in Daniel 2, whereby the eventual destruction of the Babylonian

Empire is revealed through a symbolic portrayal of the annihilation of the golden head (Dan 2:32-35). This further suggests that the king senses that this second dream was also about his demise. Moreover, within the interpretative portion of the mystery (Dan 2:36-45), Daniel describes king Nebuchadnezzar's rule much in the same way that the angel describes the cosmic tree in Daniel 4:11-12.

> You, O king, are the king of kings, to whom the God of heaven has given the kingdom, the power, the strength and the glory; and wherever the sons of men dwell, *or* the beasts of the field, or the birds of the sky, He has given *them* into your hand and has caused you to rule over them all. You are the head of gold." (Dan 2:37-38)

> The tree grew large and became strong
> And its height reached to the sky,
> And it *was* visible to the end of the whole earth.
> Its foliage *was* beautiful and its fruit abundant,
> And in it was food for all.
> The beasts of the field found shade under it,
> And the birds of the sky dwelt in its branches,
> And all living creatures fed themselves from it. (Dan 4:11-12)

The strong connection between Daniel 2 and 4 is well documented, and if this connection is valid, then the king most likely believed that his vision of the cosmic tree somehow involved himself, even before Daniel interpreted it for him. Whether or not this is the case, Daniel's interpretation of Nebuchadnezzar's dream in Daniel 4:19-27 is a further unpacking or full interpretation of a partially existing interpretation that was already known by the king himself. The king already knew that the symbolic tree that was felled represented some leader or king somewhere, and if he had a sense that the dream was about his own demise, then he knew even more about the interpretation of the symbolic dream. In other words, Daniel fully interprets a partial interpretation that the king already possessed!

This line of thinking may be confirmed in comparing the Old Greek translation of Daniel 4:15 (Dan 4:18 Eng.; see table 13.1). Both the MT and Theodotion read simply "interpretation" (*pišrā'/to synkrima*), whereas the Old Greek says, "entire interpretation" (*pasan tēn synkrisin*). By suggesting that the king may indeed have had a partial understanding or interpretation of his dream, the Old Greek may offer an interpretation in line with our own.

Table 13.1

Masoretic Text (NASB)	Old Greek	Theodotion
Dan 4:18 "This is the dream which I, King Nebuchadnezzar, have seen. Now you, Belteshazzar, tell me its interpretation, inasmuch as none of the wise men of my kingdom is able to make known to me the interpretation [*pišrā*]; but you are able, for a spirit of the holy gods is in you."	**Dan 4:15** (18) And when I arose in the morning from my bed, I called Daniel, the ruler of the savants and the leader of those who decide dreams, and I described the dream for him, and he showed me its entire interpretation [*pasan tēn synkrisin*].	**Dan 4:15** (18) "This is the dream that I, King Nabouchodonosor, saw. And you, Baltasar, tell the meaning, since all the sages of my kingdom are unable to explain to me the meaning [*to synkrima*]. But you, Daniel, are able, because a holy, divine spirit is in you."

Perhaps Nebuchadnezzar's dream in Daniel 2 follows suit. According to Daniel 2:30b, Daniel claims to interpret "for the purpose of making the interpretation known to the king, and that you may understand the thoughts of your mind" ("thoughts" already in his mind, which may have been more than the mere recollection of the symbolic dream; cf. Dan 7:1). This verse may reveal that Nebuchadnezzar had *some* insight into the interpretation of his dream in Daniel 2.

Similar to Daniel 4, the king was "was troubled and his sleep left him . . . [and he was] anxious to understand the dream" (Dan 2:1-3). Though Nebuchadnezzar withholds the symbolic dream from the Babylonian wise men, we may speculate that he may very well have told Daniel a portion of his dream and perhaps even told Daniel part of what he thought the dream meant. It is difficult to say either way, as the text is silent. Nevertheless, if Daniel 2 and Daniel 4 involve similar content, identical characters (the king, Nebuchadnezzar, the Babylonian diviners and Daniel) and the same revelatory framework (both are labeled a "mystery"; Dan 2:18-19; 4:9), then what is true of the dream report in Daniel 4 could also be true of dream report of Daniel 2.

This discussion of Daniel 2 and especially Daniel 4 is important, since the New Testament writers often make actual allusions to the "mystery" in these chapters (e.g., cf. Mt 13:11; 1 Cor 2:6-16; Eph 3:3-5; Col 1:26-27; 2 Thess 2:7; Rev 1:20; 10:7; and Rev 17:5, 7). Thus, the contextual use of *mystery* in Daniel 2 and above all in Daniel 4 likely are formative for the way New Testament writers would have understood the term. The hermeneutical upshot of this discussion is how Old Testament authors perceive their own words. If king Nebuchadnezzar possessed a portion of the interpretation of his dream before Daniel provided the fuller interpretation, then it may not be a stretch to conclude that

Old Testament authors, like Nebuchadnezzar, possessed some understanding of the full and final interpretation that would later be given. In line with the concept of mystery in Daniel, New Testament writers would then be providing the more complete meaning of the mystery—that is, of what Old Testament writers only partly perceived, even if they barely understood. And, in fact, this is just what we found in our detailed analysis of the use of *mystery* throughout the New Testament. And we believe this finding is not coincidental in light of what we have discovered about Daniel 2 and Daniel 4. If New Testament writers understood mystery in Daniel 2 and Daniel 4 contextually, then it should not be surprising that they believed that they were giving a fuller interpretation of what was only partially revealed in the Old Testament.

In this respect, it is relevant to recall that Ephesians 3:3-6 is the clearest formal New Testament use of a revealed mystery as a fuller disclosure of something already partially known in the Old Testament: the mystery "which in other generations was not made known to the sons of men *as* [*hōs*] now it has been made known to his apostles and prophets by the Spirit" (Eph 3:6). It may not be coincidental that Ephesians 3:3 ("by <u>revelation there was made known to me the mystery</u>") is an explicit allusion to Daniel 2:28 ("there is a God <u>revealing mysteries, and he has made known</u> to King Nabouchodonosor what must happen at the end of days"; for the comparison in Greek, see p. 168). Paul's view of the "partial to fuller" revelation here may be a reflection of his awareness of the fuller context of the mystery from Daniel 2 and Daniel 4, where the same "partial to fuller" revelation is expressed between the king's dream and its interpretation.

The model of hermeneutics from Daniel is clear enough, but whether or not this model ought to be used elsewhere in the Scriptures is difficult to say. Based on our investigations, this model seems to be used by the New Testament authors when they quote Old Testament texts in conjunction with mystery. The question remains, however, whether we should view in a similar manner other Old Testament texts that are quoted in the New Testament (but without the occurrence of mystery).

The benefit of this model is that it allows for difficult and "creative" uses of Old Testament quotations, while maintaining some continuity—even if just a small degree—with the immediate context of the Old Testament passage. Continuity between the original contexts of Old Testament quotations is maintained because the New Testament writers perceive that the fuller meaning of the quotation was "hidden" or encoded in the Old Testament. Since this new meaning was really "there" in the Old Testament, the original context is never completely severed. Certainly the meaning of some Old Testament quotations is "newer" or more creative than others, but if the biblical model of mystery is upheld, the original context is to some degree retained. For example, D. A. Carson comments on how Christ is understood typologically as the Passover lamb in its broader canonical context:

> Sometimes there is a considerable conceptual gap between the type and the antitype: the Passover lamb versus the Messiah as the Passover lamb. . . . Paul certainly does not insist that when the stipulations regarding Passover lamb were first written down, both the writer and the readers understood that they were pointing to the ultimate "lamb," the Messiah himself. So, it would be fair to say that such notions were still hidden—hidden in plain view, so to speak, because genuinely [they are] there in the text (once one perceives the trajectory of the typology), but not yet revealed. And that perhaps is why a 'mystery' must be revealed, but also why it may be revealed through the prophetic writings.[6]

In recent years, it has become fashionable for some to use the term *mystery* or *pesher* in discussion with how New Testament authors make use of the Old Testament.[7] Since mystery constitutes a new revelation, the New Testament authors were likewise given a new revelation of Old Testament texts. There is nothing inherently wrong with this position, but some advocates of this position claim that the New Testament writers quote the Old Testament in a completely "new" and radical way, leaving behind the Old Testament context and often interpreting the passage in a way that is diametrically opposed to that original context. They proceed to support their position with examples of the use of *mystery* in the New Testament. The Achilles heel of this position is that it fails to reckon adequately with the biblical conception of mystery. Mystery, according to the book of Daniel, *always* consists of two parts—hidden revelation and interpreted revelation. These scholars leave behind the first half of mystery while seizing the latter. The problem is that a revealed mystery *must* contain both: the

---

[6]D. A. Carson, "Mystery and Fulfillment: Toward a More Comprehensive Paradigm of Paul's Understanding of the Old and the New," in *Justification and Variegated Nomism: Vol. 2—The Paradoxes of Paul*, ed. D. A. Carson, Peter T. O'Brien and Mark A. Seifrid (Grand Rapids: Baker Academic, 2004), p. 427.

[7]E.g., Richard Longenecker, *Biblical Exegesis in the Apostolic Period*, 2nd ed. (Grand Rapids: Eerdmans, 1999), pp. 113-16; Peter Enns, *Inspiration and Incarnation: Evangelicals and the Problem of the Old Testament* (Grand Rapids: Baker Academic, 2005), pp. 128-32.

formerly hidden revelation still had some elements of anticipation, however subdued, which are significantly and sometimes surprisingly expanded and illumined in the interpreted form of the revelation. We have repeatedly seen in all the occurrences of *mystery* that the unveiled mystery is in some way organically linked to strands of meaning in the Old Testament, however slender those strands are. Sometimes the organic connection between the two testaments is stronger than at other times. In each case, however, the revealed mystery retains some continuity with the Old Testament. This notion of "partial to fuller revelation" may be comparable to a room with differing degrees of light. If a room is richly furnished but very dimly lit, one can barely make out what objects are in it; they cannot be clearly seen. When the room is fully lit, the illumination does not reveal anything that was not already in the room, but the objects are more clearly seen, with all their distinctive shapes in view.[8]

The Old Testament authors' intended meaning. Another related aspect of our discussion in the directly preceding section and earlier throughout our study could prove helpful for how the Old Testament authors understand their *own* words. According to the book of Daniel, Nebuchadnezzar and Daniel (both recipients of "mysteries") knew that they had only received the initial form of revelation. For example, in Daniel 2 and Daniel 4, Nebuchadnezzar had two symbolic dreams, and he knew both dreams were symbolic (Dan 2:1-3; 4:5-6). Since both dreams were symbolic, Nebuchadnezzar summoned the Babylonian wise men, and after they failed to interpret the dreams he summoned Daniel. The point is that King Nebuchadnezzar was aware that his dreams required an additional revelation of the symbolism. The same could be said for Daniel's visions in the latter portion of the book. If we apply this model to Old Testament authors, then we may be able to shed some light on how they understood their own writings. If Old Testament authors understood their writings in the way that Nebuchadnezzar and Daniel understood their initial visions, then *the Old Testament authors had some kind of anticipation of a time when a fuller revelation would be given*. In other words, perhaps the Old Testament writers knew that the meaning of their words would eventually be eclipsed by a fuller, more complete form of revelation. Keep in mind that within the Old Testament itself, there is occasional evidence that Old Testament authors perceived that there would be a later or fuller revelation of an Old Testament text.

---

[8]Illustration adapted from B. B. Warfield, *Biblical Doctrines* (New York: Oxford University Press, 1929), 141.

Daniel, for instance, reads from Jeremiah concerning the "seventy years" (Jer 25:11-12; 29:10). But it is worthy to note that Jeremiah received the seventy-years prophecy "according to the word of the LORD" (Dan 9:2); thus Daniel is reading what God revealed to Jeremiah. Not only does Daniel "observe" (a term that connects Dan 2; 8–9 together) what God revealed to Jeremiah, but God delivers an interpretation to Daniel in a vision concerning "Jeremiah's revelation" through an angel (Dan 9:22-23). Gabriel says to Daniel, "O Daniel, I have now come forth to give you insight with understanding . . . I have come to tell *you*, for you are highly esteemed; so give heed to the message and gain under-standing of the vision" (Dan 9:22-24; cf. Dan 2:1). The interpretation of the seventy years is thus given in Daniel 9:24-27. Therefore, Daniel deems God's revelation to Jeremiah concerning Israel's exile to be incomplete or unfinished until the angel gives him a fuller revelation of Israel's Babylonian captivity.

It seems likely that the New Testament authors perceived that some Old Testament authors fell into this category, particularly when the New Testament writers quote Old Testament texts in conjunction with a revealed mystery. Paul, for example, in Ephesians 5:31-32 sees the union of Christ and the church to be really "there" in the original context of Genesis 2:24. If Paul believes that the Christ was really "there" in Genesis 2:24, then it would seem likely that the original Old Testament author had Christ somewhere in his purview. It appears that some Old Testament authors had some inkling of how the meaning of their texts would or could be later interpreted. Such inklings may become percep-tible when one tries to examine what might have been in an Old Testament author's cognitive peripheral vision. We have reserved an appendix at the end of the book on this topic in order to elaborate more fully on what we mean by authors' explicit meaning and their "cognitive peripheral vision" and how that may provide clues to authors' secondary or implicit meaning(s).[9]

Some may contend that this interpretative model, though found in Daniel, does not apply to the way in which New Testament authors cite the Old Tes-tament. In other words, what may be true of Daniel is not necessarily true of the New Testament authors. Our response is twofold: (1) the term *mystery* as found in the New Testament is tethered in some way or another to the book of Daniel. Our book has confirmed what scholars have argued in the last few decades: the New Testament conception of mystery is inextricably linked to the

---

[9]See the appendix on pp. 340-64. For an expansion of this appendix, see G. K. Beale, "The Cognitive Peripheral Vision of Biblical Authors," *WTJ* 76, no. 2 (2014).

book of Daniel. So when New Testament authors employ the term *mystery* in conjunction with Old Testament texts, they are doing so with the larger narrative of Daniel in mind, to one degree or another. (2) Throughout this project, we have repeatedly seen allusions to the book of Daniel within the immediate context of the revealed mystery. There are a few exceptions to this observation (e.g., 1 Tim 3; Rom 16), but many of the uses do occur in close proximity to allusions to Daniel. The point is that the New Testament authors who employ *mystery* demonstrate some degree of familiarity with the book of Daniel.

Using Daniel's model of interpretation can pay high dividends in our understanding of how the New Testament uses the Old Testament. If the New Testament authors follow Daniel's model, then we are in a position to glean much in the way the New Testament authors view meaning in Old Testament. Perhaps this model of understanding the use of the Old Testament in the New Testament is just one of many models the New Testament authors employ—another tool in their hermeneutical toolbox. Whatever the case may be, more research needs to be done in this area. This model from Daniel could furnish us with a new lens in grasping the New Testament's use of the Old Testament.

PRACTICAL IMPLICATIONS

The practical implications for our study, once properly grasped, are significant. Far from esotericism, the revelation of God's mysteries engenders faith and godliness. For example, several uses of *mystery* involve living a cruciform lifestyle that entails mirroring Christ's life. The New Testament spends considerable time describing the content and the nature of God's wisdom of the cross. Believers must acquire God's wisdom and, once we do, our lives will naturally conform to such knowledge. To put it another way, the church possesses a completely different way of evaluating the world. Instead of embracing our reputation and fame, the biblical worldview places the mystery of the cross as its center. This knowledge should revolutionize our behavior, as we embody the very wisdom that the earliest Christians grasped.

The upshot of the mystery of the cross is that believers must live in light of the mystery of the cross. We must realize that the world's values are completely different from God's. According to the world, appearance, rhetoric and so on are highly esteemed. On the other hand, suffering, weakness and the "foolishness" of the cross are what God favors. Christians are required to have an entirely different worldview, and at its center is the crucified Messiah. It is a new way of understanding what God expects from us and how he works through us. God's glory is manifested in our suffering, as was the case with Jesus. Christ's victory and God's glory are heralded in our weakness and defeat.

We are commanded to pattern our lives after the cross. This means that we must embrace both physical and spiritual suffering in our lives. Such suffering is a demonstration that we are his and that he is truly working in our midst. This may mean the loss of a job or rejection by a family member.

The book of Revelation places much emphasis on embracing a cruciform lifestyle. Believers who "overcome" the world are inevitably persecuted by the world. Physically the world "overcomes" true believers, but spiritually believers "overcome" the world by persevering through tribulation imposed on them. This behavior is modeled after Christ conquering and overcoming Satan and the world through his death. This is why Revelation 14:4 says that Christians "follow the Lamb wherever he goes."

Another practical application of mystery is the presence of the unexpected antichrist during the church age itself. Contrary to popular belief, the antichrist is not solely a future phenomenon, but a daunting figure that makes his presence known through his agents of deception and persecution. We as the church must be on high alert to perceive his deceit and treachery. His trickery manifests itself in various falsehoods, particularly untruths related to the person of Christ. The New Testament writers, especially Paul, Peter and Jude reinforce the need for the church to maintain sound doctrine and embrace apostolic traditions. Now that the "latter days" have been inaugurated, we must "test the spirits" (1 Jn 4:1) by constantly evaluating the ideas promulgated by modern-day teachers and preachers. In order for the church to reprove the false teaching of the antichrist, believers must be steeped in and constantly meditating on Scripture.

May God confirm us in our faith in his revealed mysteries concerning Christ and our lives.

APPENDIX

THE COGNITIVE PERIPHERAL VISION OF BIBLICAL AUTHORS

The problem that this appendix attempts to address concerns those New Testament quotations of the Old Testament that appear on the surface to have a very different meaning than the Old Testament passages from which they come.[1] This is relevant to the concern of this book, since a number of scholars believe that the revealed mystery in the New Testament is completely new and does not arise out of an Old Testament author's conscious intention. As in chapter eleven, "Mystery Without *Mystery*," in this appendix we will focus our case studies on passages where the term *mystery* is not found, though the hermeneutical theory offered here is very relevant to the uses of *mystery* that we have studied throughout this book. One classic example is John 19:36, which says that not breaking Jesus' bones at the crucifixion was a fulfillment of Exodus 12:46, which commands Israelites "not to break any bone" of the Passover lamb. The problem is that this is a historical description of a command to Israelites, not a prophecy about the Messiah. Another example is Matthew's quotation of Hosea 11:1 in Matthew 2:15. The Hosea passage says, "Out of Egypt I have called My son," and Matthew quotes it and sees it fulfilled in Jesus. The problem with this is that Hosea's wording is not a prophecy to be fulfilled but merely a historical reflection on Israel's past exodus out of Egypt. Furthermore, Hosea's wording refers to Israel as a nation and not to an individual Messiah, as Matthew takes it. Many would say that Matthew has twisted the original meaning of Hosea's words. We could add more examples, but these suffice for now.

---

[1]This appendix is an adapted and shortened version of a forthcoming article by G. K. Beale, "The Cognitive Peripheral Vision of Biblical Authors," *WTJ* 76, no. 2 (2014).

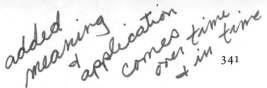

added meaning & application comes over time & in time

How do we deal with such problematic texts? There are a variety of responses to these thorny passages. There are some who say the New Testament writers were wrong. Others say their interpretative approach was wrong but what they wrote was nevertheless inspired. Still others contend that they were strange exegetes who cannot be judged by modern-day standards. And others affirm that they do legitimately exegete but their approach is so unique that we dare not try to copy their method. And then there are those who argue that with caution we can try to imitate their method.

Here we want to argue that Old Testament writers knew more about the topic of their speech act than only the explicit meaning they expressed about that topic. If so, there was an explicit intention and an implicit wider understanding related to that intention.[2] It is sometimes this implicit wider intention that New Testament writers develop instead of the Old Testament author's explicit or direct meaning. These New Testament interpretations may seem strange at a first reading, as with the John 19 and Matthew 2 texts above, as well as many of the mystery texts we have studied, but when the Old and New Testament writers' *wider implicit understanding* is explored, the interpretations become more understandable. One clarification: this appendix looks primarily at what the human biblical author understood, while realizing that the human authors were aware that they were writing under divine inspiration and that God would certainly have a more exhaustive understanding of their intention.

Modern-Day Examples of Explicit and Implicit Meaning

When a husband says he loves his wife, this can be unpacked in the following ways: I am unconditionally committed to you. I think of you before myself. I think of you as more important than myself. I love [care for] you as I love [care for] myself. I want to sacrifice myself for you. I want to sacrifice myself for you in the same manner as Christ sacrificed himself for the church. Then there could be many applications of these general principal statements (e.g., I will do house chores so that the full load of housework will not fall on you. Or, more specifically, I will cook dinner for us tonight). The point is that any one of the above statements can be unpacked further with added meaning and applica-

---

[2]Scholars (e.g., those who espouse a hermeneutical view known as "relevance theory") refer to this as explicatures and implicatures; e.g., see Gene L. Green, "Relevance Theory and Biblical Interpretation," in *The Linguist as Pedagogue: Trends in the Teaching and Linguistic Analysis of the Greek New Testament,* ed. S. E. Porter and M. B. O'Donnell, NTM 11 (Sheffield: Sheffield Phoenix Press, 2009), p. 234. Scholars can also refer to such speech acts as "linguistically underdetermined."

tions that are still truly part of the meaning of the one original statement.

Or, imagine students asking a teacher to clarify the teacher's initial interpretation of a biblical passage. There could be several more sentences of interpretation that expand on the original interpretation but were not stated explicitly with the original. For example, what does a teacher (or Paul) mean when the teacher says all believers are "in Christ." This phrase is used throughout Paul, and he focuses on different aspects of "union with Christ" in different contexts: justification, sanctification, regeneration, adopted sonship, new creation, reconciliation, image of God and so on. When Paul focuses, for example, on adopted sonship in relation to union with Christ, does that mean he does not have in mind sanctification secondarily?

The original statements in the above illustrations are what some scholars call "thick descriptive" statements, which can be unpacked layer by layer.[3] This concept of "thick description" goes a long way toward explaining some of the problematic uses of the Old Testament in the New. But more must be said to unpack this notion of "thick description."

THE CONCEPT OF COGNITIVE PERIPHERAL VISION

The notion of cognitive peripheral vision further explains the reality that human assertions have both explicit and implicit meaning. All humans have eyesight that includes direct vision and peripheral vision. Peripheral vision is typically defined as the ability to see objects and movement outside of the direct line of vision. A typical description of peripheral vision is the following:

> Peripheral vision is a part of vision that occurs outside the very center of gaze. There is a broad set of non-central points in the field of view that is included in the notion of peripheral vision. "Far peripheral" vision exists at the edges of the field of view, "mid-peripheral" vision exists in the middle of the field of view, and "near-peripheral . . . vision, exists adjacent to the center of gaze. For example, peripheral vision is practiced by jugglers. Jugglers do not directly follow the paths of individual objects with their eyes, instead they focus on a defined point in mid-air, so almost all of the information necessary for successful catches is perceived in the near-peripheral region.[4]

---

[3]See, e.g., Kevin Vanhoozer, *Is There a Meaning in This Text? The Bible, the Reader, and the Morality of Literary Knowledge* (Grand Rapids: Zondervan, 1998), pp. 264-65, 284-85, 313-14. See also John Frame, *The Doctrine of the Knowledge of God* (Phillipsburg, NJ: P & R, 1987), pp. 215-41, for his notion of the "vagueness" of language, which overlaps with Vanhoozer's idea of "thick description."
[4]See "Peripheral Vision," on Wikipedia, http://en.wikipedia.org/wiki/Peripheral_vision.

All people see and are aware of more than what their physical eyes are directly focused on and this awareness is an ongoing default setting. Likewise, there is a similar phenomenon with our mind's eye. When we make statements about anything, we are focused on our direct meaning, yet that meaning is robust and can be expanded. The expansion is not uncontrolled. In the direct vision of our physical eyes there are objects related to objects in our peripheral vision in that they are all part of one whole vision range. So likewise are things that are part of our direct focus of meaning related to things in our wider field of peripheral cognitive vision, since they are all part of one whole cognitive vision range (some scholars refer to this as the "cognitive environment"). It is thus natural to elaborate one's direct meaning by its wider range of meaning, since they are part of one unified range of meaning. Such a wider range of related meaning is a default setting for our knowledge.

We believe that something like this is going on with Old and New Testament authors when they make direct statements with an explicit meaning. There is always a related range of meaning that appropriately is an expansion of the explicit meaning that is expressed. All speakers and writers, including ancient writers, are aware of more than what they are directly saying in their speech act. Thus, cognitive peripheral vision is a theory of knowledge in itself, of which the peripheral vision that we have with our eyes is an illustration. We will delay giving biblical examples of this concept until we discuss some similar theories of human knowledge which give a more philosophical grounding to our above proposal of cognitive peripheral vision.

But at this point we can make a basic comparison between our physical peripheral vision and cognitive peripheral vision. Have you had the experience of driving, with your direct focus on the road ahead, yet you are still aware of objects in your peripheral vision to some degree? All of a sudden, you notice a car in your peripheral vision that is out of place and appears about to hit the right side of your car. You respond and immediately jerk your car to the left. Your direct focus and the direction of your car immediately changes and you veer temporarily out of your lane. However, someone in the passenger seat who was not seeing what you saw (like your spouse) thinks you are doing something radically wrong and yells out, "What in the world are you doing?!" Once the passenger learns what you saw in your peripheral vision, he or she understands why you jerked the car to the left instead of going straight. Likewise a New Testament author may quote an Old Testament passage that seems obviously to have one meaning, but he gives it a meaning that appears not to be found in that passage. What has happened is that in the author's cognitive peripheral vision, he has seen a passage three or four chapters later in the Old Testament text that is related to the meaning of the passage that he quotes and he brings in the meaning from that later passage. In keeping with our car metaphor, the biblical author quotes an Old Testament text but he steers away from its obvious meaning and goes in a different interpretative direction because of the later passage in his peripheral cognitive vision. To a later reader sitting in the interpretative passenger seat, it appears that the New Testament author has gone in the wrong interpretative direction and given a wrong meaning to the passage that he cites. However, once the interpretative passenger understands that the author saw the verse four chapters later out of his cognitive peripheral vision and has brought that meaning in, then the passenger understands why the author went in another interpretive direction. This does not distort the meaning of the focus passage but it does, at first, seem to be different.

E. D. Hirsch's Concept of a "Willed Type"

In this regard, E. D. Hirsch's notion of a "willed type" may be helpful as a further explanation of intentional verbal meaning. For Hirsch, a willed type has two characteristics: (1) a broad cognitive entity (a broad idea) with a boundary, which includes other related specific ideas that belong within the boundary, while other ideas would be excluded because they are not the same "type" of idea; (2) the type as a broad cognitive entity can be represented by more than a single conceptual expression, as long as the other representing expressions fall within the boundary and are part of the same conceptual "type."[5]

That is an abstract explanation. Let us illustrate and put flesh on it. Let us say that one of my students visits me for a lemonade on my back lawn porch during the summer while Bach's Brandenburg Concertos are playing in the background. While the student is visiting me (Greg Beale), I say to him, "There is nothing I like more on a summer day than sipping lemonade and listening to Bach's Brandenburg Concertos." The student replies, "Do you like sipping lemonade and listening to Bach more than playing golf on a warm summer day?" The student has has misunderstood and taken me too literally. My intention was to refer only to the fact that no *work of musical art* pleased me so much as Bach's

---

[5]E. D. Hirsch, *Validity in Interpretation* (New Haven: Yale University Press, 1987), pp. 49-50.

Brandenburg Concertos. I was not speaking of all other possible things that I could enjoy on a summer day. But the student, in response to my reply, then asks me, "Do you also like to listen to other compositions by Bach, as well as by Handel, Albinoni, Pachelbel, Haydn and Vivaldi?" The answer to the student's question would be yes. In fact, other Baroque composers would be included and even some classical musicians like Beethoven. Thus my statement about enjoying Bach's Brandenburg Concertos actually included and represented not only all of Bach's works but also all Baroque music. If the student had asked if my statement about Bach included hard rock music, rap music or even soft rock, like Elvis Presley's "You Ain't Nothing but a Hound Dog," the answer would be no. Some overriding principle in my original meaning about Bach's Brandenburg must have determined that Elvis Presley's "You Ain't Nothing but a Hound Dog" was not included in my meaning, along with a number of other non-Baroque musical compositions. This is the case because my peripheral or tacit vision included *a particular type of thing* that I enjoy and excluded other possible musical art pieces not belonging within the boundary of the Baroque type. Certainly my narrowly focused direct or explicit intention did not include all the kinds of musical works that please me, but only Bach's Brandenburg Concertos. There was before my mind's eye only this particular piece by Bach, but if the student proposed more within the Baroque genre, I would agree that that was within my implicit or peripheral cognitive vision and should be secondarily included in my original meaning to some conscious degree. In this case, even my specific explicit reference was a part for a larger whole, though not every piece of the whole would be explicitly before my conscious mind's eye. Such implicit meanings within my "willed type" can be called interpretative "implications" of the explicit verbal meaning.[6]

It could be asked how my student would be able to figure out the *implicit* representative meaning of the explicit reference to Bach's Brandenburg Concertos. The answer is that the students would need to have some knowledge about my life. If students came to my house, they would without too much effort find CDs of many kinds of Baroque music. They might well find such music playing in my house. They might notice books about Baroque music on the coffee table in the living room. In various conversations with me or my wife, they would likely hear me express my enjoyment of such music. Such

---

[6]Ibid., pp. 61-67.

comments might come as illustrations in class lectures. And so on. In other words, some research into the context of my life would help the students appreciate the implicit meaning in my explicit mention of the Brandenburg Concertos. So discovering such implicit meanings is not a shot in the dark. Likewise research into biblical authors' lives, their historical contexts and the full context of their own writings should help interpreters toward a better grasp of their implicit meanings.

In this respect, such implicit or subsidiary meanings are like icebergs: the greater part may be under the water, but that which is under the water must be organically connected to the part above the surface. The metaphor conveys the notion that the implicit or submerged authorial meaning must be organically connected to that explicit meaning. Even though the visible tip of the iceberg (explicit meaning) is the smaller part of the larger submerged iceberg (implicit meaning), it determines what is a part of the whole and what is not part of the whole (e.g., other separately floating ice, debris or sea life). "Any part of the whole that is not continuous with the mass above the surface cannot be part of the iceberg."[7] While such physical metaphors are sometimes misleading, this one seems relevant since the identity of a verbal meaning is dependent on coherence that is somewhat comparable to physical connectedness. If there are features in a text that point to implicit meanings, they are a part of the verbal meaning of the text "only if they are coherent with a consciously willed type which defines the meaning as a whole."[8] Other proposed meanings that are incoherent are then not a part of the willed verbal meaning. Therefore, in the words of Hirsch, it is possible to will an "et cetera" without in the least being aware of all the individual members that belong to it. The acceptability of any given candidate applying for membership in the et cetera depends entirely on the type of whole, determinate meaning I willed.[9]

Such subconscious "implications" of explicit meaning fall within the overall

---

[7] Ibid., p. 54.

[8] Ibid.

[9] Ibid., p. 49. Hirsch's view of a determinant meaning is based on Husserl's epistemological presupposition that the mind can perceive an idea of something experienced and that it can "demarcate" that mental act so that it remains the same idea over a period of time. See Hirsch, *Aims of Interpretation* (Chicago: University of Chicago Press, 1978), pp. 4-5. An explicitly theistic hermeneutical perspective would add to this the presupposition that the omniscient God's immutable, sovereign transcendence is the enduring foundation for "an absolute transcendent determinant meaning to all texts." D. McCartney and C. Clayton, *Let the Reader Understand* (Wheaton, IL: Victor Books, 1994), p. 284; the determinant meaning of all texts is known completely by the all-knowing God who is "not mutable or time bound, and so the meaning which He understands of a text is unchanging" (p. 284).

pattern of what the author willed.[10] One negative trait of all implicit meanings is that they are meanings on which the author was not immediately focused. Such a feature is not reassuring, since there are no limits for what a particular author may not have been aware of. Hirsch's notion of a willed type is an approach that offers some guidelines, albeit still broad and not formulaic, for determining such implicit meanings that may be included in an author's full verbal meaning.[11]

In this light, a New Testament writer may quote an Old Testament passage but give it a meaning that is not found explicitly in that passage but one that comes from the wider context of another chapter in the Old Testament book or from elsewhere in the Old Testament that has some kind of conceptual connection (i.e., it is the same "type" of idea) to the passage being quoted. In other words, a New Testament writer may cite an Old Testament passage but interpret it from the peripheral view of later chapters in the Old Testament book, where the cited passage is developed.

Michael Polanyi's Notion of Tacit or Subsidiary Knowledge

Hirsch's view of a willed type and our concept of cognitive peripheral vision can be supplemented by Michael Polanyi's similar philosophical view, which though not identical significantly overlaps with the two above perspectives.[12]

Some scholars understand that New Testament writers are respecting Old Testament contexts from which they quote only when they quote the passages with their explicit historical sense.[13] Otherwise, they are not respecting the context.

---

[10]Cf. Jeannine Brown, *Scripture as Communication: Introducing Biblical Hermeneutics* (Grand Rapids: Baker Academic, 2007), p. 39, and her summary of Hirsch.

[11]Hirsch, *Validity in Interpretation*, pp. 51-52.

[12]My former doctoral student and research assistant, Mitch Kim, has alerted me to the significance of Polanyi with respect to my own developing approach, and, in addition to consulting Polanyi for myself, this section on Polanyi is indebted to a significant degree to Mitch Kim's article on this topic, "Respect for Context and Authorial Intention: Setting the Epistemological Bar," in *Paul and Scripture,* ed. Christopher D. Stanley, SBL Early Christianity and Its Literature 9 (Atlanta: Society of Biblical Literature, 2012), pp. 115-29, though I have tried to flesh out Polanyi's view a bit more, especially with the help of Esther L. Meek, *Longing to Know: The Philosophy of Knowledge for Ordinary People* (Grand Rapids: Brazos, 2003) and her *Loving to Know: Covenant Epistemology* (Eugene, OR: Cascade, 2011), in which she develops Polanyi's epistemological approach. Furthermore, in the conclusion of the longer version of this essay in *WTJ* I attempt to respond to Steve Moyise's objection to Kim's article in his use of Polanyi in application to the Old Testament in the New Testament. See Steve Moyise, "Latency and Respect for Context: A Response to Mitchell Kim," in Stanley, *Paul and Scripture,* pp. 131-39.

[13]E.g., see Steve Moyise, "Does Paul Respect the Context of His Quotations?" in Stanley, *Paul and Scripture,* pp. 97-99, 112.

I believe that the concepts already introduced on peripheral cognitive vision and Hirsch's willed type show this criterion of respecting context to be too narrow. Before we further evaluate this overly restricted view of some scholars, it will be helpful also to reflect on the insights of Michael Polanyi. Polanyi has given some perspectives to help further define authorial intention. He says that knowledge entails a subsidiary or tacit dimension and thus entails that "we know more than we can tell."[14] Polanyi applies this to all realms of human knowledge. Before we apply his insights to authorial intention and meaning, Polanyi's view needs brief explanation and illustration.

There are two aspects of knowing for Polanyi: tacit (subsidiary) and explicit (focal). In any act of knowing one is tacitly aware of one thing that is necessary for the carrying out of another thing, which is the focus of our awareness.

When playing a musical piece, an expert pianist does not focus on the elementary foundations for playing the piano nor does she focus on her hand movements when playing—otherwise she would be paralyzed and could not play the piece. Rather, the foundations of piano playing and her hand movements become secondary in her awareness (tacit or subsidiary knowledge) and her explicit attention is directed toward playing a comprehensible piece of music.

Consider a person who wants to learn the mechanics of a racecar engine but knows nothing about it. He looks at a motor removed from a car and separated into all its smallest parts. The novice sees the parts but does not know how they fit together nor how they work in harmony. Over time, after reading about motors and learning as an apprentice with hands–on work, the connectedness of the parts and their harmonious operation become apparent. The novice learns from a racecar mechanic who is also a skilled racecar driver (and the novice also watches his teacher race his racecar in various races). As this learner becomes skilled at understanding the engine of a racecar, the overall pattern of the motor is revealed and even makes more sense of each particular part. The unconnected parts are what Polanyi calls *tacit* or *subsidiary awareness* and the overall pattern of how the motor fits together is the *focus*, since that is the goal the mechanic is trying to achieve. The former has merged with the latter but is

---

[14]Polanyi, *The Tacit Dimension* (Garden City, NY: Doubleday, 1966), p. 10; along the same lines, see his other two works, where he selectively discusses the same notion: *Personal Knowledge* (Chicago: University of Chicago Press, 1958) and Michael Polanyi and Harry Prosch, *Meaning* (Chicago: University of Chicago Press, 1975).

not the main focus. Polanyian followers refer to the subsidiary focus as being "like our peripheral vision," since "by definition you can't focus on your peripheral vision! But you rely on it all the time."[15]

Then this mechanic decides he wants to be a racecar driver like his teacher whom he has been watching. The mechanic has to learn a new skill set to learn to race a racecar. The skill of a race driver cannot be expressed by a mere knowledge of the mechanics of the car motor and its other workings, but on paying direct attention to the various aspects of driving the car: attending to the gear shift, curves of the roadway, speed, brakes, length of the race and relationship to the other cars in the race. The knowledge of the way the parts of the motor are connected and work together now becomes *tacit* or *subsidiary awareness,* and the direct concentration on how all the facets of racecar driving fit together into a successful race is the *explicit focus.* The former has merged with the latter but is not the main focus. Again this subsidiary focus is like our peripheral vision.

Thus Polanyi also makes a distinction between focal awareness (explicit/ distal awareness) and subsidiary awareness (tacit or proximate awareness).[16] The tacit is that which is unspoken or not explicitly expressed but is implied or inferred (see *OED*).[17] It is important to note that Polanyi does not view tacit awareness as "unconscious"; rather, a person has varying degrees of awareness of tacit meaning.

Therefore, when a New Testament writer refers to an Old Testament passage, both the explicit and subsidiary understanding of the Old Testament author's meaning comprise what we would call the New Testament writer's respect for the Old Testament contextual meaning. In addition to the explicit meaning from the specific text quoted, the wider contextual meaning may include ideas from the immediate or nearby Old Testament context that are in mind, as well as ideas from other chapters of the book or even from other Old Testament books, which are related to the meaning of the focus text (in this respect, see further below on the section titled "Subsidiary Presuppositional Perspectives of the New Testament Writers in Their Use of the Old Testament").

---

[15]Meek, *Longing to Know,* p. 84.

[16]Polanyi, *Personal Knowledge,* pp. 55-59, 61-62, 92-93.

[17]A synonym of "subsidiary" or "tacit" knowledge used more rarely by Polanyi is "latent" knowledge (e.g., ibid., pp. 103, 317), i.e., that which is "hidden, concealed," or "present or existing, but not manifest, exhibited or developed" (*OED*).

Some Old-Testament-in-the-New Examples of Tacit Knowledge, Willed Type or Cognitive Peripheral Vision

So far we have looked at my own view of "cognitive peripheral vision," Hirsch's "willed type" theory and Polanyi's notion of "tacit knowledge," and we have given illustrations of them.[18] I believe these three perspectives are significantly overlapping. That is, they all have in common the notion that *we know more than we intend to tell.* This is true of biblical authors: they focus on an explicit idea but included in this idea are related ideas from the wider context or peripheral vision of the author, and these ideas in the peripheral vision supplement the idea of explicit focus. Now we will apply these concepts to some actual uses of the Old Testament in the New.

The use of Hosea 11:1 in Matthew 2:15.[19] Matthew 2:15 says Joseph took Jesus and his mother into Egypt in order "that what was spoken by the Lord through the prophet might be fulfilled, saying 'Out of Egypt I called My Son.'" How can Matthew say a historical statement made by Hosea about Israel's exodus is a prophecy fulfilled by Jesus entering and returning from Egypt? On the surface, it seems as though Matthew is wrongly reading a prophecy into a text that is only historical. However, a fuller study reveals that Hosea himself in Hosea 11 and elsewhere in the book already had a view of Israel's first exodus as a typological foreshadowing of an end-time exodus, with the Messiah leading it.

In this respect, mention of a first exodus from Egypt outside of Hosea 11:1 occurs elsewhere in Hosea and a future return from Egypt would appear to be implied by repeated prophecies of Israel returning to Egypt in the future, though Hosea 1:10-11 (see below) and Hosea 11:11 are the only texts explicitly affirming a future return from Egypt (though there are several texts in Isaiah that are also explicit about this; see appendix table 1). Thus we can see that by extending Hosea's peripheral vision to the end of the chapter and to other parts of the book, he understood that the first exodus was a pattern foreshadowing a second, end-time exodus. So Matthew is just following Hosea's own wider peripheral typological hermeneutic, which he sees beginning to be fulfilled in Jesus.

---

[18]See Beale, "Cognitive Peripheral Vision," for more in-depth summary and discussion of the views of Hirsch and Polanyi.

[19]For an expansion of this section, see G. K. Beale. "The Use of Hosea 11:1 in Matthew 2:15: One More Time," *JETS* 55 (2012): 697-715.

Appendix Table 1

First Exodus Out of Egypt	Future Return to Egypt (implying a future return from Egypt)
Hos 2:15b "And she will sing there as in the days of her youth, / As in the day when she came up from the land of Egypt" (though this passage compares the first exodus with a future exodus)	**Hos 7:11** "So Ephraim has become like a silly dove, without sense; / They call to Egypt, they go to Assyria."
Hos 12:13 "But by a prophet the Lord brought Israel from Egypt, / And by a prophet he was kept."	**Hos 7:16b** "Their princes will fall by the sword Because of the insolence of their tongue. This *will be* their derision in the land of Egypt."
Cf. Hos 12:9 "But I have been the Lord your God since the land of Egypt."	**Hos 8:13b** "Now He will remember their iniquity, / And punish *them* for their sins; They will return to Egypt."
Cf. Hos 13:4 "Yet I have been the Lord your God since the land of Egypt, and you were not to know any god except me, for there is no savior besides me."	**Hos 9:3** "They will not remain in the Lord's land, But Ephraim will return to Egypt, And in Assyria they will eat unclean <u>food</u>."
	Hos 9:6 "For behold, they will go because of destruction; Egypt will gather them up, Memphis will bury them. Weeds will take over their treasures of silver; Thorns *will be* in their tents."
	See also **Hos 1:11** "And they [Israel] will go up from the land [of Egypt]."
	Hos 11:5 "He [Israel] assuredly will return to the land of Egypt."
	Note the implication of a future exodus from Egypt in Hos 2:15 above.

But how can Matthew say that Jesus fulfills Hosea 11:1, when Hosea 1:11 is about the corporate nation Israel and not about an individual? Note that Hosea 1:11 sees that the Messiah will lead this future exodus. That Jesus, the individual, can be corporately identified with the "many" of Israel in Hosea 11:1 shows that Matthew was assuming a presupposition of corporate solidarity between Christ and Israel: Christ sums up true Israel in himself. Kings represented Israel in the Old Testament, so that what could be said about the king was true of the nation, and vice-versa. Hosea 1:11 shows that Israel's end-time king will lead them out of Egypt again. Matthew sees Jesus as that king, so the king can appropriately be said to be Israel. This corporate identification is further apparent from Matthew's later recording of Jesus' name as "Son of the living God" (Mt 16:16), which itself is an allusion to Hosea 1:9, where the nation Israel is called "sons of the living God." By extending Matthew's peripheral vision from Hosea 11 back to Hosea 1:9-10 and to a previous chapter in his own book (Mt 16), we see justification for him understanding that Jesus was Israel. Later we will see further why Matthew can use this corporate hermeneutic.

The use of Hosea 1:10; 2:23 in Romans 9:25-26. A comparison of the texts is shown in appendix table 2. Some scholars would say that Paul is merely using the Hosea texts as illustrations of salvation, which would pose no interpretative problem: Israel's prophesied salvation is now taken as an illustration of Gentile salvation. However, the majority of scholars more correctly understand that Paul is indicating the beginning fulfillment of the Hosea prophecies.[20] This would mean that what was prophesied for Israel's salvation is fulfilled not only among a remnant of Jews but also among Gentiles. This is why some scholars contend that Paul has not respected the original meaning and context of Hosea.

Appendix Table 2

Hosea 2:23; 1:10 NASB	Romans 9:25-26 (authors' trans.)
Hos 2:23 "And I will sow her for Myself in the land. And I will have mercy on No Mercy. And I will say to Not My People, 'You are my people,' and he shall say, 'You are my God.'"	**Rom 9:25** "As indeed he says in Hosea, 'Those who were not my people, I will call my people, and her who was not beloved, I will call "beloved."'"
Hos 1:10 And in the place / Where it is said to them, / "You are not My people," / It will be said to them, / "You are the sons of the living God."	**Rom 9:26** "And it shall be that in the place where is was said to them, "You are not My people," there they shall be called sons of the living God."

However, some have pointed out that the position of Israel as "not my people" before they become "my people" is really a Gentile position. Unbelieving Gentiles are also "not my people." Seen in this way, Hosea would be prophesying that Israel would be in an unbelieving Gentile status before they would come to faith. Thus it is a natural extension to see that the prophecy would be applied

---

[20]This is in line with the connection of Rom 9:24-26 with the immediately following Old Testament prophecies cited in Rom 9:27-29, which are clearly viewed as inaugurated prophetic fulfillments among a remnant of Israelites.

to ethnic Gentiles who were in the same position as unbelieving Jews.[21]

This identification of unbelieving Israel with unbelieving Gentiles is strikingly underscored in Hosea 11:8-9:

> How can I give you up, O Ephraim?
> How can I surrender you, O Israel?
> How can I make you like Admah?
> How can I treat you like Zeboiim?
> My heart is turned over within Me,
> All My compassions are kindled.
> I will not execute My fierce anger;
> I will not destroy Ephraim again.
> For I am God and not man, the Holy One in your midst,
> And I will not come in wrath.

In Hosea 11:8 God asks the question of how he could judge Israel "like" Admah and Zeboim. Hosea 11:9 then says that he will not judge them that way. But why? Part of the explanation is that he "will not destroy Ephraim <u>again</u>." Apparently, Ephraim which had not formerly been destroyed as a tribe, in some way was corporately identified with Admah and Zeboim, which were cities destroyed along with Sodom and Gomorrah. In some mysterious way, Ephraim, therefore, was considered to have been destroyed already with these other Gentile cities. So God says in Hosea 11:9 that he "will not destroy Ephraim <u>again</u>." This is more than an analogical comparison of the destruction of these Gentile cities with that of Ephraim.[22] Rather, this is an actual corporate identification of these Gentile cities with Ephraim,[23] much like Paul says that all of humanity was corporately identified with Adam in his sinful disobedience and condemnation.[24]

---

[21]E.g., see Mark Seifrid, "Romans," in *Commentary on the New Testament Use of the Old Testament*, ed. G. K. Beale and D. A. Carson (Grand Rapids: Baker Academic, 2007), p. 648.

[22]Note that often the prophets compare the sin or destruction of Sodom to the sin of Israel (Is 1:9-10; 3:9; Jer 23:14; Lam 4:6; Ezek 16:46, 48, 55-56; Amos 4:11). However, these appear to be mere comparisons, not any kind of corporate identification.

[23] On the corporate identification of Ephraim with these cities associated with Sodom see further Derek D. Bass, "Hosea's Use of Scripture: An Analysis of His Hermeneutics" (PhD diss., Southern Baptist Theological Seminary, 2008), pp. 222-26.

[24]This is much like the preceding kingdoms of Babylon, Medo-Persia, and Greece were corporately identified with the fourth and last world kingdom's destruction in Dan 2:31-45 (and as also suggested by Dan 7:1-12. Likewise, another example of Israel not merely being like the Gentiles but actually corporately identified with Gentiles is Mt 21:43-45, where Mt 21:44b is an allusion to Dan 2:34-35: "And he who falls on this stone will be broken to pieces; but on whomever it falls, it will

One of the implications of Hosea 11:8-9 is that Ephraim was not merely like these Gentile cities but was actually in some way a corporate part of them! Perhaps Hosea 7:8 alludes to the same thing: "Ephraim mixes himself with the nations." This enhances much more the notion that when Israel was said to be "not my people," *they really were, in fact, in the real position of unbelieving Gentiles* and not merely "like" the Gentiles.

What impact does all of this have on Paul affirming that not only Jews but Gentiles could fulfill the Hosea prophecy? It shows that the prophecy really was about people being saved out from a literal unbelieving Gentile location, whether they were ethnic Israelites or ethnic Gentiles. Hosea had direct focus on Israel coming out from that position, but, from what we have said above, it is viable that Hosea himself would have "tacitly understood" (in light of, e.g., Hosea 11:8-9) that his prophecy could just as well apply to Gentiles, who would also be saved out of an unbelieving Gentile position. Paul would be developing both Hosea's direct meaning and his tacit meaning, or his willed type, or what was in his broader cognitive peripheral vision.

Part of Paul's rationale may well also have been his latent understanding and presupposition that Christ was true Israel and that anyone, whether Jew or Greek, who identified with Christ was corporately understood to be also true Israel. This rationale, together with Paul's above understanding of unbelieving Jews' corporate identification with Gentiles, would have made it relatively easy for Paul to see Gentiles also fulfilling the Hosea prophecy about Israel's salvation.[25] We will discuss this latent presupposition about Christ as true Israel further below.

The use of Exodus 12:46 in John 19:36. This passage is perhaps the most difficult so far, including the examples of *mystery* discussed in earlier chapters, since the historical narrative about the exodus Passover lamb is taken by John to be a prophecy of Jesus' death. After narrating that the Roman soldiers did

---

scatter him like dust." This is startling, since the image that is broken in Dan 2 represents the evil Gentile kingdoms, but now Jesus applies the Daniel passage to the Jews, and they realized it ("they understood that he was speaking about them"). Thus in this passage Jesus apparently sees the Jewish leaders as corporately identified with the Gentiles.

[25]That this latent idea may be in mind is suggested by the phrase "sons of the living God" in Rom 9:26 (quoting from Hosea 1:10), the statement that Christ was "the Son of God" (Rom 1:4) and the repeated abbreviated references in Romans to him as God's "Son" (Rom 1:3, 9; 8:3, 29, 32). The three references to "Son" in Rom 8 are not far from the context of Rom 9:25-26. The corporate identification with Jesus as God's son is also enhanced from noticing the mention of "adoption as sons," referring both to believing Jews and Gentiles in Rom 8:15, 23, and the reference to Israelites in the older epoch being in a position of "adoption as sons" (Rom 9:4).

not break Jesus' bones at the crucifixion, John 19:36 says, "For these things came to pass that the Scripture might be fulfilled, 'NOT A BONE OF HIM SHALL BE BROKEN.'"

To be specific, this quotation is prophetic in the sense that Hosea 11:1 is prophetic. It speaks of an event that points forward implicitly to what John is narrating about Jesus' death. The statement "NOT A BONE OF HIM SHALL BE BROKEN" most likely comes from Exodus 12:46 (or Num 12:9, which repeats the Exodus statement).[26] Certainly, Moses' statements in the Exodus and Numbers texts refers to the historical event of the Passover Lamb's slaying and the requirements about how it was to be slain, which the following generations of Israelites were to obey. These statements in Exodus and Numbers are mere historical descriptions and not prophecies. So how can John 19:36 say that not breaking Jesus' bones at the crucifixion was a fulfillment of prophecy from these Exodus and Numbers texts? Many if not most scholars would say that Moses had no prophetic intent in these texts. As a result, some would merely say that John misinterpreted these Old Testament texts or read completely new ideas into them.[27] Still others would contend that John was given this insight retrospectively, after the ascension and bestowal of the Spirit. Accordingly, the prophetic sense was not at all in Moses' mind but in God's wider intention, which is then revealed later to John. This is different than the use of Hosea 11:1 in Matthew 2:15, since we saw that Hosea himself in the wider context of his book viewed Israel's exodus as typological of a future exodus. But we do not have anything like this about the Passover Lamb anywhere else in the Book of Exodus.

How can the notion of cognitive peripheral vision, together with Hirsch's and Polanyi's ideas, help in this case? These overlapping notions may illuminate why John sees a mere historically narrated event as pointing forward. It is true that Moses focused on making a historical description about the Passover Lamb, which was to be prescriptive for all succeeding generations of Israelites. This was the direct focus of meaning in his mind's eye. However, can

---

[26]It is possible that Ps 34:20 could be included, which applies the Exodus/Numbers statement to God's protection of the righteous, on which see further G. K. Beale, *Handbook on the New Testament's Use of the Old Testament* (Grand Rapids: Baker Academic, 2012), pp. 59-60.

[27]In this respect, some would flatly say that John was wrong, while others would say that his flawed exegetical method should not be followed but what he wrote, nevertheless, was inspired. Others would say that John's exegetical approach could be construed as wrong, but, on the other hand, would also say that modern scholars should be cautious in judging ancient writers by modern exegetical standards.

we not legitimately ask the question of how Moses would have related his statement in Exodus 12:46 to other parts of his own writings in the Pentateuch? Some would say that to ask such a question is pure speculation! But what we are really asking is whether or not the rest of his writings that are related significantly to the Exodus event were in his cognitive peripheral vision or in his subsidiary understanding when he wrote about the Passover lamb. We cannot ask uncontrolled questions about what would have been in his wider understanding (e.g., about what he had for breakfast or whether he had a family quarrel), but we can ask only those questions that are related to and prompted by his direct focus concerning the Passover lamb and its relation to the Exodus event. We have only what he has written in Exodus 12 and elsewhere in the Pentateuch. Thus we are not trying to enter into the mind of the author to discover all of his encyclopedic knowledge about redemptive history that has *not* been written down elsewhere in his own writings but came later through Old Testament authors.

For example, we could ask if Moses would have related this event to other similar redemptive-historical events that he narrated in his own writings. While the Exodus event was the greatest event in the history of God's people up until that time, Moses had earlier written about an even greater redemptive-historical event in Genesis 3:15 in which the seed of the woman was to deal a fatal blow to the satanic serpent.[28] Yet Genesis 3:15 says that the seed of the woman will be "bruised" by the serpent. So there is the idea of this end-time conqueror winning a battle over an eschatological adversary yet suffering in the midst of that battle.[29] If we were to ask Moses, "Is the slain Passover lamb (which leads to Israel's victory over Egypt and their deliverance) related to the even greater historical deliverance of a conqueror who will suffer yet still win a decisive victory over Satan (Gen 3:15)?" We think that he would have said there was an analogical relation between the Exodus event and Genesis 3:15, and that this was a divinely intended analogy.

Thus, we are saying that the similar but greater event of Genesis 3:15 was in Moses' subsidiary understanding or within his "willed type," or what we

---

[28]We take this in the traditional sense that it refers to the Messiah who will decisively defeat the Devil. We do not think this is limited only to humans judging serpents by stepping upon them, as some scholars think, which is a very "thin" and unlikely description of the Gen 3 narrative. See further G. K. Beale, *A New Testament Biblical Theology* (Grand Rapids: Baker Academic, 2011), pp. 29-58.

[29]For the idea that Gen 1–3 contains eschatological implications, see Beale, *New Testament Biblical Theology*, pp. 29-63.

have called his cognitive peripheral vision. If so, John may have understood the same thing, and this may be the reason that John sees the slain lamb of the Exodus as an analogical pointer to the slain lamb at the cross, which was a greater redemptive-historical event than the Exodus. Thus the messianic lamb could be understood as "fulfilling" what was implicitly related to the Exodus lamb.

But that is not all. Moses writes in Genesis 49:1, 9-12 that in "the latter days" Judah would rule over all Israel and all the "peoples," as well as winning a decisive battle. Similarly Numbers 24:14-19 says "in the latter days," a leader from Jacob would defeat nations that are likely representative of Gentile enemies in general. Part of the description is that this leader will "crush through the forehead of Moab" (Num 24:17), which is likely a reflection back to the "bruising of the head" of the serpent.[30]

These latter two texts plausibly develop Genesis 3:15 in a conceptual way, and the latter may even be an inner-biblical exegesis of that text.[31] These passages, since they are related developments to Genesis 3:15, are also good candidates for passages that would have been in Moses' latent understanding when he wrote about the Passover lamb. The eschatological nature of Genesis 49 and Numbers 24 would have facilitated all the more John's prophetic understanding of the exodus Passover lamb, if he had some insight into Moses' subsidiary knowledge.

Hebrews 11:25-26 may be but the "tip of the iceberg" in revealing that indeed Moses did have such tacit knowledge or cognitive peripheral vision. Moses chose "rather to endure ill-treatment with the people of God than to enjoy the passing pleasures of sin, considering the reproach of Christ greater riches than the treasures of Egypt; for he was looking to the reward." And then on the heels of this statement, only two verses later there is reference to Moses who "kept the Passover and the sprinkling of blood, so that he who destroyed the firstborn might not touch them. By faith they passed through the Red Sea" (Heb 11:28-29). This is striking since the reference to Moses considering the suffering of

---

[30]See further James Hamilton, "The Skull Crushing Seed of the Woman: Inner-biblical Interpretation of Genesis 3:15," *SBJT* 10 (2006): 34, 49-50, who makes this connection and also traces other later inner-biblical Old Testament allusions (and allusions by Judaism) to Gen 3:15 and understands many of them to be related to the coming Messiah's defeat of evil (see pp. 30-54), though some would question some of his allusive connections.

[31]On these Genesis and Numbers texts and their eschatological and messianic development of Gen 1–3, see Beale, *New Testament Biblical Theology*, pp. 92-101.

the "Christ," (which is related to Moses receiving an eschatological "reward" in Heb 11:26) is closely related to the Passover lamb's slaying and the exodus deliverance from Egypt (Heb 11:28-29), the very connection we were earlier trying to say may have been latent in Moses' and John's minds. Some would say that Hebrews 11:26 is a good example of illegitimately reading Christ into the Old Testament. On the other hand, in the light of what we have said so far about the possibilities of Moses' subsidiary knowledge, the Hebrews text may just as plausibly be an example that our analysis is not pure speculation but is on the right track.

By the way, up to this point in this appendix, we have not appealed to God's wider understanding (compared with the human prophet), though this is applicable. We certainly do not want to affirm that we are only concerned with purely human intentions in the Bible, since biblical writers wrote under the inspiration of God and were probably conscious of writing under such inspiration. When there is a divine understanding that transcends the conscious intention of the human author, the divine understanding is still organically related to the human author's understanding or "willed type." What God knew more fully than the prophet consciously knew would be an interpretative implication that would fit within the human author's "willed type," and, if asked later, the prophet would say, "Yes, I see how that is the wider, thicker meaning of what I intended originally to say." We must say that in every case God had a more exhaustive understanding than biblical authors had of what they wrote.

There is not space here to discuss how this relates to so-called new meanings or creative meanings developed by New Testament writers, especially in those places where the term *mystery* is applied to New Testament understandings of Old Testament texts. However, we have tried to explain this in some detail in the earlier chapters of this book. Suffice it to say that the upshot of the main body of our book is that such meanings still fit within the Old Testament human author's ultimate willed type or latent knowledge, yet they are also a hidden mystery revealed. There is certainly a tension here, but perhaps Ephesians 3:4-5 is somewhat of a key to the other *mystery* texts in the New Testament: "the mystery of Christ . . . in other generations was not made known to the sons of men, as it has now been revealed to His holy apostles and prophets by the Spirit." This text affirms that the mystery was known partially (note the "as" in Eph 3:5) but not fully, as it has come to be known in the new covenantal era.[32] My contention is that the full development of such Old Testament mysteries in the New Testament is not inconsistent with and ultimately fits into the human author's willed type or potential tacit understanding. Would the Old Testament author be surprised? Yes, but on further reflection he would see how it all ultimately fit as progressive revelation into his latent understanding. This is a tricky tension, which we have attempted to tease out in earlier chapters.[33]

Coming back to the use of Exodus 12 in John 19, one does not have to affirm that when the laws respecting the Passover lamb were written, Moses (or his readers) explicitly understood that they were foreshadowing the messianic slain lamb. Our explanation of Exodus 12 in John 19 is what we would consider only a possible explanation, and will likely not be persuasive to many. Nevertheless, the examples of the use of Hosea 11:1 and Hosea 1–2 in the New Testament, we believe, are more probable or persuasive case studies. On the other hand, this possible explanation of Exodus 12 in John 19 should still be considered among the options for understanding this difficult use of the Old Testament in the New. The upshot of these three examples is to suggest that, contrary to the consensus opinion both inside and outside of evangelical scholarship, Old Testament authors may have had some inkling of how the meaning of their texts would be later understood in what would appear to us to be surprising interpretations.[34]

We have tried to unpack the idea that the typology in John 19 is *not* something revealed *only* in the New Testament but had its roots tacitly in the relation of the Passover lamb to other greater redemptive-historical events that had already been written about by Moses himself. Yet when what was foreshadowed by the Passover lamb occurred in Christ there was a fuller revelation of the

---

[32]On Eph 3:4-5 see pp. 163-64. Our view here is generally consistent with and is a further elaboration of D. A. Carson's outstanding essay "Mystery and Fulfillment: Toward a More Comprehensive Paradigm of Paul's Understanding of the Old and the New," in *Justification and Variegated Nomism*, ed. D. A. Carson, P. T. O'Brien and M. A. Seifrid (Grand Rapids: Baker Academic, 2004), 2:393-436, which stresses both continuity and discontinuity between the Old Testament and the New Testament, while arguing that the revealed mystery in the New Testament had its roots in the Old Testament, yet was a "new" revelation.

[33]Beale has also tried to elaborate on this tension throughout his *New Testament Biblical Theology*; e.g., see the discussion of the temple (chap. 19), the church as true end-time Israel (chaps. 20–21), Israel's land promises (chap. 22) and the role of the law in the Old Testament and New Testament (chap. 26).

[34]For another case study, see the study of the use of Is 22:22 in Rev 3:7 in Beale, "Cognitive Peripheral Vision."

antecedent latent typology. For example, at the least, crucifixion by Romans
in Jerusalem, which was instigated by Jews, would certainly not have been
in Moses' immediate subsidiary understanding, but it would still fit into the
broad contours of his willed type and would flesh out in detail how the fulfillment occurred.[35]

The Subsidiary Presuppositional Perspectives of the New Testament Writers in Their Use of the Old Testament

When New Testament writers cite and interpret an Old Testament text, they
may not explicitly state the presuppositions that underlie their interpretation,
but these are nevertheless present in their subsidiary or tacit understanding
and are indeed crucial for understanding how the authors formulated their
interpretation. In fact, without understanding the underlying presuppositions,
the interpretation may seem farfetched and wrongheaded. For example, the
New Testament writers sometimes, perhaps often, interpret Old Testament
texts through presuppositional lenses of which they may be explicitly conscious
or not (that is, such lenses may be tacit to the writers). These presuppositions
are all rooted in the Old Testament itself.[36] First there is the assumption of
(1) *corporate solidarity* or *representation*. Following from this is that (2) Christ
is viewed to represent corporately the *true Israel* of the Old Testament and the
true Israel, the church, in the New Testament. (3) *History is unified* by a wise

---

[35]As N. T. Wright says, Paul "claims to offer a historical reading in which the prefigurements are part
of the story [of Israel] that has now come to its climax," and, we would add, that this climax fleshes
out in new ways the preceding prefigurements, though with coherence with those prefigurements.
See *The Climax of the Covenant: Christ and the Law in Pauline Theology* (Minneapolis: Fortress,
1992), p. 265 (also p. 264). Wright, however, seems to play down a bit too much the new progressive
revelatory notion by saying, Paul "appeals" to arguments from these prefigurements "in the public
domain and not by means of an esoteric secret which other contemporary Jews could not share" (p.
265). While there is truth to this, since the prefigurements really are observable in the Old Testament
texts(!), it does not seem to leave enough room for Paul's view of the revealed mystery, which he
often speaks about (following the critique of Carson, "Mystery and Fulfillment," pp. 430-31). However, my suspicion is that Wright has somewhere in his voluminous writings qualified his statement
appropriately—e.g., see Wright, *New Testament and the People of God*, COQG 1 (Minneapolis:
Fortress, 1992), pp. 62-63.

[36]Explanation of these presuppositions can be found in Beale "Did Jesus and His Followers Preach
the Right Doctrine from the Wrong Texts? An Examination of the Presuppositions of the Apostles'
Exegetical Method," *Themelios* 14 (1989): 89-96; and Beale, *Handbook*, pp. 52-53, 95-102. There is
debate about some of these presuppositions, which we do not have space to elaborate on here. To
the above presuppositions we may also add two others: (1) the Old Testament was the inspired word
of God; (2) the Holy Spirit must open a person's eyes to understand the saving truth of the Old
Testament (see Beale, *Handbook*, pp. 95-96).

and sovereign plan so that the earlier parts are designed to correspond and point to the latter parts (cf. Mt 11:13-30). (4) The age of *eschatological fulfillment* has been launched in Christ. Finally, (5) the latter parts of biblical history function as the broader context to interpret earlier parts because they all have the same, ultimate divine author who inspires the various human authors. One deduction from this premise is that Christ as the goal toward which the Old Testament pointed and the end-time center of redemptive history is the *key to interpreting the earlier portions of the Old Testament and its promises.* These presuppositions help us understand why the New Testament interpretatively applies Old Testament texts to apparently different realities than what the Old Testament had in mind. For example, presupposition three explains why Old Testament historical events can be understood as typological prophetic pointers, as we attempted to show above with Hosea 11:1 (which is also true of Ex 12:46 in Jn 19:36, as well as Is 22:22 in Rev 3:7).

In addition, changed applications of the Old Testament in general, whether or not typology is involved, do not necessitate the conclusion that these passages have been misinterpreted. For example, Matthew applies to Jesus what the Old Testament intended for Israel (e.g. Hos 11:1 in Mt 2:14-15[37]). Or, prophecies about the Messiah are applied to the church because the church is corporately identified with Jesus the Messiah, true Israel (e.g., Is 49:6 in Acts 13:47), so that what Jesus often fulfills as representing Israel, the church is seen as taking part in also as Israel. Or, as we discussed earlier, Paul applies to the predominately Gentile church what was intended for Israel (e.g. Rom 9: 24-26), since the church is true Israel because of its identification with Christ as true Israel. What should be challenged in these kinds of apparently different applications is not the New Testament writers' interpretation of the Old Testament but the validity of the above-mentioned presuppositional framework through which they interpreted the Old Testament. In the above cases not only typological presupposition three is in mind, but also the first two, that Christ corporately represented true Israel and that all who identify with him by faith are considered to be part of true Israel. Furthermore, if Israel was corporately identified with unbelieving Gentiles (the first presupposition) in Hosea, then

---

[37]See Beale, "Use of Hosea 11:1," pp. 708-10. I.e., what is true of Israel positively is also true for the individual true Israel, Jesus, because of corporate identity. Cf. R. T. France's good discussion of this context in "The Formula-Quotations of Matthew 2 and the Problem of Communication" *NTS* 27 (1981): 233-251, where he discusses the Old Testament in Mt 2:4-22.

it makes sense that Paul could legitimately see Gentiles themselves coming to faith, together with ethnic Jews, in fulfillment of the Hosea prophecies he appealed to in Romans 9:24-26.

If the validity of these presuppositions is granted, then the viability of their interpretation of the Old Testament in the above categories of usage must also be viewed as plausible. Assuming the viability of the presuppositions, although the new applications are technically different, they nevertheless stay within the conceptual bounds (the willed type or subsidiary meaning) of the Old Testament contextual meaning, so that what results often is an extended reference to or application of a principle which is inherent to the Old Testament text.

Some suspect that whenever there is a difficult use of the Old Testament in the New, any new "presupposition" can be created by a willing exegete in order to solve the problem, so that such a position becomes unfalsifiable. However, these presuppositions were not created ex nihilo by the early Christian community but are themselves rooted in the Old Testament and its telling of the redemptive-historical story of Israel.[38] We may say that these presuppositions were part of the subsidiary mindset or peripheral vision or tacit default setting of the later Old Testament prophets and early Christians in interpreting the Old Testament.[39] These presuppositions were not chosen willy-nilly by the early church, nor can modern interpreters create their own new presuppositions to explain Old Testament uses in the New. It is within the framework of these five presuppositions that the whole Old Testament was perceived as pointing to the new covenant eschatological age, both via direct prophecy and the indirect prophetic adumbration of Israel's history. Accordingly, the broad redemptive-historical perspective of these assumptions was the dominant framework within which Jesus and his followers thought and so served as an ever-present heuristic guide to the Old Testament. Therefore, the matrix of these five perspectives, especially the last four, are the peripheral lenses through which the New Testament authors looked at (i.e., interpreted) Old Testament passages.

In this respect, the New Testament writers (like the car mechanic) learned

---

[38]On the Old Testament roots of these presuppositions, see Beale, *Handbook*, pp. 96-102. Consequently, this blunts the contention of some postmodern scholars who believe that the New Testament writers' presuppositions distorted their interpretation of the Old Testament, since they see these presuppositions as newly created by the early Christian community in the light of the coming of Christ. Accordingly, such scholars believe the New Testament was reading these foreign presuppositions into the Old Testament, which skewed the original meaning of the Old.

[39]In the case of the later Old Testament writers, the language of "Christ" in presuppositions 2, 4 and 5 would be changed to "Messiah" or eschatological king.

the "mechanics" of these presuppositions from Jesus (what they were, how they worked, how they related to one another, etc.). They strove to understand them during Jesus' earthly ministry, as they watched Jesus "run the race" of that ministry. Then as they later ran the race of their ministries to various churches (like the mechanic turned into racecar driver), their explicit focus changed to pastoral concerns and the mechanics of these presuppositions became implicit and subsidiary—that is, they were still operative but were not always front and center in their focus.

CONCLUSION

We have argued in this essay that when Old Testament or even New Testament authors make direct statements with an explicit meaning, there is always a related secondary range of meaning that is an appropriate expansion of the explicit meaning. All speakers and writers, including ancient writers, are aware of more than what they are directly saying in their speech act. New Testament authors may interpret Old Testament speech acts not directly in line with their explicit meaning but may draw meaning from their cognitive peripheral vision. It may seem like speculation to try to formulate what that latent peripheral meaning was, but at the least we can try to show the viable possibility that there was a wider meaning and that the New Testament writer may well have been aware of that meaning to various degrees in interpreting the Old Testament passage. We have tried to show that searching for the peripheral sense is not a matter of pure speculation that is uncontrolled. In some difficult cases, we may call it "controlled speculation." There is what we may call an "organic" connection between the direct and the tacit meaning. Both Hirsch and Polanyi have sketched how these two dimensions of meaning are related and how, for example, the broader willed type of one statement and its meaning can be determined to some degree. The concept of cognitive peripheral vision expresses something very similar.

There is unfortunately not space here to entertain objections to the hermeneutical approach described in this appendix, though this can be found elsewhere.[40]

---

[40]Probably the most viable objections to this view are twofold. First, it only explains how complicated interpretation is, and it explains the diversity of interpretations among commentators (e. g., most recently in this respect, see Steve Moyise, "Latency and Respect for Context," pp. 136-38). Second, and more significantly, it does not propose specific criteria for determining what is the content of the tacit meanings of Old Testament authors and which tacit meanings a New Testament author

This appendix is an attempt to expand on what J. Gresham Machen said in 1936 concerning the New Testament writers' use of the Old Testament:

> The writers of the Bible did know what they were doing when they wrote. I do not believe that they always knew all that they were doing. I believe that there are mysterious words of prophecy in the Prophets and the Psalms, for example, which had far richer and more glorious fulfillment than the inspired writers knew when they wrote. Yet even in the case of those mysterious words I do not think that the sacred writers were mere automata. They did not know the full meaning of what they wrote, but they did know part of the meaning and the full meaning was in no contradiction with the partial meaning but was its glorious unfolding.[41]

Machen is referring to meanings of Old Testament authors that lie at the "edges" of the widest part of their cognitive peripheral vision. There is a blurring at these edges, just as there is with the peripheral vision of our literal eyes.[42] Because of this blurring, one can, therefore, say that these authors may not have been very aware at all of these meanings; but God, who inspired them, was explicitly aware, and when this meaning becomes explicit in the New Testament, the "blurred vision" becomes clear and it is truly something that is organically "unfolded" from the Old Testament author's original meaning.

---

might have picked up on, in addition to the explicit meaning when the latter is, in fact, referred to. In other words, the subsidiary theory approach is unable to offer guidelines for deciding which among all the diverse possibilities of subsidiary meanings might be in mind (pp. 137-38). For a response to these objections, see Beale, "Cognitive Peripheral Vision."

[41]J. Gresham Machen, *The Christian Faith in the Modern World* (Grand Rapids: Eerdmans, 1947), p. 55.

[42]Brown, *Scripture as Communication*, pp. 101, 103, 105, 108, 111, 113.

BIBLIOGRAPHY

Aletti, Jean-Noël. *Saint Paul Épître aux Colossians.* Études bibliques 42. Paris: Gabalda, 1993.

Allo, E.-B. *Première Épitre aux Corinthiens.* 2nd ed. Paris: Gabalda, 1956.

Anderson, Chip. "Romans 1.1-5 and the Occasion of the Letter: The Solution to the Two-Congregation Problem in Rome." *TJ* 14 (1993): 25-40.

Arnold, C. E. *The Colossian Syncretism: The Interface between Christianity and Folk Belief at Colossae.* WUNT 77. Tübingen: Mohr Siebeck, 1995.

Arrowsmith, William. *Euripides,* vol. 5. The Complete Greek Tragedies. Chicago: University of Chicago Press, 1959.

Aune, David. *Prophecy in Early Christianity and the Ancient Mediterranean World.* Grand Rapids: Eerdmans, 1983.

Baker, David L. "Typology and the Christian Use of the Old Testament." *SJT* 29 (1976): 137-57.

Baldwin, Joyce G. *Daniel.* TOTC. Downers Grove, IL: InterVarsity Press, 1978.

Barker, G. W. "Mystery." In *International Standard Bible Encyclopedia,* rev. ed., edited by Geoffrey W. Bromiley, 3:451-55. Grand Rapids: Eerdmans, 1986.

Barr, James. *Biblical Words for Time.* SBT 33. London: SCM Press, 1962.

———. *The Semantics of Biblical Language.* New York: Oxford University Press, 1961.

Barrett, C. K. *The Pastoral Epistles.* Oxford: Clarendon, 1963.

Bass, Derek D. "Hosea's Use of Scripture: An Analysis of His Hermeneutics." PhD diss., Southern Baptist Theological Seminary, 2008.

Bauckham, Richard. *Climax of Prophecy: Studies on the Book of Revelation.* Edinburgh: T & T Clark, 1993.

———. *God Crucified: Monotheism & Christology in the New Testament.* Grand Rapids: Eerdmans, 1998.

———. *Jesus and the God of Israel: God Crucified and Other Studies on the New Testament's Christology of Divine Identity.* Grand Rapids: Eerdmans, 2008.

Beale, G. K. *1-2 Thessalonians.* IVPNTC. Downers Grove, IL: InterVarsity Press, 2003.

———. *The Book of Revelation: A Commentary on the Greek Text.* NIGTC. Grand Rapids: Eerdmans, 1999.

———. "The Cognitive Peripheral Vision of Biblical Authors." *WTJ* 2014.

———. "Colossians." In *Commentary on the New Testament Use of the Old Testament,* edited by G. K. Beale and D. A. Carson, pp. 841-70. Grand Rapids: Baker Academic, 2007.

———. "Did Jesus and His Followers Preach the Right Doctrine From the Wrong Texts? An Examination of the Presuppositions of the Apostles' Exegetical Method." *Themelios* 14 (1989): 89-96.

———. "Eschatological Conception of New Testament Theology." In *Eschatology in Bible & Theology,* edited by Kent E. Brower and Mark W. Elliott, pp. 11-52. Downers Grove, IL: InterVarsity Press, 1997.

———. "The Eschatological Hour in 1 John 2:18 in the Light of Its Daniel Background." *Biblica* 92 (2011): 231-54.

———. *A Handbook on the New Testament Use of the Old Testament: Exegesis and Interpretation.* Grand Rapids: Baker Academic, 2012.

———. *John's Use of the Old Testament in Revelation.* JSNTSup. Sheffield: Sheffield Academic Press, 1998.

———. *A New Testament Biblical Theology: The Unfolding of the Old Testament in the New.* Grand Rapids: Baker Academic, 2011.

———. "Revelation." In *Commentary on the New Testament Use of the Old Testament,* edited G. K. Beale and D. A. Carson, pp. 1081-1161. Grand Rapids: Baker Academic, 2007.

———. "A Surrejoinder to Peter Enns on the Use of the Old Testament in the New." *Themelios* 32 (2007): 16-36.

———. *The Temple and the Church's Mission.* NSBT 17. Downers Grove, IL: InterVarsity Press, 2004.

———. *The Use of Daniel in Jewish Apocalyptic Literature and in the Revelation of St. John.* Lanham, MD: University Press of America, 1984.

———. "The Use of Hosea 11:1 in Matthew 2:15: One More Time." *JETS* 55 (2012): 697-715.

———. *We Become What We Worship: A Biblical Theology of Idolatry.* Downers Grove, IL: IVP Academic, 2008.

Beasley-Murray, G. R. *Jesus and the Kingdom of God.* Grand Rapids: Eerdmans, 1986.

Beetham, Christopher A. *Echoes of Scripture in the Letter of Paul to the Colossians.* Boston: Brill, 2008.

Bell, R. H. *Provoked to Jealousy: The Origin and Purpose of the Jealousy Motif in Romans 9–11*. WUNT 63. Tübingen: Mohr Siebeck, 1994.

Bettenson, Henry. *Livy: Rome and the Mediterranean*. New York: Penguin, 1976.

Betz, O. "Der Katechon." *New Testament Studies* 9 (1963): 282-84.

Beyerle, Stefan. "Daniel and Its Social Setting." In *The Book of Daniel: Composition and Reception*, edited by John J. Collins and Peter W. Flint, pp. 205-28. VTSup 83. Boston: Brill, 1993.

Bird, Michael F. *Are You the One Who Is to Come? The Historical Jesus and the Messianic Question*. Grand Rapids: Baker Academic, 2009.

———. *Jesus and the Origins of the Gentile Mission*. LNTS 331. London: T & T Clark, 2006.

Blomberg, Craig L. "Matthew." In *Commentary on the New Testament Use of the Old Testament*, edited by G. K. Beale and D. A. Carson, pp. 1-109. Grand Rapids: Baker Academic, 2007.

Bockmuehl, Markus. *Revelation and Mystery in Ancient Judaism and Pauline Christianity*. WUNT 36. Tübingen: Mohr Siebeck, 1990. Reprint, Grand Rapids: Eerdmans, 1997.

Borgen, Peder. "Proselytes, Conquest, and Mission." In *Recruitment, Conquest, and Conflict: Strategies in Judaism, Early Christianity, and the Greco-Roman World*, edited by Peder Borgen, Vernon K. Robbins and David B. Gowler, pp. 57-77. Atlanta: Scholars Press, 1998.

Bornkamm, Günther. "μυστήριον, μυέω." In *Theological Dictionary of the New Testament*. 10th ed., edited by Gerhard Kittel and Gerhard Friedrich, 4:802-27. Grand Rapids: Eerdmans, 1977.

Bousset, William. *Kyrios Christos: Geschichte des Christusglaubens von den Anfängen des Christentums bis Irenaeus*. Göttingen: Vandenhoeck & Ruprecht, 1913. Translated into English by John E. Steely, *Kyrios Christos: A History of the Belief in Christ from the Beginnings of Christianity to Irenaeus*. Nashville: Abingdon, 1970.

Brown, Colin. "Secret." In *New International Dictionary of New Testament Theology*, edited by Colin Brown, 3:501-11. Grand Rapids: Zondervan, 1986.

Brown, Jeannine. *Scripture as Communication: Introducing Biblical Hermeneutics*. Grand Rapids: Baker Academic, 2007.

Brown, Raymond. *The Semitic Background of the Term "Mystery" in the New Testament*. BS 21. Philadelphia: Fortress, 1968.

Brownlee, W. H. "Biblical Interpretation Among the Sectaries of the Dead Sea Scrolls." *BA* 14 (1951): 54-76.

———. *The Midrash Pesher of Habakkuk.* SBLMS 24. Missoula, MT: Scholars Press, 1979.

Bruce, F. F. *1 & 2 Thessalonians.* WBC 45. Waco, TX: Word, 1982.

———. *1 and 2 Corinthians.* NCBC. London: Marshall, Morgan & Scott; 1971. Reprint, Grand Rapids: Eerdmans, 1986.

———. *A Mind for What Matters: Collected Essays of F. F. Bruce.* Grand Rapids: Eerdmans, 1990.

———. *Biblical Exegesis in the Qumran Texts.* Grand Rapids: Eerdmans, 1959.

———. *The Epistles to the Colossians, to Philemon, and to the Ephesians.* NICNT. Grand Rapids: Eerdmans, 1984.

Brütsch, C. *Die Offenbarung Jesu Christi I-II.* Zürcher Bibelkommentare. Zürich: Zwingli, 1970.

Buchanan, G. W. "Eschatology and the 'End of Days.'" *JNES* 20 (1961): 188-93.

Caird, G. B. *A Commentary on the Revelation of St. John the Divine.* New York: Harper and Row, 1966.

———. *The Language and Imagery of the Bible.* Philadelphia: Westminster, 1980.

———. *New Testament Theology.* Edited by L. D. Hurst. Oxford: Clarendon, 1995.

Calvin, John. *Acts 14-28, Romans 1-16.* Vol. 16 of Calvin's Commentaries. Grand Rapids: Baker, 1984.

Cambier, J. "Le grand mystère concernant le Christ et son Église: Éphésiens 5,22 33." *Biblica* 47 (1966): 43-90.

Capes, David B. *Old Testament Yahweh Texts in Paul's Christology.* WUNT 47. Tübingen: Mohr Siebeck, 1992.

Caragounis, Chrys. *The Ephesian Mysterion: Meaning and Content.* CNNTS 8. Lund: Gleerup, 1977.

Carson D. A., and Douglas J. Moo. *An Introduction to the New Testament.* 2nd ed. Grand Rapids: Zondervan, 2005.

Carson, D. A. *Exegetical Fallacies.* 2nd ed. Grand Rapids: Baker, 1996.

———. *Matthew.* EBC 8. Grand Rapids: Zondervan, 1984.

———. "Mystery and Fulfillment." In *Justification and Variegated Nomism,* vol. 2: *The Paradoxes of Paul,* edited by D. A. Carson, Peter T. O'Brien and Mark A. Seifrid, pp. 393-427. Grand Rapids: Baker Academic, 2004.

———. "Three More Books on the Bible: a Critical Review." *TJ* 27 (2006): 1-62.

Casey, Maurice. *From Jewish Prophet to Gentile God: The Origins and Development of New Testament Christology.* Cambridge: James Clarke, 1991.

Chapman, David W. *Ancient Jewish and Christian Perceptions of Crucifixion.* WUNT 244. Tübingen: Mohr Siebeck, 2008.

Chazon, Esther G. "Human and Angelic Prayer in Light of the Scrolls." In *Liturgical*

Perspectives: Prayer and Poetry in Light of the Dead Sea Scrolls, edited by Esther G. Chazon, pp. 35-47. STDJ 48. Boston: Brill, 2003.

Childs, Brevard S. *Isaiah.* OTL. Louisville, KY: Westminster John Knox, 2001.

Clinton, Kevin. "The Mysteries of Demeter and Kore." In *A Companion to Greek Religion,* edited by Daniel Ogden, pp. 342-56. Malden, MA: Blackwell, 2007.

———. "Stages of Initiation in the Eleusinian and Samothracian Mysteries." In *Greek Mysteries: The Archaeology and Ritual of Ancient Greek Secret Cults,* edited by Michael B. Cosmopoulos, pp. 50-78. New York: Routledge, 2003.

Cohen, Shaye J. D. "Crossing Boundary and Becoming a Jew." *HTR* 82 (1989): 13-33.

Cole, R. A. *The New Temple.* London: Tyndale Press, 1950.

Cole, Susan Guettel. "Finding Dionysus." In *A Companion to Greek Religion,* edited by Daniel Ogden, pp. 327-41. Malden, MA: Blackwell, 2007.

Collins, John J. *Daniel: A Commentary on the Book of Daniel.* Hermeneia. Minneapolis: Fortress, 1993.

———. *The Apocalyptic Imagination: An Introduction to Jewish Apocalyptic Literature.* 2nd ed. BRS. Grand Rapids: Eerdmans, 1998.

———. *The Scepter and the Star: The Messiahs of the Dead Sea Scrolls and Other Ancient Literature.* ABRL 10. New York: Doubleday, 1995.

Coppens, Joseph. "'Mystery' in the Theology of Saint Paul and Its Parallels at Qumran." In *Paul and Qumran: Studies in New Testament Exegesis,* edited by Jerome Murphy-O'Connor, pp. 132-58. Chicago: Priority, 1968.

Cosmopoulos, Michael B., ed. *Greek Mysteries: The Archaeology and Rituals of Ancient Greek Secret Cults.* New York: Routledge, 2003.

Cranfield, C. E. B. *A Critical and Exegetical Commentary on the Epistle to the Romans,* vol. 2. ICC. New York: T & T Clark, 1979.

Dahl, Nils Alstrup. *Jesus in the Memory of the Early Church.* Minneapolis: Augsburg, 1976.

Davidson, Richard M. *Flame of Yahweh: Sexuality in the Old Testament.* Peabody, MA: Hendrickson, 2007.

Dawes, Gregory W. *The Body in Question: Metaphor and Meaning in the Interpretation of Ephesians 5:21-33.* Boston: Brill, 1998.

Deden, D. "Le 'Mystère' paulinien." *Ephemerides theologicae lovanienses* 13 (1936): 405-42.

Dibelius, Martin, and H. Greeven. *An die Kolosser, Epheser, an Philemon.* 3rd ed. Handbuch zum Neuen Testament 12. Tübingen: Mohr Siebeck, 1953.

Dibelius, Martin, and Hans Conzelmann, *The Pastoral Epistles.* Translated by Philip Buttolph and Adela Yarbro. Hermeneia. Philadelphia: Fortress, 1972.

Dickson, John P. *Mission-Commitment in Ancient Judaism and in the Pauline Communities: The Shape, Extent, and Background of Early Christian Mission.* WUNT 159. Tübingen: Mohr Siebeck, 2003.

Diodorus of Sicily. Translated by C. H. Oldfather. 8 vols. LCL. Cambridge, MA: Harvard University Press, 1939.

Donaldson, Terence L. "Proselytes or 'Righteous Gentiles'? The Status of Gentiles in Eschatological Pilgrimage Patterns of Thought." *JSP* 7 (1990): 3-27.

Dunn, James D. G. *Jesus and the Spirit: A Study of the Religious and Charismatic Experience of Jesus and the First Christians as Reflected in the New Testament.* Philadelphia: Westminster, 1975. Reprint, Grand Rapids: Eerdmans, 1997.

———. *Unity and Diversity in the New Testament: An Inquiry into the Character of Earliest Christianity.* 3rd. ed. London: SCM Press, 2006.

Elgvin, Torleif. "Wisdom and Apocalypticism in the Early Second Century BCE: The Evidence of 4QInstruction." In *The Dead Sea Scrolls Fifty Years After Their Discovery,* edited by Lawrence H. Schiffman, Emanuel Tov and James C. VanderKam, pp. 226-47. Jerusalem: Israel Exploration Society, 2000.

Enns, Peter. *Inspiration and Incarnation: Evangelicals and the Problem of the Old Testament.* Grand Rapids: Baker Academic, 2005.

Evans, Craig A. "Daniel in the New Testament: Visions of God's Kingdom." In *The Book of Daniel: Composition and Reception,* edited by John J. Collins and Peter W. Flint, 2:490-527. Boston: Brill, 2001.

Fairbain, P. *The Typology of Scripture.* New York: T & T Clark, 1876.

Fee, Gordon D. *1 and 2 Timothy, Titus.* NIBC. Peabody, MA: Hendrickson, 1988.

———. *The First and Second Letters to the Thessalonians.* NICNT. Grand Rapids: Eerdmans, 2009.

———. *First Epistle to the Corinthians.* NICNT. Grand Rapids: Eerdmans, 1987.

Feldman, Louis H. *Josephus's Interpretation of the Bible.* Los Angeles: University of California Press, 1998.

Ferguson, Everett. *Backgrounds of Early Christianity.* 3rd ed. Grand Rapids: Eerdmans, 2003.

Fishbane, Michael. *Biblical Interpretation in Ancient Israel.* Oxford: Clarendon, 1985.

Fitzgerald, A. *The Letters of Synesius of Cyrene.* New York: Oxford University Press, 1926.

Frame, John. *The Doctrine of the Knowledge of God.* Phillipsburg, NJ: P & R, 1987.

France, R. T. "The Formula-Quotations of Matthew 2 and the Problem of Communication." *NTS* 27 (1981): 233-251.

———. *The Gospel of Matthew.* NICNT. Grand Rapids: Eerdmans, 2007.

———. *Jesus and the Old Testament: His Application of Old Testament Passages to*

Himself and His Mission. Grand Rapids: Baker, 1982.

Furfey, Paul Hanley. "The Mystery of Iniquity." *CBQ* 8 (1946): 179-91.

Gager, John G. *The Origins of Anti-Semitism: Attitudes Toward Judaism in Pagan and Christian Antiquity.* New York: Oxford University Press, 1985.

Garland, David E. *1 Corinthians.* BECNT. Grand Rapids: Baker, 2003.

———. *Colossians, Philemon.* NIVAC. Grand Rapids: Zondervan, 1998.

Garlington, D. B. "Obedience of Faith in the Letter to the Romans. Part I: The Meaning of ὑποκοὴν πίστεως." *WTJ* 52 (1990): 201-24.

Gladd, Benjamin L. "The Last Adam as the 'Life-Giving Spirit' Revisited: A Possible Old Testament Background of One of Paul's Most Perplexing Phrases." *WTJ* 71 (2009): 297-309.

———. *Revealing the* Mysterion: *The Use of Mystery in Daniel and Second Temple Judaism with Its Bearing on First Corinthians.* BZNW 160. Berlin: Walter de Gruyter, 2008.

Goff, Matthew. *The Worldly and Heavenly Wisdom of 4QInstruction.* STDJ 50. Boston: Brill, 2003.

Gooding, David W. "The Literary Structure of the Book of Daniel and Its Implications." *TynBul* 32 (1981): 43-79.

Goppelt, Leonhard. *Typos: The Typological Interpretation of the Old Testament in the New.* Translated by Donald H. Madvig. Grand Rapids: Eerdmans, 1982.

Gorman, Michael. *Cruciformity: Paul's Narrative Spirituality of the Cross.* Grand Rapids: Eerdmans, 2001.

Graf, Fritz. *Ritual Texts for the Afterlife: Orpheus and the Bacchic Gold Tablets.* New York: Routledge, 2007.

Green, Gene L. "Relevance Theory and Biblical Interpretation." In *The Linguist as Pedagogue: Trends in the Teaching and Linguistic Analysis of the Greek New Testament,* edited by S. E. Porter and M. B. O'Donnell, pp. 217-40. NTM 11. Sheffield: Sheffield Phoenix Press, 2009.

Gundry, Robert H. "The Form, Meaning and Background of the Hymn Quoted in 1 Timothy 3:16." In *Apostolic History and the Gospel: Biblical and Historical Essays Presented to F.F. Bruce,* edited by W. Ward Gasque and Ralph P. Martin, pp. 203-22. Exeter: Paternoster, 1970.

Hamilton, James. "The Skull Crushing Seed of the Woman: Inner-Biblical Interpretation of Genesis 3:15." *SBJT* 10 (2006): 30-54.

Hamilton, Victor. *The Book of Genesis: Chapters 1-17.* NICOT. Grand Rapids: Eerdmans, 1990.

Harris, Murray J. *Colossians and Philemon.* EGGNT. Nashville: B & H Academic, 2010.

Hartman, L. *Prophecy Interpreted: The Formation of Some Jewish Apocalyptic Texts and of the Eschatological Discourse Mark 13 par.* ConBNT 1. Lund: Gleerup, 1966.

Harvey, A. E. "The Use of Mystery Language in the Bible." *JTS* 31 (1980): 320-36.

Hays, Richard B. *The Conversion of the Imagination.* Grand Rapids: Eerdmans, 2005.

———. *Echoes of Scripture in the Letters of Paul.* New Haven, CT: Yale University Press, 1989.

———. *First Corinthians.* Interpretation. Louisville, KY: Westminster John Knox, 1997.

Heil, J. P. "The Fifth Seal (Rev 6, 9-11) as a Key to Revelation." *Biblica* 74 (1993): 220-43.

Hendriksen, William. *New Testament Commentary: Exposition of Ephesians.* Grand Rapids: Baker, 1967.

Hengel, M. *Crucifixion: In the Ancient World and the Folly of the Message of the Cross.* Philadelphia: Fortress, 1977.

———. *Judaism and Hellenism: Studies in their Encounter in Palestine during the Early Hellenistic Period.* 2 vols. Philadelphia: Fortress, 1974.

Hirsch, E. D. *Aims of Interpretation.* Chicago: University of Chicago Press, 1978.

———. *Validity in Interpretation.* New Haven, CT: Yale University Press, 1967.

Hoehner, Harold W. *Ephesians: An Exegetical Commentary.* Grand Rapids: Baker, 2002.

Hoekema, Anthony A. *The Bible and the Future.* Grand Rapids: Eerdmans, 1979.

Hoffmeier, J. K. "Moses." In *International Standard Bible Encyclopedia.* Revised edition, ed. Geoffrey Bromiley, 3:415-25. Grand Rapids: Eerdmans, 1995.

Horbury, William. *Messianism Among Jews and Christians: Biblical and Historical Studies.* London: T & T Clark, 2003.

House, H. W. "Tongues and the Mystery Religions at Corinth." *Bibliotheca sacra* 140 (1983): 134-50.

Hübner, Hans. *Biblische Theologie des Neuen Testaments.* 2 vols. Göttingen: Vandenhoeck & Ruprecht, 1993.

———. *Vetus Testamentum in Novo.* 2 vols. Göttingen: Vandenhoeck & Ruprecht, 1997.

Hugenberger, Gordon P. "Introductory Notes on Typology." In *The Right Doctrine from the Wrong Texts?* edited by G. K. Beale, pp. 331-41. Grand Rapids: Baker, 1994.

———. *Marriage as a Covenant: Biblical Law and Ethics as Developed from Malachi.* VTSup 52. Boston: Brill, 1994. Reprint, Grand Rapids: Baker, 1998.

Hurtado, Larry W. *How on Earth Did Jesus Become a God? Historical Questions About Earliest Devotion to Jesus.* Grand Rapids: Eerdmans, 2005.

————. *Lord Jesus Christ: Devotion to Jesus in Earliest Christianity.* Grand Rapids: Eerdmans, 2003.

Instone-Brewer, David. *Divorce and Remarriage in the Bible: The Social and Literary Context.* Grand Rapids: Eerdmans, 2002.

Jeremias, Joachim. "Flesh and Blood Cannot Inherit the Kingdom of God (1 Cor 15:50)." *NT Studies* 2 (1955-56): 151-59.

————. *Jesus' Promise to the Nations.* SBT 24. London: SCM Press, 1958.

Jewett, Robert. *Romans: A Commentary.* Hermeneia. Minneapolis: Fortress, 2007.

Johnson, A. F. "Revelation." EBC 12. Grand Rapids: Zondervan, 1981.

Johnson, A. R. *The One and the Many in the Israelite Conception of God.* 2nd ed. Cardiff: University of Wales Press, 1961.

Keener, Craig S. *The Gospel of Matthew: A Socio-Rhetorical Commentary.* Grand Rapids: Eerdmans, 2009.

Kelber, Werner. *The Kingdom in Mark: A New Place and a New Time.* Philadelphia: Fortress, 1974.

Kelly, J. N. D. *The Pastoral Epistles.* London: Black, 1963.

Kennedy, H. A. A. *St. Paul and the Mystery-Religions.* London: Hodder & Stoughton, 1913.

Khobnya, Svetlana. "'The Root' in Paul's Olive Tree Metaphor (Romans 11:16-24)." *TynBul* 64 (2013): 257-73.

Kiddle, M. with M. K. Ross. *The Revelation of St. John.* MNTC. London: Hodder and Stoughton, 1940.

Kim, Mitchell. "Respect for Context and Authorial Intention: Setting the Epistemological Bar." In *Paul and Scripture: Extending the Conversation,* edited by Christopher D. Stanley, pp. 115-29. SBLECL 9. Atlanta: Society of Biblical Literature, 2012.

Kim, Seyoon. *The Origin of Paul's Gospel.* WUNT 4. Tübingen: Mohr Siebeck, 1981. Reprint, Grand Rapids: Eerdmans, 1981.

Kitchen, Martin. "The *anakephalaiōsis* of All Things in Christ." PhD diss., University of Manchester, 1988.

Knibb, M. A. "Martyrdom and Ascension of Isaiah: A New Translation and Introduction." In *The Old Testament Pseudepigrapha,* edited by J. H. Charlesworth, 2:143-76. Garden City, NY: Doubleday, 1985.

Knight, George A. F. *Hosea: Introduction and Commentary.* London: SCM Press, 1960.

Knight, George W. *The Pastoral Epistles.* NIGTC. Grand Rapids: Eerdmans, 1992.

Köstenberger, A. J. "The Mystery of Christ and the Church: Head and Body, 'One Flesh.'" *TJ* 12 (1991): 79-94.

Krämer, H. "μυστήριον," in *Exegetical Dictionary of the New Testament,* ed. Horst Balz and Gerhard Schneider, 2:446-49. Grand Rapids: Eerdmans, 1993.

Ladd, George Eldon. *A Theology of the New Testament.* Rev. ed. Grand Rapids: Eerdmans, 1993.

———. *The Presence of the Future: The Eschatology of Biblical Realism.* Grand Rapids: Eerdmans, 1974.

Lau, Andrew Y. *Manifest in Flesh: The Epiphany Christology of the Pastoral Epistles.* WUNT 86. Tübingen: Mohr Siebeck, 1996.

Liddell, H. G., R. Scott, and H. S. Jones, *A Greek-English Lexicon.* 9th ed. Oxford: Clarendon, 1996.

Lietaert Peerbolte, L. J. *The Antecedents of Antichrist: A Traditio-Historical Study of the Earliest Christian Views on Eschatological Opponents.* JSJSup 49. Boston: Brill, 1996.

Lightfoot, J. B. *St. Paul's Epistles to the Colossians and Philemon.* 4th ed. Peabody, MA: Hendrickson, 1995.

Lincicum, David. *Paul and the Early Jewish Encounter with Deuteronomy.* WUNT 284. Tübingen: Mohr Siebeck, 2010.

Lincoln, Andrew T. *Ephesians.* WBC 42. Waco: Word, 1990.

———. *Paradise Now and Not Yet: Studies in the Role of the Heavenly Dimension in Paul's Thought with Special Reference to His Eschatology.* Grand Rapids: Baker, 1991.

Litfin, Duane. *St. Paul's Theology of Proclamation: 1 Corinthians 1-4 and Greco-Roman Rhetoric.* SNTSMS 79. New York: Cambridge University Press, 1994.

Lohse, Eduard. *Colossians and Philemon.* Hermeneia. Minneapolis: Fortress, 1971.

Longenecker, Richard N. *Biblical Exegesis in the Apostolic Period.* 2nd ed. Grand Rapids: Eerdmans, 1999.

Longman, Tremper. *Daniel.* NIVAC. Grand Rapids: Zondervan, 1999.

Lorein, G. W. *The Antichrist Theme in the Intertestamental Period.* JSPSup 44. New York: T & T Clark, 2003.

Luedemann, Gerd. *Paul, Apostle to the Gentiles: Studies in Chronology.* Translated by F. Stanley Jones. Philadelphia: Fortress, 1984.

Machen, J. Gresham. *The Christian Faith in the Modern World.* Grand Rapids: Eerdmans, 1947.

Marcus, Joel. "Mark 4:10-12 and Marcan Epistemology." *JBL* 103 (1984): 557-74.

Marshall, I. Howard. *1 and 2 Thessalonians.* NCBC. Grand Rapids: Eerdmans, 1983.

———. *The Pastoral Epistles.* ICC. New York: T & T Clark, 1999.

Mazzaferri, Frederick David. *The Genre of the Book of Revelation from a Source-Critical Perspective.* BZNW 54. Berlin: Walter de Gruyter, 1989.

McCartney, D., and C. Clayton, *Let the Reader Understand: A Guide to Interpreting and Applying the Bible*. Wheaton, IL: Victor Books, 1994.

McKnight, Scot. *A Light Among the Gentiles: Jewish Missionary Activity in the Second Temple Period*. Minneapolis: Fortress, 1991.

McNamara, Martin. *Targum Neofiti 1: Genesis: Translated, with Apparatus and Notes*. Collegeville, MN: Liturgical, 1992.

Meek, Esther L. *Longing to Know: The Philosophy of Knowledge for Ordinary People*. Grand Rapids: Brazos, 2003.

———. *Loving to Know: Covenant Epistemology*. Eugene, OR: Cascade, 2011.

Merkle, Benjamin L. "Romans 11 and the Future of Ethnic Israel." *JETS* 43 (2000): 709-21.

Metzger, Bruce. *A Textual Commentary on the Greek New Testament*. 2nd ed. Stuttgart: Deutsche Bibelgesellschaft, 1998.

Meyer, Marvin W. *The Ancient Mysteries: A Sourcebook of Sacred Texts*. Philadelphia: University of Pennsylvania Press, 1999.

Michaelis, Wilhelm. "ὁράω." In *Theological Dictionary of the New Testament*, 10th ed., edited by Gerhard Kittel and Gerhard Friedrich, 5:315-67. Grand Rapids: Eerdmans, 1977.

Mihalios, Stefanos. *The Danielic Eschatological Hour in the Johannine Literature*. LNTS 436. New York: T & T Clark, 2011.

Miller, P. D. *Deuteronomy*. Interpretation. Louisville, KY: Westminster John Knox, 1990.

Minear, P. S. *I Saw a New Earth: An Introduction to the Visions of the Apocalypse*. Washington, DC: Corpus, 1968.

Moo, Douglas J. *Epistle to the Romans*. NICNT. Grand Rapids: Eerdmans, 1996.

———. *The Letters to the Colossians and Philemon*. PNTC. Grand Rapids: Eerdmans, 2008.

———. "Nature in the New Creation: New Testament Eschatology and the Environment." *JETS* 49 (2006): 449-88.

Moritz, T. *A Profound Mystery: The Use of the Old Testament in Ephesians*. NovTSup 85. Boston: Brill, 1996.

Moyise, Steve. "Does Paul Respect the Context of His Quotations?" In *Paul and Scripture,* edited by Christopher D. Stanley, pp. 97-114. SBLECL 9. Atlanta: Society of Biblical Literature, 2012.

———. "Latency and Respect for Context: A Response to Mitchell Kim." In *Paul and Scripture,* edited by Christopher D. Stanley, pp. 131-39. SBLECL 9. Atlanta: Society of Biblical Literature, 2012.

Murray, John. *The Epistle to the Romans: Chapters 9–16*. NICNT. Grand Rapids: Eerdmans, 1965.

Nickelsburg, George W. E. *1 Enoch*. 2 vols. Hermeneia. Minneapolis: Fortress, 2001.

Nitzan, Bilhah. *Qumran Prayer and Religious Poetry*. Boston: Brill, 1994.

Nock, Arthur Darby. "Mysterion." *HSCP* 60 (1951): 201-4.

O'Brien, Peter T. *Colossians–Philemon*. WBC 44. Waco, TX: Word, 1982.

———. *Letter to the Ephesians*. PNTC. Grand Rapids: Eerdmans, 1999.

———. "Mystery." In *Dictionary of Paul and His Letters*, edited by Gerald F. Hawthorne, Ralph P. Martin and Daniel G. Reid, pp. 621-23. Downers Grove, IL: InterVarsity Press, 1993.

Ortlund, Raymond C., Jr. *Whoredom: God's Unfaithful Wife in Biblical Theology*. NSBT. Downers Grove, IL: IVP, 2001.

Orton, David E. *The Understanding Scribe: Matthew and the Apocalyptic Ideal*. JSNTSup 25. Sheffield: Sheffield Academic Press, 1989.

Osborne, Grant R. *Revelation*. BECNT. Grand Rapids: Baker Academic, 2002.

Oswalt, John. *The Book of Isaiah: Chapters 1–39*. NICOT. Grand Rapids: Eerdmans, 1986.

———. *The Book of Isaiah: Chapters 40–66*. NICOT. Grand Rapids: Eerdmans, 1998.

Patte, Daniel. *Early Jewish Hermeneutic in Palestine*. SBLDS 22. Missoula, MT: Scholars Press, 1975.

Penna, Romano. *Il «Mysterion» Paolino*. SRB 10. Brescia: Paideia, 1978.

Pennington, Jonathan T. *Heaven and Earth in the Gospel of Matthew*. NovTSup 126. Boston: Brill, 2007. Reprint, Grand Rapids: Baker, 2009.

Picket, Joseph P., ed. *The American Heritage Dictionary of the English Language*. 4th ed. Boston: Houghton Mifflin Harcourt, 2000.

Piper, Otto A. "The Mystery of the Kingdom of God." *Interpretation* 1 (1947): 183-200.

Plutarch. *Moralia*. Translated by Frank C. Babbitt. 16 vols. LCL. Cambridge, MA: Harvard University Press, 1927.

Polanyi, Michael. *Personal Knowledge*. Chicago: University of Chicago Press, 1958.

———. *The Tacit Dimension*. Garden City, NY: Doubleday, 1966.

Polanyi, Michael, and Harry Prosch. *Meaning*. Chicago: University of Chicago Press, 1975.

Porter, Joshua R. "The Legal Aspects of the Concept of 'Corporate Personality' in the Old Testament." *VT* 15 (1965): 361-80.

Porter, Stanley E. "Two Myths: Corporate Personality and Language/Mentality Determinism." *SJT* 43 (1990): 289-307.

Prigent, P. *L'Apocalypse de Saint Jean*. CNT 14. Paris: Delachaux et Niestlé, 1981.

Prinsloo, G. T. M. "Two Poems in a Sea of Prose: The Content and Context of Daniel 2.20-23 and 6.27-28." *JSOT* 59 (1993): 93-108.

Quinn, Jerome D., and William C. Wacker, *The First and Second Letters to Timothy: A New Translation and Commentary.* ECC. Grand Rapids: Eerdmans, 2000.

Rabinowitz, I. "Pesher/Pittaron: Its Biblical Meaning and Its Significance in the Qumran Literature." *RevQ* 8 (1973): 226-30.

Reitzenstein, Richard. *Die hellenistischen Mysterienreligionen nach ihren Grundgedanken und Wirkungen.* 3rd ed. Berlin: Teubner, 1927. Translated into English by John E. Steely, *Hellenistic Mystery-Religions: Their Basic Ideas and Significance.* PTMS 18. Pittsburgh: Pickwick, 1978.

Rice, David G., and John E. Stambaugh, *Sources for the Study of Greek Religion.* SBLSBS 14. Chico, CA: Scholars, 1979.

Ridderbos, Herman. *Paul: An Outline of His Theology.* Translated by John Richard de Witt. Grand Rapids: Eerdmans, 1975.

Riddlebarger, Kim. *The Man of Sin: Uncovering the Truth About the Antichrist.* Grand Rapids: Baker Academic, 2006.

Robertson, O. Palmer. "Is There a Distinctive Future for Ethnic Israel in Romans 11?" In *Perspectives on Evangelical Theology,* edited by S. N. Gundry and K. S. Kantzer, pp. 209-27. Grand Rapids: Baker, 1979.

Robinson, H. W. *Corporate Personality in Ancient Israel.* Philadelphia: Fortress, 1980.

Rogerson, John W. "The Hebrew Conception of Corporate Personality: A Re-Examination." *JTS* 21 (1970): 1-16.

Sampley, J. P. *And the Two Shall Become One Flesh: A Study of Traditions in Ephesians 5:21-33.* New York: Cambridge University Press, 1971.

Sandmel, S. "Parallelomania." *JBL* 81 (1962): 1-13.

Saucy, R. L. *The Case for Progressive Dispensationalism.* Grand Rapids: Zondervan, 1993.

———. "The Church as the Mystery of God." In *Dispensationalism, Israel and the Church,* edited by Craig Blaising and Darrell L. Block, pp. 127-55. Grand Rapids: Zondervan, 1992.

Schultz, Richard L. *The Search for Quotation: Verbal Parallels in the Prophets.* JSOTSup 180. Sheffield: Sheffield Academic Press, 1999.

Schweitzer, Albert. *The Mystery of the Kingdom of God: The Secret of Jesus' Messiahship and Passion.* Translated by Walter Lowrie. New York: Macmillan, 1950.

———. *The Quest of the Historical Jesus: A Critical Study of Its Progress from Reimarus to Wrede.* 3rd ed. Translated by W. Montgomery. London: Black, 1956.

Seifrid, Mark. "Romans." In *Commentary on the New Testament Use of the Old Testament,* edited by G. K. Beale and D. A. Carson, pp. 607-94. Grand Rapids: Baker Academic, 2007.

Silva, Moisés. *Biblical Words and Their Meaning: An Introduction to Lexical Semantics.* Grand Rapids: Zondervan, 1983.

Snodgrass, Klyne R. *Stories with Intent: A Comprehensive Guide to the Parables of Jesus.* Grand Rapids: Eerdmans, 2008.

Sohn, Seock-Tae. *The Divine Election of Israel.* Grand Rapids: Eerdmans, 1991.

Sommer, B. D. "Exegesis, Allusion and Intertextuality in the Hebrew Bible: A Response to Lyle Eslinger." *VT* 46 (1996): 479-89.

Spilsbury, Paul. "Flavius Josephus on the Rise and Fall of the Roman Empire." *Journal of Theological Studies* 54 (2003): 1-24.

Swete, II. B. *The Apocalypse of St. John.* London: Macmillan, 1906.

Syrén, Roger. *The Blessings in the Targums: A Study on the Targumic Interpretations of Genesis 49 and Deuteronomy 33.* Acta Academiae Aboensis 64/1. Abo: Abo Akademi, 1986.

Tarwater, John K. "The Covenantal Nature of Marriage in the Order of Creation in Genesis 1 and 2." PhD diss., Southeastern Baptist Theological Seminary, 2002.

Thielman, Frank. "Ephesians." In *Commentary on the New Testament Use of the Old Testament,* edited by G. K. Beale and D. A. Carson, pp. 813-33. Grand Rapids: Baker Academic, 2007.

Thiselton, Anthony C. *The First Epistle to the Corinthians: A Commentary on the Greek Text.* NIGTC. Grand Rapids: Eerdmans, 2000.

Thomas, Samuel I. *The "Mysteries" of Qumran Mystery, Secrecy, and Esotericism in the Dead Sea Scrolls.* SBLEJL 25: Atlanta: Society of Biblical Literature, 2009.

Thompson, J. A. T. *Deuteronomy.* TOTC. Downers Grove, IL: InterVarsity Press, 1974.

Towner, Philip H. *The Goal of Our Instruction: The Structure of Theology and Ethics in the Pastoral Epistles.* JSNTSup 34. Sheffield: Sheffield Academic Press, 1989.

Turner, David L. *Matthew.* BECNT. Grand Rapids: Baker Academic, 2008.

Van Der Ploeg, J. P. M. "Eschatology in the Old Testament." In *Oudtestamentische Studiën,* edited by A. S. Van Der Woude, pp. 89-99. Boston: Brill, 1972.

Vanhoozer, Kevin. *Is There a Meaning in This Text? The Bible, the Reader, and the Morality of Literary Knowledge.* Grand Rapids: Zondervan, 1998.

Vos, Geerhardus. *Redemptive History and Biblical Interpretation: The Shorter Writings of Geerhardus Vos.* Edited by Richard B. Gaffin Jr. Phillipsburg, NJ: P & R, 2001.

Wagner, J. Ross. *Heralds of the Good News: Isaiah and Paul in Concert in the Letter to the Romans.* JSNTSup 101. Boston: Brill, 2002.

Wanamaker, C. A. *Epistles to the Thessalonians.* NIGTC. Grand Rapids: Eerdmans, 1990.

Ware, James P. *The Mission of the Church in Paul's Letter to the Philippians in the Context of Ancient Judaism.* NovTSup 120. Boston: Brill, 2005.

Watts, Rikki. *Isaiah's New Exodus in Mark.* WUNT 88. Tübingen: Mohr Siebeck, 1997. Reprint, Grand Rapids: Baker, 2000.

Weima, Jeffrey A. D. "1–2 Thessalonians." In *Commentary on the New Testament Use of the Old Testament,* edited by G. K. Beale and D. A. Carson, pp. 871-89. Grand Rapids: Baker Academic, 2007.

Weinfeld, Moshe. "Berit—Covenant vs. Obligation." *Biblica* 56 (1975): 120-28.

———. *Deuteronomy and the Deuteronomic School.* Oxford: Clarendon, 1972.

Wenham, David. "The Kingdom of God and Daniel." *ExpTim* 98 (1987): 132-34.

Wilder, William N. "Illumination and Investiture: the Royal Significance of the Tree of Wisdom in Genesis 3." *WTJ* 68 (2006): 51-69.

Wiley, Galen W. "A Study of 'Mystery' in the New Testament." *GTJ* 6 (1985): 349-60.

Williams, H. H. Drake. *The Wisdom of the Wise: The Presence and Function of Scripture Within 1 Cor 1:18–3:23.* AGJU 49. Boston: Brill, 2001.

Willis, John T. "The Expression *be'acharith hayyamin* in the Old Testament." *RestQ* 22 (1979): 54-71.

Winter, Bruce. *Philo and Paul Among the Sophists.* SNTSMS 96. New York: Cambridge University Press, 1997.

Wright, N. T. *The Climax of the Covenant: Christ and the Law in Pauline Theology.* Minneapolis: Fortress, 1992.

———. *The Epistles of Paul to the Colossians and to Philemon: An Introduction and Commentary.* TNTC. Grand Rapids: Eerdmans, 1986.

———. *Jesus and the Victory of God.* COQG 2. Minneapolis: Fortress, 1996.

———. *The New Testament and the People of God.* COQG 1. Minneapolis: Fortress, 1992.

Young, C. D. *The Works of Philo.* Peabody, MA: Hendrickson, 1993.

Modern Authors Index

Scripture Index

Ancient Texts Index

Finding the Textbook You Need

The IVP Academic Textbook Selector
is an online tool for instantly finding the IVP books
suitable for over 250 courses across 24 disciplines.

---

ivpacademic.com